The Impact of Artificial Intelligence on Hospitality Education

Marius Vlad
Les Roches Global Hospitality Education, Marbella, Spain

Edmund Goh
Abu Dhabi Hospitality Academy-Les Roches Global Hospitality Education, Abu Dhabi, UAE

Rachel Germanier
Les Roches Global Hospitality Education, Crans-Montana, Switzerland

IGI Global
Scientific Publishing
Publishing Tomorrow's Research Today

Vice President of Editorial Melissa Wagner
Director of Acquisitions Mikaela Felty
Director of Book Development Jocelynn Hessler
Production Manager Mike Brehm
Cover Design Jose Rosado

Published in the United States of America by
IGI Global Scientific Publishing
701 East Chocolate Avenue
Hershey, PA, 17033, USA
Tel: 717-533-8845 | Fax: 717-533-7115
Website: https://www.igi-global.com E-mail: cust@igi-global.com

Library of Congress Cataloging-in-Publication Data

Names: Vlad, Marius, 1985- editor | Goh, Edmund, 1979- editor | Germanier, Rachel, 1969- editor
Title: The impact of artificial intelligence on hospitality education / edited by Marius Vlad, Edmund Goh, Rachel Germanier.
Description: Hershey, PA : IGI Global Scientific Publishing, [2026] | Includes bibliographical references and index. | Summary: "This book explores how AI is transforming hospitality education, enhancing learning, engagement, and career preparation. Through research, innovative pedagogy, and real-world case studies, it examines AI's role in curriculum design, assessment, student support, and ethical, strategic, and operational implications for educators and practitioners"-- Provided by publisher.
Identifiers: LCCN 2025054460 (print) | LCCN 2025054461 (ebook) | ISBN 9798337351124 h/c | ISBN 9798337351131 s/c | ISBN 9798337351148 ebook
Subjects: LCSH: Hospitality industry--Study and teaching | Artificial intelligence--Educational applications
Classification: LCC TX911.5 .I47 2026 (print) | LCC TX911.5 (ebook)
LC record available at https://lccn.loc.gov/2025054460
LC ebook record available at https://lccn.loc.gov/2025054461

British Cataloguing in Publication Data
A Cataloguing in Publication record for this book is available from the British Library.

Table of Contents

Detailed Table of Contents

Artificial intelligence integration into hotel investment analysis has created a major educational requirement change for hospitality institutions. Thos chapter investigates how AI technologies, including machine learning, predictive analytics, and automated valuation systems transform investment choices and reveals essential knowledge gaps in present educational curricula. The chapter develops a complete system to train hotel investment specialists through analysis of industry patterns and academic studies and technological progress. The framework teaches students to understand data and develop AI abilities and ethical decision skills while being suitable for worldwide for different educational systems. The chapter investigates educational methods to teach AI concepts in curricula and shows how institutions face barriers to implementation and describes the changing abilities needed for hospitality graduates who want to work in investment roles within a data-intensive business environment.

This study discusses the importance of integrating artificial intelligence (AI) into hospitality education to enhance students' industry preparation for securing internships and starting their careers. Insights from students, academia, and industry professionals show AI can positively influence training and employability. As AI

learning practices and formulates recommendations for integrating AI responsibly into hospitality education and professional development.

Few developments in early-career recruitment have created as much debate in the past three years as the use of generative artificial intelligence (Gen-AI) through tools such as ChatGPT, Gemini, DeepSeek, Claude, Jasper, and Copy.ai to write or enhance CVs, cover letters or job email applications. For the hospitality sector in particular, which is recognised in the global recruitment industry for the focus on candidates that display warmth, empathy, and authentic personal narrative, the arrival of machine-generated application text has raised urgent questions for employers and recruiters, such as: Does an AI-polished application still reveal the candidate's true voice? Can recruiters rely on the written words from resumes and cover letters to predict cultural fit and the passion for service and guest satisfaction?

This chapter examines the potential of AI as a qualitative research assistant in hospitality and tourism education. Using Braun and Clarke's (2006) six-phase Thematic Analysis as a framework, the study shows how ChatGPT can support key stages of qualitative research, including transcription, coding, and theme development, under researcher supervision. The findings indicate that ChatGPT can improve efficiency, transparency, and accessibility, reducing the manual workload associated with qualitative analysis. However, its use also presents ethical and epistemological challenges that require careful validation and critical reflection. The chapter concludes that AI should not replace the qualitative researcher, but rather function as an intelligent collaborator supporting interpretive work. From a practical perspective, the study provides guidance for hospitality educators and academic institutions on the responsible integration of generative AI into research training and curriculum design, fostering innovation while preserving critical thinking and human judgment.

Section 2
Pedagogical Approaches

Generative AI is transforming higher education by enabling accessible text creation, information retrieval, and academic support. This chapter reports on a mixed-methods study of bachelor students' engagement with an AI-integrated assessment and their views on AI in education, exploring how academic policy and assessment should adapt. A quantitative phase examined how students' perceptions of AI influenced perceived learning, followed by qualitative interviews on attitudes and practices. Data from mid-2025 showed affective attitudes toward AI were the strongest predictors of perceived learning. Thematic analysis revealed strategic use of AI for academic support, ethical boundaries, and a desire for institutional guidance. AI also offered emotional support, boosting confidence. Recommendations include a roadmap for designing assignments according to a 2-lane model and focusing on assessing learning and critical thinking in an ethical and supportive manner.

Immersive and AI technologies are reshaping how hospitality competence is taught, rehearsed and assessed, but their value depends less on novelty than on design discipline and governance. This chapter presents a conceptually grounded narrative review of extended reality (VR, AR and social VR) and AI-enabled systems (conversational agents and learning analytics), interpreted through experiential and socio-constructivist lenses and the Cognitive Affective Model of Immersive Learning. Synthesising evidence across four application clusters, it shows where these tools strengthen operational fluency, service recovery, safety and hygiene, communication and data-informed judgement, and where they raise vulnerabilities around generative AI, assessment integrity, privacy and data governance, cost and equity. Drawing on hospitality-industry cases and international policy guidance, it provides evidence-strength signposting and a five-pillar implementation architecture with a constraint-led risk register to support accountable adoption.

Preface

As artificial intelligence (AI) rapidly reshapes every aspect of service delivery, guest experiences, operational efficiency, and overall business intelligence, hospitality education faces an unavoidable imperative: to evolve as quickly as the industry it serves. This book, *The Impact of Artificial Intelligence on Hospitality Education*, represents a collaborative effort between the Les Roches campuses in Crans-Montana (Switzerland), Marbella (Spain), and Abu Dhabi (United Arab Emirates), to critically examine, document, and advance how hospitality education can respond to this transformation.

The emergence of AI technologies (such as machine learning algorithms that optimize revenue management to generative AI tools that support content creation and customer service) has fundamentally altered the competencies required of hospitality professionals. While traditional hospitality curricula remain the foundation of practical education, they now require purposeful adaptation to prepare graduates for an industry in which data analytics, algorithmic decision-making, and human-AI collaboration have become central to competitive advantage. A recent global report by Rackspace Technology suggests that 73% of the hotel operators have adopted some form of AI technology, with investments in AI-powered solutions projected to reach $1.2 billion in 2025 (Rackspace Technology, 2025). Yet, a persistent gap remains between the skills hospitality graduates possess, and those employers increasingly demand in this AI-augmented environment.

This collection of chapters addresses that gap directly. Through data-driven investigations, innovative pedagogical approaches, and applied case studies, the contributing authors provide both a critical assessment of AI's impact on hospitality education and a roadmap for meaningful integration. The following chapters herein represent the collective knowledge of educators, researchers, and staff, who have focused on fundamental questions: How do we prepare students to work alongside AI while maintaining the human touch that defines hospitality? What ethical frameworks must guide AI implementation in education and practice? How should curricula evolve to balance technical proficiency with care, empathy, and interpersonal competence that are irreplaceable across service industries?

AI IN TODAY'S HOSPITALITY LANDSCAPE

The hospitality industry has always been characterized by its responsiveness to technological innovation, from the rise of property management systems in the 1980s, to online travel agencies in the 1990s, to mobile booking ecosystems in the 2010s. However, the AI revolution represents a qualitative shift, rather than a simple continuation of automation. Earlier technologies primarily streamlined routine tasks; AI systems increasingly augment human judgement, predict consumer behavior, personalize experiences at scale, and generate insights from data volumes that would be impossible for human analysts to process in real time.

In current contemporary hotel operations, AI-powered chatbots handle initial guest inquiries 24/7, machine learning algorithms adjust room pricing based on forecasting demand, computer vision enhances security and operational monitoring, and natural language processing tools analyze guest reviews to identify service improvement opportunities (Ivanov & Webster, 2019). In food and beverage contexts, AI supports inventory management, menu optimization, and recommendation systems, including wine pairing and personalization approaches (Malheiros et al., 2025). Revenue management that was once dependent on specialist intuition and complex but relatively bounded modelling, now increasingly integrates predictive analytics that simultaneously process competitor behavior, weather patterns, local events, and historical performance trends.

Recent industry research highlights the urgency of educational response. Josephson et al. (2026) report that 84% of hospitality executives consider AI critical to competitive positioning within the next three years, yet only 29% believe their workforce has sufficient AI literacy. This disconnect highlights an industry-wide development challenge that hospitality education must help address. Huang and Rust (2021) argue that the most successful service organizations will be those that optimize human–AI collaboration, leveraging AI's computational capacity while preserving empathy, cultural intelligence, and creative problem-solving. Preparing students for this collaborative future is therefore not an optional enhancement but an industry requirement.

Importantly, AI integration extends beyond operational efficiency to reshape fundamental aspects of hospitality management. Sustainability initiatives increasingly rely on AI-driven energy management systems and waste reduction algorithms (Gössling & Mei, 2025). Wellness programs may use analytics frameworks to improve employee health, reduce injuries, and mitigate stress. AI also strengthens market intelligence, risk assessment, and strategic planning. These applications, however, demand professionals who can interpret AI outputs, question underlying assumptions, and integrate insights with domain expertise and ethical judgement (Nayak & Jagadeeswari, 2025).

INTENDED AUDIENCE AND RELEVANCE

This book is addressed to a variety of interconnected audiences, each with distinct but complementary interests at the intersection of AI and hospitality education.

Hospitality Educators and Academic Administrators will find evidence-based guidance for curriculum development, pedagogical innovation, assessment design, and program-level integration of AI competencies across undergraduate and post-graduate pathways. Whether institutions choose to introduce a dedicated AI course or embed AI literacy across the curriculum, the chapters offer both conceptual framing and practical strategies.

Industry Professionals and Human Resource Managers can gain insights into emerging competency expectations, recruitment realities, and the training gaps that may require organizational intervention. Additionally, chapters on ethics, consumer trust, and brand perception provide frameworks for responsible AI adoption and decision-making in practice.

Graduating students and Researchers will find a rich foundation for further inquiry. Each chapter highlights unresolved questions, proposes future research directions, and reflects methodological diversity. This ranges from quantitative analyses to qualitative case studies and mixed-method designs that reflects the complexity of AI's educational and operational implications.

Technology enthusiasts and developers can better understand educator and student needs, the realities of classroom implementation, and the pedagogical requirements of effective AI-enabled learning tools. Chapters focused on simulations, virtual environments, and assessment approaches provide grounded feedback on what works, what fails, and why.

Current hospitality students may find the book both empowering and practical. Understanding how AI is reshaping the industry can support strategic choices about skill development, specialization, and career pathways. The chapters on job applications, internship preparation, and competency alignment offer applicable guidance for professional development.

The global relevance of this work cannot be overstated. Even though hospitality education systems vary internationally, the AI revolution is unfolding across hotel chains and geographic boundaries. Hotels, restaurants, and resorts all face similar technological transformations. Consequently, the insights presented here, though often focused on specific educational contexts, offer transferable lessons for hospitality programs worldwide.

OVERVIEW OF CHAPTER CONTRIBUTIONS

This edited book is organized into three interconnected sections, each addressing essential dimensions of AI's impact on hospitality education.

Section I: Data-Driven Investigations

The first section sets out the empirical foundation for understanding AI's influence on hospitality education through research and data analysis across multiple domains.

Chapter 1: From Data to Decisions: Educating Future Leaders in AI-Enhanced Hotel Investment examines how AI is transforming hotel investment analysis and financial decision-making. The authors investigate current practices in AI-assisted investment evaluation, including predictive analytics modeling for market performance, automated valuated systems for due diligence processes, which are dramatically changing the investment environment. Critically, this chapter explores essential gaps in the current educational curriculum, and presents how hospitality finance can evolve to prepare students for roles where traditional financial analysis is augmented by machine learning models. By developing the framework, based on industry patterns and academic studies, the chapter guides students to understand the data and to develop their AI capacities and apply ethical decisions. The chapter argues about educational methods to be implemented in teaching AI and explores the barriers institutions face in implementation. Overall, future hospitality leaders must not only understand financial and investment principles but also possess the data knowledge to critically evaluate AI-generated insights and recognize the limitations of algorithmic predictions.

Chapter 2: Using Artificial Intelligence Tools for Internship Practice and Securing Future Job Opportunities for Hospitality Students: Developing a Critical Integration AI Model for Higher Education explores how AI-enhanced tools may be introduced into hospitality curriculum to improve internship preparation, professional development, and job placement outcomes for hospitality students. The chapter introduces a Critical Integration AI Model that supports strategic use of AI for resumes, interviews, networking, and skill gap analysis while preserving ethical professional conduct. The evidence is drawn from various stakeholder insights like students, educators, and industry professionals. The study shows that integrating AI into hospitality curricula may impact job readiness, strengthen early-career performance, and align AI-supported learning with industry requirements for a sustainable hospitality practice.

Chapter 3: Integrating Artificial Intelligence and Sustainability into Hospitality Education: A Strategic Framework for Graduate-Level Tourism Programs proposes a framework for implementing artificial intelligence and sustainability practices into graduate-level hospitality and tourism education. It examines leading international curricula to show how AI-driven tools, from energy management to waste analytics, can develop more sustainable operations, and offer program managers concrete guidance on course sequencing, learning outcomes, and assessment. The study is grounded in global standards from UNESCO, UN Tourism, OECD, and the GSTC, and it argues for an integrated curriculum that combines technological awareness, ethical reasoning, and sustainability knowledge in line with the UNESCO Recommendation on the Ethics of AI and the Education for Sustainable Development roadmap.

Chapter 4: Artificial Intelligence as a Learning Companion: Student Perceptions and Utilization Patterns in Hospitality Higher Education presents an empirical examination of how AI is currently integrated into hospitality curricula and learning practices. By surveying students, educators, and administrators, the study maps adoption rates, implementation strategies, and perceived impacts on teaching and learning outcomes. The chapter analyses how students use generative AI tools in coursework, research, career preparation, and explores their understanding of educational values, ethical boundaries, and institutional support. The findings highlight AI's potential to enhance comprehension, raise confidence levels, improve efficiency, while also revealing challenges such as uneven access, limited training, and fears of overreliance. The chapter offers baseline data on hospitality education's AI integration journey and proposes recommendations for supporting responsible, well-founded use of AI through institutional support, faculty development, and strong industry partnerships.

Chapter 5, *ChatGPT Got the Job? Hospitality Recruiters Weigh in on AI Use in Job Applications* shows the perspective of hospitality employers on the applicants' use of generative AI in resumes, cover letters, and interviews. Through in-depth interviews with human resource professionals and hiring managers, the study presents a nuanced environment in which AI assistance is increasingly expected and acceptable for some application elements yet viewed with skepticism when it obscures genuine capabilities or produces generic responses, lacking authenticity. The chapter offers practical, evidence-based guidance for students and career services on ethical AI use in job searches. Also, the investigation engages with larger questions about how AI is reshaping professional communication norms and what counts as authentic self-presentation in an era of overwhelming algorithmic support. Over the last three years, few changes in early-career recruitment have triggered such debate as using generative AI tools, like for example ChatGPT, Gemini, DeepSeek, Claude, Jasper, and Copy.ai, for drafting or refining CVs, cover letters, and job application emails. This is more obvious specifically in the hospitality sector, where recruiters traditionally prize an approachable personality, empathy, and a compelling personal narrative. In this industry, written materials have always served as a key signal of cultural adaptation and passion for guest service. The emergence of machine-generated application text forces employers to face difficult questions: can AI-polished documents still transmit the candidate's true inner voice? To what extent can recruiters continue to rely on written applications as reliable indicators of authenticity and service orientation?

Chapter 6, *Bridging the Gap: Aligning AI Competencies in Hospitality Education with Industry Needs* discusses the critical disconnect between hospitality education and industry demands by developing an AI competency framework through employer surveys, job posting analyses, and curriculum reviews. The research highlights gaps in foundational AI literacy, applied utilization, and critical evaluation of skills, while recommending a program diagnostic tool and strategic roadmap for alignment. The chapter explores ChatGPT's role as a research assistant in hospitality education, applying Braun and Clarke's (2006) Thematic Analysis framework to demonstrate efficiency gains in transcription, coding, and theme development. It underlines assisted use to navigate ethical challenges, and positions AI as a collaborative tool that enhances accessibility without excluding human judgment or overall critical thinking. Practical guidance supports its integration into academic curricula and training.

Section 2: Pedagogical Approaches

The second section of the book moves from documenting AI's impact to exploring innovative institutional strategies that effectively integrate AI into hospitality education while focusing on essential human-centered learning.

Chapter 7 on *Innovating Hospitality Finance Education through Revenue Strategies and Technology* examines how AI-powered revenue management systems are transforming hospitality finance education. The author analyses the pedagogical innovations that rely on classroom case studies to incorporate real-time data analysis, dynamic pricing simulations, and machine learning-assisted forecasting exercises. This chapter presents evidence that experiential learning with professional AI tools enhances student engagement, driving strategic thinking, adaptation to changing market conditions and applying technological innovation practices to the real live scenarios.

Using AI to Enhance Wine Education in Fine Dining Operations, chapter 8 focuses on a surprising application: how AI can enhance the highly sensory, traditionally human-centered domain of wine education and sommelier training. The authors apply innovative pedagogical approaches that combine AI-powered wine recommendation systems, chemical analysis tools, and consumer preference prediction with traditional tasting education and personal expertise development. This aligns with the UAE-appropriate approach, where learning institutions do not serve wine. Instead replacing human discernment with algorithmic recommendations, this approach teaches students to leverage AI for acquiring knowledge, justify pairings, and provide service personalization while developing their own sensory capabilities and customer relationship skills. This chapter exemplifies the broader pedagogical principle that AI integration should enhance rather than diminish the human elements that define hospitality excellence in the UAE context.

The collection continues with *Perception of Generative AI in Assessments in Higher Education.* Chapter 9 fundamentally questions academic integrity and learning evaluation in the age dominated by ChatGPT and generative technologies. Through mixed-method analysis of undergraduate student engagement with AI-integrated assessment, the author examines their views of using generative AI in academic assessments. The chapter presents quantitative evidence-based perceptions for AI's influence on student learning, complimenting the findings with qualitative interviews with student attitudes and practices. The data collection highlighted affective attitudes towards AI, as the strongest perceived learning predictors, while the thematic analysis revealed AI strategies for academic support, ethical boundaries, and a need for institutional guidance. AI was revealed as an emotional guide and a student confidence booster. The study´s recommendations focused on a comprehensive roadmap for assessment design, grounded on evaluating learning and critical thinking, using an ethical and supporting approach.

Teaching in the Virtual Worlds: Integrating Immersive AI Technologies into Hospitality Classrooms, is the 10th chapter of the book. It explores the pedagogical potential of immersive and AI technologies, extended reality, and AI-powered simulations for hospitality education. The author shows attention to implementations of experiential and socio-constructivist lenses and the Cognitive Affective Model of Immersive Learning. The research presented evidence of where these innovative immersive technologies, particularly when enhanced with AI strengthen operational delivery, increase service recovery, impact safety and hygiene, and increase the overall communication and data driven decisions. The study cautions against potential AI vulnerabilities relating to assessment integrity, data privacy, costs and equity. Importantly, the chapter addresses implementation of hospitality industry challenges and policy guidance, including cost, technical expertise requirements, and the risk that technological innovation might register to support accountable adoption.

Chapter 11 is dedicated to *Teaching the Human-AI Balance: Enhancing Technical and Interpersonal Skills in Front Office Education through AI-Powered Simulations.* It examines how AI simulations can be used to paradoxically enhance human skill development in front office operations. The authors present a pedagogical model combining AI and virtual reality for training purposes. These simulations develop students' empathy, active listening, and problem-solving skills while simultaneously familiarizing them with the front office departmental needs. This chapter models an educational approach that recognizes AI not as a threat to human-centered hospitality, but as a tool for more effectively developing the very capabilities that distinguish exceptional service professionals.

Section 3: Case Studies and Scenarios

The final section of the book grounds theoretical and pedagogical discussions in concrete examinations of AI implementation challenges, ethical dilemmas, and practical applications that educators and students will encounter.

The Ethics of Artificial Intelligence (AI) in Career Counselling and Career Development, chapter 12, presents an in-depth case examination of how AI-driven systems assist with ethical, pedagogical career guidance in hospitality programs. The authors evaluate scenarios involving algorithmic bias in internship recommendations, privacy concerns with data-driven career advising, and the potential for AI recommendations to reinforce rather than challenge existing inequities in hospitality career trajectories. The ethical framework developed here emphasizes transparency, human oversight, equity auditing, and student judgement, and provides guidance for responsible AI implementation in career services and the importance of broader professional counselling.

The final book chapter on *The Impact of Consumer Trust in AI on Hotel Brand Perception: The Dos and Don'ts* examines how consumer attitudes toward AI influence brand perception and booking behavior in the hotel industry. Through the integration of this AI model, the author proposes a framework based on critical brand touchpoints. Initially, brand appraisals focused on establishing judgement anchored on integrity. Secondary appraisals are based on performance and efforts, and these determine the perceived ability. The research reveals that perceived ethics and emotions are stronger determinants of acceptance than the overall utility. Thus, it establishes brand trust as a prerequisite for guest engagement with AI. For hospitality educators, this opens the need for evaluation and reflection. Future industry professionals must be competent in AI ethics, transparency management, and strategic brand-AI alignment. The study recommends a balanced approach between data personalization and privacy, and the AI use of enhancing trust, while preserving authentic human connection as a central core for successful hotel brands.

CONTRIBUTING TO THE FIELD: IMPACT AND FUTURE DIRECTIONS

This book makes several distinctive contributions to hospitality education and practice. First, it provides a comprehensive examination of AI's influence on hospitality education, spanning curriculum content, pedagogy, assessment, ethical governance, and industry alignment. Rather than treating AI as a single tool or isolated application, the collection recognizes that meaningful integration requires systemic educational transformation.

Secondly, the book balances empirical rigor with practical applicability. Each chapter draws on research evidence through quantitative data analysis, qualitative case studies, or mixed-method investigations, while translating findings into actionable strategies for educators, administrators, and industry partners. The proposed frameworks, models, and strategies presented here are apart from theoretical exercises, tested approaches developed for implementation. The work builds a philosophically grounded perspective on AI's role in hospitality education.

Thirdly, rather than reducing it to either technological determinism (by seeing AI adoption as inevitable, or uniformly beneficial) or neo-Luddite resistance (O'Gorman, 2017) (by promoting the fear that AI threatens hospitality's human essence), the contributing authors deploy a balanced vision. The proposed articles recognize AI as a powerful tool that can enhance educational outcomes, operational efficiency, and industry competitiveness while simultaneously insisting that hospitality's core identity is rooted in human connection, cultural sensitivity, and personalized service. AI can guide the people to provide service rather than replace them with its technological integration.

The research presented here aligns with publications exploring the impact of AI on service industries. Wirtz et al. (2018) set the stage by considering that successful service automation requires careful attention to the service context and customer preferences. Our contributors build on this foundation, demonstrating how educational programs can prepare students to make these differentiated determinations. Similarly, Huang and Rust's (2021) framework for human-AI collaboration in service delivery finds pedagogical expressions in several chapters that model how to teach students to work effectively together with AI systems.

The World Travel & Tourism Council (WTTC, 2025) has documented the rapid pace of AI adoption in hospitality operations and identified critical skill gaps in the workforce, while the American and Hotel Lodging Association (AHLA, 2025) has seen the leading brands explore the potential of tools driven by AI prioritizing trust and responsibility. This book provides hospitality educators with research foundations and pedagogical tools to align with industry expectations. Automation is not seen as a primary threat to jobs, but more likely a tool to enable employees to work more productively (WTTC, 2025), and where 88% of travelers expect AI to offer options from multiple brands (AHLA, 2025).

Looking forward, this book also identifies critical directions for further investigation and development. Several chapters note the need for longitudinal studies tracking how students educated with AI-integrated curriculum perform throughout their careers compared to traditional practical programs. Questions remain about optimal AI competency development across hospitality programs and whether certain AI skills are best introduced in foundational courses or reserved for advanced study. The rapid and constant evolution of AI technologies raised un undeniable challenge: how can hospitality study remain current when the tools and techniques may shift significantly within a single academic year?

Additionally, global perspectives on AI in hospitality education remain under research. Most studies represented here originate from Western educational backgrounds. Understanding how AI integration unfolds in diverse international hospitality programs would enrich our collective knowledge. Cultural variations in attitudes toward automation, different regulatory environments for AI deployment, and varying levels of technological infrastructure might influence suitable integration strategies. The ethical dimensions of AI in hospitality also warrant focused attention. Tussyadiah (2020) argues that traveler acceptance of AI in tourism, trust remains fragile and context dependent. Preparing students to navigate ethical dilemmas, like algorithmic bias in hiring, privacy concerns in guest data analytics, employment implications of automation, requires ongoing curriculum development as these technologies develop and their societal impacts become clearer.

CONCLUSION

The hospitality industry has always been defined by its commitment to service excellence, human connection, and the ability to create memorable experiences that extend beyond transactions. These defining characteristics are not threatened by artificial intelligence if we prepare our students wisely. AI presents an opportunity to elevate hospitality through smarter operations, better decision-making, and more personalised experiences, while reinforcing the importance of ethical judgement, cultural intelligence, and empathy.

This book is grounded in the belief that hospitality education must evolve thoughtfully and proactively rather than reactively trying to catch up with industry changes. The research, pedagogical innovations, and case analyses assembled here offer evidence-based guidance for programs committed to preparing students for the AI-augmented hospitality landscape.

For students, this is a remarkable moment to enter the profession. The competencies developed during your education will shape not only your career trajectory, but also the future of hospitality itself. Embrace AI literacy as an empowering capability paired with care, integrity, and reflective judgement, which will enable you to lead with both technological sophistication and human wisdom.

For educators, this collection is both validation and challenging. Validation that AI integration is essential and timely, and a challenge to move beyond familiar pedagogies toward innovation that genuinely serves students and industry partners. The chapters provide roadmaps, but each institution must chart its course in line with its mission, student needs, resources, and industry context.

For industry professionals, partnerships with hospitality education providers are central to building the next generation of leaders. The bridge between academic preparation and industry practice can only be sustained through ongoing dialogue, meaningful internship experiences, and transparent communication about evolving competency expectations.

Artificial intelligence in hospitality education is neither a crisis to be managed nor a solution to be embraced uncritically. It is an opportunity to reimagine how we prepare students for meaningful careers in an industry that will always depend on human excellence, even as it expands its technological capabilities. This book offers a course toward that reimagined future grounded in research, guided by pedagogical innovation, and committed to the enduring values that make hospitality a caring profession.

The Editors

Marius Vlad
Les Roches Global Hospitality Education, Marbella, Spain

Edmund Goh
Abu Dhabi Hospitality Academy-Les Roches Global Hospitality Education, Abu Dhabi, UAE

Rachel Germanier
Les Roches Global Hospitality Education, Crans-Montana, Switzerland

REFERENCES

American Hotel & Lodging Association. (2025). *2025 State of the Industry Report*. Retrieved from https://www.ahla.com/resource/2025-state-industry-report on Feb. 05, 2026.

Braun, V., & Clarke, V. (2006). Using thematic analysis in psychology. *Qualitative Research in Psychology*, *3*(2), 77–101. DOI: 10.1191/1478088706qp063oa

Buhalis, D., & Leung, R. (2018). Smart hospitality: Interconnectivity and interoperability towards an ecosystem. *International Journal of Hospitality Management*, *71*, 41–50. DOI: 10.1016/j.ijhm.2017.11.011

Gössling, S., & Mei, X. Y. (2025). AI and sustainable tourism: An assessment of risks and opportunities for the SDGs. *Current Issues in Tourism*, 1–14. DOI: 10.1080/13683500.2025.2477142

Huang, M.-H., & Rust, R. T. (2021). A strategic framework for artificial intelligence in marketing. *Journal of the Academy of Marketing Science*, *49*(1), 30–50. DOI: 10.1007/s11747-020-00749-9

Ivanov, S., & Webster, C. (2019). Perceived appropriateness and intention to use service robots in tourism. In Pesonen, J., & Neidhardt, J. (Eds.), *Information and communication technologies in tourism 2019* (pp. 237–248). Springer., DOI: 10.1007/978-3-030-05940-8_19

Josephson, M., Casullo, J., & Panzer, A. (January 2026). *Deloitte Makes Progress: The future of hospitality*. Deloitte Insights. Retrieved from https://www.deloitte.com/us/en/Industries/consumer/articles/future-of-hospitality-ai-innovation.html on Feb. 5, 2026.

Li, J., Bonn, M. A., & Ye, B. H. (2019). Hotel employee's artificial intelligence and robotics awareness and its impact on turnover intention: The moderating roles of perceived organizational support and competitive psychological climate. *Tourism Management*, *73*, 172–181. DOI: 10.1016/j.tourman.2019.02.006

Malheiros, C., Gomes, C., Lima Santos, L., & Campos, F. (2025). Monitoring Revenue Management Practices in the Restaurant Industry - A Systematic Literature Review. *Tourism and Hospitality*, *6*(1), 44. DOI: 10.3390/tourhosp6010044

Nayak, P. B., & Jagadeeswari, I. U. (2025). *Organizational performance optimization: An AI-enabled framework for employee compensation and benefits management*. Research in Globalization., DOI: 10.1016/j.resglo.2025.100328

O'Gorman, M. (2017). The Making of a Digital Humanities Neo-Luddite. *Making Things and Drawing Boundaries: Experiments in the Digital Humanities*, 116-127.

Rackspace Technology. (2025). *2025 Global AI Report The AI Acceleration Gap: Why Some Enterprises Are Surging Ahead.* Retrieved from https://fair.rackspace.com/lp/2025-ai-research-report/ty/ on Feb. 5, 2026.

Tussyadiah, I. (2020). A review of research into automation in tourism: Launching the Annals of Tourism Research Curated Collection on artificial intelligence and robotics in tourism. *Annals of Tourism Research, 81*, 102883. DOI: 10.1016/j.annals.2020.102883

Wirtz, J., Patterson, P. G., Kunz, W. H., Gruber, T., Lu, V. N., Paluch, S., & Martins, A. (2018). Brave new world: Service robots in the frontline. *Journal of Service Management, 29*(5), 907–931. DOI: 10.1108/JOSM-04-2018-0119

World Travel & Tourism Council. (2025). *The Future of Work in Travel & Tourism. The key trends shaping workforce strategies*. WTTC Global Report. Retrieved from https://researchhub.wttc.org on Feb. 4, 2026

Section 1
Data-Driven Investigation

Chapter 1
From Data to Decisions: Educating Future Leaders in AI-Enhanced Hotel Investment

Ahmed Bakri
http://orcid.org/0000-0003-4232-9683
Les Roches Global Hospitality Education, Marbella, Spain

Raúl S. Castro López
Les Roches Global Hospitality Education, Marbella, Spain

ABSTRACT

Artificial intelligence integration into hotel investment analysis has created a major educational requirement change for hospitality institutions. Thos chapter investigates how AI technologies, including machine learning, predictive analytics, and automated valuation systems transform investment choices and reveals essential knowledge gaps in present educational curricula. The chapter develops a complete system to train hotel investment specialists through analysis of industry patterns and academic studies and technological progress. The framework teaches students to understand data and develop AI abilities and ethical decision skills while being suitable for worldwide for different educational systems. The chapter investigates educational methods to teach AI concepts in curricula and shows how institutions face barriers to implementation and describes the changing abilities needed for hospitality graduates who want to work in investment roles within a data-intensive business environment.

DOI: 10.4018/979-8-3373-5112-4.ch001

INTRODUCTION

The combination of artificial intelligence with hotel investment analysis has created a new educational standard for hospitality education. The combination of machine learning algorithms with their ability to analyze thousands of data points instantly and create accurate predictive models makes traditional spreadsheet-based methods and manual market research and experiential learning insufficient (Buhalis & Leung, 2018; Ivanov & Webster, 2017). The industry demands AI-trained professionals, but hospitality graduates show insufficient preparation for these requirements. The modern job market demands data analytics abilities from candidates, yet hospitality institutions have not implemented AI tools as standard components in their educational programs (Gretzel et al., 2020; Tussyadiah, 2020), which puts their graduates at risk of professional disadvantage.

Hospitality education faces a problem that requires more than adding AI courses to current programs. The development of future hotel investment professionals demands a complete overhaul of educational goals, teaching methods, and a proper balance between teaching technical abilities and helping students develop critical thinking skills (Mulder et al., 2009). Students need to learn enough technical skills to operate AI systems, yet they must also retain their hospitality-specific expertise and ethical decision-making abilities which separate them from standard data analysts (Li et al., 2018; Mulder et al., 2009). Educational solutions need to handle the typical resource limitations and faculty expertise shortages and student diversity found in hospitality programs operating worldwide.

The framework for teaching AI competencies in hotel investment education requires students to possess fundamental investment abilities that are necessary for professional work. Students need to master advanced financial modeling skills for building their own 10-year discounted cash flow models and they must understand the Uniform System of Accounts for the Lodging Industry (USALI) and demonstrate expertise in hotel operations, revenue management, transaction structuring, due diligence procedures, and traditional market research methods (Rushmore & Baum, 2001). AI literacy serves to improve existing core competencies which determine investment success across all market segments and economic conditions.

Students who need to improve their hotel financial statement analysis skills, return metric calculations (IRR, equity multiples, cash-on-cash returns), and basic valuation methods should first master these fundamental abilities before using AI-based analytical tools. The framework presented here functions as an additional component to complete hotel investment education instead of a replacement because students who lack essential knowledge will not be ready for professional work. Investment companies state that professionals who combine fundamental investment abilities with AI knowledge gain market superiority but AI expertise without proper investment knowledge results in minimal professional worth.

The chapter investigates the current use of AI in hotel investment choices before evaluating educational shortcomings and developing a complete system to train students for AI-based investment work. The framework focuses on competencies that work worldwide while prioritizing conceptual knowledge above technical execution and combines AI education with established hospitality education content. The following sections discuss effective teaching methods for AI education and present solutions for institutions with limited resources and examine the moral aspects of AI-based investment education. Hotel investment success depends mainly on market selection, timing, capital structure optimization, operational excellence, and relationship management although AI tools help with analytical support to enhance efficiency and generate insights. Hotel investment success depends primarily on market selection and timing, followed by capital structure optimization and operational performance (Rushmore & Baum, 2001). Analytical tools and technologies, including AI applications, play a smaller but increasingly important supporting role.

The distribution shows that market selection and timing decisions along with favorable financing terms and operational excellence create the foundation for investment success. Educational programs should understand this reality because AI literacy should serve as an additional skill for professionals rather than a replacement for their core investment abilities which make them successful.

BACKGROUND AND LITERATURE REVIEW

Hotel investment analysis has shifted from using instinctive methods to using complex quantitative methods for decision-making. The traditional investment approach used capitalization rates, comparable sales data, and expert professional opinions for analysis (Rushmore & Baum, 2001). The introduction of specialized software during the 1990s-2000s improved calculation speed but human analysts maintained their role as main decision-makers (Buhalis & Leung, 2018; Ivanov & Webster, 2017).

The modern analytical process undergoes fundamental transformation through the implementation of AI technologies in contemporary analysis methods. Machine learning algorithms detect market patterns while natural language processing retrieves valuable information from unstructured data and predictive models create forecasts that use hundreds of variables at once (Buhalis & Leung, 2018). The new capabilities allow for handling vast data amounts that humans cannot process but create problems with algorithmic clarity and skill level requirements.

The adoption of AI applications experienced rapid growth in recent years due to improvements in computing power and expanding data resources. Automated valuation models use transaction data and market indicators to produce quick property value assessments (Kok et al., 2017). Predictive analytics use booking patterns, economic indicators, and demand data to generate revenue forecasts. These models are often developed using large datasets, such as hotel booking demand datasets (Antonio et al., 2019), and implemented through machine learning techniques in hospitality analytics (Sánchez et al., 2020).

Natural language processing technology retrieves market intelligence from social media and review content to evaluate brand performance (Xiang et al., 2015). Portfolio optimization algorithms help institutional investors build well-diversified investment portfolios.

The implementation of AI technology shows inconsistent adoption patterns across different sectors. Major institutional investors tend to rely on advanced analytical tools, while smaller organizations often continue to use more conventional methods, creating competitive gaps and increasing the demand for new graduate skill sets (Ivanov & Webster, 2017; Tussyadiah, 2020).

Generative AI and Recent Development in Hospitality Education

Recent advances in generative artificial intelligence, particularly large language models such as ChatGPT, have accelerated the integration of AI into higher education environments. Since late 2022, universities have increasingly recognized AI literacy as an essential competency for future professionals, with international organizations emphasizing its importance for workforce preparedness, digital inclusion, and innovation in professional education (UNESCO, 2023; Wang et al., 2024). Higher education institutions are generally adopting a cautious but proactive stance, acknowledging the potential of generative AI to enhance teaching, research, and decision-making while addressing concerns related to academic integrity, data privacy, and reliability of AI-generated outputs (Hodges & Ocak, 2023).

Business and hospitality education have begun incorporating generative AI into curricula through specialized courses, executive education initiatives, and experimental classroom applications. Some business schools have introduced interdisciplinary AI-focused programs that combine analytics, strategy, and technology skills, while hospitality programs are gradually exploring AI-assisted case analysis, market forecasting simulations, and investment scenario modelling. Early evidence suggests that AI tools can enhance analytical capabilities, student engagement, and employability prospects, although institutions continue to address ethical considerations and faculty training requirements (Ivanov & Soliman, 2023; Sigala et al., 2024).

Importantly, the need for AI competencies extends beyond students to include current hospitality professionals. Industry reports highlight significant skills gaps in data analytics, digital technologies, and AI adoption across hospitality organizations. Continuous professional training has therefore become essential as AI-driven decision-support tools increasingly influence revenue management, asset valuation, and investment planning. Organizations that combine structured training with hands-on experimentation appear more successful in developing AI-ready workforces capable of integrating technological insights with professional judgment (Deloitte, 2023; HSMAI Foundation, 2025).

Hospitality investment education already demonstrates early examples of technology integration through industry data platforms and analytical systems. Tools such as STR market datasets, CoStar real estate analytics, and revenue management systems incorporating predictive algorithms are increasingly used in teaching hotel market analysis, feasibility studies, and investment evaluation. Exposure to such tools allows students to understand both the capabilities and limitations of AI-assisted analytics while reinforcing fundamental investment competencies, including financial modelling, market assessment, and strategic decision-making.

These developments reinforce the need for structured educational frameworks that integrate AI literacy with traditional hospitality investment competencies. Rather than replacing foundational financial and operational knowledge, generative AI expands the analytical toolkit available to future hospitality investment professionals while increasing the importance of critical thinking, ethical awareness, and professional judgment.

Current State of AI in Hotel Investment Decision-Making: AI Applications in Investment Analysis

Automated valuation models (AVMs) use machine learning algorithms to process transaction data, property attributes, and market indicators to generate rapid property value assessments (Kok et al., 2017). The models analyze hotel-specific elements such as RevPAR performance, brand strength, and management quality, together with location and demographic information (Rushmore & Baum, 2001). The main use of AVMs as screening tools remains appropriate because they lack sufficient data for independent properties and thin market segments (Kok et al., 2017).

AI-based predictive analytics now uses booking patterns and demand data to support revenue forecasting and operational decision-making, including the identification of cancellation risks that directly affect revenue performance (Sánchez et al., 2020). Natural language processing technology performs sentiment analysis on review content and social media data to detect performance trends (Xiang et al., 2015). The tools deliver maximum value in unpredictable market conditions, yet their precision heavily relies on maintaining high-quality data and proper validation methods (Gretzel et al., 2020; Tussyadiah, 2020).

Industry Example: AI Applications in Hotel Investment Analysis

To illustrate practical applications, several hospitality analytics platforms already incorporate artificial intelligence into hotel investment decision-making processes. For example, STR and CoStar market intelligence platforms combine large transactional datasets, market performance indicators, and predictive analytics to support feasibility analysis, valuation benchmarking, and investment screening. These tools allow analysts to assess occupancy trends, revenue performance, competitive positioning, and pipeline developments more efficiently than traditional manual approaches.

Similarly, revenue management and forecasting systems such as IDeaS, Duetto, and Rainmaker employ machine learning algorithms to predict demand patterns, optimize pricing strategies, and evaluate revenue potential under different market scenarios. Although originally developed for operational revenue management, these tools increasingly inform investment feasibility assessments and asset management strategies by providing forward-looking performance projections.

Despite their advantages, practitioners emphasize that such systems function primarily as decision-support tools rather than replacements for professional judgment. Data limitations, structural market shifts, and qualitative factors such as management quality, brand positioning, and local market dynamics continue to require human expertise. Educational programs should therefore expose students to these tools while simultaneously strengthening their ability to critically interpret AI-generated outputs and integrate them with traditional investment analysis methods.

AI tools demonstrate different levels of effectiveness and precision when used for various hotel asset classes because of distinct operational characteristics, revenue structures, and value creation elements. The proper use of AI-enhanced analysis depends on investment professionals understanding different property types because wrong tool selection for unsuitable properties produces deceptive results that new analysts might accept without question.

The standardized operational models of limited-service and select-service properties along with their uniform revenue streams from rooms department and frequent transactions make them suitable for AI-based analysis (Rushmore & Baum, 2001). The performance of automated valuation models reaches its peak for branded limited-service hotels operating in markets with active transactions and complete STR competitive set information when they achieve R^2 values between 0.75 and 0.85 with enough training data available. Select-service properties benefit from accurate predictive revenue models because their booking patterns and competitive pricing and demand factors show stability which enables machine learning algorithms to identify patterns effectively. Full-service hotels require complex analysis because they generate multiple revenue streams from rooms, food and beverage services, meetings and events, spa and recreation, and various ancillary services which have different market behaviors and pricing systems and operational needs. The wide range of management quality between full-service hotels leads to performance differences which algorithms find difficult to measure unless they receive extensive feature engineering that includes subjective evaluation methods. The combination of brand positioning, service culture, and unique experiential elements in full-service properties represents a significant share of their value. However, these aspects are inherently qualitative and context-specific, making them difficult to capture accurately using machine learning models and limiting the ability of data-driven approaches to fully reflect value creation in hospitality assets (Gretzel et al., 2020; Rushmore & Baum, 2001). AI tools need precise tuning and thorough testing procedures to analyze full-service properties, yet human evaluators maintain authority in making investment choices and determining property values.

The analysis of luxury and resort properties through algorithms becomes difficult because their investment value stems from exclusive experiences and premium locations and established brand reputation and high-end guest relationships that cannot be measured through systematic methods. The analysis of luxury and resort properties becomes more difficult because these properties have low trading activity which results in insufficient training data that leads to inadequate model development. The application of algorithms designed for branded select-service data to luxury segments results in inaccurate valuations which unsophisticated analysts might accept but experienced professionals recognize as implausible.

AI analysis faces difficulties when evaluating conversion and repositioning opportunities because algorithms based on historical data fail to forecast future results after brand changes or major property transformations. The evaluation of these investment opportunities which create major value requires market expertise and operational projections and comparable conversion experience that AI tools based on historical patterns cannot produce reliably.

Investment professionals need to understand when data-driven algorithms enhance their analysis but traditional judgment-based methods with qualitative elements become more trustworthy. Educational programs should teach students about AI tool applications across different asset classes to show both correct usage scenarios and situations where algorithms fail to deliver useful results or produce incorrect results. The balanced approach helps students understand when to use technological solutions properly and when to rely on human judgment for analysis while learning to use AI tools effectively in beneficial situations. Students need to demonstrate their ability to use AI tools properly while explaining their appropriate use cases and algorithmic accuracy boundaries and validating computational results against investment principles and market intelligence.

Educational Gaps and Opportunities

The current educational programs for hospitality graduates fail to meet the AI competencies which employers demand in the market. The modern investment industry demands professionals who can interpret data and perform statistical analysis, but hospitality education programs focus mainly on operational management with minimal quantitative content (Gretzel et al., 2020). The growing need for investment roles has created a shortage of professionals who can interpret data and assess AI outputs and communicate technical information effectively (Tussyadiah, 2020).

The integration of AI content into hospitality education faces structural challenges, including curriculum constraints and limited available instructional time (Sigala et al., 2024). The interdisciplinary nature of AI-enhanced investment analysis demands that students learn hospitality knowledge, financial analysis, statistical literacy, and technological competence through departmental collaboration (Koseoglu et al., 2016). The diverse mathematical abilities of students make teaching more complicated for instructors.

The main obstacle to faculty expertise development among hospitality faculty members stems from their industry background without sufficient data science training. The availability of training programs for AI competency development remains limited, reflecting broader challenges in workforce readiness and skills development (Gretzel et al., 2020; Tussyadiah, 2020). Educational institutions face several resource-related obstacles, including high software costs, limited access to real-world industry data, and uneven technological infrastructure (Tussyadiah, 2020).

The implementation of AI technology creates chances for educational institutions to create unique programs that lead to better student results. Educational partnerships with industry organizations enhance curriculum content and students gain hands-on experience through practical learning opportunities (Gretzel et al., 2020; Kolb, 2015). Online learning platforms allow students to access specialized content which exceeds the capabilities of their home institutions (Tussyadiah, 2020). The institutions that adopt AI first will establish themselves as leaders in their field and gain better placement opportunities for their graduates (Gretzel et al., 2020; Tussyadiah, 2020).

The proposed educational framework for AI-enhanced investment training includes multiple core competency domains.

Hotel investment professionals need to develop four essential competency domains, including hospitality investment fundamentals, data literacy, AI technology understanding, and ethical decision-making abilities, to succeed in AI-enhanced environments. The domains work together as a system because each area of expertise strengthens the learning process and application of others.

To enhance clarity and provide a concise overview of the proposed educational framework, Table 1 summarizes the core competency domains required for AI-enhanced hospitality investment education. The table highlights the complementary relationship between traditional investment expertise and emerging AI-related capabilities.

Table 1. Core competency domains for AI-enhanced hospitality investment education

Competency Domain	Key Skills	Educational Focus
Hospitality Investment Fundamentals	Financial modelling, hotel valuation, capital structure understanding, operational knowledge	Maintain strong traditional investment expertise as the foundation for AI-supported analysis
Data Literacy & Analytics	Statistical reasoning, data interpretation, visualization, evidence-based decision-making	Develop analytical capabilities to interpret AI outputs critically
AI Technology Understanding	Machine learning concepts, predictive analytics, automated valuation tools, AI limitations	Enable effective use and validation of AI tools in investment decision-making
Ethical & Professional Judgment	Algorithmic bias awareness, data privacy, transparency, responsible decision-making	Ensure responsible, informed, and professionally sound AI-supported investment practices

As shown in Table 1, these competency domains function as complementary elements rather than independent skill sets. Hospitality investment professionals must combine traditional financial expertise with analytical literacy, technological understanding, and ethical judgment to operate effectively in AI-enhanced decision environments.

The Hospitality Investment Fundamentals domain contains extensive knowledge and capabilities which extend beyond basic investment understanding to include multiple interconnected fields that form the foundation of professional practice. The core financial competencies for students include building independent 10-year projections with detailed revenue and expense assumptions and performing sensitivity analysis across multiple scenarios, and calculating investment return metrics such as internal rate of return and equity multiples and cash-on-cash returns (Rushmore & Baum, 2001). Students need to master the Uniform System of Accounts for the Lodging Industry (USALI) to perform department-level profitability analysis and understand flow-through concepts and operating leverage and recognize how operational choices affect investment returns.

Students need to understand hotel-specific lending practices and loan-to-value ratio standards, debt service coverage requirements, the distinction between recourse and non-recourse financing, mezzanine capital applications, the relationship between cap rates and interest rates, and equity return requirements. Students need to understand how equity partnership structures work through preferred return provisions and waterfall distribution mechanisms and promote or carried interest calculations which affect investor returns. Sophisticated analysts demonstrate their expertise through their ability to understand how capital structure choices affect risk-adjusted returns and exit options and stakeholder interest alignment.

The complete acquisition process from identifying opportunities to post-closing integration falls under transaction execution capabilities. The process of letter of intent creation requires students to add suitable conditions and exclusive terms while managing a thorough due diligence assessment that includes financial verification, physical property evaluation, environmental compliance checks, and legal document assessment. Students need to understand the different structures of purchase and sale agreements and the standard representations and warranties and indemnification terms and the procedures for closing deals including the organization of third-party reports such as appraisals and property condition assessments and Phase I environmental studies. The knowledge of title insurance and survey requirements and standard closing adjustments demonstrates professional competence.

The analysis of hospitality investments requires specialized knowledge about hotels which sets it apart from standard commercial real estate assessment. The evaluation of franchised properties which make up most U.S. hotel transactions requires knowledge of franchise economics through understanding initial fees and ongoing royalty rates and marketing contributions and PIP requirements and brand value measurement. The evaluation of management agreements requires students to analyze base fee and incentive fee structures and performance termination provisions and operator selection criteria and management contract effects on property valuations and financing options. Students who understand asset class differences can develop separate investment strategies for full-service hotels and select-service hotels and extended-stay hotels and resort properties because each segment has unique operational characteristics and capital requirements and management complexities and market conditions.

Students who possess physical property assessment abilities can use their financial analytical skills to conduct effective property tours which help them detect deferred maintenance needs and capital requirements and competitive advantages and operational enhancement possibilities. The ability to assess FF&E reserve adequacy and plan replacement cycles and understand how capital reinvestment affects competitive sustainability marks the difference between theoretical education and professional readiness. Students need to develop market research abilities which include building broker connections and analyzing feasibility reports and appraise and local economic growth patterns and infrastructure projects and competitive supply pipeline assessments for market trend prediction.

The understanding of economic cycles in the lodging industry helps investors make better timing choices for their investments while enabling them to evaluate proper risk levels. Students need to grasp the past hotel performance fluctuations and recession effects on different market segments and asset types and learn to identify cycle transition indicators and how supply growth interacts with demand patterns and pricing capabilities. The cyclical understanding of the market which uses human judgment surpasses algorithmic methods when analyzing market shifts at critical points. The three core capabilities work together to help students succeed as investment analysts by performing thorough property underwriting and delivering investment recommendations to decision-makers and supporting acquisition and asset management activities. Students who receive AI literacy training after completing their foundational education will become more efficient in their analysis while generating better insights. Students who learn AI tools without first mastering these essential skills will become proficient in tool operation yet fail to evaluate AI results properly and present their findings effectively to investors.

Data Literacy consists of three essential skills which include statistical reasoning, quantitative analysis, and the ability to present data-driven findings effectively. Investment professionals need to grasp essential statistical concepts which include sampling methods and the difference between correlation and causation and statistical significance and confidence intervals and data visualization techniques. The skills allow professionals to assess AI model results and understand system boundaries while delivering results to both technical experts and non-technical decision-makers.

AI Technology Understanding requires professionals to grasp the operational principles of machine learning systems, their suitable deployment scenarios and their built-in restrictions (Tussyadiah, 2020). The essential knowledge for investment professionals includes supervised and unsupervised learning methods, training data needs, model verification methods and typical issues that occur when using algorithms such as overfitting and algorithmic bias. The required level of understanding stops at tool selection and output analysis and technical specialist partnership but does not require programming skills or algorithmic math knowledge.

Ethical decision-making capabilities focus on the responsible use of AI, helping professionals identify potential biases, ensure transparency, and evaluate how their decisions may affect different stakeholders (Gretzel et al., 2020; Tussyadiah, 2020). The implementation of AI-driven recommendations for investment decisions requires professionals to evaluate ethical factors which extend past financial optimization because these choices impact property owners and their employees and guests and surrounding communities. The ability to identify algorithmic biases and data privacy risks and maintain transparency standards allows professionals to practice responsibly in technological environments.

Knowledge and Skill Progression Model

The development of competencies advances through stages which start with basic awareness before moving to intermediate application and finish with advanced critical evaluation and innovation (Mulder et al., 2009). The progression model enables educational institutions to organize their teaching methods and evaluation methods according to the natural sequence of skill development.

The foundation level of education provides students with essential knowledge about AI technology and its applications in hospitality investments and basic data literacy principles. Students gain understanding about AI tool functionality for investment analysis, yet they do not need to work with these tools directly. The learning objectives focus on three main areas: students should identify AI usage in real-world scenarios, understand fundamental terminology and recognize both strengths and weaknesses of AI systems. Students demonstrate their knowledge through tests, brief case studies and written reflective work.

Students at the application-level work directly with AI-enhanced analytical tools through structured exercises, guided case studies and project-based assignments (Kolb, 2015). Students acquire skills to read AI output results and evaluate these results against traditional analysis methods and learn to combine different analytical methods. The learning objectives focus on correct tool operation, output assessment and clear presentation of results. The assessment process requires students to complete analytical projects and present case studies and write documented decision-making rationales that show how AI information supported their conclusions.

Students at the Integration Level need to pick suitable analytical methods independently while verifying AI results against industry knowledge and creating complete investment recommendations by combining various data sources (Mulder et al., 2009). Students face situations where the best analytical approach remains uncertain so they must decide when AI tools enhance results and when traditional methods produce better outcomes. The learning objectives focus on helping students develop professional judgment, adaptive problem-solving skills and advanced communication abilities. The assessment process includes complete case studies, capstone work and internship performance reviews.

Students who want to become specialized investment analysts or pursue graduate studies should learn at the innovation level by analyzing current AI approaches and finding ways to enhance them and advancing analytical methods. Students assess tool algorithms for bias and create new AI usage methods and create standards for AI deployment responsibility. The learning objectives focus on developing critical scholarship abilities, innovative methods and leadership skills for thought leadership. The assessment process includes research projects together with industry consulting work and thesis development.

FRAMEWORK FOR GLOBAL APPLICABILITY

Educational frameworks need to support multiple institutional settings, student demographics and industrial frameworks to achieve worldwide applicability (Mulder et al., 2009). Multiple design elements function to support educational system adaptability.

Programs can reach essential learning targets through various curricular arrangements which flexible implementation pathways provide. Educational institutions choose between creating separate AI courses or distributing AI competencies throughout their finance and revenue management and capstone curriculum. The modular design structure allows students to build competencies step by step across different delivery methods, making the program suitable for three- and four-year programs, undergraduate and postgraduate studies, and varying credit-hour requirements.

Programs that use Competency-Based Learning Outcomes instead of content specifications can teach core capabilities through suitable teaching methods for their specific context (Mulder et al., 2009). The definition of student competencies through demonstration standards allows institutions to use their own teaching methods despite differences in resources and educational approaches. The clear definition of competencies allows for outcome evaluation while maintaining freedom in teaching methods.

The framework operates at a scalable level of resource needs which prevents institutions from needing expensive technology or extensive infrastructure that only well-funded institutions can access. The use of free analytical tools, open-source software, public datasets and online educational materials help students overcome financial obstacles (Tussyadiah, 2020). The focus on conceptual learning instead of platform-specific skills enables students to build enduring abilities which do not require access to particular commercial software systems.

The framework recognizes that hotel investment practices and market structures and regulatory frameworks differ between different regions worldwide. The use of diverse geographic market examples and multiple jurisdiction references and regional context-based assessment scenarios make learning materials applicable worldwide. The implementation of framework principles by faculty members for local industry needs creates authentic learning experiences that uphold essential competency standards. The Partnership and Collaboration Mechanisms use industry relationships and inter-institutional cooperation and technology provider engagement to handle resource limitations. Educational institutions can access additional resources through frameworks which support partnership development and educational material sharing and collaborative program execution. The combination of industry advisory boards with guest speakers and internships allows students to gain valuable learning experiences regardless of their institution's location or budget.

ASSESSMENT AND CONTINUOUS IMPROVEMENT

The implementation of an effective framework depends on strong assessment systems which track student competency growth and program success and industry standards evolution. The assessment methods used in this framework evaluate student learning through multiple dimensions which measure their knowledge development and skill performance and professional decision-making abilities in all competency areas.

Students receive feedback through formative assessment which enables them to improve their skills and develop metacognitive abilities during their learning process. Students develop their capabilities through practice exercises with AI tools and peer review of analytical work and instructor feedback about algorithmic output interpretation (Kolb, 2015). The assessment method of formative evaluation focuses on learning assistance instead of summative evaluation which creates an environment for students to experiment and develop their skills.

The summative assessment process evaluates student learning outcomes through complete competency demonstrations. The assessment process includes portfolio evaluations of analytical work and case study analyses that combine traditional methods with AI tools and capstone projects which integrate various competency domains for authentic evaluation (Mulder et al., 2009). The use of rubrics which define performance targets for knowledge and skills and professional judgment elements helps maintain consistent and transparent assessment practices.

The assessment of program effectiveness relies on feedback from employers and graduate survey results and placement statistics which serve as external evaluation criteria. The systematic collection of employer feedback about graduate readiness and career advancement tracking and alumni feedback about educational quality enables ongoing program development (Mulder et al., 2009). The industry advisory board evaluates curriculum materials and learning resources and graduate competencies to maintain professional practice alignment with current developments.

The assessment data and industry feedback and technological advancements and pedagogical research form a cycle which guides program development through the Program Review process. The framework stays current through annual learning outcome assessments and periodic program evaluations and strategic planning activities that adapt to AI technology advancements and investment industry changes and educational excellence standards. The field's fast-paced nature becomes less likely to cause educational stagnation because of this ongoing improvement approach.

Pedagogical Approaches and Teaching Strategies

Students learn effectively through experiential experiences that use real-world investment scenarios with authentic data and AI tools to create meaningful learning experiences (Kolb, 2015). The learning progression starts with directed activities before students move to independent work which develops their skills progressively. The practice of reflection helps students build metacognitive skills which are vital for their professional growth (Kolb, 2015).

The educational experience becomes more authentic through industry partnerships, which provide students with guest speakers, internships, and access to specialized tools (Gretzel et al., 2020; Kolb, 2015). Advisory boards further support curriculum development by ensuring alignment with current industry needs (Gretzel et al., 2020). The combination of group work in projects helps students develop teamwork abilities while teaching them how to work with others.

The combination of portfolio development and comprehensive case analysis and reflective documentation provide better assessment of integrated problem-solving abilities than traditional exams do (Mulder et al., 2009). The practice of peer review helps students learn to evaluate work critically (Kolb, 2015).

Professional Development and Executive Education Implications

While much of the discussion around AI-enhanced hospitality investment education focuses on undergraduate and postgraduate students, the need for professional development among industry practitioners is equally significant. Many current hospitality managers, asset managers, and investment analysts were trained before the widespread adoption of artificial intelligence tools and therefore face a growing need to update their analytical capabilities. Continuous executive education and professional training programs are increasingly essential to ensure that existing professionals remain competitive in rapidly evolving data-driven investment environments.

Executive education programs differ from traditional academic curricula in several important ways. Professional participants typically possess substantial operational or financial experience but may lack exposure to recent technological developments. Educational approaches for this audience should therefore emphasize applied learning, short intensive modules, case-based teaching, and direct exposure to industry analytics platforms. Flexible delivery formats, including hybrid learning, online workshops, and industry collaborations, are particularly effective in addressing time constraints faced by working professionals.

INSTITUTIONAL READINESS FOR AI INTEGRATION IN HOSPITALITY EDUCATION

Beyond curriculum design and professional training, successful integration of artificial intelligence into hospitality investment education depends heavily on institutional readiness. Educational institutions vary significantly in technological infrastructure, faculty expertise, and access to industry partnerships, all of which influence the feasibility and effectiveness of AI-related educational initiatives. Recognizing these differences is essential when developing globally applicable educational frameworks.

Faculty development represents one of the most critical factors in institutional readiness. Many hospitality educators possess strong industry experience but may have limited exposure to data science, advanced analytics, or artificial intelligence applications. Structured faculty development programs, including workshops, industry collaborations, and interdisciplinary cooperation with business analytics or computer science departments, can help bridge this gap. Continuous professional development ensures that instructors remain confident in teaching emerging analytical tools while maintaining the contextual industry perspective that hospitality education requires.

Technological infrastructure also plays an important role. Access to industry databases, analytics platforms, and cloud-based computational resources enables students to engage with realistic datasets and decision-making scenarios. However, high-cost proprietary systems may not always be accessible to all institutions. Therefore, a balanced approach combining commercial tools, open-source analytical platforms, and publicly available datasets can provide effective learning opportunities while maintaining financial feasibility.

Institutional culture and leadership support further influence successful AI integration. Universities that encourage innovation, interdisciplinary collaboration, and industry engagement tend to adapt more quickly to technological change. Administrative backing is often necessary for resource allocation, curriculum redesign, and faculty training initiatives. Without institutional commitment, even well-designed educational frameworks may face implementation barriers.

Finally, institutional readiness should be viewed as an evolving process rather than a fixed state. Artificial intelligence technologies continue to develop rapidly, requiring ongoing adaptation of curricula, teaching methods, and partnerships. Educational institutions that adopt flexible strategies, encourage experimentation, and maintain strong industry connections are more likely to remain relevant in AI-enhanced hospitality investment education.

Industry partnerships play a crucial role in professional AI education within hospitality investment. Collaboration with hotel companies, asset management firms, data providers, and technology vendors allows educational institutions to provide access to real-world datasets, contemporary analytical tools, and current industry practices. Such partnerships enhance program credibility and ensure alignment between educational content and evolving professional requirements. Guest lectures, industry-sponsored projects, and executive mentoring programs can further strengthen this connection between academia and industry practice.

Another important consideration involves change management within organizations adopting AI-supported decision-making. Even when analytical tools are available, professionals may resist adoption due to unfamiliarity, perceived complexity, or concerns about job displacement. Educational initiatives should therefore address not only technical competencies, but also organizational adaptation, ethical considerations, and leadership skills required to integrate AI effectively within hospitality investment contexts.

Ultimately, professional education in AI-enhanced hospitality investment should complement rather than replace traditional financial and operational expertise. The most effective professionals combine domain-specific knowledge with technological literacy, enabling them to interpret AI-generated insights critically while maintaining strategic judgment. Educational institutions that successfully bridge academic training with ongoing professional development will play a central role in preparing both future graduates and current industry leaders for increasingly technology-enabled hospitality investment environments.

IMPLEMENTATION CONSIDERATIONS AND BEST PRACTICES

The implementation of successful programs depends on realistic institutional readiness assessments, strategic resource allocation, and phased implementation approaches aligned with organizational capabilities (Ivanov & Webster, 2017; Tussyadiah, 2020). The evaluation of program strengths and faculty capabilities and available resources through environmental scanning enables proper planning. Engaging stakeholders is essential for gaining organizational support and identifying potential concerns during the implementation process (Ivanov & Webster, 2017; Tussyadiah, 2020).

The development of faculty members stands as a fundamental requirement. The combination of technical workshops with collaborative learning communities and industry immersion experiences and complete support systems helps develop professional capabilities (Koseoglu et al., 2016; Law et al., 2012).

The selection of a platform requires organizations to find a balance between educational needs and financial costs and industrial relevance (Tussyadiah, 2020). Cloud-based platforms eliminate obstacles to access (Tussyadiah, 2020) while open-source tools offer free solutions with strong capabilities. The combination of different approaches enables organizations to achieve maximum capabilities while controlling their expenses.

The combination of strategic partnerships between investment firms and technology providers and industry associations enables organizations to access capabilities that exceed their internal resources (Tussyadiah, 2020).

Multiple institutions can join forces with peer hospitality programs and business schools to share resources and create joint educational content and exchange faculty members and conduct research collaborations. The combination of multiple institutions in collaborative online courses enables them to create educational programs that surpass the capabilities of individual programs. Software licensing consortiums and content development partnerships enable cost reduction while building practice-based communities that drive ongoing improvement efforts.

CHALLENGES AND ETHICAL CONSIDERATIONS: ALGORITHMIC BIAS AND FAIRNESS CONCERNS

Machine learning systems maintain and strengthen existing biases which exist in training data and algorithm design and deployment environments (O'Neil, 2016). Hotel investment applications contain the risk of algorithmic bias which could lead to unfair property value assessments and market evaluations and investment guidance. The education of future investment professionals needs to include training about bias detection methods and evaluation techniques and methods to reduce bias.

The training data used to create AI models contains biases because it contains discriminatory elements and market flaws and missing information from past times. The algorithms trained on hotel transaction databases that lack diverse market representation and property types and ownership demographics produce biased predictions for minority groups (Tussyadiah, 2020). Investment professionals need to understand that past data patterns do not guarantee future success, and they should verify recommendations which show systematic prejudice against specific markets or operators.

The selection of features, model design, and optimization criteria during algorithm development can introduce bias even when the underlying training data appears unbiased. Decisions regarding variable selection, weighting, and model objectives are inherently shaped by human judgment, which ultimately influences the outputs generated by AI systems (O'Neil, 2016; Tussyadiah, 2020). The inability to see through black-box algorithms makes it difficult to detect and fix bias in their decision-making processes. AI systems should be taught to students as developer-created constructs instead of absolute facts because they need to be evaluated instead of accepted without question.

AI systems which were created for one purpose or population become problematic when deployed in inappropriate situations, a phenomenon often referred to as deployment context bias. The performance of valuation models trained on full-service hotels deteriorates when applied to limited-service properties, while algorithms trained on stable markets fail to adapt to fast-changing market conditions (Gretzel et al., 2020; Tussyadiah, 2020). Investment professionals need to determine if AI tools match their operational needs before using complex systems that may not be suitable for their work.

Data Privacy and Security Implications

Hotel investment analysis depends on detailed information about guest activities and property metrics and market trends which create privacy and security challenges. The process of obtaining necessary information for decision-making requires investment professionals to handle privacy rights and legal requirements and ethical standards (Tussyadiah, 2020). The education system should teach students about privacy matters and ethical data handling methods together with their analytical skills.

The collection and use of personal data in hospitality settings now faces rising regulatory oversight because of GDPR and CCPA and new international privacy standards. The analysis of customer booking data and preference information and behavioral patterns for investment purposes needs to follow all relevant privacy laws that apply to the situation (Buhalis & Leung 2018). Investment professionals who work with detailed datasets need to learn about consent rules and data reduction methods and individual privacy protections. The entire analytical lifecycle needs continuous data security practices to stop unauthorized access and breaches and misuse of information. Hotel performance data together with transaction information and market intelligence hold competitive value that requires protection because personal data breaches result in legal consequences and damage to reputation (Gretzel et al., 2020). The security practices of access controls and encryption and secure data disposal need to be understood by investment professionals although specialists handle the technical implementation.

The practice of sharing data with partners and lenders and service providers in investment activities introduces new security and privacy risks because of third-party involvement. Investment professionals need to assess vendor data handling practices of vendors while creating suitable legal agreements and verifying international data transfer compliance (Ivanov & Webster, 2017). The educational approach should focus on handling real-world privacy issues instead of treating privacy as an abstract concept.

TRANSPARENCY, EXPLAINABILITY, AND PROFESSIONAL RESPONSIBILITY

The lack of transparency in deep learning, ensemble methods, and other machine learning algorithms makes it difficult to achieve explainability in investment decision processes. Stakeholders, including property owners, investors, lenders, and regulators, need to understand how investment recommendations are generated and which factors influence the results, particularly given the dense nature of many algorithmic models (O'Neil, 2016; Tussyadiah, 2020). Investment professionals need to explain and defend their AI-based decisions to stakeholders even though they cannot simplify the complex technical aspects of the algorithms.

The implementation of Explainable AI methods, including feature importance metrics, visualization techniques, and simplified model approximations, helps address the transparency problem (Gretzel et al., 2020; Tussyadiah, 2020). Students need to learn about both complex black-box algorithms and simpler interpretable methods while developing skills to present AI-derived findings to people without technical backgrounds. The ability to understand how model accuracy relates to interpretability helps professionals make suitable choices based on specific situations.

The practice of professional responsibility requires investment professionals to make ethical decisions about AI recommendation modifications when algorithms fail to detect important factors. The combination of market conditions and relationship factors and strategic business needs can lead to decisions that differ from algorithmic optimization recommendations (Tussyadiah, 2020). The educational program should teach students to trust their professional decisions which guide AI system outputs but do not follow them automatically because algorithms exist to assist human decision-making.

The practice of documentation needs specific focus because it enables both transparency and accountability. Investment professionals need to document their analytical approaches and data resources and their assumptions and reasoning that led to their final recommendations (Tussyadiah, 2020). The documentation process allows future assessments and helps organizations meet regulatory requirements and build organizational knowledge. The educational approach should teach students to view documentation as their professional duty instead of treating it as an administrative chore.

The overreliance on AI systems threatens to diminish essential analytical abilities and professional expertise and critical thinking abilities because users fail to properly assess algorithmic outputs.

The deskilling problem becomes most severe when users do not possess sufficient domain knowledge or methodological skills to identify flawed AI recommendations (O'Neil, 2016). The combination of technology adoption with fundamental professional capability development stands as a critical educational requirement.

AI output assessment needs professionals who can detect abnormal results and verify recommendations against different information sources and evaluate unusual patterns (Rushmore & Baum, 2001). The ability to perform basic financial analysis and market research and valuation assessment independently serves as the foundation for evaluating AI-generated conclusions (Rushmore & Baum, 2001). The curriculum needs to teach students essential skills first or simultaneously with AI tool training instead of substituting technology for traditional skill development.

The risk of automation bias becomes most dangerous in critical investment decisions because people tend to trust system outputs more than their own judgment even when the system shows errors (Tussyadiah, 2020). Users tend to disregard their own expertise when algorithms present different suggestions which might result in suboptimal choices. The education system needs to teach students about automation bias directly while helping them uphold their professional judgment and stay receptive to alternative perspectives.

The practice of creating scenarios for technological breakdowns and system unavailability helps professionals build their ability to adapt and become more resilient. The ability to perform meaningful analysis without AI tools becomes essential for investment professionals when their preferred tools become unavailable because of cost issues or technical problems or organizational changes (Ivanov & Webster, 2017). Students who learn transferable analytical skills instead of tool-specific knowledge will become more adaptable to different professional environments.AI systems encounter major operational constraints when markets experience inflection points and economic cycles shift between different phases.

Machine learning algorithms trained on historical data fail to deliver reliable performance during market cycle inflection points and economic shocks and regulatory changes and structural industry shifts because these events create unreliable or misleading future performance indicators from past data. The COVID-19 pandemic created a major forecasting challenge because AI models trained with pre-pandemic data produced highly inaccurate predictions during 2020-2021 while human analysts who used first-principles thinking and scenario planning and analogical reasoning from SARS and 9/11 crises produced more accurate forecasts (Gretzel et al., 2020).

Hotel market cycle awareness depends on human judgment which combines economic analysis with supply pipeline evaluation and financing market dynamics assessment and historical pattern recognition rather than on algorithmic output (Rushmore & Baum, 2001). The interpretation of leading indicators such as construction financing availability and building permit issuance trends and lending underwriting standard evolution and transaction volume patterns and cap rate movements needs human experience to understand them because algorithms cannot duplicate these patterns from historical data. The ability to detect major market changes enables investment professionals to determine when AI tools based on historical data need major updates or should be put on hold or completely replaced by fundamental analysis that does not rely on past patterns.

Educational programs need to teach students about economic cycle analysis through the study of cycle positioning indicators which include construction pipeline dynamics against demand growth and pricing power trends and lending standard evolution and transaction volume patterns and cap rate movements and investor sentiment indicators from REIT performance and private market activity levels. The analysis of investment choices made during past cycle peaks (2006-2007) and troughs (2009-2010 and 2020-2021) shows that fundamental market assessment takes precedence over algorithmic suggestions during market inflection points. The analysis of transactions made at peak market times which needed restructuring or foreclosure and successful investments made during market bottoms proves that understanding market cycles remains more important than having advanced analytical skills.

The accuracy of machine learning models deteriorates exactly when accurate predictions become essential during times of fast market shifts and economic stress and industrial transformations. The ability of algorithms to detect patterns in stable data environments fails when dealing with the non-stationary patterns that occur when cyclical industries undergo structural changes. The fundamental weakness of algorithms requires professionals to build judgment skills which help them determine when to ignore algorithmic outputs by using scenario analysis and stress testing and first-principles thinking. Students need to demonstrate their ability to analyze model assumptions and detect data regime shifts that invalidate historical patterns and explain situations where traditional methods perform better than AI-based approaches despite their technological complexity.

The training enables new graduates to handle upcoming market cycles and economic disruptions and industrial shifts because AI systems based on past stability data become ineffective for fast-evolving market situations. The combination of cycle awareness with AI literacy training produces investment experts who can use technology effectively during stable market times but also possess the analytical skills needed for successful investing through all economic cycles.

FUTURE DIRECTIONS

AI technology shows rapid development in its capabilities. The combination of advanced natural language processing with computer vision and generative AI systems will drive future changes in investment analysis according to Buhalis & Leung (2018) and Ivanov & Webster (2017). The new technologies will allow automated news tracking and property inspection through image processing and synthetic scenario development (Xiang et al., 2015) yet they introduce privacy concerns and data quality issues and appropriate automation usage.

The implementation of AI technology will reshape professional roles and create new career paths for employees. The future of work may lead to specialized roles between technical experts and business professionals, or it could create accessible tools for non-technical users or AI systems could enhance human capabilities for strategic planning and relationship building (Gretzel et al., 2020; Ivanov & Webster, 2017). Students need to develop three essential competencies which include adaptability and continuous learning orientation and meta-competencies of learning agility and critical thinking instead of focusing on specific tool mastery.

Research opportunities in AI tools, educational methods, ethical standards, and international studies of AI adoption across different global markets remain substantial (Koseoglu et al., 2016; Tussyadiah, 2020).

Future research should also look at how AI influences investment performance, decision-making quality, and organizational strategy over time. In addition, comparing different regions and industries could help explain how local conditions shape the adoption and effectiveness of AI. Bringing together perspectives from finance, technology, and hospitality will be important to better understand the broader impact of AI-driven transformation.

CONCLUSION

The implementation of AI systems in hotel investment analysis brings both positive prospects and complex difficulties for hospitality education programs. Students need to develop four essential competency areas which include hospitality investment principles and data skills and AI system comprehension and ethical decision-making abilities. The proposed framework places emphasis on conceptual knowledge instead of technical skills because hospitality graduates excel at uniting their technological skills with their deep industry expertise.

The educational methods which focus on experiential learning and industry collaboration and teamwork development match the real-world requirements of professionals. The success of implementation depends on realistic planning from institutions and development of faculty members and strategic partnership development. Systematic planning combined with institutional commitment enables the resolution of three main obstacles which include limited faculty expertise and restricted resources and ethical concerns about ethics.

Educational programs that teach AI competencies to students create a competitive edge in the job market while building stronger connections with industry partners. The future demands a balanced approach which unites hospitality knowledge with analytical skills and technological competencies to develop adaptable professionals who excel in digital environments while keeping their human judgment and relationship-building abilities which set hospitality professionals apart from basic data analysts.

As artificial intelligence continues to reshape hospitality investment analysis, educational institutions must remain adaptable, ensuring that graduates and professionals develop both technological literacy and the critical judgment required for responsible decision-making.

REFERENCES

Antonio, N., de Almeida, A., & Nunes, L. (2019). Hotel booking demand datasets. *Data in Brief, 22*, 41–49.

Buhalis, D., & Leung, R. (2018). Smart hospitality: Interconnectivity and interoperability towards an ecosystem. *International Journal of Hospitality Management, 71*, 41–50.

Deloitte. (2023). *State of Generative AI in the Enterprise Survey*. Deloitte Insights.

Gretzel, U., Fuchs, M., Baggio, R., Hoepken, W., Law, R., Neidhardt, J., & Xiang, Z. (2020). e-Tourism beyond COVID-19: A call for transformative research. *Information Technology & Tourism, 22*, 187–203.

Hodges, C., & Ocak, C. (2023). Integrating generative AI into higher education: Considerations. *EDUCAUSE Review*.

HSMAI Foundation. (2025). *The state of generative AI in talent management for hotel sales, marketing and revenue management*. https://global.hsmai.org/wp-content/uploads/2025/02/02122025-AI-Research-Report-Final.pdf

Ivanov, S., & Soliman, M. (2023). Game of algorithms: ChatGPT implications for the future of tourism education and research. *Journal of tourism futures, 9*(2), 214-221.

Ivanov, S., & Webster, C. (2017). Adoption of Robots, Artificial Intelligence and Service Automation by Travel, Tourism and Hospitality Companies – A Cost-Benefit Analysis. Prepared for the *International Scientific Conference "Contemporary Tourism – Traditions and Innovations"*, Sofia University, 19-21 October 2017.

Kok, N., Koponen, E. L., & Martínez-Barbosa, C. A. (2017). Big data in real estate? From manual appraisal to automated valuation. *Journal of Portfolio Management, 43*(6), 202–211.

Kolb, D. A. (2015). *Experiential learning: Experience as the source of learning and development* (2nd ed.). Pearson Education.

Köseoglu, M. A., Rahimi, R., Okumus, F., & Liu, J. (2016). Bibliometric studies in tourism. *Annals of Tourism Research, 61*, 180–198.

Law, R., Leung, D., & Cheung, C. (2012). A systematic review, analysis, and evaluation of research articles in the Cornell Hospitality Quarterly. *Cornell Hospitality Quarterly, 53*(4), 365–381.

Li, J., Xu, L., Tang, L., Wang, S., & Li, L. (2018). Big data in tourism research: A literature review. *Tourism Management, 68*, 301–323.

Mulder, M., Gulikers, J., Biemans, H., & Wesselink, R. (2009). The new competence concept in higher education: Error or enrichment? *Journal of European Industrial Training, 33*(8/9), 755–770.

O'Neil, C. (2016). *Weapons of math destruction: How big data increases inequality and threatens democracy*. Crown.

Rushmore, S., & Baum, E. (2001). *Hotels and motels: Valuations and market studies*. Appraisal Institute.

Sánchez, , E. CSánchez-Medina, , A. JPellejero, , M. (2020). Identifying critical hotel cancellations using artificial intelligence. *Tourism Management Perspectives*, 35, 100718

Sigala, M., Ooi, K. B., Tan, G. W. H., Aw, E. C. X., Buhalis, D., Cham, T. H., & Ye, I. H. (2024). Understanding the impact of ChatGPT on tourism and hospitality: Trends, prospects and research agenda. *Journal of Hospitality and Tourism Management, 60*, 384–390.

Tussyadiah, I. (2020). A review of research into automation in tourism. *Annals of Tourism Research, 81*, 102883.

UNESCO. (2023). *ChatGPT and Artificial Intelligence in Higher Education*. Quick Start Guide.

Wang, H., Dang, A., Wu, Z., & Mac, S. (2024). Generative AI in higher education: Seeing ChatGPT through universities' policies, resources, and guidelines. *Computers and Education: Artificial Intelligence, 7*, 100326.

Xiang, Z., Fuchs, M., Gretzel, U., & Höpken, W. (2015). What can big data and text analytics tell us about hotel guest experience and satisfaction? *International Journal of Hospitality Management, 44*, 120–130.

ADDITIONAL READING

Agrawal, A., Gans, J., & Goldfarb, A. (2018). *Prediction machines: The simple economics of artificial intelligence*. Harvard Business Review Press.

Brynjolfsson, E., & McAfee, A. (2017). The business of artificial intelligence. *Harvard Business Review Digital Articles*, 1-20.

Davenport, T. H., & Ronanki, R. (2018). Artificial intelligence for the real world. *Harvard Business Review, 96*(1), 108–116.

Huang, M. H., & Rust, R. T. (2018). Artificial intelligence in service. *Journal of Service Research, 21*(2), 155–172.

Makridakis, S. (2017). The forthcoming artificial intelligence (AI) revolution: Its impact on society and firms. *Futures, 90*, 46–60.

McAfee, A., & Brynjolfsson, E. (2017). *Machine, platform, crowd: Harnessing our digital future*. W. W. Norton & Company.

Russell, S., & Norvig, P. (2020). *Artificial intelligence: A modern approach* (4th ed.). Pearson.

Schwab, K. (2017). *The fourth industrial revolution*. Currency.

Stone, P., Brooks, R., Brynjolfsson, E., Calo, R., Etzioni, O., Hager, G., & Teller, A. (2016). *Artificial intelligence and life in 2030: The one hundred year study on artificial intelligence*. Stanford University.

Wilson, H. J., & Daugherty, P. R. (2018). Collaborative intelligence: Humans and AI are joining forces. *Harvard Business Review, 96*(4), 114–123.

KEY TERMS AND DEFINITIONS

AI-Enhanced Investment Analysis: AI-Enhanced Investment Analysis represents a method that combines artificial intelligence systems with traditional financial methods and market research to enhance decision accuracy and efficiency for hotel property evaluation.

Algorithmic Bias: The systematic errors in machine learning systems produce unfair results through biased algorithms which stem from unrepresentative training data and inappropriate feature selection and algorithm design that incorporates human prejudices and historical discrimination.

Automated Valuation Model (AVM): The Automated Valuation Model (AVM) uses statistical methods and machine learning algorithms to analyze historical data and property characteristics and market indicators for fast and consistent real estate value assessments without needing traditional appraisal methods.

Competency-Based Education: The pedagogical framework of Competency-Based Education focuses on developing measurable professional skills which match industry requirements instead of traditional content-based or credit hour systems to let learners prove their mastery through performance assessments regardless of time or teaching methods.

Data Literacy: Data Literacy represents the ability to handle data information through reading and understanding and creation and communication while showing expertise in statistical output interpretation and data quality assessment and analytical boundary identification and evidence evaluation and quantitative information delivery to various groups through suitable visualizations and storytelling methods.

Digital Investment Literacy: Digital Investment Literacy involves the ability to assess and use technology-based investment tools and platforms and methods by understanding their appropriate uses and algorithmic boundaries and validating computational results against professional knowledge and combining multiple analytical methods.

Experiential Learning: The educational philosophy of Experiential Learning supports learning through direct experience followed by reflective observation and abstract conceptualization and active experimentation which suits professional judgment development and complex skill integration in real-world problem-solving situations.

Franchise Agreement: A hotel owner receives the right to use a specific brand name and reservation system through a franchise agreement which requires them to pay initial fees and ongoing royalties and marketing contributions and maintain brand standards and execute property improvement plans and follow operational rules that impact property value and financing options and investment performance through brand value generation versus fee expenses and operational restrictions.

Machine Learning Applications in Hospitality: The hospitality industry uses machine learning applications to develop algorithms which learn from data patterns to enhance predictions and classifications and decision-making for hospitality operations through revenue forecasting and customer segmentation and market trend prediction and operational optimization and investment risk assessment.

Management Agreement: A management agreement lets a professional hotel management company run a property for the owner while receiving payment through base management fees and incentive fees and reimbursement payments which determine investment returns and operational control and financing terms and property marketability.

Natural Language Processing (NLP): Natural Language Processing (NLP) represents an artificial intelligence subfield which enables computers to process human language effectively for valuable purposes in hospitality investment through review sentiment analysis and market intelligence extraction and automated report summarization.

Predictive Analytics: Investment professionals use predictive analytics to analyze historical data and statistical methods and machine learning algorithms to create accurate and consistent forecasts about future events and behaviors and market trends.

Uniform System of Accounts for the Lodging Industry (USALI): The Uniform System of Accounts for the Lodging Industry (USALI) provides standardized financial reporting tools which help hotels track departmental revenues and expenses and create profit statements and financial ratios and reporting standards for accurate investment analysis and operational improvement decisions. Hotel investment professionals need USALI proficiency to evaluate property financial statements and create pro forma projections and identify operational efficiency opportunities.

Chapter 2

Using Artificial Intelligence Tools for Internship Practice and Securing Future Job Opportunities for Hospitality Students:

Developing a Critical Integration AI Model for Higher Education

Marius Vlad
http://orcid.org/0009-0006-3953-2823
Les Roches Global Hospitality Education, Marbella, Spain

Jon Loiti
Les Roches Global Hospitality Education, Marbella, Spain

ABSTRACT

This study discusses the importance of integrating artificial intelligence (AI) into hospitality education to enhance students' industry preparation for securing internships and starting their careers. Insights from students, academia, and industry professionals show AI can positively influence training and employability. As AI transforms guest interactions and operational routines, including it in hospitality educational curricula becomes essential. Automated systems and guest service applications can boost industry productivity and streamline operations, directly

DOI: 10.4018/979-8-3373-5112-4.ch002

impacting students' practical experience. To prepare future professionals, hospitality educational institutions must develop their own balanced AI learning model, based on the theoretical and hands-on training, while maintaining an ethical awareness.

INTRODUCTION

Artificial intelligence (AI) technologies have significantly impacted the inter-human interactions and the overall environmental perception of the individuals (Benckendorff et al., 2019). Organisations must develop a clear approach for identifying what AI means to their specific context and to effectively leverage the AI potential into a coherent strategy. Gartner (n.d.) saw AI as using advanced analytical and logic-based technologies to interpret data, support making decisions and automate tasks. For educational institutions and hospitality organisations it has been especially important to develop this clear strategy for preparing their students or trainees for the workplace.

A well-defined and balanced AI strategy enables institutions to design training programs and internship opportunities that reflect real-world applications of AI (Nartey, 2024; Pericleous et al., 2025). Students learning technologies and skills that align with industry expectations become more competitive candidates for internships and employment opportunities.

Moreover, when companies formulate and communicate how AI delivers value – for example through automation, customer experience enhancement, or operational efficiency (Ivanov & Webster, 2020; Koo et al., 2021; Kong et al., 2024; Lestari et al., 2021; Lu et al., 2019; Mori et al., 2012; Murphy et al., 2019; Nartey, 2024; Owoeye, 2024; Pericleous et al., 2025; Santiago & Gil, 2025; Veletsianos, 2016) - they strengthen their collaboration with academic partners to build meaningful work placements (Baum, 2019; Lestari et al., 2021; Owoeye, 2024; Santiago & Gil, 2025). Thus, defining AI within an organisation is both a strategic necessity and step toward creating connections for students to transition successfully from education to employment in AI-enhanced roles (Chen et al., 2020; Gartner, n.d.).

The hospitality industry, particularly the hotels and service associated industries, are sectors experiencing profound technological transformation (Baum, 2019; Ivanov & Webster, 2020; Lestari et al., 2021; Lukanova & Ilieva, 2019). Originally regarded as a "people-oriented" (Lukanova & Ilieva, 2019, p.4) industry, hospitality is being redefined by AI-driven systems such as chatbots, facial recognition, service robots, and automated check-in kiosks (Ivanov & Webster, 2020; Lu et al., 2019; Van Dis et al., 2023; Wang et al., 2023). These technologies are becoming progressively more embedded in operational practices. It is relevant to evaluate how AI can be utilised within hospitality education, especially in practical training classrooms (Cassidy et al. (2023) to prepare students for the evolving demands of industry. This study discusses how AI tools can be integrated into educational frameworks to support instructors and academia to reflect on what skills students need to succeed in a technological-enhanced hospitality world.

By incorporating AI into classroom instruction and hands-on learning environments, students gain, apart from technical knowledge, critical competencies such as analytical reasoning, effective communication, and ethical decision-making skills (Koo et al., 2021; Kong et al., 2024; Lu et al., 2019; Murphy et al., 2019; Nartey, 2024; Pericleous et al., 2025; Veletsianos, 2016) which are vital in navigating AI-driven workplaces. Additionally, exposing students to AI applications during their studies enhances adaptability and confidence (Cassidy et al., 2023; Kong et al., 2024; Nartey, 2024; Pericleous et al., 2025; Santiago & Gil, 2025; Veletsianos, 2016) in using further emerging technologies.

AI implementation in hospitality education can contribute to securing work opportunities and internship placements for graduating students (Lestari et al., 2021; Nartey, 2024; Owoeye, 2024). The immediate transformation of the industry requires professionals who understand and can manage these AI systems, so students with practical experience in these technologies become highly attractive to potential employers. During internships, students gain hands-on experience and these are their entries to employment (Kong et al., 2024; Nartey, 2024; Santiago & Gil, 2025; Veletsianos, 2016). AI proficiency in customer service automation, data analytics, and smart room technologies (Baum, 2019; Kong et al., 2024; Murphy et al., 2019) better position students to meet the expectations of modern hospitality employers. Furthermore, AI can assist in the job search itself, through intelligent career platforms, resume screening tools, and personalised job matching systems (Yu & Meng, 2025).

In essence, the strategic integration of AI into hospitality education enhances the students' learning experience and expands their career pathways. By aligning academic training with technological advancements, institutions can empower students to enter the workforce with confidence, competence, and a competitive edge.

Research Aim

Since AI has drastically transformed the way hospitality and related industries deliver service and interact with guests, this study discusses how AI tools can be integrated into classroom and educational frameworks. The recommendations are meant to assist instructors and academia delivering on the approaches students need to succeed in a technologically enhanced hospitality world and secure internship and job opportunities in the field of hospitality.

LITERATURE REVIEW

The integration of AI into hospitality education has turned into a fundamental driver of change, rather than just a technological upgrade. While the post-pandemic accelerated the implementation of digital learning tools in hospitality higher education curriculum, the literature reveals significant competing visions of how AI can impact the student preparation for professional practice.

This literature review is meant to examine these approaches, by discussing how different theoretical frameworks explore AI's transformative potential and the limitations in bridging the gap between classroom learning and industry demands (El Hajal & Yeoman, 2024; Portocarrero Ramos et al., 2025). While hospitality subjects have traditionally relied on in-person and hands-on training (Ivanov & Webster, 2020), AI has brought new modalities of discovery, interaction and learning, through virtual simulations (Botero-Gómez et al.(2023), chatbots, and AR/VR technologies (Al-Hyari et al., 2023; Deri et al., 2024; Murphy et al., 2019; Sigala et al., 2024; Tacgin, 2020; Van Der Meulen & De Vries, 2023; Veletsianos, 2016). These tools provide opportunities not only to replicate real-world environments (hotels, restaurants, event areas), but also to prepare the students for the technology-driven society (Benckendorff et al., 2019; European Commission, 2023; Nartey, 2024; Owoeye, 2024; Tiwari, 2023) and modern service industries (Deri, et al., 2024; Murphy et al., 2019; Santiago & Gil, 2025).

Pedagogical Exploration

Considering the immersive and interconnected nature surrounding AI environments, the studies of Chytas et al. (2023) and Hilken et al. (2020) analyse how AI can develop two crucial dimensions for future employability: decision-making and problem-solving skills. Santiago and Gil (2025) found that providing clear structural guidelines, receiving meaningful tasks, followed by step-by-step quality mentorship, strong academic integration, or personalised feedback mechanisms can support student growth. Ressin (2025) focused on mentorship and providing constant feedback. These approaches have been repeatedly identified as crucial for internship satisfaction and effectiveness (Villegas-Ch. et al., 2023). The importance of AI for university-level studies has already been postulated (Holmes et al., 2019), while recently Thomson et al. (2024) found that students were ever more eager to learn AI, believing that these are skills essential for future employment. The study highlighted the importance of integrating AI into curricula to enhance career readiness and transferable skills. Nonetheless, Westman et al. (2021) see AI as a support and career guide for higher education institutions. The framework developed by El Hajal and Yeoman (2024) integrates AI in tourism and hospitality talent management. It relies on scenario planning to identify ethical considerations and a balanced use of AI, complementing the human roles. This turns AI into a valuable tool for developing competencies that are directly transferable to the workplace.

Furthermore, the studies explored whether AI based learning environments are sufficient and actually prepare students for hospitality work. Research supporting immersive AI technologies considers that virtual simulations, chatbots and AR/VR applications (Al-Hyari et al., 2023; Deri et al., 2024; Murphy et al., 2019) can sufficiently replicate real word environments to develop actual skills. The assumption is that practicing decision making and problem-solving situations in the virtual world will enable a smooth transfer of the practices to actual hotel lobbies (Chytas et al., 2023; Hilken et al., 2020).

On the other hand, Ivanov and Webster (2020) stand behind the traditional approach of in-person training as the historical basis for the industry's practice. Connecting with guests has always required interpersonal interactions, fostering reading guests' body language, navigating the physical demands of service, and being spontaneous and empathetic. Du et al. (2022), Sigala et al. (2024), and Sung et al. (2022) discuss that even though AR and VR can help bridge the gap between theory and practice, technology is insufficient, especially in the fields where human connection is needed.

Nonetheless, a critical gap in literature lies in analysing whether AI is truly transforming practical education or just updating the context of traditional mentorship with the current technological advancements.

Technical Proficiency and Human Expertise

The published studies reveal different approaches about what are the most employable profiles of hospitality graduates, in an industry augmented by AI. On one hand technical proficiency with generative AI-tools, data analytics and digital service platforms is currently a true and undeniable asset (Portocarrero Ramos et al., 2025; Thomson et al., 2024). Graduates who master generative AI-tools and associate technologies position themselves positively in the labour market. Kong et al. (2024), Nhan et al. (2022), and Heller et al. (2019) demonstrate that AI contributes to developing personalised guest experiences and improves operational efficiency. This suggests that understanding and using the intricacies of algorithms impacts job performance.

However, the technological value comes into conflict with the current industry demands for human abilities. Even though Du et al. (2022) found there is a niche need in the market for smart hotels service robots, facial recognition, Benckendorff et al. (2019) debate the complex industry reality, shifting the dynamics from people-to-people connections to people-to-systems and people-to-robot relationships. These new technologies cannot be used without human expertise. The critical question lies whether hospitality students, as future industry managers, are able to take advantage of human connections and AI solutions.

The AI integration framework for tourism and hospitality talent management developed by El Hajal and Yeoman's (2024) claimed that through scenario planning and ethical considerations, AI is positioned as complimentary to human roles. This contrasts also with the drastic opinions that adopting technology is inevitable and without problems.

Creating Opportunity or Displacing Jobs

The most obvious debate of literature relies on AI's promises and the threats to employment. There are studies that promote AI's use for its skill development (Nartey, 2024; Tiwari, 2023), personalised learning (Westman et al., 2021), which align with the industry expectations. Santiago and Gil (2025) researched where students were using AI to solve genuine operational challenges and drive digital transformation, showing AI can foster entrepreneurial mindsets and practical engagement.

However, the studies of Owoeye (2024) and Tiwari (2023) support the notion of AI threatening to displace entry-level positions, which are occupied usually by hospitality students during their internships. The controversy lies in the very educational systems training students with AI competencies, maybe leading to irreversibly making their students' work redundant. The solution to this problem is in upskilling initiatives and new roles in data science and AI ethics. Thus, preparing hospitality workers for transitioning into higher level analytical positions. Baum (2019) has already cautioned against this approach, however mostly because of the nature of the stratified nature of the hospitality labor market and the overall deskilling observed in the service roles.

A noticeable optimism based on growth and the creation of new roles may omit crucial questions about labour and work security. Deri et al. (2024) analyse the role of AI and robotics in redefining service delivery and the need for new technological competencies. However, there is limited discussion about who benefits from these transformations. If AI increases the efficiency of the operations and reduces costs for employees but requires workers to constantly gain new skills and retrain to be employed, the overall benefits are less desirable than the literature actually suggests.

Pedagogical Innovation and Ethical Ambiguity

An overall recurring discord is noticeable between the studies who recommend integrating AI into the educational curriculums, and the persistence of uncertainty about the ethical implementation and overall effectiveness of these strategies. Various studies support the incorporation of AI tools into hospitality education for preparing the students for technology-driven industries (Benckendorff et al., 2019; Lestari et al., 2021), while the European Commission, (2023) has issued guiding principles about the AI implementation in higher education. Supporting this approach, Thomson et al. (2024) has revealed that students are eager to learn AI skills, which they perceive as essential for future employment, which underlines the existing demand for such integration.

On the other hand, these recommendations are balanced by significant ambiguity regarding the appropriate methods of integration. Even though Nartey (2024) asks for an ethical and transparent AI integration, rooted in developing critical thinking, it remains unclear what constitutes ethical AI use in hospitality education. The ethical concepts are mostly treated in published studies as additional considerations, rather than a foundational basis on which AI implementation is built. For example, when using AI to complete internship assignments, or to deal with operational problems (Santiago & Gil, 2025), it is unclear how educators differentiate between the use of a legitimate learning tool and the breach of academic integrity. Furthermore, considering AI as a necessity to reduce skill gaps (Portocarrero Ramos et al., 2025; Tiwari, 2023), overlooks how the industry demands are reflecting the particular labour market strategies and relations of power. A critical pedagogical analysis should discuss primarily whether education should be focused on serving the interests and the needs of the industry, or on developing students to reflect on the industry practices and the usefulness of AI implementation itself.

Methodological Limitations and Knowledge Gaps

The literature findings highlight a noticeable methodological limitation, focusing on technological capabilities and potential applications, rather than documenting educational outcomes, and, due to the relative novelty of the topic, its long-term career impacts. Since there is limited research on how AI affects internship performance and job placement and insufficient investigation of ethical implications on service-driven industries, this gap is particularly sensitive, given the topic's rapid evolution. The claims of AI's benefits solely rest on speculation and pilot studies, rather than on longitudinal evidence.

Also, the literature shows little attention on how AI integration might function differently in various educational contexts, with different levels of resources or in different cultural settings. By focusing on results from well-resourced institutions, mostly undertaken in developed economies, the results meant to transfer universally to all hospitality educational contexts require further analysis, to avoid fueling the geographical and institutional biases. At the same time, the prior exposure of the student population to technology, their learning preferences and career paths, which vary drastically, are not explored by current literature.

Furthermore, by focusing on student perspectives and the educational institutions, the requirements of the employers are underexamined. Even though the needs of the industry and the technological trends are mentioned (Chassignol et al., 2018), there is insufficient evidence whether AI-trained graduate students perform better in internships and entry level positions. Nonetheless, it is unclear whether managers actually value AI competencies as much as literature assumes. This critical gap should be further explored, in order to justify the investment in curricular AI integration.

Longitudinal studies, tracking student development from AI-integrated programs through internships and employment would provide grounds for claims about career readiness and job placement. These types of studies could examine not only the employment rates, but also job quality, career progression and overall satisfaction. Furthermore, comparative studies across different types of integrated models – intensive AI environments, selective incorporation or traditional teaching methods with minimal Ai intervention, would help clarify which approaches generate which outcomes and under what circumstances. At the moment literature treats AI integration uniformly beneficial, while in reality, the effectiveness of the strategies varies considerably based on implementation practices, resources or student background.

Nevertheless, a critical analysis of evaluating the dynamics between what counts as necessary AI competencies and the alternative visions for hospitality work and education are needed.

A genuine ethical framework for AI in hospitality education must take into account not only the procedural concerns about transparency but move beyond and discuss substantive aspects about the core educational purposes. Is AI facilitating more efficient job training, should education broaden capacities for professional judgement, and critically engage with technological change? By limiting the discussion of AI as a means of employment, the deeper discussion about the educational role in shaping, not only the individual careers, but the overall future of the hospitality industry as a whole, is overlooked.

Currently, the studies on the impact of AI in hospitality education reveal a variety of questions. The themes of immersive learning and authentic practice, technological proficiency and personal expertise, creating opportunities and displacing jobs, and the pedagogical innovations and the ethical ambiguous context, suggest that AI integration is not a straightforward discussion. Its effects depend on the implementation of choices, institutional context, and labour market dynamics, that the current studies insufficiently scrutinize.

Nevertheless, given the technological development, the industry pressure or the student expectations seem to make increased AI integration inevitable. This integration should not exclude the academic critical examination. Academia must navigate the competing demands of preparing students for a technologically developed workplace, while enhancing the evaluation of the very usefulness of that technology. The AI implementation includes ambiguities, trade-offs, and potential damaging practices. Only by discussing these aspects can hospitality education develop AI integrated models that genuinely serve the student development and not only respond to the technological and market requirements.

Framing the Hypotheses

The reviewed literature reveals AI-enabled environments, as virtual simulations, chatbots, AV/VR, as promising spaces for developing decision-making and problem-solving skills that are directly transferable to hospitality workplaces. At the same time, when looking at pedagogical value, structured guidance, meaningful tasks, mentorship and personalized feedback remain focal to student growth and internship satisfaction. The recommendation is that AI should function best when embedded within strong pedagogical designs, rather than a stand-alone solution. Building on this competing vision, this study's hypothesis is to examine whether student AI engagement is actually reflected in quantifiable expertise:

- Null Hypothesis (H_0): No correlation exists between AI usage frequency and expertise level (ρ|0).
- Alternative Hypothesis (H_1): A positive correlation exists between AI usage frequency and expertise level (ρ|0).

By placing these hypotheses within the debate on immersive AI environments, as opposite to traditional hospitality hands-on training, this study aims to explore whether frequent engagement with AI-based tools, translates into higher levels of expertise, or the usage is just an update of the mentorship context, which does not transform the underlying educational outcomes. Testing whether AI usage frequency correlates with expertise level, directly addresses whether a positive significant correlation would support arguments that AI-based learning environments truly enhance students' readiness to assume complex roles in the hospitality industry.

METHODOLOGICAL FRAMEWORK AND SAMPLING STRATEGY

The current study relies on a convergent research design, integrating quantitative survey data with qualitative interview insights, in order to examine the AI adoption in hospitality education. The purposive sampling strategy targeted three specific stakeholders: graduating students (GS) with a minimum of 1 year of work experience in a hospitality company, hospitality industry professionals (HIP) with at least 5 years of management experience in the chain hotel properties, and academia representatives (A) with more than 10 years of higher educational experience (Figure 1), totaling 117 participants. Among the GS (n = 57), females represented 57.9% and males 42.1%, with most respondents (75.5%) born between 2002 and 2005. The majority were from Europe (63.2%), followed by Asia (15.8%), North America (12.3%), and Africa (8.8%). The group of HIP (n = 49) consisted of 59.2% females and 40.8% males, predominantly from Europe (69.4%) and Asia (24.5%), with participants mostly born between 1986 and 2003. Lastly, the A (n = 11) were primarily male (72.7%), with the largest representation from Europe (81.8%), and birth years ranging from 1965 to 1996. This distribution reflects a diverse sample across gender, professional background, continent, and age, providing a balanced foundation for the study's comparative analysis. Even though the purposive sampling helps target the investigation of populations with relevant AI experience (Saunders et al., 2023), it adds limitations about the overall generalizability of the overall findings.

The data was collected through a survey with 10 multiple choice questions delivered through social media platforms, which volunteers took an average of 2 minutes to complete. Quantitative methods relied on two inferential procedures to the sample Pearson correlation, using a t-test to assess statistical significance and Fisher's z-transformation, to build the confidence intervals for the population correlation.

Figure 1. The profiles of the participants

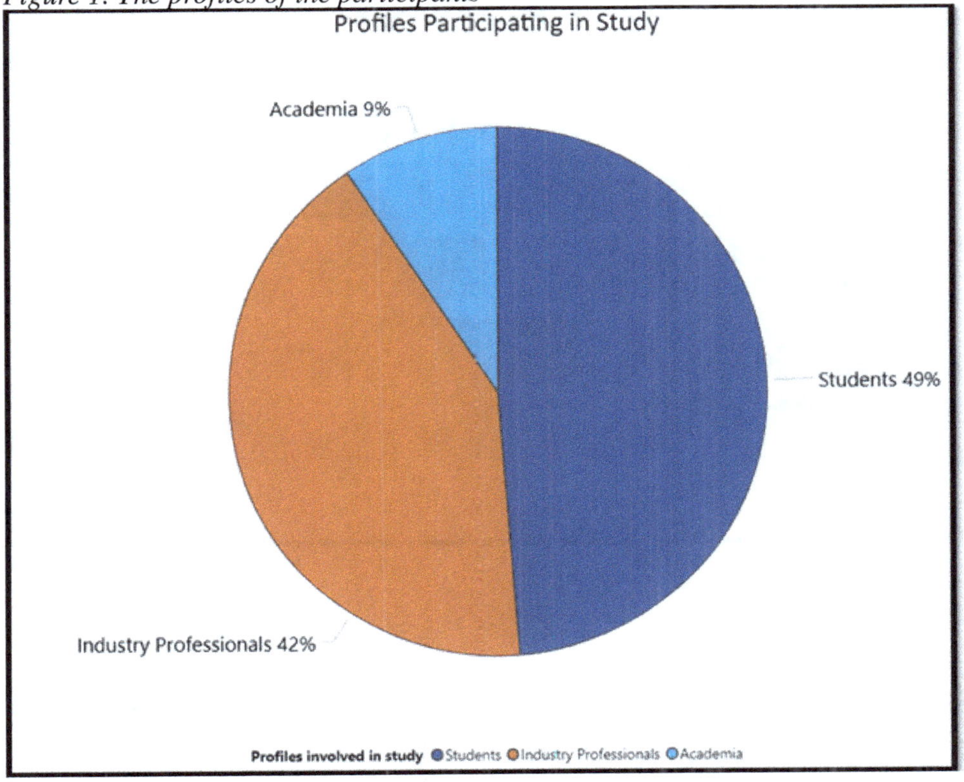

Figure 2. AI use

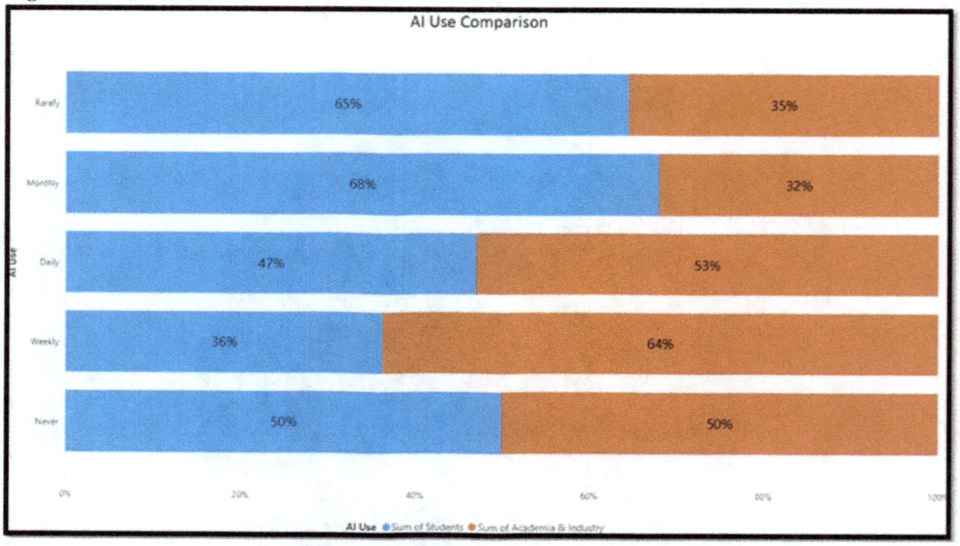

Figure 3. AI expertise

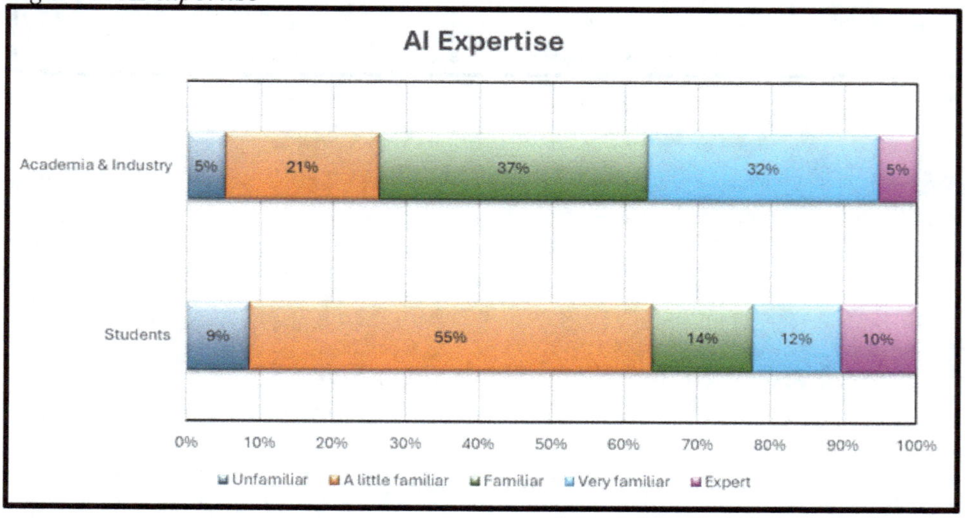

Figure 4. Comparison of AI expertise

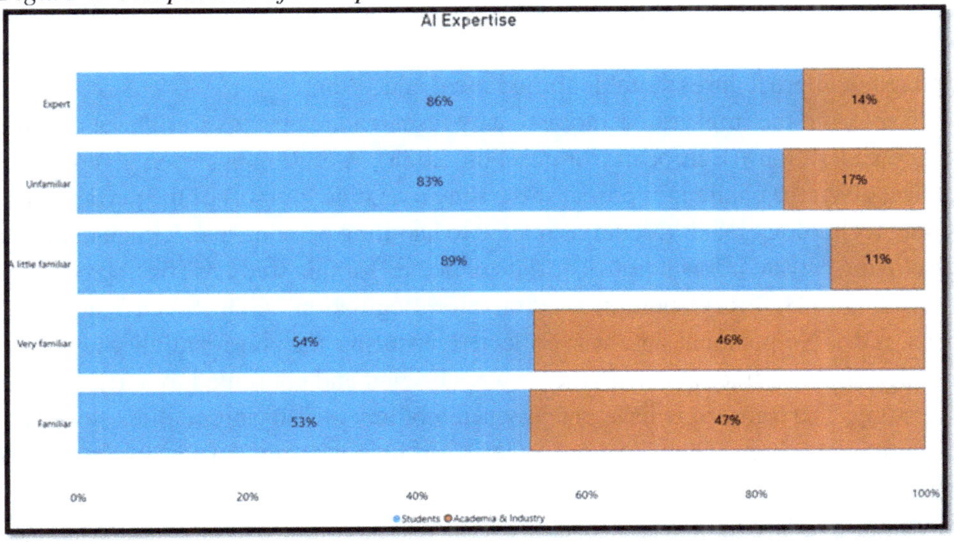

By selecting deliberately participants with existing AI familiarity, the positive selection bias is created, systematically excluding individuals who have avoided, or rejected AI tools. The reasoning for this sampling method was to develop patterns, but it cannot explore the challenges preventing non-users from engaging with AI technologies. The findings only reflect the perspectives of early adopters, rather than representing the larger population`s experience. The AI use, combined with the level familiarity rates and expertise (over 80% of graduating students showing different degrees of competence, Figure 2, 3 and 4), are explained by the high technological awareness of the participants, and the fact that digitally disengaged individuals are underrepresented.

The lack of socio-economic and geographical information limits the assessment of the how structural inequalities shape the AI access and adoption. As the geographical bias was already acknowledged by the literature towards developed economies (as discussed in the theoretical framework), it likely extends to this sample, raising issues about transferability to resource-constrained destinations and regions with limited technological development.

Thematic analysis was applied to 19 in-depth interviews conducted with 10 academia and 9 hospitality professionals, both with more than 10 years of experience. The interviews were conducted in English and took in average 30 minutes, discussing the AI impact on students' preparation for job opportunities. The recorded and transcripted data generated coded themes, which enabled qualitative analysis. For developing visual representations of the collected data, Power BI (Microsoft

Power Platform, n.d.) tool was used, adding significant meaning and facilitating later interpretation. Clark et al. (2021) recommend the mixed approach for small samples, while Bryman (2008) supports the thematic analysis for understanding the pedagogical procedures suitable for practical education.

Exploring the impact of AI tools in any research area brings forth a set of ethical considerations (European Commission, 2023). Attention has been given to the ethics, given the challenges posed by the sensitive topic for most of the participants. Using technology raises dilemmas related to handling personal participant data and disclosing private information. The data collected for this study has been processed according to GDPR (General Data Protection Regulation - GDPR – Official Legal Text, n.d.). No personal data was collected, ensuring the confidentiality and anonymity of the sources. The volunteers were briefed and consented to participate in the study. The transcripts have been redacted of any identifying markers, specifics or company names. They have only been used for academic purposes, and the recordings will be kept on a safe drive for 5 years. Afterwards, the raw data will be completely deleted.

Furthermore, an ethical committee formed by 2 senior academics and 1 senior academic manager, all with over 20 years of higher education experience, have approved the methodology, before pilot testing and data collection.

The participants' experience and knowledge of the topic ensure the reliability of the findings. Relying on stakeholders with academic and industry experience, the discussion focused only on current, relevant, and useful technology applicable to job opportunities. The interview questions were based on the relevant literature sources (Chytas et al., 2023; Du et al., 2022; Naveed et al., 2023; Villegas-Ch et al., 2023; Wang et al., 2023), focused on the implementation of AI tools in internship and full-time employment opportunities. The approach was pilot-tested, and the research gap identified was represented by applying these technological approaches to practical and hospitality education.

Finally, all the participants will be provided with a copy of the chapter once the study is published.

RESULTS AND DISCUSSION

Statistical Analysis: Modeling AI Adoption Predictors

The study reveals strong positive correlations between AI usage frequency and expertise levels across all stakeholder groups. For students, the correlation coefficient ($r^2 = 0.8117$, Figure 5) indicates that approximately 81% of variance in AI expertise can be explained by usage frequency. For combined the HIP and A groups, a similar relationship emerges ($r^2 = 0.7883$, Figure 6), explaining over 78% of expertise variance through usage patterns.

Figure 5. Correlation between student AI use and AI expertise

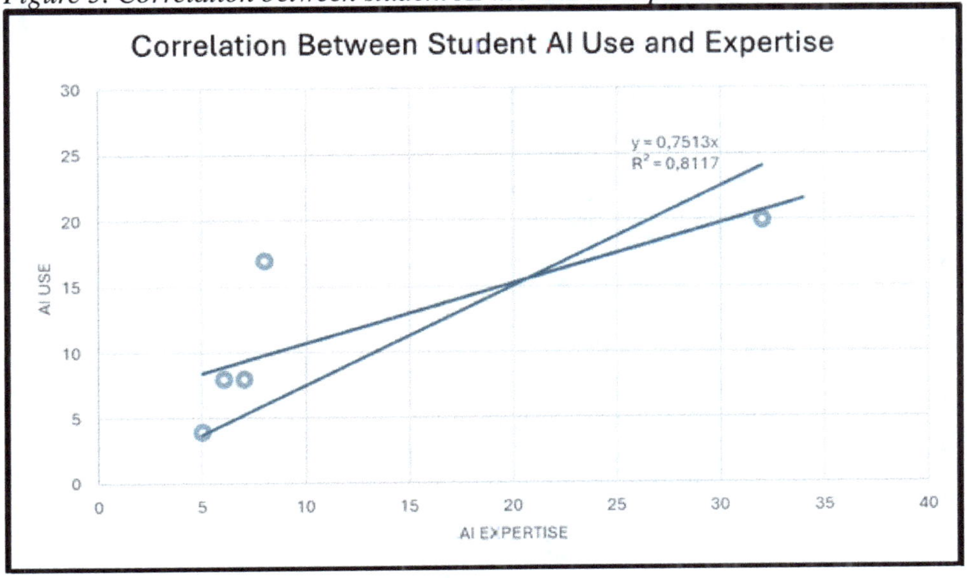

Figure 6. Correlation between academia and industry AI use and AI expertise

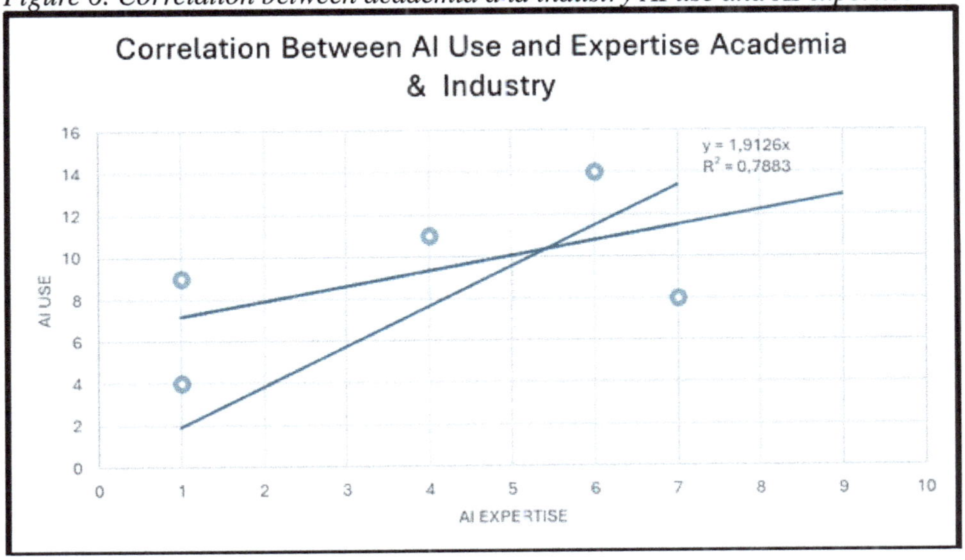

Figure 7. Types of AI used by students

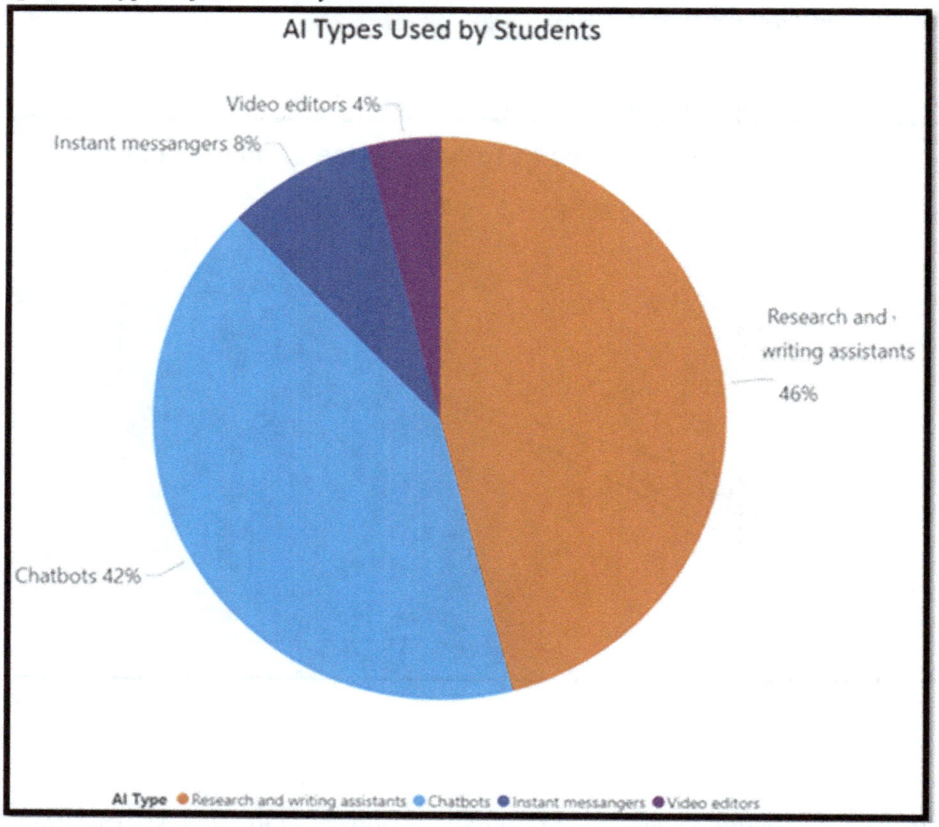

Figure 8. Types of AI used by academia and industry representatives

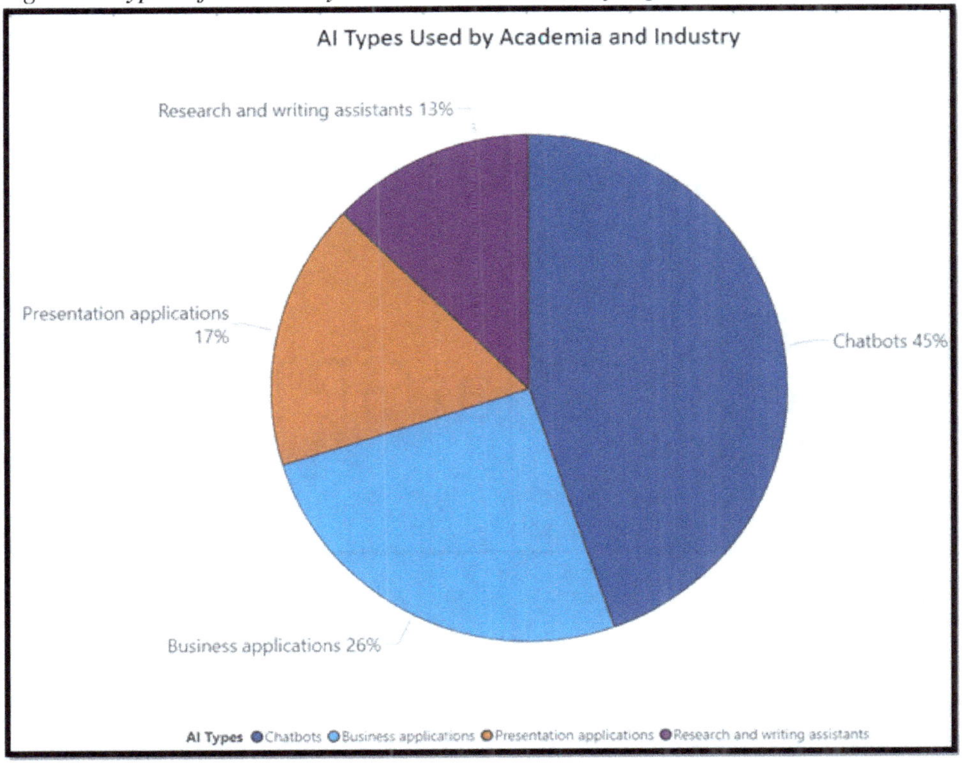

Figure 9. Word cloud of AI tools used by students, academia and industry representatives

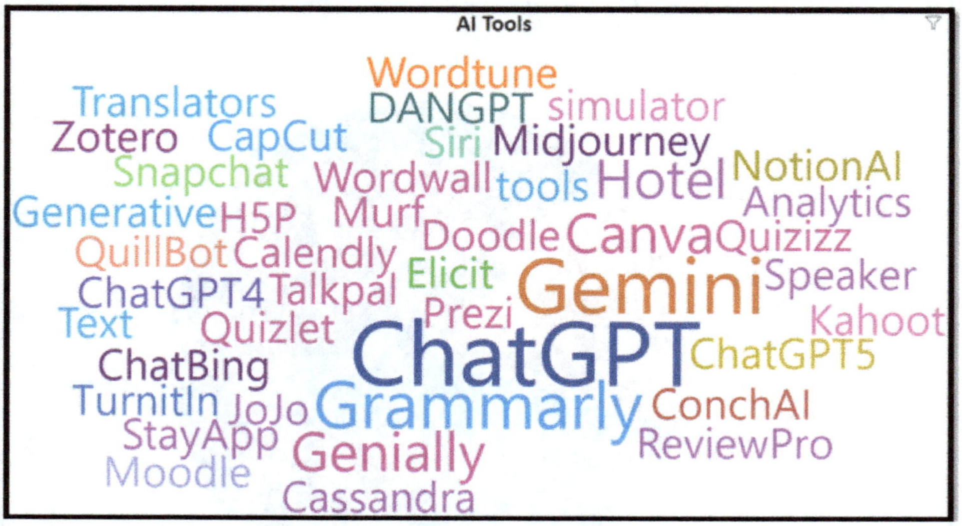

(Generated using Power BI)

Figure 10. Student considerations of using AI for job opportunities

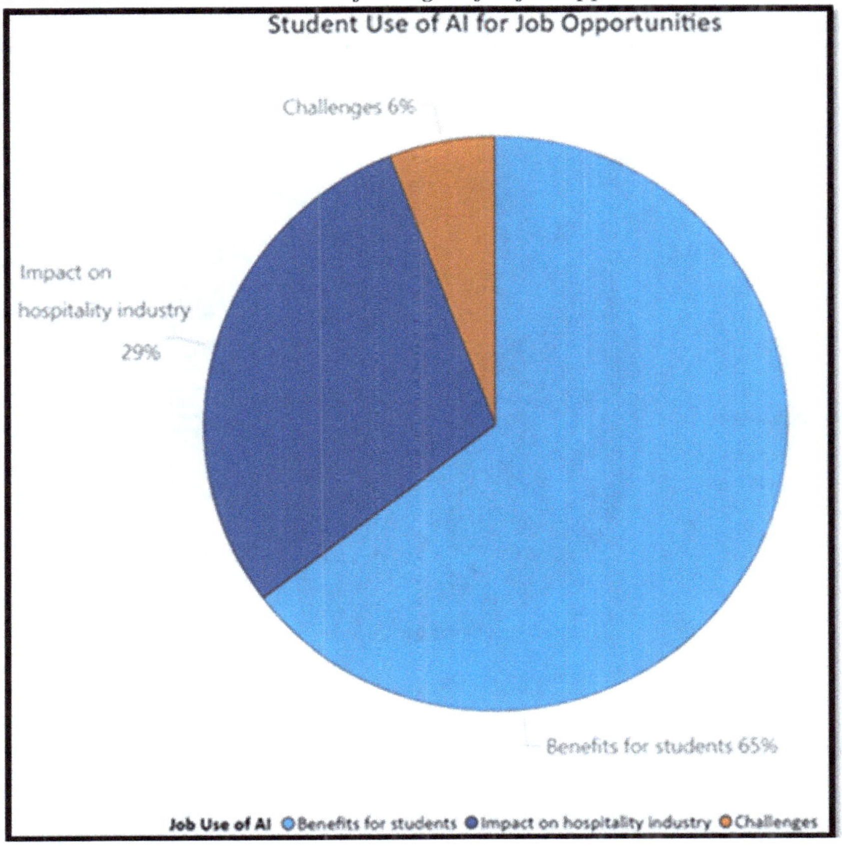

Figure 11. Considerations from academia and industry representative about using AI for job opportunities

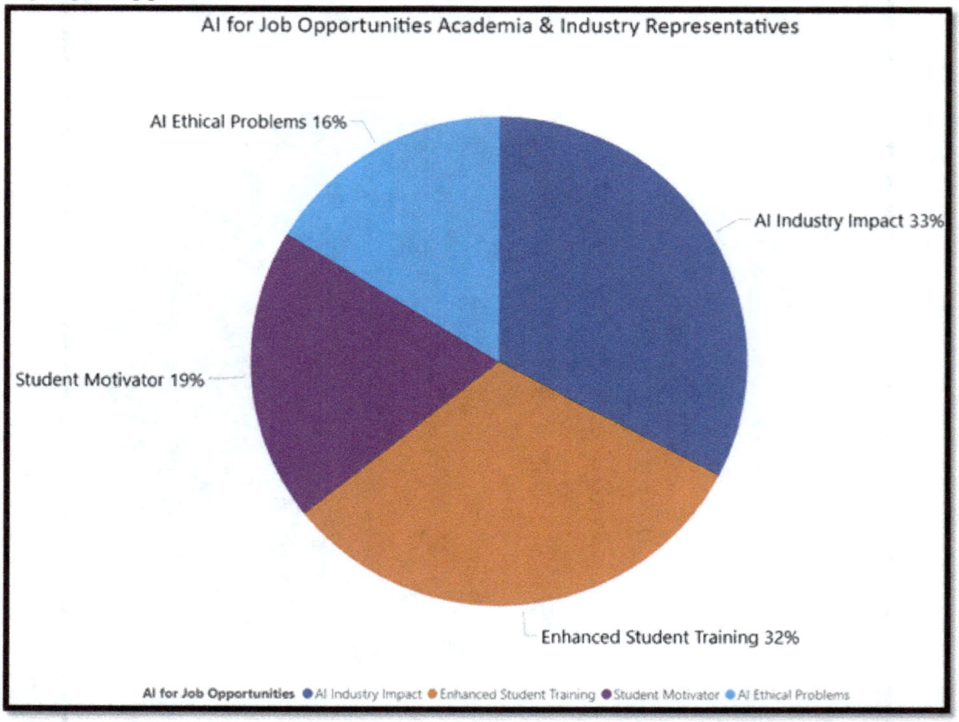

Under H_0 and standard assumptions (bivariate normality, linear relationship, independent observations), the following correlation can be converted:

$$t = \frac{r\sqrt{n-2}}{\sqrt{1-r^2}}.$$

This statistic follows a t-distribution with n–2 degrees of freedom when ρ=0. For GS:

(r = $\sqrt{0.8117} \approx 0.901$): t = r$\sqrt{(n-2)}/\sqrt{(1-r^2)}$.

With n = 57: t = 0.901$\sqrt{28}/\sqrt{(1-0.812)} \approx 10.99$, the critical value at $\alpha = 0.05$,

df = 55 (two-tailed): t_crit ≈ 2.048.

Applying it to HIP/A (r = $\sqrt{0.7883} \approx 0.888$): with similar calculations:

$$t = \frac{0.888\sqrt{55}}{\sqrt{0.2117}} \approx 9.82.$$

Again with 28 degrees of freedom: t ≈ 9.82 greatly exceeds t_crit ≈ 2.048. The p-value is therefore < 0.001, as a result H_0 at $p < 0.001$ is rejected as well.

For 95% confidence intervals: Using Fisher's z-transformation to establish confidence intervals for the population correlation. While t-test shows whether the correlation is significantly different from zero, it does not provide a range of plausible values to the population correlation p. Fisher´s z-transformation stabilizes the variance of the correlation, allowing an approximately normal distribution for constructing confidence intervals.

The Fisher z-transfor is:

$$z = \frac{1}{2}\ln\left(\frac{1+r}{1-r}\right).$$

For GS with r ≈ 0.901:

$$z = 0.5\ln\left(\frac{1+0.0901}{1-0.901}\right) \approx 1.47$$

Standard error of z depends only on the sample size:

$$SE_z = \frac{1}{\sqrt{n-3}}.$$

With n=57,

$$SE_z = \frac{1}{\sqrt{55}} \approx 0.192.$$

For a 95% confidence interval, using the normal critical value z for $z_{0975} \approx 1.96$. The 95% CI for z is:

$$z \pm 1.96\ SE_z.$$

For GS:

$$1.472 \pm 1.96 \times 0.192 \approx [1.095, 1.849].$$

By converting the endpoints from z back to r, using the inverse Fisher transform:

$$r = \frac{e^{2z} - 1}{e^{2z} - 1}.$$

By applying this to 1.095 and 1.849 gives the 95% CI for the population correlation for GS, approximately [0.799, 0.951].

Repeating the same steps for HIP/A with r ≈ 0.888 yields z ≈1.410, the same Sez ≈ 0.192, and after transforming back, a 95% CI for ρ of about [0.771, 0.943].

To develop a comprehensive model of AI adoption success, the study proposes extending the bivariate analysis to multiple regression, incorporating additional predictor variables suggested by the data:

Proposed Regression Model:

AI Expertise

$= \beta_0 + \beta_1$ (Usage Frequency) $+ \beta_2$ (Tool Diversity) $+ \beta_3$ (Stakeholder Type) $+ \beta_4$ (Perceived Benefits) $+ \beta_5$ (Training Access) $+ \varepsilon$

Where:

Usage Frequency: Daily (5), Weekly (4), Monthly (3), Rarely (2), Never (1) (Figure 2).
Tool Diversity: Count of distinct AI tools used (ChatGPT, Gemini, Grammarly, etc., from Figure 9).
Stakeholder Type: Categorical dummy variables (GS = baseline, HIP, A).
Perceived Benefits: Scale score from attitudes toward AI job opportunities (Figures 10, 11).

Based on the strong correlations, the expectation for the full model is to achieving $R^2 \geq 0.85$, with usage frequency remaining the dominant predictor (β_1 likely accounting for 60-70% of explained variance). However, multicollinearity concerns arise given the overlap between usage frequency and tool diversity (both reflect engagement intensity). The Variance Inflation Factor (VIF) diagnostics would be essential to assess whether these predictors can be simultaneously retained.

The following models are proposed:

- Model 1 (Baseline): Usage frequency only (establishes baseline $R^2 \approx 0.81$).
- Model 2: Add tool diversity (tests incremental variance explained).
- Model 3: Add stakeholder type (examines group differences).
- Model 4 (Full): Add attitudinal and access variables.

By comparing ΔR^2 between models using F-tests would identify which additional factors could significantly enhance the prediction apart from the usage frequency alone. This hierarchical approach addresses whether the relationship between usage and expertise is moderated by stakeholder identity or mediated through attitudes and opportunities.

Critical Integration of the Theoretical Framework

Figure 12. AI challenges faced by students

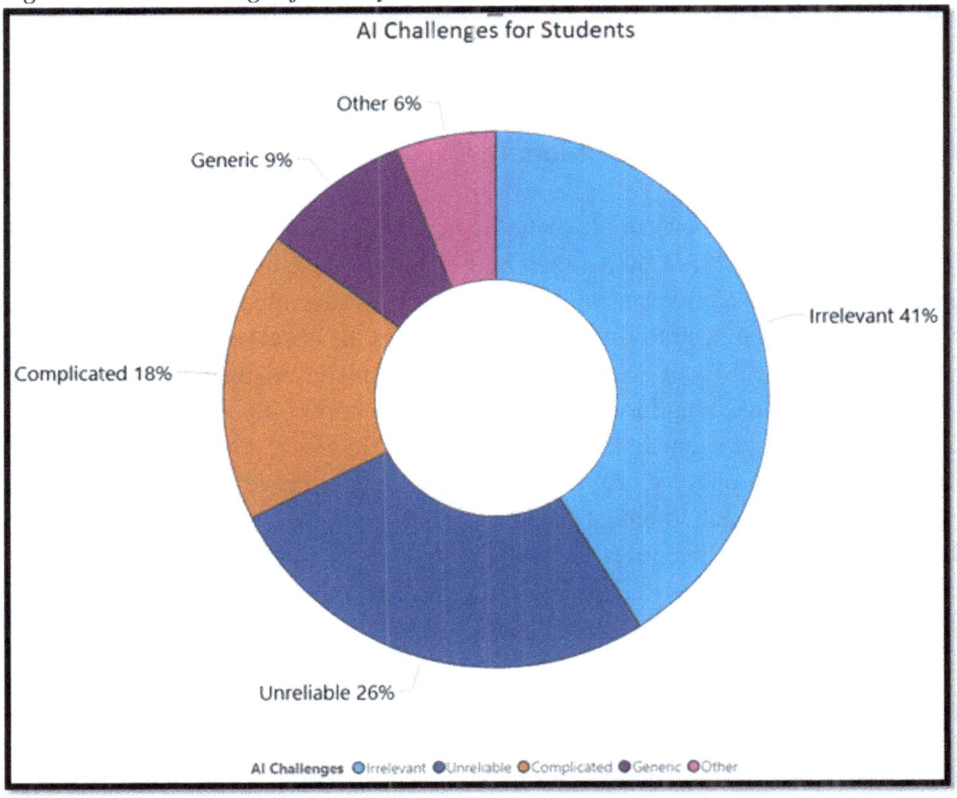

The strong usage-expertise correlation aligns with Holmes et al. (2019), Santiago and Gil (2025), and Portocarrero Ramos et al. (2025), which elaborated on the relationship between AI engagement and competency development. The challenge raised in this case is definitely interpretative: does the frequency of use cause expertise development, or does existing expertise enable frequent use? The design cannot establish causal directionality, so the following models are proposed:

A. Usage → Expertise (Skill Development Model):

Through consistent use practice opportunities are provided, thus enabling competency growth through experiential learning. This interpretation supports educational interventions recommending AI exposure to GS.

B. Expertise → Usage (Capability Model):

By focusing on hospitality students with pre-existing technical aptitude or digital literacy this model predicts both initial AI adoption and sustained engagement. As a result, GS comfortable with technology adopt the AI tools, while digitally anxious individuals avoid them regardless of potential benefits.

C. Bidirectional (Complex Model):

Other variables (for example technological self-efficacy, institutional support, peer norms) could drive both usage and expertise development simultaneously. Alternatively, measurement of self-reported expertise correlating with self-reported usage due to social desirability bias) could impact the observed relationships.

A dominating Model A aligns with the optimistic AI agenda advocated by Thomson et al. (2024) and Nartey (2024) receives support. By exposing students to AI tools, work competencies could be developed. However, if Models B or C better explains the data, only by providing AI access would prove insufficient. Further interventions into technological anxiety, digital divide issues, or systemic barriers become necessary. The collected data cannot adjudicate between viewing AI competency as democratically achievable only through exposure, as opposite viewing it as stratified. Cultural, economic, or educational background may determine who adopts effectively.

The quantitative results show high adoption rates between chatbots and writing assistants (88% GS, Figures 7, 8), similar with the immersive learning findings of Al-Hyari et al. (2023) and Sigala et al. (2024). On the other hand, the qualitative data reveal obvious contrasts. A6's discussion of chatbots providing "*scenarios and problems to face*" exemplifies simulation-based pedagogy, still GS challenges (85% reporting unreliable, irrelevant answers, Figure 12) expose the authenticity gap critique raised in the published literature.

By developing this triangulation approach, the conceptual disconnection between the high adoption rates claimed by the GS and the reported dissatisfaction with the AI quality of results, suggests students use these AI tools despite, and not because of, their pedagogical values. The pattern of adoption is rather pragmatic, likely driven by necessity (completing tasks and assignments, meeting employer's expectations and deadlines), rather than due to genuine learning effectiveness. As a result, students may develop procedural familiarity with AI algorithms, without developing the critical evaluation needed by authentic hospitality practice demands.

This finding goes against the recommendations of Chytas et al. (2023) and Hilken et al. (2020), who reflected that immersive environments automatically transfer decision-making skills. The qualitative evidence suggests AI interactions can remain superficial. Students learn to generate acceptable outputs without developing deeper problem-solving capabilities. Under these circumstances, Ivanov and Webster's (2020) regarding the replacement of bodied practice gains support: high usage statistics may mask questionable learning quality.

Thematic Analysis: Qualitative Dimensions of AI Integration

Theme 1: Efficiency - Quality Analysis

Industry representatives emphasized during their discussions efficiency as the main AI gain (HIP8: *"improve efficiency and customer satisfaction*", HIP6: "*AI can contribute to innovation*"), aligning thus with the reflections of Kong et al. (2024) and Holmes et al. (2019). The concerns about the quality of the outputs emerged as a counterbalance to this theme (HIP3: "*overwhelming number of AI options of questionable quality*", A7: time investment required to "*refine the answers*"). The reporting of 85% of unreliable/irrelevant AI outputs (Figure 12) confirms these qualitative concerns.

The convergence of the results suggests a systematic implementation of the problem: stakeholders recognize the AI potential for efficiency, but the lack of standardized framework results in questionable quality of results. The gap between the aspirational expectations and experiences quality issues represents a barrier to effective integrating the algorithms into learning and working environments.

This point brings a new level of complexity when faced with the findings of Thomson et al. (2024) and Westman et al. (2021), who treat AI as straightforwardly beneficial once implemented. The results align more likely to the cautious perspectives of Murphy et al., (2019) and Nartey (2024), emphasizing implementation challenges and ethical considerations.

The efficiency – quality theme reveals that the technological capabilities do function, and AI can comfortably automate tasks, but this does not guarantee educational value.

Theme 2: The Guidance Analysis

Interview participants pointed out the importance of AI for structured mentorship (A3: "*familiarity with systems*", A6: chatbots requiring pedagogical scaffolding, A8: teachers providing "*ethical guidance*"). The need for human guidance contradicts the autonomous learning paths, aligning thus with findings of Santiago and Gil (2025) and Ressin (2025), who highlighted mentorship as crucial for AI learning effectiveness.

If AI requires intensive human support to function educationally, it should be treated as a technological advanced teaching aid, rather than a transformative independent learning platform. Thus, the interpretation clashes with the radical transformation proposed by Deri et al. (2024) and Murphy et al. (2019) and supports integration models, where technology augments rather than replaces the traditional pedagogy.

Looking back to the correlation between usage and expertise (Figures 5, 6), this may actually reflect supervised practice quality, rather promote the algorithm´s effectiveness. Hospitality students who are receiving better mentorship (variable which should be measured by future research), may use AI more frequently, and develop greater expertise, and the mentorship may be the causal mechanism. The interpretation puts the human relation in the focal point, being critical for the AI´s educational value.

Theme 3: Job Security and Labor Market Transformation

Industry professionals expressed their concerns during the interviews about automation displacing roles (HIP6: "*revenue management jobs at risk*", HIP8: "*implementing training...adapting employees...difficult*"). This is aligned with the literary theme pointing the opposition between the creative opportunity (Portocarrero Ramos et al., 2025; Tiwari, 2023), and job insecurity (Owoeye, 2024).

While more than 60% of GS perceived AI as beneficial for employment (Figure 10), only 50% of HIP/A shared this opinion (Figure 11). This contradiction may point out that GS are lacking industry experience, while professionals observing the technological impact on the labour market maintain a justified skepticism. Baum (2019) and Benckendorff et al. (2019) acknowledged the industry transformation but minimized labor implications. The implication may be that GS may be disadvantaged when entering into an AI-reshaped labour market, where most of the entry level positions have been or are in the process of being automatized. The claim that "*AI tools should be designed to complement the work of humans, not replace them*" (HIP9) may represent an aspiration rather than observed reality.

Regarding cost reduction and efficiency maximization, AI integration may potentially be misaligned with the hospitality worker's overall welfare.

Theme 4: Ethical Implementation Barriers

Interview participants raised concerns about discrimination, privacy, and over-reliance, aligning thus with Nartey (2024), Murphy et al. (2019), and Pericleous et al. (2025). However, the ethical considerations appeared as acknowledged risks, rather than active implementation principles. A8's statement about teachers providing "*ethical guidance*" suggests ethics remain pedagogical add-ons rather than foundational design principles.

The quantitative and qualitative data collected was insufficient to demonstrate a systematic ethical framework guiding the AI integration. Even though stakeholders recognize the ethical issues conceptually, there is limited evidence of clear accountability mechanisms, or student critical thinking development. This gap has been identified, so even though ethics are acknowledged, there is insufficient operational implementation.

The findings' generalisability is constrainted by sampling bias, being an obvious limitation for global applicability. Cultural dimensions substantially shape AI adoption but remain unexamined. In high power-distance cultures as per Hofstede's (Guan et al., 2022, Kim et al., 2024) implementation of AI may be limited, regardless of the algorithmic availability, in order to maintain the clear hierarchy between students and the authoritative sources of knowledge. Conversely, in low-power distance contexts, the democratizing potential of AI may be enthusiastically embraced.

When considering personalised learning (A3: "*personalise presentation letters*", A4: "*personalise prices and promotions*") this reflects individualistic cultural assumptions (Guan et al., 2022, Kim et al., 2024). In such aspects, educational cultures focused on individual performance may embrace AI, while collectivist educational context may find AI personalisation culturally inappropriate or unsuitable in the classroom environment. Cultures with high uncertainty avoidance may resist AI's unpredictability (85% reporting unreliable outputs) stronger than uncertainty-tolerant cultures. Thus, the implementation success likely varies systematically across this dimension.

Nonetheless, the current study implicitly assumes reliable internet connectivity, device access, and institutional technology budgets. Such conditions may be absent in many educational contexts globally. Findings from presumably well-resourced institutions cannot be reflected in settings where basic technological prerequisites remain unmet. The data reflects a particular pedagogical western European tradition emphasising experiential learning, student independence, and industry alignment, due to sampling bias. Alternative educational philosophies may integrate AI differently or resist integration altogether based on competing educational priorities and should be further explored.

At the same time, even in a global industry, hospitality and tourism aspects vary greatly. Small and medium enterprises, such as family-owned hotels dominate in some regions. They will likely face different AI implementation realities compared to the large international chain hotels represented by the sample. In these conditions, students working for hotels with more informal interaction with the guests during their employment may find AI competencies very different compared to the actual work conditions.

Figure 13. AI challenges faced by academia and industry representatives

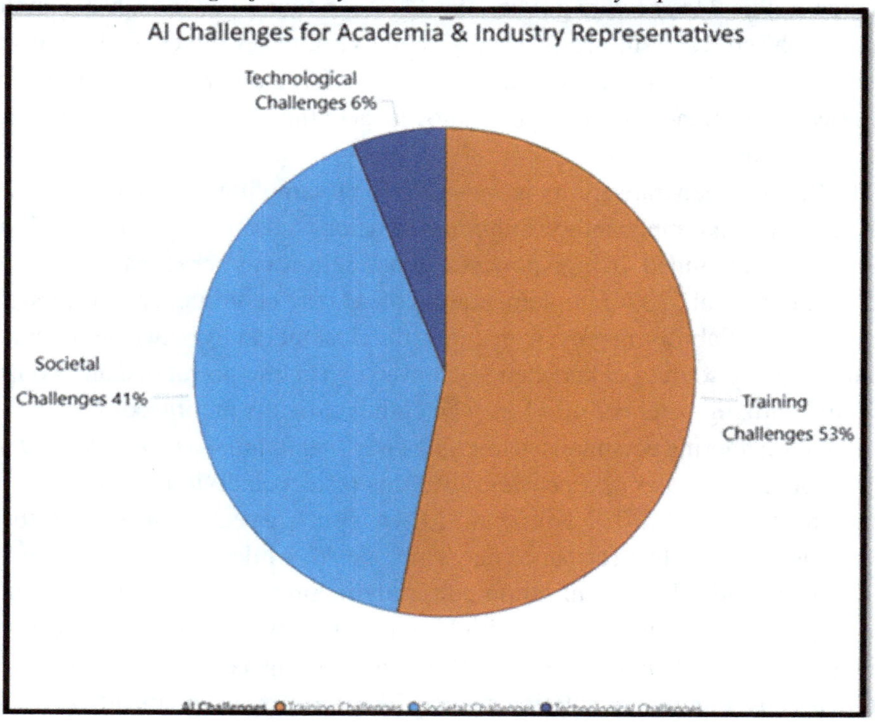

Figure 14. Differentiation of AI challenges faced by academia and industry representatives

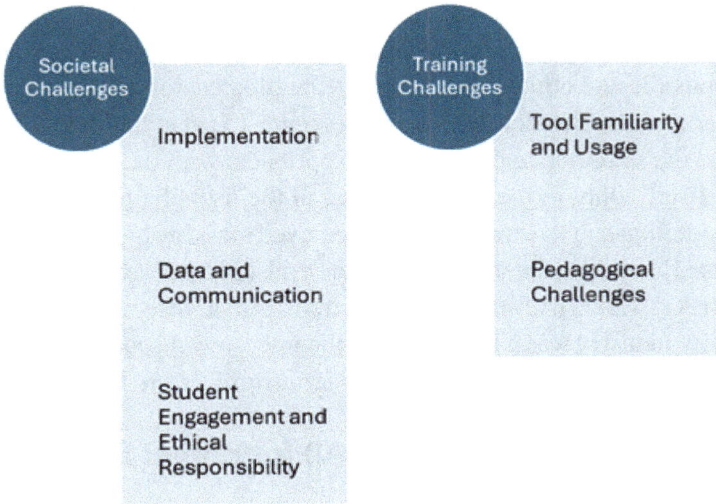

Figure 15. Word cloud for using AI for student job opportunities from interviews with academia and industry representatives

(Generated using Power BI)

Furthermore, the AI challenges faced by A and HIP were grouped into 2 major categories, impacting the society overall and the specific training aspects (Figure 13, 14). The level of the implementation was driven by the quality of the data, so the impact to the industry was determined using high-quality AI algorithms. This translated into the communication importance of knowing how to speak to AI and having a foundational understanding of the subject. The result for the GS was an increased understanding how to use AI effectively. The surveyed participants encouraged a responsible and ethical use of these technologies, for a high impact for their future career and benefits for the industry (Figure 15). The industry professionals have aligned the importance of a smooth experience, with the correct set up of the technology itself. Only in these conditions can the users be properly trained. The systemic modelling and its impact over the received message have been similar to the ones discussed already in the studies of Hilken et al. (2020), Naveed et al. (2020), and Villegas-Ch et al. (2023). Overall, theme of transformative technological impact for the hospitality industry was a focal point in the interview discussions (HIP3: *AI can be a valuable tool for decision-making and innovation in the hospitality industry*).

Critical Integration AI Model (CRIAI) for Higher Education

Overall, the study developed a set of educational practical and policy recommendations for implementing AI in hospitality education, in preparing students for their practical internships and entering the workforce. The Critical Integration AI (CRIAI) model was built on usage quality, faculty capacity, ethical governance, adaptation and critical inquiry, and is meant as a framework for pedagogical AI integration of hospitality practical approaches in higher education.

Reconceptualise Integration Goals

AI integration should not be associated with educational innovation. The CRIAI model proposes quality based integration, where the institutional goals are anchored in learning outcomes, critical digital literary and ethical awareness. The study has demonstrated that high usage rates without learning quality do not confirm successful implementation. Thus, the key performance indicators should move from counting usage percentages towards assessing value competency development and ethical approaches. Successful AI implementation is defined by pedagogical depth and cognitive development.

Developing Pedagogical Capacity

The persistent necessity for mentorship and guidance (Theme 2) shows that faculty development is a proper AI drive implementation. By training educators to facilitate meaningful AI engagement, students are offered the possibility to actively and critically explore the algorithmic opportunities, rather than just receiving answers for their requests. This likely requires professional development programs, collaborative learning communities, and reflexive teaching practices that integrate AI as a co-learning tool, instead of a replacement for human pedagogical judgment.

Institute Ethical Governance Frameworks

A responsible AI use requires a proactive ethical infrastructure. The CRIAI model embeds governance as a core structural dimension. These are the following proposed principles:

- Transparent institutional policies on permissible AI use.
- Academic integrity frameworks tailored to AI contexts.
- Mechanisms for ensuring data protection, bias detection, and accountability.
- Collaborating and participatory dialogue involving stakeholders to evaluate emerging ethical dilemmas (students, academia, and industry representatives).

This ethical governance adds a layer of reflection, becoming not only a reactive measure, but rather an institutional ongoing practice.

Contextual Implementation

The generalizability limitations of the study suggest that a one-size-fits-all approach will likely be unsuitable. Institutions must assess their specific cultural contexts, student populations, resource constraints, and educational philosophies before adopting AI integration models developed elsewhere. The CRIAI model proposes context-sensitive adoption, rather than a universal integration template. The institution may need to evaluate the following points:

- Cultural and linguistic contexts
- Institutional mission and resource availability
- Disciplinary differences in AI applicability
- Student readiness and educational background

Implementation strategies, therefore, must align with the institution's pedagogical philosophy and community needs to avoid superficial or misaligned adoption.

Establishing Critical Distance

The employment paradox (Theme 3) reflects on the need for critical alignment with the industry's demands. Educational institutions must maintain this space for reflection on the AI´s societal impact, ethical and epistemological implications. Thus, AI becomes a tool for inquiry and not just a industrial conformity.

Overall, the CRIAI model positions AI as catalyst for reflective transformation, rather than an endpoint of educational modernisation. By aligning the five interdependent dimensions (purpose redefinition, faculty empowerment, ethical governance, contextual adaptation, and critical inquiry) the model proposes a comprehensive roadmap for institutions seeking to balance innovation with integrity.

FUTURE RESEARCH DIRECTIONS

Exploring the career path of students who have graduated from AI-integrated programs in longitudinal studies, not only through their internship, but also by following their employment, would test empirically the causal claims about skill development and career outcomes. At the same time, comparing cohorts with varying degrees of AI exposure levels (undergraduate and graduate students) would provide experimental evidence, which at the moment is lacking. By comparing different AI integration approaches, controlled trials could be set for intensive immersion, elective incorporation and traditional teaching methods. Thus, effective practices may be highlighted and the aspects impacting observational studies may be controlled.

Nevertheless, systematic investigation across diverse cultural, economic and educational contexts are needed to set boundary conditions and to identify culturally appropriate integration models. This can be done in conjunction with labour market analysis, by surveying the employers. Job placement data may help to validate whether AI competencies actually improve employability.

CONCLUSION

The mixed method analysis reveals AI integration in hospitality education as more complex than the optimistic literature suggestions. The links between usage and expertise provide some support for integration advocates, however profound implementation challenges, quality concerns and unresolved ethical issues moderate the enthusiasm. The importance of mentorship, stakeholder divergence about employment impacts and the generalizability concerns show that AI would function as a pedagogical augmentation, instead as a revolutionary transformation.

The data collected does not validate overall rejection, neither does it confirm uncritical adoption of AI. It does however recommend a careful approach keeping in mind context-sensitive integration by highlighting the critical functions of the educational institutions, and the prioritization of genuine learning outcomes over superficial adoption metrics. Hospitality education requires move beyond the optimistic narrative towards rigorous assessments of actual educational values. This shift cannot begin without complete and comprehensive longitudinal and comparative research addressing the methodological limitations.

REFERENCES

Al-Hyari, H.S., Al-Smadi, H.M., & Weshah, S.R. (2023). The Impact of Artificial Intelligence (AI) on Guest Satisfaction in Hotel Management: An Empirical Study of Luxury Hotels. *GeoJournal of Tourism and Geosites*, 48(2spl), 810–819. DOI: 10.30892/gtg.482spl15-1081

Baum, T. (2019). Does the hospitality industry need or deserve talent? *International Journal of Contemporary Hospitality Management, 31*(10), 3823–3837. DOI: 10.1108/IJCHM-10-2018-0805

Benckendorff, P. J., Xiang, Z., & Sheldon, P. J. (2019). *Tourism Information Technology* (3rd ed.). CABI. DOI: 10.1079/9781786393432.0000

Botero-Gómez, V., Ruiz-Herrera, L. G., Valencia-Arias, A., Romero Díaz, A., & Vives Garnique, J. C. (2023). Use of Virtual Tools in Teaching-Learning Processes: Advancements and Future Direction. *Social Sciences (Basel, Switzerland), 12*(2), 70. DOI: 10.3390/socsci12020070

Bryman, A. (2008). Of methods and methodology. *Qualitative Research in Organizations and Management, 3*(2), 159–168. DOI: 10.1108/17465640810900568

Cassidy, D., Borgne, Y.-A. L., Bellas, F., Vuorikari, R., Rondin, E., Sharma, M., Niewint-Gori, J., Gröpler, J., Gilleran, A., & Kralj, L. (2023). *Use Scenarios & Practical Examples of AI Use in Education*. DOI: 10.48550/ARXIV.2309.12320

Chassignol, M., Khoroshavin, A., Klimova, A., & Bilyatdinova, A. (2018). Artificial Intelligence Trends in Education: A Narrative Overview. *Procedia Computer Science, 136*, 16–24. DOI: 10.1016/j.procs.2018.08.233

Chen, X., Xie, H., Zou, D., & Hwang, G.-J. (2020). Application and theory gaps during the rise of Artificial Intelligence in Education. *Computers and Education: Artificial Intelligence, 1*, 100002. DOI: 10.1016/j.caeai.2020.100002

Chytas, K., Tsolakidis, A., Triperina, E., & Skourlas, C. (2023). Educational data mining in the academic setting: Employing the data produced by blended learning to ameliorate the learning process. *Data Technologies and Applications, 57*(3), 366–384. DOI: 10.1108/DTA-06-2022-0252

Clark, T., Foster, L., Bryman, A., & Sloan, L. (2021). *Bryman's Social Research Methods*. Oxford University Press.

Deri, M. N., Zaazie, P., & Singh, A. (2024). Digital future of the hospitality industry and hospitality education globally. In *International handbook of skill, education, learning, and research development in tourism and hospitality* (pp. 221–243). Springer Nature Singapore., DOI: 10.1007/978-981-97-4318-6_14

Du, Z., Liu, J., & Wang, T. (2022). Augmented Reality Marketing: A Systematic Literature Review and an Agenda for Future Inquiry. *Frontiers in Psychology, 13*, 925963. DOI: 10.3389/fpsyg.2022.925963 PMID: 35783783

El Hajal, G., & Yeoman, I. (2024). AI and the future of talent management in tourism and hospitality. *Current Issues in Tourism*, 1–18. DOI: 10.1080/13683500.2024.2439395

European Commission. (2023, October 30). *Directorate-General for Communications Networks, Content and Technology - G7 Leaders' Statement on the Hiroshima AI Process Shaping Europe's Digital Future.* Retrieved September 2, 2025, from https://digital-strategy.ec.europa.eu/en/library/g7-leaders-statement-hiroshima-ai-process.

Gartner (n.d.). *What Is Artificial Intelligence (AI)?* (n.d.). Retrieved September 20, 2025, from https://www.gartner.com/en/topics/artificial-intelligence

General Data Protection Regulation (GDPR) – Official Legal Text. (n.d.). *General Data Protection Regulation (GDPR)*. Retrieved October 31, 2024, from https://gdpr-info.eu/

Google. (n.d.). *Gemini 2.5 Flash*. Retrieved September 20, 2025, from https://gemini.google.com

Grammarly Inc. (2025). *Grammarly*. Retrieved September 20, 2025, from https://app.grammarly.com/

Guan, C., Hung, Y. C., & Liu, W. (2022). Cultural differences in hospitality service evaluations: Mining insights of user generated content. *Electronic Markets, 32*(3), 1061–1081. DOI: 10.1007/s12525-022-00545-z

Heller, J., Chylinski, M., De Ruyter, K., Mahr, D., & Keeling, D. I. (2019). Touching the Untouchable: Exploring Multi-Sensory Augmented Reality in the Context of Online Retailing. *Journal of Retailing, 95*(4), 219–234. DOI: 10.1016/j.jretai.2019.10.008

Hilken, T., Keeling, D. I., De Ruyter, K., Mahr, D., & Chylinski, M. (2020). Seeing eye to eye: Social augmented reality and shared decision making in the marketplace. *Journal of the Academy of Marketing Science, 48*(2), 143–164. DOI: 10.1007/s11747-019-00688-0

Holmes, W., Bialik, M., & Fadel, C. (2019). *Artificial intelligence in education: Promises and implications for teaching and learning*. The Center for Curriculum Redesign.

Ivanov, S., & Webster, C. (2020). Robots in tourism: A research agenda for tourism economics. *Tourism Economics, 26*(7), 1065–1085. DOI: 10.1177/1354816619879583

Kim, J., Erdem, M., & Kim, B. (2024). Hi Alexa, do hotel guests have privacy concerns with you?: A cross-cultural study. *Journal of Hospitality Marketing & Management, 33*(3), 360–383. DOI: 10.1080/19368623.2023.2251157

Kong, H., Yin, Z., Chon, K., Yuan, Y., & Yu, J. (2024). How does artificial intelligence (AI) enhance hospitality employee innovation? The roles of exploration, AI trust, and proactive personality. *Journal of Hospitality Marketing & Management, 33*(3), 261–287. DOI: 10.1080/19368623.2023.2258116

Koo, B., Curtis, C., & Ryan, B. (2021). Examining the impact of artificial intelligence on hotel employees through job insecurity perspectives. *International Journal of Hospitality Management, 95*, 102763. DOI: 10.1016/j.ijhm.2020.102763

Lestari, N. S., Rosman, D., & Putranto, T. S. (2021). The Relationship Between Robot, Artificial Intelligence, and Service Automation (RAISA) Awareness, Career Competency, and Perceived Career Opportunities: Hospitality Student Perspective. *2021 International Conference on Information Management and Technology (ICIMTech)*, 690–695. DOI: 10.1109/ICIMTech53080.2021.9535054

Lu, L., Cai, R., & Gursoy, D. (2019). Developing and validating a service robot integration willingness scale. *International Journal of Hospitality Management, 80*, 36–51. DOI: 10.1016/j.ijhm.2019.01.005

Lukanova, G., & Ilieva, G. (2019). Robots, Artificial Intelligence, and Service Automation in Hotels. In S. Ivanov & C. Webster (Eds.), *Robots, Artificial Intelligence, and Service Automation in Travel, Tourism and Hospitality* (157–183). Emerald Publishing Limited. DOI: 10.1108/978-1-78756-687-320191009

Microsoft Power Platform. (n.d). *Power BI - Data Visualization*. Retrieved September 6, 2025, from https://www.microsoft.com/en-us/power-platform/products/power-bi

Mori, M., MacDorman, K., & Kageki, N. (2012). The Uncanny Valley [From the Field]. *IEEE Robotics & Automation Magazine, 19*(2), 98–100. DOI: 10.1109/MRA.2012.2192811

Murphy, J., Gretzel, U., & Pesonen, J. (2019). Marketing robot services in hospitality and tourism: The role of anthropomorphism. *Journal of Travel & Tourism Marketing, 36*(7), 784–795. DOI: 10.1080/10548408.2019.1571983

Nartey, E. K. (2024). Guiding principles of generative AI for employability and learning in UK universities. *Cogent Education, 11*(1), 2357898. DOI: 10.1080/2331186X.2024.2357898

Naveed, Q. N., Choudhary, H., Ahmad, N., Alqahtani, J., & Qahmash, A. I. (2023). Mobile Learning in Higher Education: A Systematic Literature Review. *Sustainability (Basel), 15*(18), 13566. DOI: 10.3390/su151813566

Nhan, V. K., Tam, L. T., Dung, H. T., & Vu, N. T. (2022). A conceptual model for studying the immersive mobile augmented reality application-enhanced experience. *Heliyon, 8*(8), e10141. DOI: 10.1016/j.heliyon.2022.e10141 PMID: 36039131

Open, A. I. (n.d.). *ChatGPT 4o*. Retrieved September 20, 2025, from https://chatgpt.com/

Owoeye, G. (2024). The Influence of Artificial Intelligence on Employment Trends in the United States (US). [IJISRT]. *International Journal of Innovative Science and Research Technology, 1368–1372*, 1368–1372. Advance online publication. DOI: 10.38124/ijisrt/IJISRT24JUN328

Pericleous, K., Liasidou, S., & Dyankov, T. (2025). AI and hotel employees' coexistence: A helpful tool or a threat to job loss? *Worldwide Hospitality and Tourism Themes, 17*(1), 132–143. DOI: 10.1108/WHATT-01-2025-0001

Portocarrero Ramos, H. C., Cruz Caro, O., Sánchez Bardales, E., Quiñones Huatangari, L., Campos Trigoso, J. A., Maicelo Guevara, J. L., & Chávez Santos, R. (2025). Artificial intelligence skills and their impact on the employability of university graduates. *Frontiers in Artificial Intelligence, 8*, 1629320. DOI: 10.3389/frai.2025.1629320 PMID: 40741284

Ressin, M. (2025). Innovations in the process of training young entrepreneurs: Achieving a balance between theory, practice, and market conditions. *Education and Information Technologies, 30*(7), 9841–9858. DOI: 10.1007/s10639-024-13217-6

Santiago, T., & Gil, M. (2025). Preparing graduates for digital futures: Critical insights from High-Tech internships in business administration. *Education and Information Technologies, 30*(17), 24259–24289. Advance online publication. DOI: 10.1007/s10639-025-13751-x

Saunders, M. N., Lewis, P., & Thornhill, A. (2023). *Research Methods for Business Students* (9th ed.). Pearson International Content.

Sigala, M., Ooi, K.-B., Tan, G. W.-H., Aw, E. C.-X., Buhalis, D., Cham, T.-H., Chen, M.-M., Dwivedi, Y. K., Gretzel, U., Inversini, A., Jung, T., Law, R., & Ye, I. H. (2024). Understanding the impact of ChatGPT on tourism and hospitality: Trends, prospects and research agenda. *Journal of Hospitality and Tourism Management*, *60*, 384–390. DOI: 10.1016/j.jhtm.2024.08.004

Sung, E., Han, D. D., & Choi, Y. K. (2022). Augmented reality advertising via a mobile app. *Psychology and Marketing*, *39*(3), 543–558. DOI: 10.1002/mar.21632

Tacgin, Z. (2020). *Virtual and augmented reality: an educational handbook*. Cambridge Scholars Publishing.

Thomson, S. R., Pickard-Jones, B. A., Baines, S., & Otermans, P. C. J. (2024). The impact of AI on education and careers: What do students think? *Frontiers in Artificial Intelligence*, *7*, 1457299. DOI: 10.3389/frai.2024.1457299 PMID: 39610850

Tiwari, R. (2023). The Impact of AI and Machine Learning on Job Displacement and Employment Opportunities. *International Journal of Scientific Research in Engineering and Management*, *07*(01). Advance online publication. DOI: 10.55041/IJSREM17506

Van Der Meulen, F. J., & De Vries, M. (2023). A literature review of implementing virtual reality in hospitality education. *Research in Hospitality Management*, *13*(1), 55–61. DOI: 10.1080/22243534.2023.2239584

Van Dis, E. A. M., Bollen, J., Zuidema, W., Van Rooij, R., & Bockting, C. L. (2023). ChatGPT: Five priorities for research. *Nature*, *614*(7947), 224–226. DOI: 10.1038/d41586-023-00288-7 PMID: 36737653

Veletsianos, G. (Ed.). (2016). *Emergence and innovation in digital learning: Foundations and applications*. AU Press.

Villegas-Ch, W., García-Ortiz, J., Urbina-Camacho, I., & Mera-Navarrete, A. (2023). Proposal for a System for the Identification of the Concentration of Students Who Attend Online Educational Models. *Computers*, *12*(4), 74. DOI: 10.3390/computers12040074

Wang, T., Lund, B. D., Marengo, A., Pagano, A., Mannuru, N. R., Teel, Z. A., & Pange, J. (2023). Exploring the Potential Impact of Artificial Intelligence (AI) on International Students in Higher Education: Generative AI, Chatbots, Analytics, and International Student Success. *Applied Sciences (Basel, Switzerland)*, *13*(11), 6716. DOI: 10.3390/app13116716

Westman, S., Kauttonen, J., Klemetti, A., Korhonen, N., Manninen, M., Mononen, A., Niittymäki, S., & Paananen, H. (2021). Artificial Intelligence for Career Guidance – Current Requirements and Prospects for the Future. *IAFOR Journal of Education*, *9*(4), 43–62. DOI: 10.22492/ije.9.4.03

Yu, J., & Meng, T. (2025). Image Generative AI in Tourism: Trends, Impacts, and Future Research Directions. *Journal of Hospitality & Tourism Research (Washington, D.C.)*, *50*(2), 1–42. DOI: 10.1177/10963480251324676

Chapter 3

Integrating Artificial Intelligence and Sustainability Into Graduate-Level Hospitality and Tourism Education:

A Framework of Guidelines Based on Recognized International Standards

Roberto Rodriguez-Garcia
http://orcid.org/0000-0001-7006-6716
Les Roches Global Hospitality Education, Marbella, Spain

ABSTRACT

The accelerating convergence of artificial intelligence (AI) and sustainability imperatives has redefined the skill sets required in the global hospitality and tourism industry. Yet, graduate-level education often lags behind these transformations, with curricula that remain fragmented and disconnected from evolving international standards. This study develops a framework of guidelines for integrating AI and sustainability into graduate-level hospitality and tourism education, drawing upon recognized global frameworks from UNESCO, the United Nations World Tourism Organization (UNWTO), the Organization for Economic Co-operation and Development (OECD), and the Global Sustainable Tourism Council (GSTC).

DOI: 10.4018/979-8-3373-5112-4.ch003

Findings underscore the need for an integrative curriculum that unites technological fluency, ethical reasoning, and sustainability literacy, guided by established principles such as the UNESCO Recommendation on the Ethics of Artificial Intelligence and the Education for Sustainable Development (ESD) roadmap.

INTRODUCTION

Background and Rationale

The hospitality and tourism industry is undergoing an unprecedented transformation shaped by rapid digitalization, sustainability imperatives, and the socio-economic disruptions of the COVID-19 era. As a sector contributing over 10% to global GDP and employing more than 320 million people prior to the pandemic (World Travel & Tourism Council, 2022), hospitality remains a key driver of sustainable development and cultural exchange. However, as technological innovation accelerates, the integration of artificial intelligence (AI) systems into service operations, destination management, and marketing raises new challenges for workforce preparedness, ethics, and curriculum design.

Simultaneously, the sustainability agenda, anchored in the United Nations Sustainable Development Goals (SDGs), calls for tourism education to cultivate environmentally literate, socially responsible, and innovation-driven graduates (UNWTO, 2022).

The purpose of this paper is to address this gap by proposing a globally aligned framework of guidelines for integrating AI and sustainability into graduate-level hospitality and tourism education. Grounded in recognized international standards, including UNESCO's Education for Sustainable Development (ESD) framework and Recommendation on the Ethics of Artificial Intelligence (2021), the OECD's Principles on AI (2019) and Learning Compass 2030 (2020), and the GSTC's sustainability criteria, the study aims to synthesize best practices into a coherent educational model. The framework provides direction for curriculum designers, policy institutions, and accreditation agencies seeking to future-proof hospitality and tourism education.

Research Objectives

The study pursues three interrelated objectives:

1. To examine the current global landscape of AI and sustainability integration in graduate-level hospitality and tourism programs through comparative case study analysis.
2. To analyze international frameworks and standards relevant to AI ethics, sustainability, and educational transformation.
3. To propose an evidence-based framework of guidelines for higher education institutions to align curricula with the competencies required for AI-enabled sustainable hospitality and tourism.

Significance of the Study

This study contributes to educational and tourism scholarships by synthesizing global policy frameworks and evidence from leading institutions into actionable academic guidelines. By integrating AI and sustainability education, it seeks to bridge the gap between digital transformation and responsible leadership development.

For universities, the proposed framework offers a structured pathway for curriculum innovation aligned with international quality benchmarks. For policymakers, it serves as a reference for accreditation, capacity-building, and policy coherence in higher education.

Furthermore, this research responds to calls from the UNWTO (2022) and OECD (2023) to strengthen future-oriented competencies that balance technological capability with ethical and environmental responsibility. The inclusion of comparative case studies from leading programs provides concrete evidence of successful implementation strategies, enhancing the framework's practical applicability. As Fernández-Villarán et al. (2024) argue, higher education institutions play a pivotal role in advancing sustainable tourism development through innovative curriculum design and industry partnerships. As such, this study advances both theoretical understanding and practical policy relevance.

LITERATURE REVIEW

Contemporary Challenges in Hospitality and Tourism Education

Hospitality and tourism education has long struggled to balance vocational training with intellectual development. Globalization, sustainability, and technological disruption now require a more adaptive educational paradigm (Baum et al., 2020). The COVID-19 crisis exposed the fragility of traditional hotel management models and underscored the urgent need to equip future hospitality managers with robust sustainability competencies, preparing them to respond with agility to complex and uncertain global environments — qualities increasingly essential for graduates expected to navigate the interconnected economic, social, and environmental challenges facing the industry (Rodríguez-García et al., 2025).

The OECD (2023) identifies future-oriented learning as a process of cultivating cognitive, social, and emotional capabilities that enable learners to act with autonomy and responsibility. However, the absence of unified international guidelines complicates curriculum alignment and accreditation.

Artificial Intelligence in Hospitality and Tourism: Applications and Educational Implications

Artificial intelligence now permeates nearly every aspect of tourism operations, from predictive analytics in revenue management to automated guest services and real-time customer engagement (Ivanov & Webster, 2019). Robots and AI-driven systems perform check-ins, housekeeping coordination, and sentiment analysis, enhancing efficiency and personalization while reshaping labor structures (Tussyadiah, 2020).

International policy frameworks provide a moral and procedural compass. UNESCO's Recommendation on the Ethics of Artificial Intelligence (2021) advocates for human-centered AI grounded in human rights, inclusivity, and environmental sustainability. Similarly, the OECD's AI Principles (2019) emphasize transparency, accountability, and robust governance. Integrating these frameworks into hospitality curricula ensures that technological competencies are accompanied by critical reflection and ethical literacy.

Pedagogically, AI integration supports experiential and interdisciplinary learning. Simulation-based projects allow students to model AI-enabled sustainability scenarios, such as optimizing hotel energy consumption or predicting waste patterns, thereby bridging theory and practice (Filho et al., 2025). This learning design aligns with constructivist approaches, where students co-create knowledge through problem-solving and collaboration (Creswell & Poth, 2018).

Sustainability and Responsible Tourism in Graduate Education

Sustainability education in tourism has evolved from niche interest to global necessity. Anchored in the UN Sustainable Development Goals (SDGs)particularly SDG 4 (Quality Education), SDG 8 (Decent Work and Economic Growth), and SDG 12 (Responsible Consumption and Production), hospitality programs are urged to integrate ecological, social, and economic sustainability principles (UNWTO, 2018).

The Global Sustainable Tourism Council (GSTC) provides a global baseline for sustainability standards in hotels and destinations, focusing on environmental management, cultural preservation, and socio-economic equity. The UNESCO Education for Sustainable Development (ESD) roadmap (2020) similarly outlines the competencies of systems thinking, anticipatory learning, and collaboration as central to transformative education.

In graduate hospitality education, sustainability pedagogy has advanced through approaches such as transformative learning (Mezirow, 2000), systems thinking (Senge, 2006), and the triple bottom line model (Elkington, 1997). These frameworks promote reflection, ethical awareness, and problem-based learning. Berjozkina and Melanthiou (2021) observe that effective sustainability education requires moving beyond theoretical knowledge to develop practical competencies through industry engagement and real-world problem-solving.

The challenge lies in reimagining sustainability education not as an isolated subject but as a dynamic context where AI and data-driven tools enhance responsible management and innovation capacity. This convergence is essential for aligning curricula with international sustainability and digital education agendas. Fernández-Villarán et al. (2024) emphasize that integrating sustainability into tourism curricula requires addressing both pedagogical challenges and institutional barriers, including faculty development, resource allocation, and assessment strategies.

Integrating AI and Sustainability: Converging Competencies

Recent research indicates that AI can accelerate sustainability outcomes across hospitality and tourism sectors (Filimonau et al., 2025). AI-powered analytics can optimize energy use, minimize waste, and personalize sustainable guest experiences (Ivanov & Webster, 2019).

Educationally, integrating AI with sustainability creates opportunities for interdisciplinary competency development. Students learn to analyze ethical trade-offs, use digital tools for sustainability monitoring, and apply data-driven insights to responsible decision-making. The OECD Learning Compass 2030 (2020) conceptualizes these skills as "transformative competencies" the ability to create new value, reconcile tensions, and act responsibly.

The UNWTO's Digital Transformation Strategy (n.d.) also calls for the alignment of technological innovation with sustainable tourism principles. These convergences suggest that AI and sustainability should be taught not as separate domains but as interdependent capabilities underpinning responsible innovation.

Identified Research Gap

Despite mounting attention, the literature reveals a persistent lack of cohesive, internationally aligned frameworks for integrating AI and sustainability in hospitality and tourism education. Studies typically focus on either digital transformation or sustainability pedagogy in isolation (Filimonau et al., 2025).

Consequently, educators and policymakers face challenges in designing programs that simultaneously address technological fluency, ethical reasoning, and sustainability literacy. This study therefore aims to fill this gap by constructing a comprehensive framework based on international standards (UNESCO, UNWTO, OECD, GSTC) and validated through comparative analysis of leading graduate programs, establishing shared guidelines for educational innovation.

METHODOLOGY

Research Design

The study employs a qualitative exploratory research design combining documentary analysis and comparative case study methodology to derive a framework of guidelines for integrating AI and sustainability into graduate-level hospitality and tourism education. This design is appropriate for exploring emerging, multidimensional phenomena where theoretical consensus remains limited (Creswell & Poth, 2018).

The approach integrates three methodological components:

1. Documentary analysis of international frameworks, policy reports, and academic literature.
2. Comparative case study analysis of leading graduate programs that have pioneered AI and/or sustainability integration.
3. Thematic synthesis to identify converging principles and best practices.

This design reflects a constructivist–interpretivist paradigm, emphasizing meaning-making, contextual interpretation, and pattern recognition across multiple contexts (Yin, 2018).

Data Sources

Documentary Sources

Primary documents analyzed include:

- UNESCO's Recommendation on the Ethics of Artificial Intelligence (2021).
- UNESCO's Education for Sustainable Development: A Roadmap (2020).

- OECD's Principles on Artificial Intelligence (2019) and Learning Compass 2030 (2020).
- UNWTO's Tourism and the SDGs Roadmap (2018, 2022).
- GSTC's Sustainability Criteria for Hotels and Destinations (2019).

Secondary sources consist of peer-reviewed articles published between 2015 and 2025 in journals such as *Tourism Management*, *Sustainability*, and *Journal of Hospitality, Leisure, Sport & Tourism Education*. The inclusion criteria focused on research addressing AI in hospitality, sustainability education, or competency-based curriculum design.

Case Study Programs

Seven graduate programs were purposively selected based on the following criteria:

- Recognition for innovation in AI integration and/or sustainability education
- Geographic diversity (representing Europe, North America, Asia-Pacific, and Middle East)
- Accreditation alignment with international standards (UNWTO TedQual, AACSB, or equivalent)
- Public accessibility of curriculum information

Selected Programs:

1. Cornell University, School of Hotel Administration (USA) – Master of Management in Hospitality
2. University of Surrey, School of Hospitality and Tourism Management (UK) – MSc International Hotel Management
3. Hong Kong Polytechnic University, School of Hotel and Tourism Management (Hong Kong) – MSc in International Hospitality Management
4. Lausanne Hotel School (EHL) (Switzerland) – MSc in Global Hospitality Business
5. Griffith University, Department of Tourism, Sport, and Hotel Management (Australia) – Master of Business (Tourism and Hospitality)
6. IE University, School of Global and Public Affairs (Spain) – Master in Tourism and Hospitality Management
7. Les Roches Global Hospitality Education (Switzerland/Spain/UAE) – Master of Science in International Hospitality Management

Data sources for each case included: program websites, course syllabi (publicly available), accreditation reports, promotional materials, and published program descriptions in academic databases.

Data Collection

Phase 1: Documentary Analysis

Following PRISMA guidelines (Moher et al., 2009), a systematic documentary review identified overlapping themes and competencies among the international frameworks. Key categories included AI ethics, sustainability literacy, curriculum integration, and global standard alignment.

A total of 58 peer-reviewed articles and 12 policy documents were analyzed. Documents were coded for: (1) competency areas, (2) pedagogical approaches, (3) alignment mechanisms with international standards, and (4) implementation strategies.

Phase 2: Comparative Case Study Analysis

For each selected program, the following data were systematically extracted and analyzed:

- Curriculum structure: Core and elective courses related to AI, data analytics, sustainability, and responsible tourism
- Learning outcomes: Stated competencies in technology, ethics, and sustainability
  -Pedagogical methods: Experiential learning, interdisciplinary collaboration, industry partnerships
- Alignment mechanisms: Explicit references to UNESCO, UNWTO, OECD, GSTC, or SDG frameworks
- Innovation practices: Unique approaches to integrating AI and sustainability

Data Analysis

Data were analyzed using thematic analysis (Braun & Clarke, 2006) and cross-case synthesis (Yin, 2018), supported by NVivo software for coding and organization.

Analysis Process:

1. Initial coding: Open coding of documentary sources and case study data to identify recurring themes

2. Axial coding: Grouping codes into thematic categories aligned with research objectives
3. Cross-case pattern matching: Identifying convergent and divergent practices across the seven programs
4. Framework synthesis: Integrating documentary insights and case study patterns into coherent principles
5. Validation: Triangulating findings against international standards to ensure alignment and comprehensiveness

Reliability, Validity, and Ethics

Reliability was ensured through:

- Systematic documentation of data collection and analysis procedures
- Use of an audit trail for transparency
- Intercoder reliability checks (Cohen's Kappa = 0.84)

Validity was established through:

- Construct validity: Aligning analysis with established frameworks (UNESCO ESD, OECD Learning Compass)
- Triangulation: Combining documentary analysis with multiple case studies
- Member checking: Verification of publicly available program data through official institutional sources

Ethical considerations

- All data sources were publicly available; no human subjects were involved
- Institutional confidentiality was maintained by focusing on publicly accessible information
- Analysis followed UNESCO's AI Ethics principles, ensuring transparency and respect for institutional contexts

Limitations

The study acknowledges several limitations:

- Case selection bias: Focus on internationally recognized programs may not represent emerging or regional institutions

- Data accessibility: Reliance on publicly available information limited depth of curricular analysis
- Temporal constraints: Rapid evolution of AI and sustainability education means findings reflect a specific moment in time (2024-2025)
- Geographic representation: Limited representation from African and Latin American institutions due to accessibility of English-language materials

Despite these limitations, the combination of international standards analysis and comparative case studies provides a robust foundation for framework development.

Justification for Methodological Approach

The shift from expert consensus methodology to comparative case study analysis offers several advantages aligned with the study's objectives:

1. Evidence-based: Grounds the framework in actual practices of leading institutions
2. Replicability: Other researchers can verify findings through the same publicly accessible sources
3. Feasibility: Eliminates dependency on expert availability and multi-round consensus processes
4. Richness: Provides concrete examples of how principles are operationalized in diverse contexts
5. International perspective: Captures diverse approaches across educational systems and cultural contexts

This methodology maintains the study's qualitative exploratory nature while providing empirical grounding that strengthens the framework's credibility and applicability.

FINDINGS: COMPARATIVE ANALYSIS AND FRAMEWORK DEVELOPMENT

Comparative Analysis of Case Study Programs

The comparative analysis of seven leading graduate programs reveals distinct yet complementary approaches to integrating AI and sustainability into hospitality and tourism education.

Key Patterns Identified

Pattern 1: Integrated Rather Than Isolated Approach

Leading programs embed AI and sustainability across multiple courses rather than confining them to standalone modules. Cornell integrates predictive analytics into revenue management while simultaneously addressing energy optimization. Hong Kong PolyU combines smart hospitality systems with green operations in capstone projects. Les Roches explicitly integrates AI-driven personalization with sustainable design across its curriculum, demonstrating the convergence of digital transformation and sustainability in luxury hospitality contexts.

Pattern 2: Experiential and Applied Learning

All seven programs emphasize hands-on learning through industry partnerships, consulting projects, and technology labs. Surrey's sustainability audits, Griffith's community-based projects, and Les Roches' international business field trips exemplify how theoretical knowledge translates into practical competencies.

Pattern 3: Explicit Alignment with International Standards

Programs consistently reference UNESCO, UNWTO, GSTC, and SDG frameworks in learning outcomes and program documentation. This alignment facilitates international recognition and graduate mobility while ensuring curricular relevance.

Pattern 4: Interdisciplinary Collaboration

Successful integration requires collaboration across departments. IE University's innovation labs bring together technology, sustainability, and business faculty. EHL's consulting projects engage students with real-world stakeholders across disciplines. Les Roches' multi-campus model (Switzerland, Spain, UAE) provides unique opportunities for cross-cultural and interdisciplinary learning embedded in diverse regional hospitality contexts.

Pattern 5: Ethical and Critical Perspectives

Programs increasingly incorporate ethical dimensions of AI, addressing bias, transparency, and social impact. Cornell's AI ethics modules and Surrey's sustainability analytics courses exemplify this commitment to responsible technology use. Les Roches emphasizes guest experience personalization through data while maintaining focus on responsible luxury and sustainable operations.

Pattern 6: Global and Multi-Campus Perspectives

Les Roches' distinctive three-campus model spanning Switzerland, Spain, and the UAE offers students exposure to diverse luxury hospitality markets, regulatory environments, and cultural contexts. This geographic diversity enhances students' ability to apply AI and sustainability principles across different regional and cultural settings, preparing graduates for truly global careers in hospitality management.

Framework of Guidelines: Seven Thematic Principles

Drawing upon international standards (UNESCO, UNWTO, OECD, GSTC) and validated through comparative case analysis, the framework identifies seven thematic principles that underpin curriculum design, pedagogical strategy, and policy alignment. Each principle includes practical implications and evidence from case studies.

Principle 1: Alignment with Global Standards and Competency Frameworks

Description: Graduate programs should align AI and sustainability curricula with recognized international standards. UNESCO's Education for Sustainable Development (ESD) framework (2020) emphasizes competency development in systems thinking, anticipatory learning, and collaborative problem-solving. OECD's Learning Compass 2030 (2020) and AI Principles (2019) provide additional guidance on integrating transformative competencies and ethical AI literacy. UNWTO's tourism and SDG roadmap (2018, 2022) and GSTC criteria (2019) define sustainable tourism objectives that can anchor educational content.

Evidence from Case Studies

All seven programs explicitly reference international frameworks in program descriptions and learning outcomes. Hong Kong PolyU aligns capstone projects with UNESCO ESD competencies, while IE University structures its curriculum around UN SDG targets. Surrey holds UNWTO TedQual accreditation, demonstrating systematic alignment with global tourism education standards. Les Roches' accreditation by both Swiss (SAC) and U.S. (NECHE) bodies demonstrates dual commitment to European and North American quality standards, facilitating global recognition and graduate mobility.

Practical Implications

Curriculum designers should map course outcomes, learning objectives, and assessment strategies to these international frameworks. Embedding global competencies ensures graduates are prepared to meet both ethical and operational expectations in AI-driven sustainable tourism. Policymakers can use alignment with these standards as a benchmark for accreditation and quality assurance.

Principle 2: Integration of AI Competencies Across the Curriculum

Description: AI literacy should be embedded throughout the curriculum rather than confined to isolated modules. Core competencies include data literacy, algorithmic thinking, predictive analytics, human–machine collaboration, and AI ethics (Ivanov & Webster, 2019). Students should engage with AI applications in service management, revenue optimization, and customer experience personalization, alongside ethical and regulatory considerations.

Evidence from Case Studies

Cornell integrates AI analytics across revenue management, operations, and marketing courses. Hong Kong PolyU embeds machine learning in service design and smart hospitality systems. Surrey combines data science with hospitality management in core curriculum, ensuring all graduates achieve baseline AI literacy regardless of specialization. Les Roches integrates "Hospitality Analytics & Revenue Management" and "Guest Experience and Personalization through Data" as core courses, demonstrating systematic embedding of AI competencies in revenue optimization and service delivery contexts.

Practical Implications

Universities should design interdisciplinary modules where AI concepts are taught in tandem with sustainability topics, allowing students to apply AI tools to environmental management, waste reduction, and energy optimization. Policy alignment ensures AI literacy remains consistent with UNESCO and OECD recommendations for ethical and inclusive technology use.

Principle 3: Embedding Sustainability Literacy and Transformative Learning

Description: Sustainability education should foster critical awareness of environmental, social, and economic systems. Transformative learning approaches (Mezirow, 2000; Barth & Rieckmann, 2012) encourage reflective thinking and responsible decision-making. Incorporating GSTC standards and UN SDGs provide actionable content on sustainable operations, cultural preservation, and responsible tourism practices.

Evidence from Case Studies

Griffith University emphasizes Indigenous tourism and climate change adaptation through community-based projects. EHL integrates responsible luxury and sustainable gastronomy across its curriculum. Surrey conducts sustainability audits as experiential learning, while IE University structures courses around SDG achievement. Les Roches offers "Sustainable Design & Facilities Management" as a core course and embeds sustainable gastronomy throughout its curriculum, aligning luxury hospitality education with environmental responsibility and resource efficiency.

Practical Implications

Educators should integrate case studies, project-based learning, and fieldwork that demonstrate sustainability challenges in real-world hospitality contexts. As Berjozkina and Melanthiou (2021) emphasize, moving beyond theoretical knowledge to practical application enhances student engagement and competency development. Policy frameworks can incentivize institutions to incorporate sustainability as a measurable outcome in accreditation criteria and program review.

Principle 4: Interdisciplinary and Experiential Learning Approaches

Description: Integrating AI and sustainability requires pedagogical strategies that bridge disciplines. Experiential learning, simulations, and project-based assignments enable students to apply AI tools to sustainability challenges, such as predictive energy management or sustainable destination planning (Filho et al., 2025).

Evidence from Case Studies

All seven programs employ experiential learning as a core pedagogical strategy. Cornell's hospitality labs and consulting projects, Surrey's industry partnerships and sustainability audits, Hong Kong PolyU's service-learning initiatives, EHL's global immersion programs, Griffith's fieldwork in conservation tourism, IE's hackathons and case competitions, and Les Roches' international business field trips and mandatory six-month internships, demonstrate diverse approaches to applied learning.

Practical Implications

Programs should foster collaboration across technology, management, and sustainability faculties. Universities can establish partnerships with industry and policy organizations to provide hands-on learning, while policymakers can support incentives for interdisciplinary programs that meet international competency benchmarks. Sarpong et al. (2025) underscore that university-industry partnerships are essential for translating academic knowledge into sustainable tourism practices.

Principle 5: Ethical and Responsible AI in Hospitality Education

Description: Ethical considerations must permeate AI instruction, emphasizing fairness, transparency, accountability, and environmental responsibility (UNESCO, 2021; OECD, 2019). Students should explore the social implications of automation, data privacy, and algorithmic decision-making in tourism and hospitality contexts.

Evidence from Case Studies

Cornell offers dedicated AI ethics modules examining bias, transparency, and accountability. Surrey integrates ethical considerations into data science courses, addressing privacy and algorithmic fairness. Hong Kong PolyU and IE University incorporate social impact assessments into AI-related projects. Les Roches' integration of AI-driven personalization within "Guest Experience and Personalization through Data" provides opportunities to address ethical considerations of data collection, privacy, and algorithmic decision-making in luxury hospitality contexts.

Practical Implications

Curriculum developers should include modules on AI ethics and sustainability impact assessments. Policy bodies and accreditation agencies can encourage institutions to adopt mandatory ethical AI competencies, ensuring graduates act responsibly in technology-mediated environments. This aligns with UNESCO's call for human-centered AI that respects human rights and environmental sustainability.

Principle 6: Digital Sustainability and Innovation

Description: AI should be leveraged to advance sustainability objectives, including resource optimization, waste reduction, and operational efficiency (Ivanov & Webster, 2019). The integration of smart technologies, predictive modeling, and digital tools supports evidence-based decision-making in hospitality operations while reinforcing sustainability principles.

Evidence from Case Studies

Surrey combines sustainability analytics with AI applications in environmental management systems. Hong Kong PolyU's smart hospitality systems optimize energy consumption and waste management. Cornell's predictive analytics courses address resource optimization in hotel operations. Griffith applies digital tools to conservation tourism and climate adaptation strategies. Les Roches' "Sustainable Design & Facilities Management" course provides opportunities to apply AI and digital tools for optimizing energy efficiency, resource utilization, and environmental performance in luxury hospitality facilities.

Practical Implications

Students should engage in applied projects demonstrating the environmental and economic benefits of AI deployment. Policymakers can incentivize innovation through grants, collaborative industry projects, and recognition programs for sustainable technology integration. This principle responds to UNWTO's call for aligning digital transformation with sustainable tourism objectives.

Principle 7: Continuous Evaluation and Curriculum Adaptation

Description: Programs must be dynamic, responding to rapid technological advances and evolving sustainability priorities. Continuous evaluation, informed by feedback from students, industry, and international standards, ensures curricula remain relevant and globally aligned (Oloyede et al., 2024).

Evidence from Case Studies

All programs demonstrate commitment to curriculum review and adaptation. IE University conducts annual program evaluations incorporating industry feedback. Surrey maintains advisory boards with industry representatives. Cornell and EHL regularly update course content to reflect emerging technologies and sustainability practices. Les Roches' recent launch (2025) of its updated MSc in International Hospitality Management across all global campuses demonstrates institutional commitment to curriculum evolution aligned with industry demands for digital transformation and sustainability competencies.

Practical Implications

Universities should implement periodic curriculum audits and maintain adaptive learning pathways, while policymakers can promote mechanisms for continuous program improvement, benchmarking institutions against international standards and emerging best practices. This ensures that education remains responsive to the rapidly changing landscape of AI and sustainability.

Framework Synthesis and Integrated Model

The seven principles collectively constitute a cohesive, action-oriented framework for integrating AI and sustainability in graduate hospitality education. They establish a curriculum design philosophy where international standards guide both content and pedagogy, fostering graduates who are technologically competent, ethically grounded, and sustainability-literate.

Figure 1. Integrated Framework for AI and Sustainability in Graduate Hospitality Education

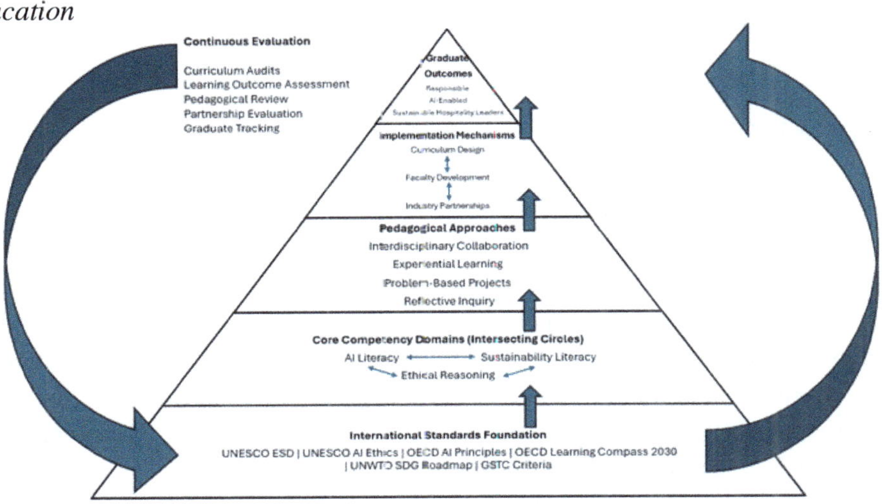

Source: Own elaboration based on the outcome

Importantly, the framework balances conceptual rigor with practical applicability, ensuring it is actionable for curriculum designers, educational policymakers, and accreditation bodies. By grounding principles in evidence from leading programs, the framework demonstrates not only what should be done but also what can be done within existing institutional contexts.

By applying this framework, institutions can:

1. Enhance interdisciplinary learning, bridging technology, management, and sustainability through integrated curriculum design and cross-departmental collaboration.
2. Align program outcomes with global standards, supporting international recognition, graduate mobility, and quality assurance through explicit mapping to UNESCO, OECD, UNWTO, and GSTC frameworks.
3. Foster ethical and responsible application of AI in the hospitality and tourism sector through dedicated ethics modules and impact assessments integrated throughout the curriculum.

4. Support lifelong learning through continuous curriculum adaptation, reflecting industry and societal shifts while maintaining alignment with evolving international standards.
5. Prepare graduates for dual transitions, equipping them with competencies to navigate both digital transformation and sustainability imperatives in an increasingly complex global industry.

DISCUSSION

Theoretical Contributions

This study makes several theoretical contributions to hospitality and tourism education scholarships. First, it synthesizes previously fragmented discussions of AI and sustainability education into a unified conceptual framework grounded in international standards. By demonstrating the interdependence of technological and sustainability competencies, the research challenges the traditional separation of these domains in curriculum design.

Second, the framework extends the OECD Learning Compass 2030 concept of "transformative competencies" to the specific context of hospitality and tourism education. It operationalizes abstract concepts such as "reconciling tensions" and "taking responsibility" through concrete curricular and pedagogical strategies evidenced in leading programs.

Third, the comparative case study methodology provides empirical validation for theoretical principles derived from policy documents. This approach bridges the gap between international policy frameworks and institutional practice, demonstrating how global standards can be translated into actionable educational strategies across diverse cultural and institutional contexts.

Fourth, the inclusion of Les Roches' multi-campus model reveals the importance of geographic and cultural diversity in delivering globally relevant hospitality education. The study demonstrates how institutions can leverage multiple campus locations to provide contextual learning experiences that prepare graduates for diverse regional markets while maintaining coherent alignment with international standards.

Practical Implications for Curriculum Design

For curriculum designers, the framework offers a structured pathway for innovation that balances international standards with institutional autonomy. The seven principles provide clear direction while allowing flexibility in implementation based on institutional strengths, regional contexts, and resource availability.

The evidence from case studies demonstrates that successful integration does not require wholesale curriculum redesign. Rather, strategic embedding of AI and sustainability competencies across existing courses, combined with targeted experiential learning opportunities, can achieve significant impact. This incremental approach may be more feasible for institutions with limited resources or regulatory constraints.

The framework also highlights the importance of faculty development. As case studies reveal, successful programs invest in continuous professional development to equip faculty with AI literacy, sustainability expertise, and interdisciplinary teaching methods. Without faculty capacity building, even well-designed curricula may fail to achieve their intended learning outcomes.

Les Roches' recent curriculum update across all campuses demonstrates the feasibility of implementing coordinated curriculum innovation across multiple geographic locations while maintaining program coherence and quality standards. This model offers insights for other multi-campus or international hospitality education providers.

Policy and Accreditation Implications

For policymakers and accreditation bodies, the framework provides a benchmark for quality assurance in graduate hospitality and tourism education. By aligning with UNESCO, OECD, UNWTO, and GSTC standards, the framework facilitates international recognition and comparability while respecting diverse educational traditions and institutional contexts.

The study suggests that accreditation criteria should evolve beyond traditional metrics of operational competency to include explicit assessment of AI literacy, sustainability competence, and ethical reasoning. Programs that demonstrate alignment with international standards and evidence of integrated curriculum design should receive recognition and support through policy incentives.

Furthermore, policymakers can use the framework to guide investment in educational infrastructure, including technology labs, sustainability research centers, and industry partnership programs. The comparative analysis reveals that leading institutions benefit from dedicated resources that support experiential learning and interdisciplinary collaboration.

The dual accreditation model exemplified by Les Roches (Swiss and U.S. accreditation bodies) demonstrates the value of pursuing multiple quality assurance frameworks, enhancing program credibility across different educational systems, and facilitating graduate mobility in an increasingly globalized hospitality industry.

Addressing the Education-Industry Gap

One of the persistent challenges identified in the literature is the mismatch between educational outcomes and industry expectations (Commey et al., 2023). This framework addresses this gap by grounding competency development in both international standards and evidence from programs with strong industry connections.

The emphasis on experiential learning, industry partnerships, and applied projects ensures that graduates develop not only theoretical knowledge but also practical skills directly applicable to workplace contexts. Case studies demonstrate various models of industry engagement, from Cornell's consulting projects to Griffith's community-based fieldwork to Les Roches' mandatory six-month internships, providing templates for institutions seeking to strengthen industry connections.

However, the framework also maintains that education should not merely respond to immediate industry demands but should prepare graduates to lead transformation. By integrating ethical reasoning and sustainability competencies alongside technological skills, the framework positions graduate as change agents capable of shaping industry practices rather than simply adapting to them.

Limitations and Future Research Directions

While this study provides a comprehensive framework grounded in international standards and validated through comparative case analysis, several limitations suggest directions for future research.

First, the focus on leading programs in developed countries may limit transferability to institutions in developing regions with different resource constraints and educational priorities. Future research should explore how the framework can be adapted to diverse institutional contexts, including emerging economies and resource-constrained settings.

Second, the reliance on publicly available data, while ensuring replicability and ethical rigor, limits depth of analysis regarding actual implementation challenges, student learning outcomes, and long-term graduate impacts. Longitudinal studies tracking graduate employment, career trajectories, and contributions to sustainable tourism development would provide valuable insights into framework effectiveness.

Third, the rapid evolution of both AI technologies and sustainability imperatives means that the framework requires continuous updating. Future research should monitor emerging technologies (such as generative AI and quantum computing) and evolving sustainability challenges (including climate adaptation and regenerative tourism) to ensure the framework remains relevant.

Fourth, while the study identifies key principles and provides evidence of successful practices, it does not empirically test the framework's effectiveness through controlled implementation studies. Future research employing quasi-experimental designs or action research methodologies could assess framework impact on student learning outcomes, graduate competencies, and institutional change.

Finally, the study focuses on graduate-level education, but similar challenges exist at undergraduate and professional development levels. Expanding the framework to encompass the full spectrum of hospitality and tourism education would enhance its comprehensive utility.

CONCLUSION

The integration of artificial intelligence (AI) and sustainability into graduate-level hospitality and tourism education has emerged as a defining challenge and opportunity for twenty-first-century higher learning. As global tourism undergoes profound transformation driven by digitalization, environmental imperatives, and post-pandemic socio-economic shifts, the boundaries between technology, ethics, and sustainability are becoming increasingly blurred. This study has responded to that convergence by developing a globally informed, evidence-based framework grounded in recognized international standards (UNESCO, UNWTO, OECD, and GSTC) and validated through comparative analysis of seven leading graduate programs across five continents.

The findings demonstrate that successful integration requires more than the mere addition of AI or sustainability courses. It necessitates a systemic pedagogical realignment in which technology and environmental stewardship are treated as complementary, mutually reinforcing dimensions of professional competence. The seven thematic principles identified (alignment with global standards, embedded AI literacy, transformative sustainability learning, interdisciplinary and experiential pedagogy, ethical AI practice, digital sustainability innovation, and continuous evaluation) collectively articulate a holistic pathway for curricular transformation.

At a conceptual level, the framework advances the theory of transformative hospitality education by linking the OECD's "transformative competencies" and UNESCO's Education for Sustainable Development (ESD) competencies to concrete curricular and institutional practices. It demonstrates how hospitality education can transcend traditional vocational boundaries to become a platform for developing critical, ethical, and creative thinkers who can navigate the complexity of AI-enabled sustainability transitions. By connecting policy frameworks with comparative institutional evidence, the research bridges the persistent gap between international aspiration and institutional implementation.

From a practical standpoint, the framework offers a blueprint for actionable reform. Universities can adopt a mapping approach that explicitly aligns learning outcomes with international standards, ensuring coherence and comparability across regions. Policymakers and accreditation bodies can employ the framework as a benchmark for evaluating institutional quality and fostering global recognition. Industry partners, whose role has historically been limited to internship provision, are invited to become co-architects of curricular innovation, embedding real-world challenges, data-driven case studies, and ethical technology applications directly into learning experiences. In doing so, industry engagement transitions from transactional to transformational, strengthening the feedback loop between academia and practice.

Equally significant is the framework's emphasis on ethical responsibility and human-centered innovation. AI, while promising efficiency and personalization, also introduces risks of bias, exclusion, and environmental externalities. Embedding UNESCO's Recommendation on the Ethics of Artificial Intelligence (2021) and OECD's AI Principles (2019) within hospitality curricula ensures that future leaders possess not only technical fluency but also moral imagination, the capacity to evaluate how technological decisions shape human experiences, labor relations, and planetary wellbeing.

The comparative case studies provide persuasive evidence that curricular transformation is achievable within existing institutional structures. Programs such as Cornell's data-analytics integration, Griffith's community-based sustainability fieldwork, and Les Roches' global multi-campus model illustrate diverse yet convergent strategies that balance innovation with contextual relevance. Their experiences confirm that curriculum integration can be gradual and iterative, driven by reflective assessment, faculty development, and sustained industry collaboration.

Moreover, the research underscores the strategic importance of faculty empowerment. Without continuous professional development that cultivates digital literacy, sustainability expertise, and interdisciplinary pedagogy, even well-designed curricula may falter in implementation. Institutions must therefore view faculty not merely as content deliverers but as change agents, and mediators between evolving knowledge systems and the ethical responsibilities of education.

Beyond individual programs, the study contributes to global policy dialogue by illustrating how educational frameworks can operationalize the Sustainable Development Goals (SDGs) in higher education. Specifically, it reinforces SDG 4 (Quality Education), SDG 8 (Decent Work and Economic Growth), and SDG 12 (Responsible Consumption and Production), situating graduate hospitality education within the larger UN agenda for inclusive, equitable, and sustainable societies. The integration of AI further supports SDG 9 (Industry, Innovation, and Infrastructure), ensuring that technological progress advances rather than undermines sustainability objectives.

Looking forward, the framework invites a paradigm shift toward regenerative and anticipatory education; one that not only mitigates negative impacts but also proactively shapes sustainable futures through foresight, creativity, and systems thinking. As emerging technologies such as generative AI, quantum computing, and the Internet of Things transform hospitality operations, educational institutions must cultivate graduates capable of leading adaptive, ethical, and innovative responses. This entails re-conceptualizing hospitality management as a knowledge ecosystem where data, culture, and environmental responsibility converge.

The implications extend beyond academia. Industry stakeholders stand to benefit from graduates who possess hybrid competencies, therefore data analytics integrated with sustainability reasoning, AI ethics paired with cultural intelligence, and entrepreneurial agility informed by global citizenship values. These capabilities will define competitive advantage in a marketplace increasingly regulated by sustainability standards, digital transparency, and consumer expectations for ethical practice.

At the societal level, embedding AI and sustainability within hospitality education contributes to resilient human capital development, equipping professionals to address grand challenges such as climate change, social inequity, and technological disruption. Graduates trained under this framework will be prepared not only to operate within existing paradigms but to question, reform, and reinvent them acting as catalysts for responsible innovation and transformative leadership across the global tourism ecosystem.

While this study acknowledges inherent limitations, such as geographical concentration, reliance on publicly available data, and the evolving nature of AI and sustainability discourse, it lays a robust foundation for subsequent empirical inquiry. Future research should test the framework through longitudinal studies assessing graduate outcomes, institutional transformation processes, and measurable sustainability impacts. Comparative analyses involving institutions in emerging economies can further illuminate pathways for inclusive adoption and contextual adaptation.

Ultimately, the convergence of AI and sustainability represents an inflection point in the evolution of hospitality and tourism education. The framework proposed herein offers a roadmap for navigating this transformation through international alignment, ethical stewardship, and interdisciplinary collaboration. It challenges universities to transcend disciplinary silos, policymakers to rethink accreditation paradigms, industry to assume co-creative responsibility, and researchers to sustain an evidence-based dialogue between innovation and ethics.

In essence, integrating AI and sustainability into graduate-level hospitality and tourism education is not solely a curricular innovation; it is a moral and strategic imperative for shaping a future in which digital intelligence and environmental consciousness coexist in service of human and planetary well-being. If adopted with commitment and reflexivity, this framework has the potential to redefine the identity of hospitality education, transforming it from a discipline of service excellence into a driver of global sustainability and responsible technological progress.

The integration of artificial intelligence (AI) and sustainability into graduate-level hospitality and tourism education is no longer optional but imperative. This study has developed a globally informed, evidence-based framework grounded in recognized international standards (UNESCO, UNWTO, OECD, GSTC) and validated through comparative analysis of seven leading graduate programs across five continents. By identifying seven thematic principles, the framework offers a comprehensive blueprint for curriculum design, pedagogical innovation, and policy alignment.

The framework emphasizes alignment with international standards, interdisciplinary and experiential learning, integrated AI literacy, transformative sustainability competence, ethical responsibility, digital sustainability innovation, and continuous curriculum adaptation. It underscores the critical role of ongoing evaluation to respond to rapid technological changes and evolving sustainability imperatives. Collectively, these principles support the preparation of graduates capable of navigating complex, AI-enabled, and sustainability-driven hospitality and tourism systems.

Evidence from leading programs demonstrates that successful integration requires not merely adding new courses but fundamentally rethinking curriculum architecture, pedagogical approaches, and institutional partnerships. The comparative analysis reveals diverse yet complementary strategies, from Cornell's analytics-focused approach to Griffith's community-based model to Les Roches' global multi-campus immersive learning, illustrating that multiple pathways can achieve similar outcomes while respecting institutional contexts and regional priorities.

Integrating AI and sustainability is not solely about imparting technical knowledge or environmental awareness. It represents a transformative educational approach that fosters critical thinking, ethical reasoning, and global citizenship. As Giousmpasoglou (2025) emphasize, higher education institutions bear responsibility for advancing sustainable tourism development through innovative curriculum design and leadership preparation. Universities adopting this framework will produce graduates who are technologically fluent, ethically grounded, and equipped to lead sustainable innovation in the hospitality and tourism sector.

The framework contributes to both educational scholarship and policy dialogue by providing an actionable, internationally aligned model that bridges the gap between global standards and institutional practice. It responds to calls from UNWTO (2022) and OECD (2023) for future-oriented competencies that balance technological capability with ethical and environmental responsibility. By grounding abstract principles in concrete evidence from successful programs, the framework demonstrates not only the necessity but also the feasibility of transformative curriculum innovation.

As the hospitality and tourism industry continues its dual transition toward digitalization and sustainability, education must evolve correspondingly. This framework provides a roadmap for that evolution, one that honors international standards, respects institutional diversity, and prioritizes the development of responsible, innovative leaders capable of shaping a more sustainable and equitable future for global tourism.

RECOMMENDATIONS

Based on the findings, framework development, and comparative analysis, the following recommendations are proposed for different stakeholder groups:

For Universities and Curriculum Designers

1. Integrated Curriculum Design: Embed AI and sustainability across all graduate-level courses rather than confining them to isolated modules. Ensure that competencies in data analytics, ethical AI, and responsible tourism are integrated throughout the program architecture. Map learning outcomes explicitly to UNESCO ESD, OECD Learning Compass, UNWTO SDG roadmaps, and GSTC standards.
2. Adopt Experiential Pedagogies: Implement interdisciplinary, project-based, and experiential learning approaches as demonstrated by leading programs. Establish industry partnerships, consulting projects, sustainability audits, and community-based fieldwork to bridge theory and practice.
3. Invest in Faculty Development: Create continuous professional development programs that equip faculty with expertise in AI technologies, sustainability practices, and interdisciplinary teaching methods. Ensure faculty familiarity with international ethical standards and policy frameworks. Consider faculty exchanges and collaborative teaching across departments.
4. Establish Innovation Infrastructure: Develop dedicated spaces and resources for AI and sustainability integration, including technology labs, sustainability research centers, and collaborative workspaces that facilitate interdisciplinary learning.
5. Create Assessment Mechanisms: Design assessment strategies that evaluate not only technical knowledge but also ethical reasoning, systems thinking, and sustainability competencies. Incorporate portfolio assessments, capstone projects, and reflective journals that demonstrate integrated learning.
6. Leverage Multi-Campus Models: For institutions with multiple campus locations, develop coordinated curriculum frameworks that maintain coherence while leveraging regional diversity to provide contextual learning experiences across different cultural and market contexts.

For Policymakers and Accreditation Bodies

1. Update Accreditation Criteria: Recognize and incentivize curricula that integrate AI and sustainability by incorporating these elements into accreditation standards. Benchmark programs against international standards (UNESCO, OECD, UNWTO, GSTC) to ensure quality, relevance, and international comparability.
2. Provide Financial Incentives: Support curriculum innovation through grants, research funding, and infrastructure investment targeted at AI and sustainability integration. Recognize exemplary programs through awards and best practice dissemination.
3. Facilitate International Collaboration: Promote partnerships between institutions across regions to share best practices, develop joint programs, and enhance global perspectives. Support faculty and student mobility programs that expose participants to diverse approaches.
4. Mandate Continuous Evaluation: Require institutions to implement mechanisms for ongoing curriculum evaluation and adaptation, leveraging feedback from students, industry partners, and evolving international standards.
5. Align with SDG Frameworks: Ensure that educational policies explicitly support UN Sustainable Development Goals, particularly SDG 4 (Quality Education), SDG 8 (Decent Work), and SDG 12 (Responsible Consumption), creating coherence between education policy and broader sustainability agendas.
6. Support Dual and Multiple Accreditation Pathways: Recognize the value of institutions pursuing multiple quality assurance frameworks across different educational systems, facilitating international recognition and graduate mobility.

For Industry Partners

1. Engage in Co-Creation: Actively participate in curriculum design through advisory boards, guest lectures, and collaborative project development. Share real-world challenges that require AI and sustainability solutions, providing authentic learning contexts.
2. Offer Experiential Opportunities: Provide internships, consulting projects, and industry placements that allow students to apply AI and sustainability competencies in professional settings. Support student research and capstone projects aligned with organizational sustainability goals.
3. Support Faculty Development: Facilitate faculty industry immersions, provide access to organizational data and technologies, and collaborate on applied research that bridges academic and industry knowledge.

4. Recognize Graduate Competencies: Value and prioritize AI literacy, sustainability competence, and ethical reasoning in recruitment and professional development, creating market signals that reinforce educational priorities.

For Students and Graduates

1. Seek Integrated Programs: Prioritize graduate programs that explicitly integrate AI and sustainability, demonstrate alignment with international standards, and offer experiential learning opportunities.
2. Develop Interdisciplinary Competencies: Actively engage with courses and projects that bridge technology, sustainability, and management. Seeking opportunities for collaborative learning across disciplines and cultural contexts.
3. Cultivate Ethical Awareness: Critically examine the social and environmental implications of AI technologies. Develop competencies in ethical reasoning and responsible innovation that will guide professional practice.
4. Engage in Lifelong Learning: Recognize that both AI and sustainability fields evolve rapidly. Commit to continuous professional development and stay current with emerging technologies, sustainability practices, and international standards.
5. Leverage Global Learning Opportunities: Seek programs that offer international experience, multi-campus options, or field trips that provide exposure to diverse hospitality markets and cultural contexts.

For Researchers and Scholarly Community

1. Conduct Implementation Studies: Develop empirical research that tests framework effectiveness through controlled implementation studies, tracking student learning outcomes and long-term graduate impacts.
2. Expand Geographic Scope: Extend research to include diverse institutional contexts, particularly in emerging economies and underrepresented regions. Explore how frameworks can be adapted to different cultural, economic, and regulatory environments.
3. Investigate Longitudinal Outcomes: Track graduate career trajectories, contributions to sustainable tourism development, and long-term impacts of integrated education on industry practices and innovation.
4. Monitor Emerging Trends: Continuously update research to address emerging technologies (generative AI, quantum computing), evolving sustainability challenges (climate adaptation, regenerative tourism), and changing industry requirements.

5. Foster International Collaboration: Build research networks that span institutions, regions, and disciplines to advance collective understanding and accelerate knowledge translation into practice.
6. Examine Multi-Campus and Transnational Education Models: Investigate how multi-campus institutions and transnational education partnerships can effectively deliver integrated AI and sustainability curricula while maintaining quality and coherence across diverse contexts.

These comprehensive recommendations provide actionable guidance for all stakeholders involved in graduate hospitality and tourism education. Collectively, they support the development of responsible, technologically adept, and sustainability-oriented leaders capable of driving positive change in a complex, interconnected global industry.

REFERENCES

Barth, M., & Rieckmann, M. (2012). Academic staff development as a catalyst for curriculum change towards education for sustainable development: An output perspective. *Journal of Cleaner Production, 26*(1), 28–36. DOI: 10.1016/j.jclepro.2011.12.011

Baum, T., Mooney, S. K. K., Robinson, R. N. S., & Solnet, D. (2020). COVID-19's impact on the hospitality workforce–new crisis or amplification of the norm?. *International Journal of Contemporary Hospitality Management, 32*(9), 2813–2829.

Berjozkina, G., & Melanthiou, Y. (2021). Is tourism and hospitality education supporting sustainability? *Worldwide Hospitality and Tourism Themes, 13*(6), 744–753. https://doi.org/10.1108/whatt-07-2021-0101

Braun, V., & Clarke, V. (2006). Using thematic analysis in psychology. *Qualitative Research in Psychology, 3*(2), 77–101. DOI: 10.1191/1478088706qp063oa

Commey, V., Sarkodie, N. A., & Kokt, D. (2023). Hospitality Management Competency: Framework to match expectations of academia and industry in Ghana. *Journal of Tourism and Hospitality Studies, 1*(2), 09–20. https://doi.org/10.32996/jths.2023.1.2.2

Creswell, J. W., & Poth, C. N. (2018). *Qualitative inquiry and research design: Choosing among five approaches* (4th ed.). SAGE Publications.

Elkington, J. (1997). *Cannibals with forks: The triple bottom line of 21st century business*. Capstone Publishing.

Fernández-Villarán, A., Guereño-Omil, B., & Ageitos, N. (2024). Embedding Sustainability in tourism Education: Bridging curriculum gaps for a Sustainable Future. *Sustainability, 16*(21), 9286. https://doi.org/10.3390/su16219286

Filimonau, V., Ashton, M., Derqui, B., & Hernandez-Maskivker, G. (2025). Exploring how artificial intelligence (AI) can enable sustainability in the hospitality industry. *Sustainable Development, 33*(6), 9123–9143. https://doi.org/10.1002/sd.70146

Giousmpasoglou, C. (2025). Reclaiming Hospitality Education: A critical reflection. *Journal of Hospitality & Tourism Education*, 1–11. https://doi.org/10.1080/10963758.2025.2578541

Global Sustainable Tourism Council (GSTC). (2019). *GSTC criteria for hotels and tour operators: Version 3.0*. GSTC. https://www.gstcouncil.org/gstc-criteria

Ivanov, S., & Webster, C. (2019). *Robots, artificial intelligence, and service automation in travel, tourism and hospitality*. https://doi.org/10.1108/9781787566873

Leal Filho, W., Kim, E., Borsatto, J. M. L. S., & Marcolin, C. B. (2025). Using artificial intelligence in sustainability teaching and learning. *Environmental Sciences Europe, 37*(1). https://doi.org/10.1186/s12302-025-01159-w

Mezirow, J. (2000). *Learning as transformation: Critical perspectives on a theory in progress*. Jossey-Bass.

Moher, D., Liberati, A., Tetzlaff, J., & Altman, D. G. (2009). Preferred reporting items for systematic reviews and meta-analyses: The PRISMA statement. *PLoS Medicine*, 6(7), e1000097. https://doi.org/10.1371/journal.pmed.1000097

Oloyede, A., Lameed, A. A., Adelakun, M., Saka, A., Olarinde, R., & Olaniyan, B. (2024). Analyzing the influence of hospitality industry trends on home economics education and family consumer sciences. *European Journal of Hospitality and Tourism Research, 12*(3), 46–60. https://doi.org/10.37745/ejhtr.2013/vol12n34660

Organization for Economic Co-operation and Development (OECD). (2019). *OECD principles on artificial intelligence*. https://oecd.ai/en/ai-principles

Organization for Economic Co-operation and Development (OECD). (2020). *OECD Learning Compass 2030*. https://www.oecd.org/education/2030-project/

Organization for Economic Co-operation and Development (OECD). (2023). *The future of education and skills: Trends shaping education 2023*. OECD Publishing. DOI: 10.1787/6ae8771a-

Rodríguez-García, R., Ferrero-Ferrero, I., & Fernández-Izquierdo, M. A. (2025). The impact of crises on the relevance of three pillars of sustainability among hospitality and hotel management students. In *International Thematic Monograph. Modern Management Tools and Economy of Tourism Sector in Present Era* (pp. 121–136). https://doi.org/10.31410/tmt.2024-2025.121

Sarpong, D., Meissner, D., Moraes, G. H. S. M. D., & Vismara, S. (2025). The impact of university-industry engagement and the rise of competency transfer partnerships. *The Journal of Technology Transfer*. https://doi.org/10.1007/s10961-025-10251-5

Senge, P. M. (2006). T*he fifth discipline: The art and practice of the learning organization* (Revised ed.). Doubleday/Currency.

Tussyadiah, I. (2020). A review of research into automation in tourism: Launching the Annals of Tourism Research Curated Collection on Artificial Intelligence and Robotics in Tourism. *Annals of tourism research, 81*, 102883. https://doi.org/10.1016/j.annals.2020.102883

United Nations Educational, Scientific and Cultural Organization (UNESCO). (2020). *Education for sustainable development: A roadmap*. UNESCO Publishing. https://unesdoc.unesco.org/ark:/48223/pf0000374802

United Nations Educational, Scientific and Cultural Organization (UNESCO). (2021). *Recommendation on the ethics of artificial intelligence*. UNESCO Publishing. https://unesdoc.unesco.org/ark:/48223/pf0000381137

United Nations World Tourism Organization (UNWTO). (n.d.). *Digital transformation*. UN Tourism. https://www.unwto.org/digital-transformation

United Nations World Tourism Organization (UNWTO). (2018). *Tourism and the Sustainable Development Goals: Journey to 2030*. UNWTO., DOI: 10.18111/9789284419401

United Nations World Tourism Organization (UNWTO). (2022). *Tourism Futures 2030: Digital transformation and sustainability*. UNWTO. https://www.unwto.org/tourism-data/unwto-tourism-dashboard

World Travel & Tourism Council (WTTC). (2022). *Economic impact reports 2022*. https://wttc.org/Research/Economic-Impact

Yin, R. K. (2018). *Case study research and applications: Design and methods* (6th ed.). SAGE Publications.

Chapter 4
Artificial Intelligence as a Learning Companion:
Student Perceptions and Utilization Patterns in Hospitality Higher Education

Krisztina Soreg
http://orcid.org/0000-0003-1229-431X
Les Roches Global Hospitality Education, Marbella, Spain

ABSTRACT

This study presents the findings of a cross-institutional survey examining how students in hospitality education programs use artificial intelligence (AI) tools. The analysis focuses on patterns of generative AI adoption across academic work, research activities and career preparation, while also assessing perceived educational value, ethical boundaries, and institutional support. Results highlight both the opportunities of AI as a learning companion, enhancing comprehension, confidence and efficiency, as well as the challenges posed by limited training, uneven access, and concerns over overreliance. The study provides empirical analysis on how AI is reshaping learning practices and formulates recommendations for integrating AI responsibly into hospitality education and professional development.

INTRODUCTION

There is little doubt that the evolving integration of artificial intelligence (in what follows, referred to as "AI") into higher education has created a transformative period for academic institutions all across the globe. Among the most significant

DOI: 10.4018/979-8-3373-5112-4.ch004

technological advances is the expansion of generative AI tools, including ChatGPT, Claude, Gemini, and others, which now support a wide spectrum of educational tasks such as content generation, research support, summarization, language translation and data analysis (Cotton et al., 2023; Zawacki-Richter et al., 2019). As it might be observed, these tools are no longer limited to technical or engineering disciplines; rather, they are being adopted across various domains, including the applied and service-oriented field of hospitality education.

This chapter is structured around a clear argument. First, it summarizes what is already known about student access, usage patterns, perceived educational value, and ethics of generative AI in higher education. Then it briefly explains why hospitality education is a particularly revealing context, as its learning outcomes depend on experiential practice, interpersonal performance, and service judgement. Finally, a student-centered survey is introduced to provide a focused baseline of how hospitality students are currently accessing, using and negotiating generative AI as part of their academic and professional development.

Conceptual Framing: AI as a Learning Companion and Utilization Patterns

The current study adopts the conceptual lens of AI as a "learning companion": a term that was originally used in the context of intelligent tutoring systems to describe systems that offer personalized support, scaffolding and collaboration in learning processes (Chan, 2009). Earlier work on educational agents defines a learning companion as a non-authoritative agent that supports interaction within learning environments (Chou et al., 2002).

Building on earlier work on intelligent tutoring systems and human-AI collaboration in education (Chan, 2009), this study adopts a deliberately bounded interpretation of AI as a learning companion. Rather than treating AI as a generic efficiency tool or content generator, the concept is used here to capture forms of student-AI interaction that relate to learning support and educational judgement. In particular, the analysis focuses on four interrelated aspects that recur in the literature and are salient to hospitality education: AI's role in supporting conceptual understanding and task structuring (scaffolding), its contribution to students' confidence and reflective awareness (metacognitive support), its perceived influence on learning autonomy and independence, and its ethical implications in terms of responsibility, rule interpretation, and institutional trust. These dimensions inform the formulation of the research objectives and guide the interpretation of students' reported usage patterns and perceptions in later sections of the chapter.

Alongside this conceptual framing, current research also investigates utilization patterns, referring to how AI applications are structured and used across educational tasks and learning environments (Chen et al., 2020; Zawacki-Richter et al., 2019). This includes variables such as how often AI is used for writing assignments, exam preparation, professional documents, simulations, time management, etc. It is crucial to understand these patterns more accurately, as this is how we might facilitate the identification of adoption trends, areas of pedagogical dependency or enhancement, and potential gaps in training or access. Moreover, the goal is to provide critical observations and strategies to apply for curriculum design and possible institutional policies in hospitality education as informed by primary data.

Purpose and Relevance of the Study

This study investigates how students enrolled in tertiary-level hospitality education programs (from undergraduate – BBA/BSc level – to doctoral and postdoctoral studies) access, use and perceive generative AI tools throughout their academic and professional development. The research is grounded in a multi-institutional quantitative survey conducted in 2025, focusing specifically on generative AI usage since 2023, when these technologies became widely accessible, and began to penetrate learning environments globally. The year 2023 marks a critical inflection point in the integration of generative artificial intelligence into higher education. As it is well-known, this was provoked by the global public release and mass adoption of tools such as OpenAI's ChatGPT (GPT-3.5 and GPT-4), Google's Bard (currently Gemini), and others, which rapidly became integral parts of educational workflows. OpenAI's ChatGPT was launched publicly in November 2022, but its widespread adoption in educational settings peaked in early 2023, following the release of GPT-3.5 and GPT-4 with improved capabilities and user interfaces. As it is known, by March 2023, ChatGPT had surpassed 100 million active users, many of whom were students, educators and researchers (OpenAI, 2025). Google launched Bard in March 2023, incentivizing further application of generative AI tools across educational contexts. Numerous universities began issuing policies, guidance or statements on AI use in classrooms and assessments from the early to mid-2023 (Cotton et al., 2023; Qadir et al., 2023). Studies and surveys conducted in 2023 confirmed a significant increase in both awareness and experimentation with AI tools among students and faculty (OpenAI, 2025; EDUCAUSE, 2023).

On these grounds, understanding how AI is currently engaged by students in hospitality education is especially urgent (Qadir et al., 2023). At the same time, concerns about overreliance on AI can be interpreted through the concept of cognitive offloading, whereby learners delegate certain mental tasks to external tools, potentially affecting independent cognitive engagement (Risko & Gilbert, 2016).

Why Hospitality Education Is a Special Case

Unlike many academic disciplines, hospitality education is dedicated to experiential learning, real-world application, and service-based learning environments (Buhalis & Leung, 2018; Lin et al., 2017). We must also add that these competencies are not easily replicated or assessed through traditional AI tools, making hospitality a critical test case for studying the possibilities and existing vulnerabilities of AI in education. The broadly interpreted hospitality industry itself is currently undergoing rapid AI-driven transformation, as reflected in the growing body of research on artificial intelligence applications in tourism and hospitality (Knani et al., 2022; Mariani & Borghi, 2021). As such, hospitality graduates are expected to be not only highly digitally literate but also critically aware of how AI can be ethically and effectively applied in professional environment. Despite this, very limited quantitative research exists on how hospitality students are currently engaging with AI in their academic training. It is also a fact that much of the existing literature has focused on institutional implementation, system design, and educator perspectives, while the learner's experience remains comparatively underexplored (Bond et al., 2024). Furthermore, institutional readiness for AI integration varies significantly across the global hospitality education, and little is known about whether students are receiving consistent access, training or proactive support in using these tools effectively.

Given the recency of widespread adoption of generative AI (since 2023) and the absence of large-scale, student-focused empirical studies in the hospitality domain, this research employs primary data collection through a structured quantitative survey. The study's methodology is intentionally centered on direct student input and feedback in order to capture how AI tools are reshaping their learning behaviors, ethical attitudes, and career aspirations, observations that cannot be drawn only from institutional or theoretical analyses. Collecting such data is essential to inform evidence-based strategies for AI integration, curriculum development, and academic support systems. Furthermore, early empirical understanding or rather clarity is also crucial to guide institutional responses before habits and policies become more solid, particularly in an area where practical learning and interpersonal interaction are fundamental. As AI tools become crucial part of academic and professional workflows, it is straightforward to assume that hospitality schools must adapt proactively rather than reactively. This shift thus requires accurate, context-specific data for formulating strategies that may further support those taking crucial decisions.

Research Focus and Guiding Framework

The study is guided by a single overarching research question:

How have hospitality higher education students been accessing, utilizing and perceiving the impact of generative AI tools on their academic development, ethical awareness and career preparedness since 2023?

This research question is explored through the following three objectives:

RO1: To assess students' access to, training in, and utilization patterns of AI tools in hospitality higher education.

This objective investigates the infrastructural and practical nature of AI tool usage among students, namely, whether students are trained to use AI, have institutional access, and how frequently they engage with AI in various academic and professional tasks.

RO2: To explore students' perceptions of the educational value and impact of AI on academic performance, learning autonomy, and critical thinking.

The focus is on how students perceive the academic affordances and outcomes of using AI tools, as well as whether AI boosts their comprehension, critical thinking, confidence and preparedness for assessments and the workforce.

RO3: To evaluate students' awareness, attitudes, and ethical considerations surrounding AI use in hospitality education.

This objective addresses students' ethical positioning, institutional guidance and expectations around responsible AI usage, including concerns about plagiarism, fairness, faculty practices and institutional responsibility.

Through this framework, the study aims to bridge a significant empirical and pedagogical gap in the current discourse on AI in higher education. By focusing on student responses within hospitality programs, it aims at proposing practical insights that can propose more inclusive, responsible and effective AI adoption strategies across the sector to hospitality institutions and beyond.

LITERATURE REVIEW

Literature Review Roadmap

This review is organized around the three previously mentioned research objectives. First, it summarizes what is known about student access and utilization patterns of generative AI in higher education (RO1). Second, it reviews evidence on perceived learning value and cognitive impact (RO2). Third, it synthesizes current debates on ethics, integrity, and institutional responsibility (RO3). Across each strand, we distinguish between findings from higher education generally and what remains limited or fragmented in hospitality and tourism education specifically.

The growing role and influence of artificial intelligence in higher education has already provoked diverse academic discussions regarding its pedagogical, ethical and institutional implications. While the rapid expansion of generative AI tools, especially since 2023, has drawn global attention, empirical research specific to hospitality education remains rather limited and, to some extent, underdeveloped in its current form. This literature review critically evaluates the state of academic research in relation to the three central domains of inquiry of the study: access and utilization patterns (RO1), educational perceptions and learning impact (RO2), and ethical awareness as well as attitudes toward AI (RO3).

AI Access and Utilization Patterns in Higher Education

To begin with, current studies examining AI access and usage behaviors across higher education have mainly focused on institutional adoption, technical readiness and tool functionalities, often neglecting the student perspective or discipline-specific contexts. Several large-scale reviews and cross-disciplinary surveys mention increasing student experimentation with AI tools for academic purposes (Cotton et al., 2023; EDUCAUSE, 2023; Holmes et al., 2023). However, these patterns are quite heterogeneous based on accessibility, training and cultural acceptance, demonstrating a solid lack of consistent institutional support structures. More research focuses on the observation that access to generative AI tools is not equitably distributed. For example, while some universities provide licensed access to advanced AI applications (such as GPT-4, Jasper, etc.), others restrict usage due to concerns over academic integrity (Qadir et al., 2023; EDUCAUSE, 2023). This inconsistency may directly affect how students learn to use AI, creating a divide between structured, curriculum-supported engagement and unsupervised, trial-and-error exploration. This concern is consistent with recent work showing that higher education institutions vary considerably in the clarity and scope of their generative AI guidance (An et al., 2025). In hospitality and tourism education specifically, emerging studies increasingly discuss ChatGPT and AI integration in teaching, curriculum design, and digital capability development, yet student behavior and lived learning practices remain comparatively underexplored (Zhang et al., 2024)

Concerning the measurement of utilization patterns, research categorizes AI use into functional educational applications such as intelligent tutoring, feedback systems, and adaptive learning support (Chen et al., 2020). Yet, this approach often lacks a more specific focus in terms of discipline-specific needs. For example, hospitality students are likely to engage with AI differently than engineering students, through simulations, service scenario analysis and customer experience modeling. This component is still relatively scarce in current research, creating a methodological "blind spot" in survey design and data disaggregation. This matters because hospitality learning outcomes are often evaluated through applied performance (service scripts, guest recovery decisions, role-play, and operational trade-offs), not only written outputs, so AI usage patterns may concentrate differently than in content-heavy disciplines.

Furthermore, existing studies also differ in how they quantify frequency and purpose of AI use. Some utilize Likert scales based on self-reported frequency (Cotton et al., 2023), while others rely on behavioral tracking or system log analysis (Gomez et al., 2024). Each method brings trade-offs in validity and feasibility, yet not many studies take advantage of multiple data sources or contextualize metrics within specific pedagogical environments like hospitality. The limited available evidence of methodological convergence further limits the generalizability of current findings. Overall, current literature lacks student-focused, domain-specific and methodologically robust studies that explore how AI tools are accessed, supported, and regularly utilized across hospitality education programs. It can be assumed that the absence of such evidence does not fully allow institutions to develop responsive, inclusive AI strategies supporting the actual practices and challenges students might face in their learning environments.

Perceived Educational Value and Cognitive Impact of AI

The debate surrounding the educational value of AI tools in higher education is marked by rather polarized perceptions. On one side, researchers argue that artificial intelligence can support self-directed learning, enhance aspects of critical thinking, and enable more personalized feedback and adaptive learning experiences (Holmes et al., 2023; Chen et al., 2020). On the other hand, scholars warn that overreliance on such tools may lead to forms of cognitive offloading, reduced retention, and a potential decline in independent academic skills (Risko & Gilbert, 2016; Cotton et al., 2023). When considering cognitive outcomes such as critical thinking, metacognition, and academic confidence, there is limited consensus on whether AI ultimately enhances or undermines these skills. Some studies suggest that AI-supported systems can facilitate comprehension of complex topics through real-time feedback and simplified explanations, particularly in language-intensive and knowledge-based disciplines (Holmes et al., 2023; Chen et al., 2020). In contrast, conceptual concerns persist regarding the passivity of interaction, as students may receive information rather than actively construct knowledge, especially when using AI for summarization or writing support. This raises questions about the pedagogical framing of AI as a true "learning companion," as opposed to a content-generation tool.

Interestingly, few studies assess whether students feel more autonomous, efficient, or self-confident when using AI. While large-scale surveys frequently report positive attitudes, for example, that students perceive AI as saving time or simplifying tasks, they rarely connect these perceptions to deeper educational constructs such as epistemic agency, reflective learning, or self-regulated learning (Holmes et al., 2023; Cotton et al., 2023; EDUCAUSE, 2023). Existing approaches often rely on general sentiment measures, offering limited insight into how AI reshapes learners' confidence, identity, or long-term skill development. From a theoretical perspective, this concern can be related to cognitive offloading, where reliance on external tools may reduce independent cognitive effort (Risko & Gilbert, 2016). Studies that do explore such questions often do so in abstract or decontextualized ways, without accounting for how disciplinary practices shape learning autonomy and cognition. Moreover, even fewer studies examine these dynamics from a discipline-specific perspective, despite clear variation in cognitive demands across academic fields. For example, existing reviews highlight that most AI-in-education research has focused on STEM and language-related domains, with comparatively limited attention to applied professional fields such as hospitality, tourism, or business (Zawacki-Richter et al., 2019; Chen et al., 2020). This disciplinary imbalance is particularly problematic given the experiential, interpersonal, and service-oriented pedagogy central to hospitality education, which often relies on embodied learning, case-based reasoning, and affective labor (Buhalis & Leung, 2018; Lin et al., 2017).

In hospitality, perceived "learning value" therefore includes whether AI supports judgement under uncertainty, tone and empathy in guest interaction, and reflective service professionalism, not only comprehension or writing quality. In light of these considerations, a more precise understanding is required of AI's role in supporting, rather than replacing, cognitive engagement and interpersonal competence. The integration of AI into hospitality-specific learning tasks, such as service scenario planning, customer journey mapping, or operational simulations, remains relatively underexplored. Where AI is discussed in hospitality education, the focus is often placed on digital transformation, curriculum design, and future-oriented skills, rather than on how students currently engage with AI in their learning processes (Zhang et al., 2024; Zawacki-Richter et al., 2019). This forward-looking orientation tends to overlook present-day student experiences and may lead to decisions based on assumed rather than empirically grounded educational benefits.

There is thus a significant conceptual and empirical gap in understanding how AI influences student learning perceptions in hospitality programs. The existing literature offers insufficient evidence regarding how AI affects student confidence, autonomy, or preparedness for academic tasks and assessments within this context.

On such grounds, current study addresses this gap by investigating generative AI not simply as a technical tool, but as a co-agent in learning, exploring how students perceive its cognitive and educational value.

Ethical Attitudes and Institutional AI Governance in Hospitality Education

It is crucial to emphasize that the ethical implications of artificial intelligence in education predate the rise of generative AI, with concerns ranging from algorithmic bias and surveillance to authorship, autonomy, and institutional responsibility. A well-established body of literature has long argued that AI's integration in education must be guided by robust ethical frameworks addressing fairness, accountability, transparency, and inclusivity (Williamson & Eynon, 2020; Selwyn, 2019; Floridi et al., 2018). Researchers have consistently highlighted the risks of relying on opaque or "black-box" algorithmic systems in educational contexts, where such systems may influence grading, behavior monitoring, or performance prediction without sufficient transparency or accountability (Knox et al., 2020; Zawacki-Richter et al., 2019). Yet, these concerns are further compounded by the growing asymmetry between students and institutions, where learners are expected to adapt to rapidly evolving technologies without being adequately informed or consulted about their rights, risks, or responsibilities.

What is more, ethical discourse around AI in education has largely been framed through policy, governance, and institutional lenses, often overlooking students' lived experiences and day-to-day ethical decision-making (Qadir et al., 2023; Bond et al., 2024). Particularly absent are studies that examine how students internalize, interpret, or negotiate ethical boundaries in practice. Hospitality education, where human-centric values such as empathy, trust, and accountability are central to professional identity, remains especially underrepresented in these discussions. For hospitality students, AI ethics extends beyond issues of plagiarism to include authenticity of communication, trust in guest interactions, and the responsible use of data in service contexts, making ethical guidance in education particularly consequential. Existing work in the hospitality domain tends to focus on operational and industry-level ethics, such as privacy, automation, and AI-enabled service delivery, rather than on the pedagogical dimension of how future professionals are trained to use AI responsibly (Knani et al., 2022; Samala et al., 2022).

To narrow the scope of existing academic results, it is crucial to add that the ethical dimensions of AI use in higher education have received significant attention since 2023. However, the scope and depth of this research vary considerably, often prioritizing policy-level concerns over the lived experiences and moral reasoning of students or other participants. Most frameworks for AI ethics in education revolve around academic integrity, often limiting the conversation to AI-assisted cheating or plagiarism detection (Cotton et al., 2023; Qadir et al., 2023). Some studies argue that students lack adequate guidance on when and how AI use constitutes ethical misconduct (Kasneci et al., 2023), while others suggest that institutional silence contributes to normative ambiguity, leaving students to interpret AI use based on peer behavior and perceived risk (Holmes et al., 2023).

To continue, there is a notable divergence between institutions that have developed clear AI usage guidelines often in response to policy pressure or reputational risk, and those that remain reactive or ambiguous. Hospitality education institutions (particularly those operating globally) face additional complexity due to cross-cultural norms of academic honesty, yet this intersection has not been thoroughly explored in academic literature. Also, while studies on business or computer science education occasionally examine student attitudes toward AI misuse, the hospitality sector has been largely absent of these ethical conversations. In addition, there is little empirical work on how students perceive the institutional responsibility to educate them about ethical AI use. Some earlier findings indicate that students expect clearer rules and feel unprepared to deal with AI ethics independently (EDUCAUSE, 2023), but few studies test whether students actually follow policies, understand their rationale or critically engage with the ethical boundaries of AI-enhanced learning. The clear absence of structured ethics education around AI in hospitality programs creates another blind spot in moral and professional development curricula, especially as these students transition into an industry already grappling with the ethical implications of AI deployment in areas such as guest interaction, automation, and data-driven decision-making (Samala et al., 2022).

Crucially, very few student-centred empirical studies can be identified that would systematically evaluate how hospitality students take into account ethical considerations in practice, such as whether they knowingly violate AI-use rules or how they respond to faculty use of AI in teaching and grading. This leaves both institutional policy and pedagogy on rather unstable ground, especially in a sector that rewards professionalism, trust and service ethics. Addressing this issue is vital to ensure that hospitality graduates are not only competent but also conscientious digital citizens.

RESEARCH DESIGN AND DATA COLLECTION

This chapter outlines the methodological framework employed to investigate how students in hospitality higher education access, utilize and perceive the role of generative AI in their academic and professional development. The study employs a quantitative research design grounded in primary data collection, with the aim of capturing current patterns, perceptions, and ethical considerations surrounding AI integration in hospitality education. The methodological approach was carefully chosen to address the three previously defined research objectives (RO1-RO3), and to ensure the relevance, validity and applicability of findings in light of the limited presence of domain-specific data in this emerging field.

Data Source and Sampling Approach

The data used in current study consists of primary data collected through an online survey administered between July and October 2025. This survey was designed and distributed using Google Forms, and shared through social media platforms (e.g., LinkedIn, Facebook academic groups) as well as targeted email outreach to relevant academic networks, hospitality schools and professional contacts in the field. In total, 158 valid responses were collected. Participation was strictly limited to students enrolled in hospitality-related tertiary education programs, including undergraduate (BBA/BSc), master's (MSc/MBA), PhD and other postdoctoral levels. This sampling frame was intended to reflect the diversity of academic progression and present a range of student experiences with AI across hospitality education. The survey consisted of 32 questions, of which 31 were closed-ended and structured using various formats such as Likert scales, multiple choice, and frequency scales. Only the final question (Q32) was open-ended, inviting respondents to reflect on the role hospitality institutions should play in preparing students to use AI ethically and effectively in their future careers.

Instrument Design and Validity

The questionnaire was designed to align directly with RO1–RO3 and to capture both behavioural usage patterns and attitudinal perceptions. Items were informed by widely used constructs in educational technology and AI-in-education research (e.g., perceived usefulness, confidence, autonomy/self-regulation, and ethical awareness) and were adapted to the hospitality education context where necessary. Prior to distribution, the survey was reviewed informally for clarity and relevance and adjusted for wording and redundancy. Given the exploratory aim of providing a descriptive baseline, the instrument relies primarily on face validity; however, where multiple items are used to reflect a common construct (e.g., perceived educational value), internal consistency checks can be reported to strengthen reliability (e.g., Cronbach's alpha), and representative items can be listed in an appendix or table to increase transparency, however, these were not conducted given the exploratory nature of the study.

Ethics Approval and Safeguards

The study involved adult participants, collected no personal identifiers or sensitive data, and posed minimal risk. Participation was voluntary and anonymous, and respondents were informed about the study purpose and data handling prior to completion. In line with institutional guidelines for minimal-risk educational research, formal ethics committee approval was not required (or an exemption applied, if applicable); nevertheless, the study followed standard principles of informed consent, confidentiality, and GDPR-compliant data storage and use.

The survey was structured according to the three research objectives:

RO1 (Q5–Q11): questions on access, institutional support, training and frequency of AI usage across different tasks.
RO2 (Q12–Q19, Q27–Q31): questions assessing students' perceptions of AI's impact on their learning, cognitive development and preparedness.
RO3 (Q20–Q26, Q32): questions addressing ethical awareness, institutional guidance, and attitudes toward responsible AI use.

This structure enabled both horizontal (across student groups) and vertical (within thematic areas) analysis of student responses. The design is consistent with survey research practices in educational technology studies (Zawacki-Richter et al., 2019; Cotton et al., 2023), where structured questionnaires are widely used to gather attitudinal and behavioral data on emerging technologies.

Table 1. Overview of research design

Research Objective	Core Concept	Survey Sections & Questions	Question Types	Thematic Dimensions	Analytical Techniques
RO1: Access, training & usage	Access, institutional support and actual use of AI tools	**Section 1**: Personal Background & Digital Readiness (Q1–Q7) **Section 2**: AI Usage Patterns (Q8–Q11)	Multiple choice; frequency Likert scale	Formal training, institutional access, usage across academic and professional tasks, perceived challenges	Frequency distributions, comparative tables, bar charts
RO2: Value, learning & cognition	Cognitive impact and learning value of AI tools	**Section 3**: Learning Impact & Educational Value (Q12–Q19) + Priority improvement areas (Q20)	5-point Likert scale (agreement); multiple response (select all that apply)	Critical thinking, academic confidence, independence, exam preparation, AI as learning companion, areas of improvement	Weighted averages, response comparison by academic level, bar/ column graphs
RO3: Ethics, awareness & responsibility	Ethical awareness, institutional responsibility and norms	**Section 4**: Ethics, Confidence & Institutional Guidelines (Q21–Q27) **Section 5**: Self-Perception, Trust & Future Outlook (Q28–Q31) + role of hospitality schools (Q32)	5-point Likert scale; scenario-based perceptions; 1 open-ended question	AI policy clarity, plagiarism, fairness, ethical boundaries, faculty role, long-term outlook, institutional responsibility	Descriptive analysis, thematic clustering of Q32, illustrative quotes

Source: own elaboration

Method of Analysis

Given the exploratory and diagnostic goals of the study, a quantitative descriptive approach was adopted to analyze the survey data. The analysis was conducted using standard spreadsheet and statistical software tools (Microsoft Excel), with the following techniques applied:

- Descriptive statistics: Frequency distributions, percentage breakdowns and cross-tabulations to examine usage trends, subgroup differences (e.g., study level, gender, campus), and institutional support.
- Likert-scale analysis: Weighted averages, mean scores, standard deviations (SD) and coefficients of variation (CV) to assess central tendencies and internal consistency.
- Visualizations: Bar, column and pie charts to clearly display response distributions and highlight key findings.

- Analytical structuring: Matrix approaches (e.g., internal vs. external, cognitive vs. procedural challenges) to interpret clusters of AI-related barriers.
- Qualitative synthesis: Thematic review of open-ended responses (Q32) to extract recurring themes, illustrative quotes and outliers, providing context to the quantitative findings.

The open-ended responses (Q32) were not subjected to full qualitative coding but were reviewed thematically to identify recurring ideas and outliers. The selected methods are consistent with similar research in educational and hospitality contexts (Holmes et al., 2023), where descriptive statistical techniques are used for capturing early-stage trends in technology adoption and student perceptions.

Limitations and Considerations

While the study offers valuable insights, several methodological limitations should be taken into account:

- Sampling bias: The self-selection of participants via social media and institutional mailing lists likely favored students who are more digitally literate or AI-curious. As a result, the sample may overrepresent individuals with stronger awareness or interest in AI tools, limiting its representativeness of the broader hospitality student population (Bethlehem, 2010; Wright, 2005).
- Geographic concentration: Most responses came from Europe, with only minimal representation from other regions. While this reflects the institutional reach of the survey, it constrains the cross-cultural generalizability of the findings. Differences in institutional policy, technological infrastructure and cultural attitudes toward AI adoption may be underexplored this way (Robson & McCartan, 2016; Ruel et al., 2016).
- Self-reporting limitations: All data were based on self-reported attitudes and behaviors. Such measures are susceptible to social desirability bias, recall errors and differences in interpretation of key terms (e.g., "formal training" or "AI access"), which could influence reported frequency and levels of agreement (Chan, 2009; Paulhus & Vazire, 2007).
- Analytical scope: The study employed descriptive statistics (frequencies, percentages, means, SD, CV) and thematic synthesis for open responses. While appropriate for an exploratory baseline study, the absence of inferential testing, multivariate modeling or longitudinal tracking limits the ability to identify causal relationships or generalize beyond the sample (Creswell & Creswell, 2018; Babbie, 2020).

The next chapter presents the findings of the empirical study. It offers a structured analysis of student responses in relation to the three research objectives, and explores patterns of AI usage, perceived academic value, and ethical attitudes among hospitality students across different levels of higher education.

RESULTS AND DISCUSSION

This chapter introduces the findings of the survey on students' access to, usage of, and perceptions toward AI in hospitality education. The results are organized in relation to the three research objectives, combining descriptive statistics with thematic insights to offer a structured analysis of patterns, challenges and implications.

A total of 158 participants responded to the survey. The majority were undergraduate (Bachelor) students (75%), followed by postgraduates (18%), with a smaller share of doctoral (6%) and executive MBA (1%) participants, and just one respondent from a vocational diploma background. The sample was strongly concentrated at the undergraduate level, though it also included perspectives from more advanced study stages. In terms of academic specialization, the responses were highly concentrated in International Hospitality Management (88%). A small number of students represented related disciplines, such as hotel and resort management (3%), event management (1%), sustainable hospitality (1%), and tourism/destination management (1%), while 6% were enrolled in other programs. These findings are particularly reflective of hospitality management students, though with some input from broader fields relevant to tourism and hospitality. Gender distribution was relatively balanced, with 54% female and 44% male participants, along with a small proportion (1%) identifying as non-binary. Finally, the primary campus location of respondents shows a strong concentration in Europe.

Table 2. Profile of the survey participants

Current level of study (Q1)	**Responses**	**Frequency**
Undergraduate (Bachelor)	75%	119
Postgraduate (Master)	18%	28
Doctoral (PhD)	6%	9
EMBA	1%	1
Vocational Diploma	1%	1
Current program of study (Q2)	**Responses**	**Frequency**

continued on following page

Table 2. Continued

International Hospitality Management	88%	139
Other programs	6%	9
Hotel and Resort Management	3%	4
Event Management	1%	2
Sustainable Hospitality	1%	2
Tourism / Destination Management	1%	2
Gender (Q3)	**Responses**	**Frequency**
Female	54%	86
Male	44%	70
Non-binary	1%	2
Primary campus location (Q4)	**Responses**	**Frequency**
Europe	95%	150
Middle East & Africa	3%	5
Asia-Pacific	1%	2
Latin America	1%	1
Total	**100%**	**158**

Source: own elaboration

The sample is highly concentrated in Europe and in hospitality management programs, and responses were collected via academic networks and social media channels. As a result, the dataset likely over-represents students who are more digitally engaged or more motivated to reflect on AI. In interpreting levels of confidence and adoption, it is therefore important to consider potential self-selection and institutional-context effects (e.g., private or internationally oriented schools may provide stronger digital infrastructure and peer norms around AI use).

As per results, Figure 1 demonstrates a significant training gap: two-thirds of students (66%) reported not having received formal AI training but expressed a desire for it, while only a minority had exposure through compulsory courses (9%), electives or workshops (6%), or extracurricular initiatives (10%). A further 9% indicated no interest in training, and 15% selected "Other." This pattern shows that while students clearly recognize the importance of AI for their studies and careers, institutional provision remains limited and inconsistent, reflecting broader trends in higher education where access to AI support varies considerably (Cotton et al., 2023; EDUCAUSE, 2023).

Figure 1. Have you received any formal training in AI or digital tools during your studies?

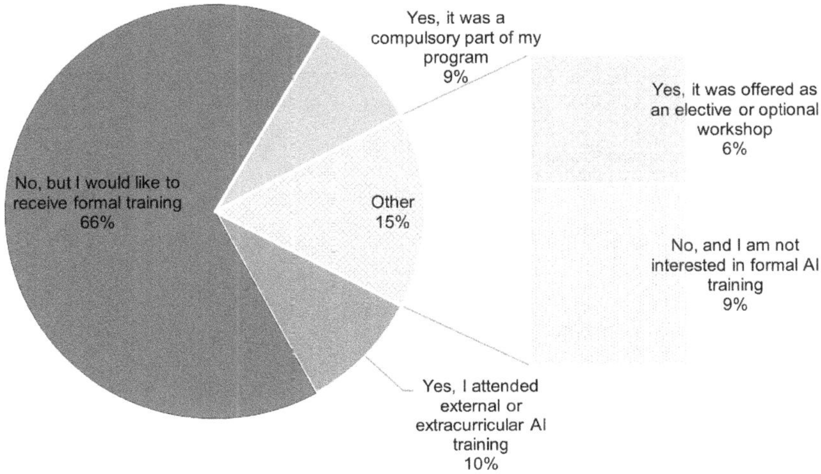

Source: Own elaboration

The high demand for structured training reflects students' awareness that AI has strong potential to boost learning, but also that its educational value depends on proper guidance, ethical boundaries and integration into curricula. With limited or no access to these tools we can assume that students are left to experiment with AI through unsupervised, trial-and-error approaches, raising risks of misuse, overreliance and academic integrity concerns (Holmes et al., 2023; Qadir et al., 2023). For hospitality education specifically, this finding highlights an urgent institutional responsibility: to embed AI training not only to build technical proficiency but also to promote critical thinking, creativity, and ethical awareness in line with the human-centered values of the discipline (Zhang et al., 2024; Lin et al., 2017; Holmes et al., 2023).

Figure 2. Does your university or institution provide you with full access to any professional AI tools as part of your academic program?

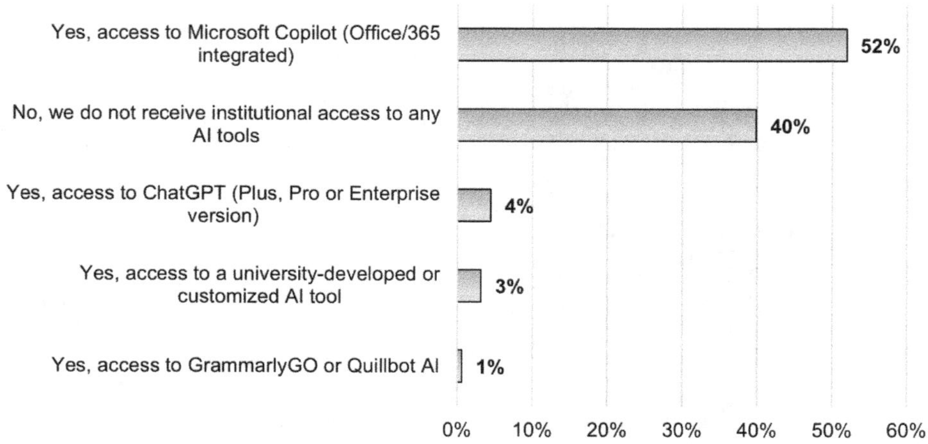

Source: Own elaboration of the Author

To continue, more than half of the respondents (52%) reported that their university provides access to Microsoft Copilot through Office/365 integration, while 40% indicated that they receive no institutional access at all. Only small proportions reported access to specialized tools: ChatGPT Plus/Pro/Enterprise (4%), university-developed tools (3%) or writing-support tools such as GrammarlyGO or Quillbot (1%). From the perspective of RO1, this finding demonstrates strong reliance on mainstream productivity platforms rather than tailored, hospitality-specific AI tools. It also shows uneven distribution of institutional support, aligned with recent studies claiming that universities vary widely in whether and how they provide licensed AI resources (Cotton et al., 2023; EDUCAUSE, 2023).The data also suggests that while institutions have begun to embed AI into widely used platforms like Microsoft Office, they are less proactive in granting access to advanced or domain-specific applications, leaving students dependent on personal subscriptions or informal use of generative AI tools. This could also present a structural gap between institutional offerings and the types of AI tools that may be most relevant to hospitality education, particularly those supporting teaching, content development, and applied learning tasks (Zhang et al., 2024; Mariani & Borghi, 2021). In connection with RO2 and RO3, the lack of comprehensive access raises questions about equity, preparedness and ethical consistency: if students are expected to master AI responsibly, institutions must go beyond generic integration and provide targeted, structured access to tools that align with both academic development and industry practice.

Table 3. AI Learning Challenges by Source and Nature (number of responses)

Source / Nature	Cognitive Nature	Procedural Nature
Internal Challenge	I lack confidence in evaluating AI-generated content (9) - I'm afraid of misusing AI / violating academic rules (54)	I don't know where to start or which tools to use (17) - I feel overwhelmed by too many tools (40)
External Challenge	I don't see how AI applies to my field (4)	I don't have time to explore or experiment (10) - I don't receive enough support/ guidance (14)

Source: Own elaboration

The analysis of students' perceived challenges with AI use (Table 3) reveals a more dominant presence of internalized barriers, particularly those related to cognitive and procedural uncertainty. A matrix structure distinguishing internal vs. external and cognitive vs. procedural dimensions was created to interpret the possible underlying structure of self-reported obstacles (Luckin et al., 2016). The most frequently mentioned issues fall into the internal-procedural quadrant, such as feeling overwhelmed or uncertain about tool selection, followed closely by internal-cognitive concerns like fear of academic misconduct. On the other hand, external challenges, such as lack of institutional support or disciplinary relevance, were less frequently mentioned, suggesting that students perceive the primary barriers to AI engagement as individual rather than structural. Even when institutions provide access to AI tools, students often hesitate to adopt them fully because of low confidence, lack of clear guidance and uncertainty about ethical use. Responses marked as "none" or "other" were excluded due to lack of analytical relevance.

Table 4. Frequency of AI usage

	Always = 5; Frequently = 4; Occasionally = 3; Rarely = 2; Never = 1					**Results**		
	5	**4**	**3**	**2**	**1**	**Mean**	**SD**	**CV**
Research projects or industry analysis	23%	44%	25%	6%	3%	**3.77**	**0.16**	**4.35%**
Academic writing and formatting related to course assessments	13%	41%	26%	14%	6%	**3.42**	**0.14**	**4.05%**
Professional development	21%	28%	28%	13%	10%	**3.36**	**0.08**	**2.43%**
Simulations and case studies	17%	31%	30%	14%	8%	**3.35**	**0.10**	**2.99%**

Source: Own elaboration of the Author

Table 4 shows that AI tools are most frequently used for research projects or industry analysis (M = 3.77), while their application in simulations, professional development, and academic writing tasks is less common. The relatively low coefficients of variation (2.4%-4.3%) indicate consistent response patterns across students, suggesting broadly shared usage habits. AI adoption in hospitality education remains more concentrated on research-related tasks than on experiential or skill-development activities.

Figure 3 shows that the vast majority of students believe AI tools help them better understand complex topics in hospitality, with 45% completely agreeing and 41% somewhat agreeing. Only a small minority expressed reservations, with 9% somewhat disagreeing and 3% completely disagreeing, while 2% reported never having used AI in this context. This strong overall agreement reinforces the role of AI as a supportive learning tool, particularly in simplifying complex material and fostering comprehension (Holmes et al., 2023; Chen et al., 2020). At the same time, the small group of skeptics reflects concerns raised in the literature about overreliance and the risk of superficial learning, indicating the need for structured guidance to maximize AI's educational value (Risko & Gilbert, 2016; Cotton et al., 2023).

Figure 3. AI tools help me better understand complex topics in hospitality

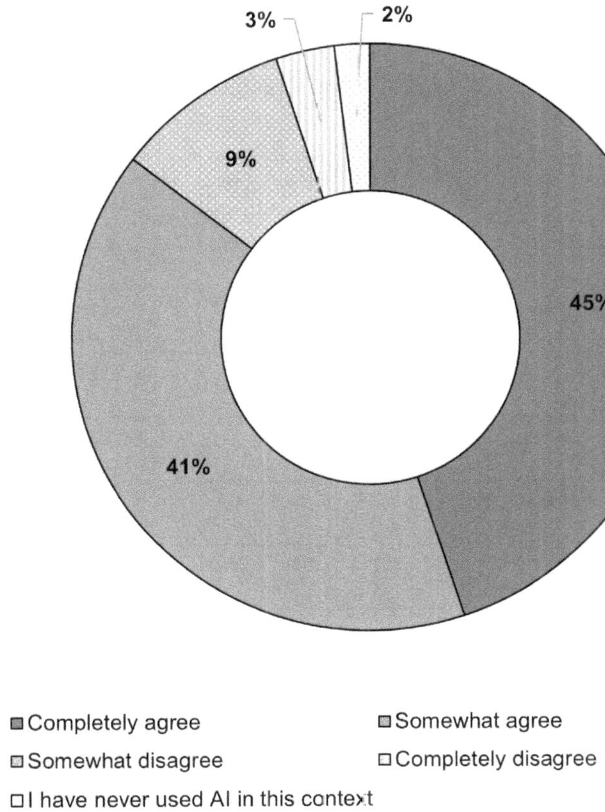

Source: Own elaboration

The results in Table 5 provide broader view of students' perceptions of AI's educational value. The strongest agreement was observed for the statement that AI helps manage time more effectively (M = 4.43), followed by its role in supporting understanding of complex topics (M = 4.16) and improving academic confidence (M = 4.13), all with relatively low variation (CV < 5%), suggesting broad consensus. Students also largely agreed that AI improves the quality of academic work (M = 4.05) and should be more deeply integrated into hospitality education (M = 4.23), reinforcing its perceived relevance for both learning outcomes and curriculum design. By contrast, weaker agreement was reported regarding AI's impact on critical thinking (M = 3.11), learning independence (M = 2.34), and exam or presentation preparation (M = 2.38), indicating that students remain skeptical about AI fostering higher-order or autonomous learning skills.

Table 5. Perceived benefits and limitations of AI use in hospitality education

	Completely agree = 5; Somewhat agree = 4; Somewhat disagree = 3; Completely disagree = 2; Never used AI in this context = 1							
	5	**4**	**3**	**2**	**1**	**Mean**	**SD**	**CV**
AI tools help me better understand complex topics in hospitality	42%	42%	9%	6%	1%	**4.16**	**0.20**	**4.82%**
AI improves the quality of my academic work	33%	47%	14%	3%	3%	**4.05**	**0.20**	**4.85%**
AI helps me manage my time more effectively	41%	47%	14%	3%	3%	**4.43**	**0.21**	**4.77%**
Using AI has made me more confident in my academic performance	37%	34%	23%	11%	4%	**4.13**	**0.14**	**3.36%**
AI enhances my ability to think critically	15%	27%	27%	19%	9%	**3.11**	**0.08**	**2.43%**
I feel more independent in my learning thanks to AI	1%	35%	21%	9%	4%	**2.34**	**0.14**	**5.97%**
AI helps me prepare more effectively for exams or presentations	6%	42%	8%	4%	6%	**2.38**	**0.16**	**6.72%**
AI should be more deeply integrated into hospitality education programs	45%	41%	9%	3%	2%	**4.23**	**0.21**	**4.96%**

Source: Own elaboration

Figure 4. Perceived educational value of ai applications in hospitality programs

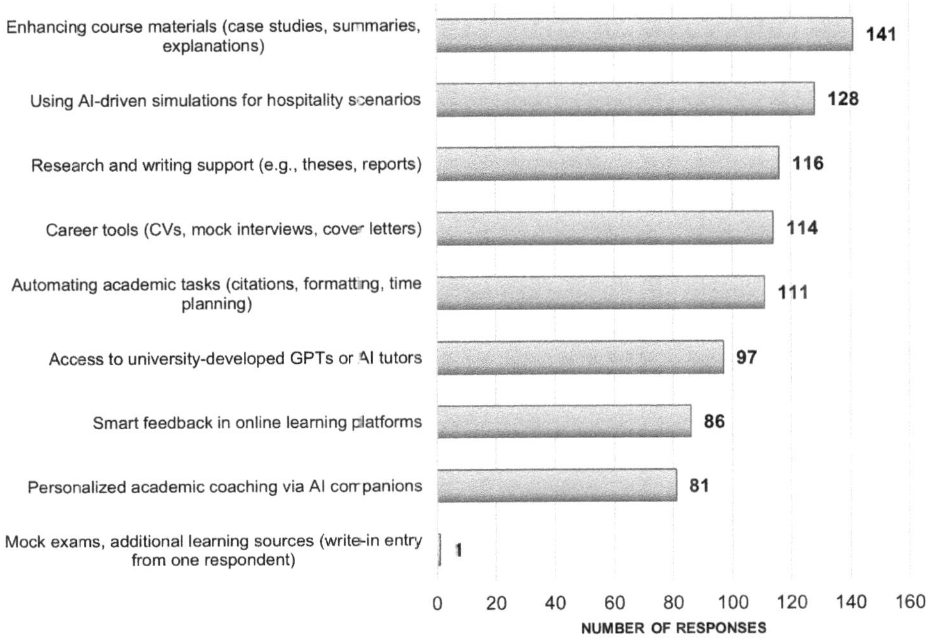

Source: Own elaboration

Students see the greatest potential of AI in hospitality education in enhancing course materials (141 responses), AI-driven simulations for hospitality scenarios (128), and research as well as writing support (116), showing a strong preference for tools that directly improve comprehension and applied learning (Fig. 4). Secondary priorities included career preparation tools (114) and automating academic tasks (111), which clearly shows AI's perceived value in supporting employability and efficiency. These findings align with existing literature that emphasizes the dual role of AI in facilitating deeper learning and skill development while also streamlining procedural tasks (Holmes et al., 2023; Chen et al., 2020). By contrast, fewer students highlighted university-developed GPTs (97), smart feedback systems (86), or personalized coaching (81), suggesting that while adaptive technologies are recognized, students currently prioritize discipline-specific applications over generalized AI support. These results suggest that students primarily value AI as a learning companion that can enrich academic content and experiential practice, provided it complements rather than replaces the critical, interpersonal and creative dimensions of hospitality education.

Figure 5. If faculty use AI tools to generate content or manage tasks, I believe it

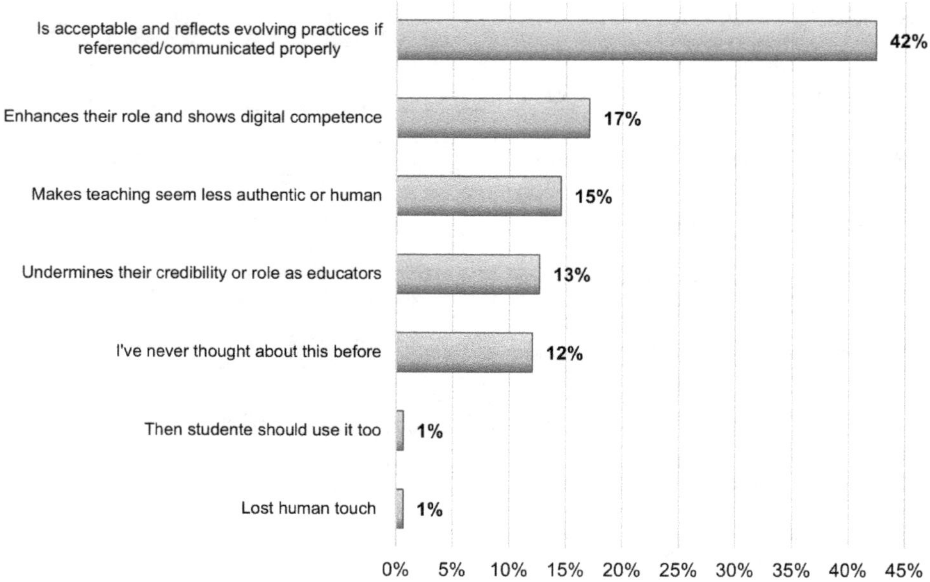

Source: Own elaboration

It is interesting that most students (42%) view faculty use of AI tools as acceptable if properly referenced and communicated, while 17% believe it enhances educators' digital competence (Fig. 5). However, a notable minority perceive risks, with 15% suggesting it makes teaching less authentic and 13% fearing it undermines educators' credibility.

Figure 6. Level of agreement on AI's impact and role in hospitality education

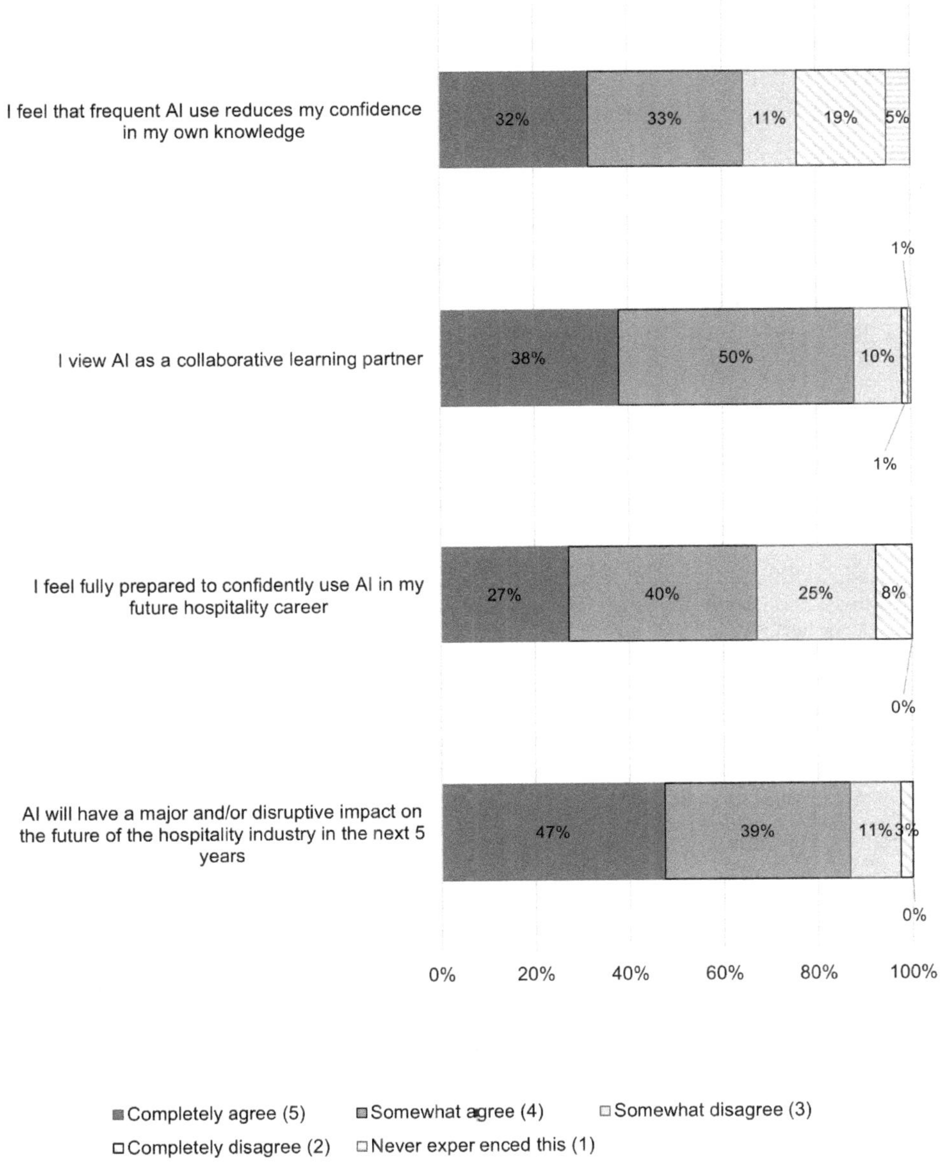

Source: Own elaboration

Overall, students expressed strong agreement on the role and impact of AI in hospitality education, though with some variation across statements (Fig. 6). Nearly nine in ten respondents (47% completely agree; 39% somewhat agree) expect AI to have a major or disruptive impact on the industry within five years, confirming its perceived transformative potential (Knani et al., 2022; Samala et al., 2022). A similarly high proportion (88%) view AI as a collaborative learning tool, reinforcing its perceived role in supporting learning processes (Holmes et al., 2023). In contrast, confidence in personal preparedness was more divided: while two-thirds felt ready to use AI in their careers, one-third expressed doubts, highlighting a persistent training gap (Cotton et al., 2023). Opinions were also mixed on whether frequent AI use reduces confidence in one's own knowledge, reflecting concerns about overreliance and cognitive offloading (Risko & Gilbert, 2016). Descriptive statistics in Table 6 reinforce these trends, with highest agreement on AI's disruptive potential (M = 4.32) and perceived learning support (M = 4.23), but lower consensus on preparedness (M = 3.87) and knowledge erosion (M = 3.67).

Table 6. Results on level of agreement on AI's impact and role

Statements	**Completely agree = 5; Somewhat agree = 4; Somewhat disagree = 3; Completely disagree = 2; Never experienced this = 1**							
	5	**4**	**3**	**2**	**1**	**Mean**	**SD**	**CV**
AI will have a major and/or disruptive impact on the future of the hospitality industry in the next 5 years	47%	39%	11%	3%	0%	**4.32**	**0.2**	**5%**
I feel fully prepared to confidently use AI in my future hospitality career	27%	40%	25%	8%	0%	**3.87**	**0.2**	**4%**
I view AI as a collaborative learning partner	38%	50%	10%	1%	1%	**4.23**	**0.2**	**5%**
I feel that frequent AI use reduces my confidence in my own knowledge	32%	33%	11%	19%	5%	**3.67**	**0.1**	**3%**

Source: Own elaboration

To add nuance beyond overall averages, responses were examined descriptively by level of study (undergraduate vs postgraduate/doctoral combined). While overall patterns remained similar, advanced students tended to report higher perceived preparedness for professional AI use and slightly lower uncertainty around ethical boundaries, whereas undergraduates expressed stronger demand for structured training and clearer institutional guidance. These differences should be interpreted cautiously due to subgroup size imbalance, but they suggest that confidence and ethical navigation may develop with academic maturity and exposure to assessment norms.

Last but not least, the analysis of the open-ended question reveals that the survey participants have developed a strong and multifaceted role for hospitality schools in preparing students to use AI tools responsibly and effectively. Using a contextual content analysis approach (Schreier, 2012), four major themes can be clearly detected: the need for structured training and ethical guidelines, the positioning of AI as a supportive tool rather than a replacement for human interaction, the cultivation of critical thinking and academic integrity, and the integration of AI into curricula through practical, industry-relevant applications. Overall, participants highlighted the importance of being taught how to use AI in ways that boost efficiency, personalization, and data-driven decision-making, while avoiding misuse or overdependence. We can assume that schools must not only focus on technical competence but also promote digital literacy grounded in ethical responsibility (Selwyn, 2022). At the same time, the responses also underline some tensions: many students see AI as essential for future success, while others express concern about over-reliance, reduced creativity, or the erosion of the human touch central to hospitality. This contradictory perspective reflects some wider debates in higher education, where AI is recognized as both an enabler of innovation and a potential threat to authentic learning and professional identity (Holmes et al., 2021).

Participants also emphasized that hospitality schools should act as gatekeepers, balancing innovation with caution, and embedding AI into teaching alongside explicit training on ethics, bias, and critical reflection.

These themes are further illustrated by selected student comments. For example, several respondents highlighted the lack of structured guidance and training:

"I think hospitality schools should conduct mandatory sessions to widely inform students about how to use AI effectively, the ethical implications, and what is acceptable or not. Right now, there is no clear guidance."

Others emphasized the need to avoid over-reliance on AI:

"AI should be used as a tool and not a crutch. Many students already rely on it too much, and this risks reducing critical thinking and independent learning."

Ethical ambiguity also emerged as a recurrent concern:

"Schools should clearly explain what is valid versus invalid use of AI. Simply saying 'don't use AI' does not help students understand responsible use."

Finally, several respondents stressed the importance of preserving hospitality's human-centred nature:

"Hospitality is based on human relations, and AI should never undermine that. It can support learning and operations, but it should not replace the human element that defines this industry."

Taken together, the open-ended responses indicate that hospitality students expect their institutions to provide structured and transparent AI training, to frame AI as a supportive rather than substitutive learning resource, to clarify ethical boundaries and acceptable use, and to ensure that AI integration remains aligned with the human-centered values that underpin hospitality education and professional practice.

Key Issues and Trends Emerging from the Findings

Synthesizing across RO1-RO3, four trends emerge:

1. Training and guidance gap: most students want formal AI training, yet provision remains uneven, reinforcing trial-and-error adoption.
2. Efficiency-first usage: students mainly use AI for comprehension and productivity (research, writing, time management) rather than autonomy or critical thinking development.
3. Ethical ambiguity: students internalize concerns about misuse and boundaries, often in the absence of clear institutional rules or consistent modelling.
4. Hospitality-specific opportunity: students prioritize AI-enhanced materials and simulations, indicating demand for experiential, discipline-relevant integration (e.g., service recovery scenarios, guest communication, operational decision-making).

CONCLUSION

This study set out to examine how students in hospitality higher education access, utilize, and perceive generative AI tools in their academic and professional development. Using a structured survey design with 158 participants, it combined descriptive statistical analysis with thematic synthesis to provide a baseline view of adoption patterns, perceived learning impact, and ethical awareness. This methodological approach enabled not only the quantification of distributions but also their contextualization against the lived experiences of students. The findings address the three research objectives and collectively respond to the overarching research question: How have hospitality higher education students been accessing, utilizing and perceiving the impact of generative AI tools on their academic development, ethical awareness and career preparedness since 2023?

With respect to RO1 (access, training, and usage patterns), the results reveal both opportunities and structural shortcomings. Most students reported using AI frequently for research and academic writing, but formal training was largely absent and institutional access inconsistent, with reliance on mainstream tools like Microsoft Copilot rather than hospitality-specific applications. This uneven provision reflects wider studies that highlight fragmented institutional support and a reliance on generic platforms (Cotton et al., 2023; EDUCAUSE, 2023). In the survey, students expressed strong demand for structured AI training, underscoring the need for universities to move beyond informal or trial-and-error adoption and toward systematic integration aligned with disciplinary needs.

Findings under RO2 (perceptions of educational value and learning impact) indicate that students generally view AI positively as a supportive learning tool. High levels of agreement were observed for AI's role in improving efficiency, comprehension, and academic confidence, aligning with existing research suggesting that AI can support student agency and aspects of metacognitive development (Holmes et al., 2023; Chen et al., 2020). However, skepticism remained regarding its contribution to critical thinking, independent learning, and exam preparation, reflecting broader concerns in the literature about overreliance and cognitive offloading (Risko & Gilbert, 2016; Cotton et al., 2023). Based on these findings, it can be assumed that while students appreciate AI's supportive functions, they remain cautious about its ability to foster deeper and higher-order learning.

Regarding RO3 (ethical awareness and institutional responsibility), the findings reveal ambivalence and normative ambiguity. Internalized concerns (fear of misuse, lack of confidence in evaluating AI content) were more dominant than external ones such as missing institutional guidelines. This opens doors for wider debates suggesting that students often navigate AI ethics in the absence of clear policies, leaving responsibility to individual interpretation (Selwyn, 2019; Qadir et al., 2023). Within hospitality education, where ethics, trust and empathy are central to professional identity, such ambiguity is particularly challenging, especially in the long term. Students also expressed expectations that faculty model responsible AI use and institutions provide explicit, contextualized guidance.

Taken together, these findings show that hospitality students definitely recognize AI's transformative potential and value its role as a learning partner, but their engagement remains so far rather fragmented, unevenly supported, and ethically uncertain. AI is primarily used for efficiency and comprehension rather than for cultivating independence or critical reflection, signaling the duality highlighted in the literature: AI as both enabler of innovation and a threat to authentic learning (Holmes et al., 2021; Cotton et al., 2023). For hospitality schools, this implies that AI integration cannot remain generic or reactive: it must be deliberate, supported by structured training, discipline-specific tools, and ethical frameworks that align with the service-oriented ethos of the field.

Implications for Hospitality Educators and Program Leaders

Based on the findings, it is advisable that hospitality schools should respond with targeted, practical actions such as:

- Embed AI literacy early and repeatedly (and not as a one-off workshop), focusing on evaluating outputs, prompting responsibly, and reflective learning habits.

- Clarify ethical boundaries beyond plagiarism, including acceptable AI support levels for different assessment types and disclosure expectations.
- Provide discipline-relevant AI use cases, such as guest-interaction scripts, service recovery simulations, revenue-management scenarios, and operations analytics exercises.
- Align tool access with learning outcomes, moving beyond generic productivity tools toward curated, curriculum-linked applications.
- Train faculty (both internal and external) as role models, ensuring transparent AI use in teaching materials and consistent messaging across modules.
- Use assessment design to protect human skills, emphasizing judgement, empathy, and decision-making under uncertainty where hospitality competence is demonstrated.

Recommendations and Future Research

Future research should expand this exploratory baseline by adopting larger, cross-cultural samples to account for regional and institutional differences, pairing self-reported perceptions with behavioral usage data (Gomez et al., 2024), and applying mixed-method approaches that integrate student, faculty, and industry perspectives. For practice, hospitality institutions should prioritize three areas: embedding structured AI training across curricula to close skill gaps, aligning institutional access with discipline-specific needs, such as service simulations and operational analytics and integrating explicit ethical education to cultivate responsible, confident use of AI. By doing so, hospitality education can ensure its graduates are not only digitally literate but also critically reflective, ethically grounded, and well-prepared for an AI-driven industry future.

Declaration of Generative AI and AI-Assisted Technologies in the Writing Process

During the preparation of this manuscript, the author used ChatGPT (OpenAI, 2025), Grammarly (Grammarly Inc., 2025), and Microsoft Copilot (Microsoft, 2025) as supportive tools in the writing process. ChatGPT and Grammarly were used to assist with language refinement and to improve clarity, coherence, and readability. Microsoft Copilot was additionally used to support the checking of reference formatting and the verification of bibliographic details (e.g., DOIs and URLs). These tools were not used to generate substantive academic content, develop original ideas, or interpret research findings. The author carefully reviewed and edited all outputs generated with the assistance of these tools and takes full responsibility for the accuracy, integrity, and originality of the final manuscript.

REFERENCES

An, Y., Yu, J. H., & James, S. (2025). Investigating the higher education institutions' guidelines and policies regarding the use of generative AI in teaching, learning, research, and administration. *International Journal of Educational Technology in Higher Education, 22*(1), 10. https://doi.org/10.1186/s41239-025-00507-3

Babbie, E. (2020). *The practice of social research* (15th ed.). Cengage Learning.

Bethlehem, J. (2010). Selection bias in web surveys. *International Statistical Review, 78*(2), 161–188. DOI: 10.1111/j.1751-5823.2010.00112.x

Bond, M., Khosravi, H., De Laat, M., Bergdahl, N., Negrea, V., Oxley, E., & Siemens, G. (2024). A meta systematic review of artificial intelligence in higher education: A call for increased ethics, collaboration, and rigour. *International journal of educational technology in higher education, 21*(1), 4. https://doi.org/10.1186/s41239-023-00436-z

Buhalis, D., & Leung, R. (2018). Smart hospitality—Interconnectivity and interoperability towards an ecosystem. *International Journal of Hospitality Management, 71*, 41–50. DOI: 10.1016/j.ijhm.2017.11.011

Chan, D. (2009). So why ask me? Are self-report data really that bad? *Organizational Research Methods, 12*(4), 309–336. DOI: 10.1177/1094428107308927

Chen, X., Xie, H., Zou, D., & Hwang, G.-J. (2020). Application and theory gaps during the rise of artificial intelligence in education. *Computers & Education: Artificial Intelligence, 1*, 100002. https://doi.org/10.1016/j.caeai.2020.100002

Chou, C.-Y., Chan, T.-W., & Lin, C.-J. (2002). Redefining the learning companion: The past, present, and future of educational agents. *Computers & Education, 40*(3), 255–269. https://doi.org/10.1016/S0360-1315(02)00130-6

Cotton, D. R. E., Cotton, P. A., & Shipway, J. R. (2023). Chatting and cheating: Ensuring academic integrity in the era of ChatGPT. *Innovations in Education and Teaching International, 61*(2), 228–239. DOI: 10.1080/14703297.2023.2190148

Creswell, J. W., & Creswell, J. D. (2018). *Research design: Qualitative, quantitative, and mixed methods approaches* (5th ed.). SAGE.

EDUCAUSE. (2023). 2023 EDUCAUSE *Horizon Report: Teaching and Learning Edition*. https://www.educause.edu/horizon-report-teaching-and-learning-2023

Floridi, L., Cowls, J., Beltrametti, M., Chatila, R., Chazerand, P., Dignum, V., Luetge, C., Madelin, R., Pagallo, U., Rossi, F., Schafer, B., Valcke, P., & Vayena, E. (2018). AI4People – An ethical framework for a good AI society: Opportunities, risks, principles, and recommendations. *Minds and Machines, 28*(4), 689–707. https://doi.org/10.1007/s11023-018-9482-5

Grammarly Inc. (2025). *Grammarly [AI-powered writing assistant]*. Grammarly. https://www.grammarly.com/

Holmes, W., Bialik, M., & Fadel, C. (2021). *Artificial intelligence in education: Promises and implications for teaching and learning* (2nd ed.). Center for Curriculum Redesign. (No DOI)

Holmes, W., Porayska-Pomsta, K., Holstein, K., Sutherland, E., Baker, R. S., Ocumpaugh, J., Rodrigo, M. M. T., d'Mello, S., Shum, S. B., du Boulay, B., Santos, O. C., Nkambou, R., Bull, S., Luckin, R., Koedinger, K. R., & Rosé, C. P. (2023). Ethics of AI in education: Towards a community-wide framework. Computers & Education. *Artificial Intelligence*, *4*, 100131. https://doi.org/10.1007/s40593-021-00239-1DOI: 10.1016/j.caeai.2023.100131

Kasneci, E., Sessler, K., Küchemann, S., Bannert, M., Dementieva, D., Fischer, F., & Kasneci, G. (2023). ChatGPT for good? On opportunities and challenges of large language models for education. *Learning and Individual Differences, 103*, 102274. https://doi.org/10.1016/j.lindif.2023.102274

Knani, M.,, Echchakoui, S., & Ladhari, R. (2022). Artificial intelligence in tourism and hospitality: Bibliometric analysis and research agenda. *International Journal of Hospitality Management, 107*, 103317. https://doi.org/10.1016/j.ijhm.2022.103317

Knox, J., Williamson, B., & Bayne, S. (2020). Machine behaviourism: Future visions of 'learnification' and 'datafication' across humans and digital technologies. *Learning, Media and Technology*, *45*(1), 31–45. DOI: 10.1080/17439884.2019.1623251

Lin, P. M., Kim, Y.,, Qiu, H.,, & Ren, L. (2017). Experiential learning in hospitality education through a service-learning project. *Journal of Hospitality & Tourism Education, 29*(2), 71–81. https://doi.org/10.1080/10963758.2017.1297716

Luckin, R., Holmes, W., Griffiths, M., & Forcier, L. B. (2016). *Intelligence unleashed: An argument for AI in education*. Pearson. (No DOI)

Mariani, M. M., & Borghi, M. (2021). Customers' evaluation of mechanical artificial intelligence in hospitality services: A study using online reviews analytics. *International Journal of Contemporary Hospitality Management, 33*(11), 3956–3976. https://doi.org/10.1108/IJCHM-06-2020-0622DOI: 10.1016/j.techfore.2023.122480

Microsoft. (2025). *Microsoft Copilot* [AI-powered assistant]. https://copilot.microsoft.com/

OpenAI. (2025). *ChatGPT [Large language model]*. OpenAI. https://chat.openai.com/

Paulhus, D. L., & Vazire, S. (2007). *The self-report method.* In R. W. Robins, R. C. Fraley, & R. F. Krueger (Eds.), *Handbook of research methods in personality psychology* (pp. 224–239). Guilford Press. (No DOI)

Qadir, J., Al-Fuqaha, A., & Iqbal, W. (2023). Engineering education in the era of ChatGPT: Promise and pitfalls of generative AI for education. *IEEE Access : Practical Innovations, Open Solutions, 11*, 53508–53530. DOI: 10.1109/ACCESS.2023.3273245

Risko, E. F., & Gilbert, S. J. (2016). Cognitive offloading. *Trends in Cognitive Sciences, 20*(9), 676–688. https://doi.org/10.1016/j.tics.2016.07.002

Robson, C., & McCartan, K. (2016). Real world research (4th ed.). Wiley-Blackwell. (No DOI)

Ruel, E., Wagner, W. E., III, & Gillespie, B. J. (2016). *The practice of survey research: Theory and applications*. SAGE. (No DOI)

Samala, N., Katkam, B. S., Bellamkonda, R. S., & Rodriguez, R. V. (2022). Impact of artificial intelligence and robotics in the tourism sector: A critical insight. *Journal of Tourism Futures, 8*(1), 73–87. https://doi.org/10.1108/JTF-07-2019-0065

Schreier, M. (2012). *Qualitative content analysis in practice*. SAGE. (No DOI)

Selwyn, N. (2019). *Should robots replace teachers? AI and the future of education. Polity*. No DOI.

Selwyn, N. (2022). Education and technology: Key issues and debates (3rd ed.). Bloomsbury. (No DOI)

Williamson, B., & Eynon, R. (2020). Historical threads, missing links, and future directions in AI in education. *Learning, Media and Technology, 45*(3), 223–235. DOI: 10.1080/17439884.2020.1798995

Wright, K. B. (2005). Researching internet-based populations: Advantages and disadvantages of online survey research, online questionnaire authoring software packages, and web survey services. *Journal of Computer-Mediated Communication, 10*(3), JCMC1034. Advance online publication. DOI: 10.1111/j.1083-6101.2005.tb00259.x

Zawacki-Richter, O., Marín, V. I., Bond, M., & Gouverneur, F. (2019). Systematic review of research on artificial intelligence applications in higher education—Where are the educators? *International Journal of Educational Technology in Higher Education, 16*(1), 39. DOI: 10.1186/s41239-019-0171-0

Zhang, K., Li, X., Ye, H., Lin, K. J., Chen, S., & Law, R. (2024). How can ChatGPT assist hospitality and tourism education? *Journal of Teaching in Travel & Tourism, 24*(4), 438-448. https://doi.org/10.1080/15313220.2024.2384743

KEY TERMS AND DEFINITIONS

AI Literacy: The competency to critically evaluate, apply, and adapt AI tools in hospitality education, balancing technical skills with ethical awareness and academic integrity.

Cognitive Offloading: The act of delegating mental tasks such as summarizing or problem-solving to AI tools, which may enhance efficiency but risks weakening independent critical thinking

Digital Readiness: The preparedness of hospitality students to adopt AI tools, shaped by prior digital training, confidence levels, and institutional access to technology.

Ethical Boundaries: The clear limits and guidelines that define acceptable AI use in academic and hospitality contexts, preventing plagiarism, bias, or overreliance.

Experiential Simulation: AI-generated practice scenarios replicating hospitality service situations, designed to enhance hands-on learning and professional preparation.

Institutional Support: Structured provision by universities, including AI access, training sessions, and guidelines, that enables responsible and equitable student use of AI.

Learning Companion: A conceptual model where AI functions as a supportive partner in education, fostering comprehension, confidence, and engagement without replacing human learning processes.

Chapter 5

ChatGPT Got the Job?

Hospitality Recruiters Weigh in on AI Use in Job Applications

Alexandru Stoinea
http://orcid.org/0009-0006-1686-8631
Les Roches Global Hospitality Education, Crans-Montana, Switzerland

Jonathan Meehan
Les Roches Global Hospitality Education, Crans-Montana, Switzerland

ABSTRACT

Few developments in early-career recruitment have created as much debate in the past three years as the use of generative artificial intelligence (Gen-AI) through tools such as ChatGPT, Gemini, DeepSeek, Claude, Jasper, and Copy.ai to write or enhance CVs, cover letters or job email applications (Fernandez-Mateo, 2025). For the hospitality sector in particular, which is recognised in the global recruitment industry for the focus on candidates that display warmth, empathy, and authentic personal narrative (Rosado-Pinto & Loureiro, 2023), the arrival of machine-generated application text has raised urgent questions for employers and recruiters, such as: Does an AI-polished application still reveal the candidate's true voice? Can recruiters rely on the written words from resumes and cover letters to predict cultural fit and the passion for service and guest satisfaction?

INTRODUCTION

Few developments in early-career recruitment have created as much debate in the past three years as the use of generative artificial intelligence (Gen-AI) through tools such as ChatGPT, Gemini, DeepSeek, Claude, Jasper, or Copy.ai to write or

DOI: 10.4018/979-8-3373-5112-4.ch005

enhance CVs, cover letters or job email applications (Fernandez-Mateo, 2025). For the hospitality sector in particular, which is recognised in the global recruitment industry for the focus on candidates that display warmth, empathy, and authentic personal narrative (Rosado-Pinto & Loureiro, 2023), the arrival of machine-generated application text has raised urgent questions for employers and recruiters, such as:

Does an AI-polished application still reveal the candidate's true voice? Can recruiters rely on the written words from resumes and cover letters to predict cultural fit and the passion for service and guest satisfaction?

While students and graduates often defend AI as a pragmatic language support tool, that makes a job, internship or management training application process easier (Paster, 2025), the decision makers of this AI opportunity are the hiring managers who must decide whether to view AI-generated polish on written materials as legitimate professional support or as a veil that obscures the individuality of each applicant.

This chapter gives priority and focuses on the employer perspective in the hospitality industry recruitment, drawing on the existing literature, industry latest news, and an original survey data from the Les Roches Career Day 2025 in the Crans Montana campus, where 52 recruiters from luxury hotels, resorts, cruise lines, event agencies and restaurant groups were asked how they perceive, detect, and evaluate AI-assisted applications.

Background: Hospitality Recruitment Norms, Digitalisation, and the Shift to AI-Mediated Hiring

The Career Services office at Les Roches Crans Montana teaches students that a well-written cover letter should "tell your story" and highlight a moment of guest care, a cross-cultural encounter, or an operational challenge overcome with specific examples and details that can be further presented in a one-to-one interview situation. The implicit assumption was that the student who wrote that cover letter was the author of that story and that the written version would not be different from the spoken one in an interview setup.

However, the COVID-19 pandemic, together with the social distancing and sanitary restrictions imposed during that time, inadvertently accelerated dependence on written communication, digital materials, and, as a result, a large majority of job application interviews moved online on Zoom or Teams (Samuk Carignani & Burchi, 2022). Global hotel chains started to use Applicant-Tracking Systems (ATS) for large-scale hiring after the pandemic, and the resume-cover letter package became the primary new norm for first impressions (Pinpoint, 2025). Because of this, a keyword optimization was introduced through ATS to filter efficiently the large number of applications received and to improve the duration and accuracy of the screening process (Pinpoint, 2025).

This was also followed by the rapid developments all over the world in alternative large-language-model (LLM). By the beginning of 2023, Gen-AI tools started to be used not just to proof-read existing content and text but instead to create completely new and optimised applications. These new applications were both tailored for ATS keyword filters and recruiter storytelling and this further blurred the line between applicants and algorithms (Hamilton, 2024).

The Rapid Adoption of Generative AI by Early-Career Applicants

According to a talent recruitment report published by LinkedIn (2024), 45% of job seekers under age 27 admit to using some form of AI to improve or draft CVs and cover letters. The figure is higher in countries and environments where there are many international residents who live, study or work there. In this case, the local language might not be their mother tongue and the young generations use AI more frequently. A relevant example is showcased in a survey at the University of Zurich done in March 2024. The university has students from more than 120 nationalities on campus and the study found that AI tools are widely used among their students, especially for writing or improving texts (von Doniken, 2024). In addition, the study also showed that 97% of their students mentioned that they used AI at least once in the past six months for writing any kind of text material for personal or academic purpose.

Erosion of Trust in Written Applications

For recruiters, the sudden shift meant that documents such as an intention letter or resume, once valued as authentic self-expressions of every single applicant, could no longer be assumed to represent the candidate's own words and experiences. This results in a loss of trust in written materials as a defining feature of the new hiring landscape. This new norm raises even more challenges for hospitality employers in particular, because they frequently highlight that a genuine personality fit with their brand and evidence of service passion are decisive criteria in the application screening of applicants (Kilson, 2025). These soft-skill indicators, hard to capture via automated scoring tools, have traditionally been noticed by recruiters from anecdotes, reflective language and specific examples in a cover letter and from the tone of voice of the candidates during the face-to-face interview process.

AI can generate a grammatically impeccable text, with perfect spelling, punctuation and flow, yet it is strangely generic, over-polished, or emotionally flat. This makes the text almost impossible to transmit those subtle cues of the individual personality, and a genuine case for guests that hospitality recruiters seek in the received applications. This tension between an industry built on human care and warmth and a new technology recognised and praised for linguistic efficiency sets the stage for the concerns voiced by employers throughout this chapter.

Authenticity, Equity, and the Emerging Digital Divide

Advocates of Gen-AI sometimes describe it as a levelling tool that reduces disadvantages for non-native speakers and candidates without access to private editing services for their job application. Early evidence in education supports that view because students report higher confidence when submitting AI-checked documents (Bui & Tong, 2025). Yet equity concerns remain. Premium subscription models and hybrid human-AI resume-coaching services give students with financial resources access to more sophisticated prompts, where they can control the text/voice tone and style of the text, making it more genuine and difficult to detect by ATS systems or recruiters. Such features can be accessed in the paid versions of AI platforms such as ChatGPT and are not available in the free versions (Lim et al., 2025), potentially creating a new digital divide between users, such as university students. As a result, it is now the responsibility of recruiters to distinguish between applications that use authentic levelling and those that use outsourced professional ghost-writing services.

Institutional Responses and the Rise of AI Literacy in Hospitality Education

Les Roches Global Hospitality Education and other universities have issued guidelines encouraging disclosure when AI tools are used. The aim of such policies is to ensure that students maintain editorial control and authorship in their academic work and in their professional premises, such as job applications for their future career. The policies warn that heavy, undisclosed AI reliance could amount to misrepresentation of authorship that is similar to plagiarism in academic writing. These institutional debates and changes signal a wider realisation that AI literacy has become integral to professional communication skills (Wright & Sapkota, 2024), and hospitality recruiters must recalibrate expectations accordingly and update recruitment practices.

This chapter further explores how hospitality recruiters perceive and respond to AI-generated written applications and identifies employer priorities, detection strategies, and policy needs. The discussion is structured in five further sections:

1. Understanding Authenticity in AI-Mediated Communication.

    An outline of the theoretical foundations of the key conceptual perspectives on authenticity in AI-mediated communication which aims to clarify how originality is understood in communication theory, organisational psychology, and digital ethics.

2. The Problem: Employer Expectations vs AI-Enhanced Submissions.
   An inside view of the recruiters' definitions of authenticity and personal voice for their job applicants
3. How Recruiters Spot AI-Generated Applications.
   What surveying linguistic, structural, and behavioural markers are most frequently mentioned in human resources literature and latest news?
4. Comparing Hospitality with Other Service Industries
5. Employer Perspectives: Findings from Les Roches Career Day 2025 survey.
   An in-depth analysis that presents original survey data from 52 recruiters present during a recruitment fair event at Les Roches Crans Montana
6. Legal, Ethical, and Practical Implications.
   An evaluation of the existing legislation on AI use, focusing on the recruiter concerns in emerging transparency and fairness frameworks.
7. Best Practices: Recommendations for Applicants and Employers.
   A guide that offers both recruiters and candidates guidance for clearer policy and communication on the use of AI in job applications

By focusing and listening to the voices of hiring professionals, the chapter contributes to ongoing debates about authenticity, fairness, and the future of human-centred selection processes in a technologically mediated era driven by AI use.

UNDERSTANDING AUTHENTICITY IN AI-MEDIATED COMMUNICATION

From Service Ethos to Contested Construct: Authenticity in Hospitality Hiring

The discussion of AI in recruitment inevitably leads to the question of authenticity- a concept deeply embedded in the ethos of hospitality, yet increasingly difficult to define in a digital hiring landscape. In the hospitality profession, authenticity has long been understood as a defining quality of guest care, emotional intelligence, and service excellence. When this notion extends to job applications, however, it becomes a complex and contested construct-something that is not simply possessed by individuals but perceived, performed, and negotiated between candidates, recruiters, and the technologies that mediate their communication.

The Performance of Self: Goffman and the Digital "Exhibition"

Sociologist Erving Goffman (1959) introduced the idea of self-presentation as a performance shaped by audience and context. Just as hospitality professionals perform authenticity for guests through gestures, tone, and personal warmth, job applicants perform authenticity through their written self-expression. When generative AI intervenes-editing, rephrasing, or even composing the text-the performance gains a new actor: a machine co-author. The "presentation of self" becomes co-constructed, as AI enhances linguistic fluency but risks diluting personal nuance. Building on Goffman's model, Hogan (2010) suggested that digital environments shift self-presentation from performance to exhibition, where individuals curate artefacts such as posts or profiles rather than engage in spontaneous interaction. In this sense, AI-generated cover letters resemble curated exhibitions: grammatically perfect and visually impeccable, yet potentially lacking emotional texture or spontaneity.

Perceived Sincerity: The Psychology of Authenticity Assessment

From the perspective of marketing and organisational psychology, authenticity is often defined as a perceived coherence between one's expressed identity and underlying values or intentions (Morhart et al., 2015). It is less about factual truth and more about perceived sincerity and consistency across contexts. In recruitment, this translates into the recruiter's intuitive assessment of whether an applicant's narrative-how they describe motivation, brand affinity, or service experiences-feels believable and aligns with observed behaviour in interviews. Schlegel et al. (2011) further associate authenticity with self-knowledge and meaning, suggesting that individuals appear authentic when their communication reflects internal clarity and reflection. AI tools that rewrite or over-edit a cover letter may polish language at the expense of this reflective quality, creating what recruiters often describe as "too perfect" or "robotic" prose.

The Sociotechnical Turn: Authenticity as a Co-Constructed Negotiation

In the broader field of digital ethics and human-AI interaction, authenticity is increasingly seen as sociotechnical-an emergent property arising from collaboration between humans and intelligent systems rather than a purely human characteristic. Suchman (2007) and Introna (2016) argue that authenticity is negotiated within human-machine configurations, where technology influences both the content and the perception of communication. In the context of AI-assisted recruitment, authenticity emerges not solely from the text but from the relationship between the applicant, the AI tool, and the recruiter interpreting the message. A candidate who uses AI transparently and thoughtfully may still project genuine self-awareness, while one who delegates authorship entirely to a machine risk losing credibility. The issue, therefore, is not whether AI was used but whether the resulting narrative preserves the relational integrity of the human voice that hospitality recruiters value most.

Recent work in digital ethics extends this relational view by examining how algorithms shape perceptions of "realness." Floridi (2011) proposes that authenticity in the information age depends on maintaining informational integrity-ensuring alignment between content and its human source. Vössing et al. (2022) further suggest that digital authenticity in human-AI interactions arises when technology is used transparently and in ways consistent with the communicator's identity. This aligns closely with the equity concerns discussed throughout this chapter: while AI can democratise access for non-native English speakers, excessive or undisclosed use may erode perceived sincerity in an industry that prizes emotional labour and interpersonal warmth.

Toward a Relational Model: Agency, Transparency, and Perceived Integrity

Taken together, these perspectives suggest that authenticity in AI-mediated job applications is performed (Goffman, 1959), perceived (Morhart et al., 2015), and co-constructed (Suchman, 2007). It depends less on the presence of AI and more on how it is used, whether the applicant retains agency, reflection, and ownership of their own narrative. This chapter therefore adopts a relational view of authenticity: a perception negotiated among candidates, recruiters, and the mediating AI systems that shape written communication.

THE PROBLEM: EMPLOYER EXPECTATIONS VS AI-ENHANCED SUBMISSIONS

The Traditional Role of the Application: A Window to the Candidate

Recruiters across service-oriented industries such as the hospitality industry have long seen the written application, particularly the cover letter, as a window into an applicant's personal and authentic motivations, personality and work ethics (Waung et al., 2017). Hospitality-management literature further notes that luxury hotels and hospitality companies in general often prioritise candidates that possess attitude-related attributes such as genuine warmth and enthusiasm for service delivery, emotional intelligence, and alignment with the organisation's service culture or brand values, alongside other technical skills required in the industry (Dimanche & Lo, 2022; Lee & Choi, 2022).

Because these skills are identified partly from how a candidate narrates their own experiences, historically, many hiring managers view the cover letter as a personal voice of the candidate's resume (McDowell, 1987). Inside a resume, a recruiter can easily identify what a candidate has done professionally and educationally in the past. In addition, the cover letter is expected to bring the personality of the candidate into play, as this could show, in a subjective way, who they are and why they seek to join that particular property or brand (Waung et al., 2017).

Defining "Authenticity" in Hospitality Hiring

This particular focus on the candidate's voice in the decision of the recruitment process for a particular role explains why the influx of AI-generated text is perceived by many employers not as a neutral formatting support system for the written application but as a potential loss of the authentic feeling of the candidate.

While authenticity is a contested concept in social psychology and marketing, recruiters often use the term pragmatically to denote the link between written self-presentation and observed interpersonal behaviour (Schmitz-Wilhelmy & Truxillo, 2025). In the hospitality hiring context, authenticity generally comprises three dimensions:

- Narrative Credibility: the sense that shows the motivations described in writing are personally experienced and verifiable (Collins & Martinez-Moreno, 2022)
- Voice Consistency: alignment between the linguistic style of the written application and the candidate's speech during interviews or networking conversations (Heimann & Schmitz-Wilhelmy, 2025)
- Brand Alignment: evidence that the applicant understands and resonates with the specific culture, guest-service philosophy, or sustainability mission of the property or chain (Auer et al., 2021)

The Homogenizing Effect of AI on Applicant Voice

Gen-AI tools, by design, optimise grammar, vocabulary, and structure for fluency and professionalism (Mekheimer, 2025), but often flatten and hide the personal expressions that recruiters are looking for as cues of the genuine personality of candidates for hospitality careers. The dimensions above mirror the triadic view of authenticity discussed later in this chapter, where authenticity is performed, perceived, and co-constructed through human–AI interactions.

Hospitality employers in the luxury segment, for example, Four Seasons, Mandarin Oriental, and Raffles, repeatedly stress the need for applications that demonstrate personalised motivation, such as references to memorable stays at hotels, shared brand values, or cultural nuances of a destination (Four Seasons, 2025; Delgado, 2023; Caira, 2024). On the other hand, AI generated content tends to generate non-specific text such are formulated phrases "I am passionate about delivering exceptional guest experiences in a luxury hotel environment". A genuine and personal sentence could be "I admire the brand's 2019 partnership with local farms in Thailand that allow you to enhance guest connection with the local environment. AI-generated text can be easily perceived as perfectly written and flawless, but it might sound impersonal. This impression weakens that genuineness signal employers rely on and search for and might reduce the chances of the applicant to successfully secure the role that they applied for.

Another common paradox in recruitment is that while many employers welcome tools that help non-native English speakers reduce grammar errors, such as Grammarly or Microsoft Word. For example, these grammar support tools can over polish and even completely remove distinctive personality markers, which could make the applications feel less authentic. Recruiters note that they now read with scepticism when all applicants, regardless of their background, education and work experience, submit their applications and personal cover letter with an identical structure, flow of sentences and words used (Yip, 2024). This similarity and homogenisation of the text found in individual applications complicates efforts to identify that individual personal voice. Discrepancies often become evident only in live or online interviews when, for example, the candidate's spoken English differs significantly from the application's style and fluency.

The Promise-Performance Gap: A Core Recruiter Fear

In addition, hospitality work is deeply interpersonal by delivering on written promises of guest-centric creativity and care, emotional intelligence, or leadership in crisis requires observable behaviour once hired. A genuine fear for recruiters is that if the written application over-promises, especially when written by AI, the promise-performance gap may widen (Bárány, 2023), leading to a high early-stage staff turnover and to guest-service inconsistency. For example, Cui et al. (2025) argue that the increasing similarity and polish of AI-assisted cover letters reduce their ability to signal true ability and knowledge, which encourages recruiters to rely more on behavioural evidence or past performance assessment that can only be confirmed through recommendation letters or on-demand references.

Faced with AI-enhanced submissions, some employers have begun to change the focus from expecting a perfectly polished written application in the initial candidate screening, instead prioritising behavioural indicators such as teamwork, adaptability or resilience. This could be collected through situational-judgement questions or video-recorded responses that allow the recruiters to evaluate the different soft and hard skills, and last but not least, the brand alignment (OECD, 2021).

Generational Divides in Perceptions of AI Use

One more important source of tension comes from the generational difference in attitudes toward the use of AI. Gen Z applicants and early-career millennials often view AI assistance in the same way as using grammar-checking software or a resume template, which is seen as a practical and normal step in a competitive, digitalised job market (Lin & Parker, 2025). By contrast, many mid-career hiring managers, educated before the rise of LLMs, see the cover letter as a writing sample demonstrating reflection and communication ability of the individual who applies for a role in a company (Gillespie et al., 2023). The resulting expectation gap can, unfortunately, lead to mutual frustration because students perceive recruiters as supporting and following outdated notions of authenticity, while recruiters perceive students as outsourcing to an AI assistant the very qualities that the hospitality industry prizes most.

Four Dominant Themes in Recruiter Concerns

Synthesising the recruiters' concerns reveals four dominant themes shaping recruiter concerns:

I. Everyone Sounds the Same: Written materials are flawless and follow a generic standard, making it difficult to distinguish between the soft skills of the candidates and identify their unique personal voice.

II. Harder to Judge Character: Traditional written cues that once signalled a candidate's motivation or service mindset are no longer reliable indicators of their genuine qualities.

III. The Interview Doesn't Match: A growing discrepancy between the refined style of written applications and a candidate's real natural communication style during live interviews.

IV. Demand for New Policies: A pressing need for organisations to establish clear guidelines on the acceptable use of AI in the hiring process and requirements for disclosure of the AI use.

HOW RECRUITERS SPOT AI-GENERATED APPLICATIONS

Automated Screening: ATS and Beyond

Identifying AI-authored material has lately become an expected part of the recruiter's daily tasks and responsibilities (Tursunbayeva et al., 2025). Identifying an AI generated application can be fully done through an ATS platform that can identify AI generated text in addition to manage, filter, rank the candidates whose resumes and cover letters match specific keywords, qualifications, or experience criteria set by the hiring company (O'Halloran et al., 2018).

While using ATS can increase the efficiency of the screening process, ATS also introduces several limitations and risks for the recruiters. Keyword-based filtering can result in both false positives answers, where over-optimized CVs and applications can easily pass the filters despite the candidates having limited real-work competence and skills. On the other hand, the false negatives, miss the capable candidates who not been taken into consideration because they didn't know how to properly highlight their experience, skills or motivation. In addition, ATS systems are largely unable to assess and clearly identify interpersonal skills, cultural sensitivity, or the service orientation of candidates which are critical in hospitality. For this reason, the unique reliance of ATS systems on textual content only, makes them vulnerable to manipulation by AI-generated applications, potentially leading recruiters to make mistakes and not continue the application process for some strong candidates. Furthermore, ATS evaluates applications in isolation, without understanding the narrative context or situational nuances that convey a candidate's fit for brand values or guest experience excellence that can be supported through a recommendation letter or referral. All these limitations underscore that while ATS can support efficiency, it should complement, rather than replace the human judgment of the recruiter.

Although this can be seen as a race between job applicants and detection software of AI content, recruiters reveal a more subtle reality. Detection in hospitality is rarely fully automated and remains largely a human, interpretive practice done by the recruiter or hiring manager (Preda, 2025). What the recruiters are looking for in an application is a combination of linguistic intuition, comparative reading across documents such as resume, cover letter and candidate profile, and matching real-time behavioural cues from the candidate during the face-to-face or online interviews.

The "Too-Perfect" Application: Linguistic Red Flags

A common observation and red flag in identifying an AI generated application is what is sometimes called the "too-perfect" cover letter. These are intention letters whose grammar and punctuation are flawless, but that can read and sound flat or impersonal (Jakesch et al., 2023). Such letters often have sentences with a similar rhythm and length, lacking idiosyncrasies, which can make them read more like a brochure than an honest personal introduction from a real person. This sense of over-polish was repeatedly cited as the first hint that a generative model, rather than the applicant, may have been responsible for the phrasing of that text. The phenomenon resonates with what press accounts in mainstream business media, where editors describe being able to "hear the robot in the room" when evaluating open application submissions (The New York Times, 2025; Shibu, 2024).

The Evidence Gap: Generic Claims vs. Specific Narratives

Recruiters also note that AI-assisted documents often rely heavily on general phrasing that is not supported by specific personal evidence. Declarations such as "I am deeply passionate about delivering exceptional guest experiences" or "I possess outstanding leadership and communication skills" are used by applicants very frequently; however, they lack real examples of service situations or project-specific outcomes (Cui et al., 2025). In contrast, applications made by humans, even from early career candidates, tend to include small story details such as an example of a memory of resolving a difficult guest complaint, or a reference to the particular style of a manager who influenced them (Harris-Watson et al., 2023).

Voice Inconsistency: From Page to Interview

Another linguistic pattern that triggers a warning for recruiters is the inconsistency of voice between the written application and a candidate's spoken language. In several cases, human resources professionals described students who submitted highly articulate written intention letters but struggled to explain the same points and with the same level of detail during the interview (Jakesch et al., 2023).

Non-Linguistic Cues: Speed of Submission as a Detection Cue

Finally, the application process itself provides non-linguistic behavioural data that can give recruiters different clues. For example, a significant red flag emerges from a disconnect between the speed of submission of an application and the perceived effort implied by the content of the application. Receiving a meticulously written, multi-page, bespoke-looking cover letter within minutes of a job posting going live is often an obvious sign of automation. The rationale is simple in this case. A human requires time to read the job description carefully, research the company, think about their relevant experiences, and then draft and edit their cover letter. An AI, however, can perform this task almost instantaneously. This immediate turnaround time suggests the application was most likely done by AI, using the job title and a few keywords, lacking the genuine customisation that a human applicant would normally do.

Overall, AI detection in hospitality recruitment remains a predominantly qualitative exercise. The over-polished CVs and cover letters, the use of general adjectives, the absence of narrative evidence, along with the inconsistency of voice, all illustrate the field's current reliance on human recruiter input rather than technology-driven certainty. This reliance on intuition empowers recruiters to make context judgments and decisions, but at the same time exposes them to the risk of implicit bias or error.

COMPARING HOSPITALITY WITH OTHER SERVICE INDUSTRIES

While recruiters across all service-oriented industries increasingly encounter generative AI-assisted applications, the hospitality sector presents unique challenges that distinguish it from other service fields such as airlines, luxury retail, and healthcare, even in the early-career hiring for university graduates. For example, airlines often prioritize technical certifications, minimum age and education requirements and compliance, which are easier to quantify and verify, making AI-polished documents less likely to pose a problem for the recruiters as long as the information is authentic and real (Brannigan et al., 2019). In the example of the healthcare industry, the recruitment process prioritizes licensure, clinical experience, and regulatory credentials that are straightforward for both humans and algorithms to assess (Barriball et al., 2015). On the other hand, for the luxury retail sector that also values storytelling and brand alignment such as the hospitality industry, recruiters and hiring decision makers also include in the recruitment process an in-person or boutique-level assessments that reveals the human face behind the candidate profile from the CV preserve the human element (Nickson et al., 2017).

While there are differences in the competencies and requirements searched by recruiters in their candidates across different sectors, industries such as airlines, healthcare and luxury retail, their customer-facing roles share the core requirement of a genuine customer-centric mindset. As a result, the recruiters across all these sectors face the common significant challenge like their colleagues in the hospitality field: how to reliably identify authentic interpersonal skills, empathy, and service orientation, whether hiring for entry-level positions or senior managerial roles.

EMPLOYER PERSPECTIVES: FINDINGS FROM LES ROCHES CAREER DAY 2025 SURVEY

To complement the existing literature and research with empirical evidence, an original survey was conducted during the Les Roches Career Day in March 2025, an annual recruitment event that gathers leading hospitality brands and current students of the Les Roches Crans Montana campus. A self-administered questionnaire was distributed to 60 recruiters representing luxury hotels, boutique properties, resort operators, food & beverage groups, cruise lines, and hospitality-technology firms, with an 83% response rate. Respondents were primarily human resources directors and talent-acquisition managers with operations across Europe, the Middle East, Asia, and the Americas.

The survey explored the perception of recruiters on AI-generated application materials, their ability to detect AI in applications, and the implications for authenticity, fairness, and selection outcomes.

How often do Students use AI and do Employers use ATS to track it?

The findings in Figure 1 reflect both curiosity and concern regarding AI-assisted writing in early-career recruitment. 82% of recruiters indicated they "frequently" or "occasionally" encountered cover letters or CVs that appeared AI-generated, a pattern consistent with recent international research showing that between 40% and 60% of job seekers under 30 now experiment with generative tools for professional writing (Grieve, 2024).

Figure 1. Perceived increase in the use of AI-generated CVs and cover letters among candidates

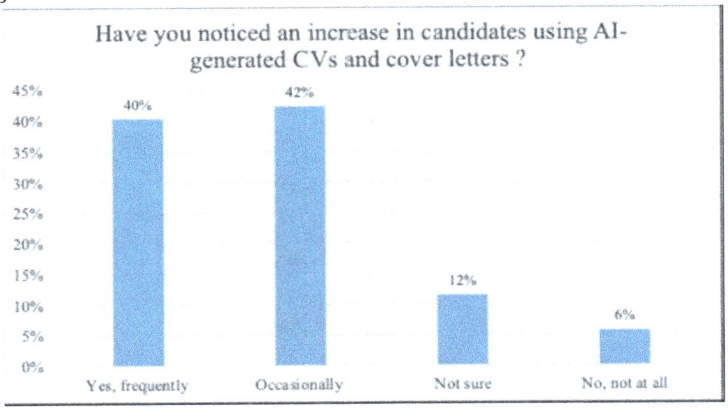

However, even though 82% of recruiters noticed frequently of occasionally the use of AI in applications, Figure 2 shows that only 12% of surveyed employers reported using any form of AI detection or Application Tracking System (ATS) capable of identifying algorithmic text. The majority of 88% still rely on human judgment, looking for linguistic cues such as overly formal phrasing or lack of personal details. Most hospitality firms, unlike large corporations, have limited technological infrastructure for automated screening (Kumawat et al., 2025). This reliance on intuition reinforces the findings of Harris-Watson et al. (2023), who note that human recruiters continue to play the decisive role in evaluating affective fit and personal warmth, qualities difficult to quantify algorithmically.

Figure 2. Use of AI detector systems or Applicant Tracking Systems for CVs and cover letters

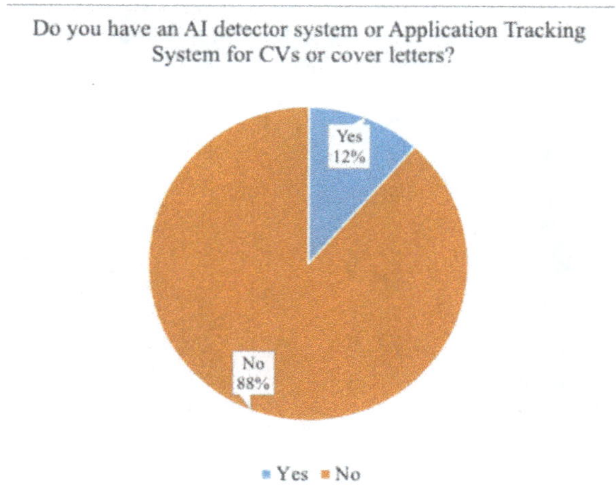

Rejection Behaviour and Authenticity Concerns

Figure 3 shows that 31% of respondents admitted to rejecting or downgrading candidates whose applications appeared to be AI-generated. However, most of the recruiters noted that rejection was not automatic with 69% of them mentioning that this does not impact their selection process. This occurred primarily when there was a marked discrepancy between written and spoken communication, such as identifying a faultless, fluent English level in cover letters mixed with a weaker oral fluency during interviews, a mismatch that triggers doubt about authenticity and skills.

Yet perceptions of authenticity remain divided. In the Les Roches survey, 54% of respondents said that AI use made applications feel "less personal," while 38% considered it acceptable provided that the content was accurate and relevant. These findings reinforce earlier research on authenticity in hospitality communication, which emphasises a focus on recruitment in identifying warmth, empathy, and the perceived sincerity of self-expression as defining professional traits from candidates (Weiss et al., 2022).

Figure 3. Rejection of candidates due to CVs or cover letters appearing AI-generated

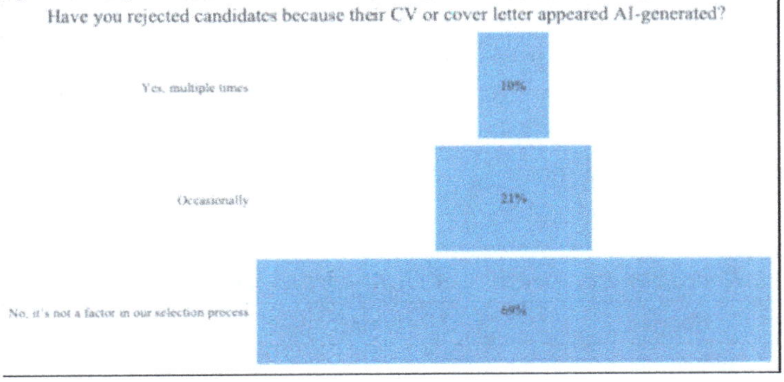

Disclosure and Acceptable Use Policies

Transparency emerged as a contentious but widely discussed theme. 56% of respondents believed that applicants should disclose AI use when preparing their CVs or cover letters, regarding openness as a sign of integrity. Others saw disclosure as not required if the factual information provided in the resume or cover letter was consistent with the candidate's professional profile.

When asked which AI tools were acceptable for candidates to use, recruiters most commonly cited Grammarly, ChatGPT, and Microsoft Word editor. These were viewed by recruiters as approved aids for proofreading and clarity of content rather than for generating entire narratives and texts. The distinction reflects the ethical boundary proposed in recent higher-education literature that mentions the use of AI for linguistic support is acceptable, but delegating the ownership and authorship rights by generating completely new texts crosses into misrepresentation (Aljabr & Al-Ahdal, 2024).

Recruiter Consensus on Key AI Concerns

The survey offers significant information also on what recruiters are most worried about when receiving an AI written application. Table 1 shows that most recruiters present at the Les Roches Career Day event, 71.2%, believe that using AI too much could damage candidates' writing and communication skills, which are crucial for service-oriented jobs. The second biggest worry is that all applications start to sound the same. More than half, 57.7% of recruiters see a serious lack of originality, making it very hard for them to identify the true person behind the application. Trust was also mentioned as a major issue, with almost half (48.1%) of the recruiters not fully trusting that the information in AI-written applications that they receive is always true or accurate. Importantly, only a small group of recruiters, 32.7%, see AI as just a helpful tool with no downsides. This shows that most recruiters are cautious about the information received and that their main worries are not about the use of AI technology itself, but about how it might harm the real human skills and originality they value most.

Table 1. The Recruiter Perspective: A Data-Driven Hierarchy of AI Concerns

Concern	Strongly Agree	Agree	Total % Agreeing
Loss of Personal Writing Skills	32.7%	38.5%	**71.2%**
Lack of Originality	23.1%	34.6%	**57.7%**
Risk of Inaccurate Information	13.5%	34.6%	**48.1%**
AI as a Positive Tool (No Concerns)	3.8%	28.8%	**32.7%**

Differences Between Industries

Luxury and lifestyle hotel brands, where brand storytelling and personal warmth of employees are key differentiators in their businesses, were the most critical of the candidate applications written by AI. On the other hand, recruiters from corporate offices and tech companies related to hospitality, were more pragmatic, as they value efficiency and coherence over a certain stylistic individuality. Recruiters involved in large hotels and resorts that have high numbers of employees were mostly indifferent. In this case, their focus lies more on the availability of candidates and the reliability of completing their tasks.

Finally, when asked how AI-generated content affected their selection process, most recruiters said that suspicion of AI use will make them read the applications received more careful and at the same time more critical, but not necessarily in a negative way.

Overall, these results illustrate that hospitality recruiters embrace the technological change and the new challenges that come with AI supported applications with caution but openness. Recruiters admit and understand that AI can enhance writing skills and proofread texts, but they remain concerned about its impact on genuineness and trust in the information that they read in the applications. The data suggest that recruiters prefer transparency, balanced use, and contextual judgment rather than a complete interdiction on AI use. This highlights that the hospitality recruiters are in need for clearer policies and shared ethical frameworks in their profession.

LEGAL AND PRACTICAL IMPLICATIONS

The use of AI in recruitment raises concerns that reach beyond the individual applications and hiring process by integrating broader areas such as regulatory frameworks, professional ethics, and day-to-day human resources practice.

Legal and Regulatory Landscapes: A Global Patchwork

The legal landscape for AI in hiring is complex and fragmented, requiring international hospitality employers to navigate differing rules depending on the country where they are based or the local legislation they follow. From a global perspective, the most comprehensive regulation is the European Union's Artificial Intelligence Act. Approved in 2024, it classifies AI systems used in recruitment as high-risk, mandating strict transparency, human oversight, and data governance. A core principle is that individuals must be informed when an AI system is used to evaluate them (Artificial Intelligence Act, 2024). In contrast, regulation in the United States is emerging at the individual state level (ex. laws in Illinois, Maryland, New York City), creating a patchwork of rules around notice, consent, and bias audits for automated employment decision tools. In regions like the Middle East and Asia, approaches vary. Tech-forward hubs like the UAE and Singapore actively promote AI adoption, potentially normalising its use in hiring faster, while other jurisdictions may emphasize different aspects like data privacy (ex. China's PIPL). At a national level, countries like Switzerland impose specific constraints through laws like the revised Federal Act on Data Protection, which restricts sending personal documents to external servers. This represents a direct concern for any hotel group using cloud-based Application Tracking Systems (ATS) or AI detectors (New Federal Act on Data Protection, 2023). This global inconsistency means a single multinational hotel chain must comply with multiple, sometimes conflicting, regulatory regimes.

Practical Realities: The Policy Gap

On the practical level, the findings of the survey done in Les Roches during the Career Day show that most hospitality recruiters currently operate without formal internal guidance on the use of AI by applicants, and they do not use ATS systems. A handful of multinational hotel chains have begun to experiment with voluntary disclosure statements, brief checkboxes on application portals asking whether generative AI was used to draft any part of the submission, but uptake has been limited, and policies remain inconsistent across markets.

Some organisations have made trials with different AI detection software to identify suspiciously text written by AI, however human resources professionals continue to doubt on the reliability of such tools and their potential vulnerability to legal challenges. In this case, for the majority of recruiters, making a decision about applications written by AI around remains at the discretion of the recruiter, dependent on their individual judgment rather than following an individual policy and a standardised process.

The absence of clear rules risks producing inequitable outcomes for different candidates. For example, two candidates who did their entire cover letters using AI may be judged very differently because of the personal perception of the recruiter. As generative tools continue to improve and be increasingly used, employers in the hospitality industry will need to create more explicit decision-making processes. This could mean to encourage the transparent disclosure of artificial intelligence use in addition to investing in technologies that could assist them in the process. In addition, this disruption could lead to a shift from the emphasis on written a perfectly written application, towards having live assessments to that help discover the individual competences of the candidates.

BEST PRACTICES: RECOMMENDATIONS FOR APPLICANTS AND EMPLOYERS

Although the main focus of this chapter is the voice of recruiters, the existing literature and the survey done at Les Roches Career Day suggest that constructive steps can be taken by both sides of the hiring equation in order to navigate the AI transition and ensure fairness, transparency, and originality. The following recommendations could offer a frame for both applicants and employers to strengthen ethical hiring culture across the hospitality industry.

Recommendations for Applicants: Preserving Authenticity and Professional Integrity

Use AI as a Linguistic Aid, Not A Ghostwriter

Present studies agree that using AI to refine grammar, structure, or vocabulary can enhance clarity and confidence. However, over trusting and relying on generative tools risks removing the personal voice of the applicant that the hospitality companies are looking for. Recruiters who took part in the Les Roches survey consistently mentioned that what differentiates strong applications is the inclusion of specific, real lived experiences, such as examples of guest interactions, teamwork moments with colleagues, or problem-solving situations under pressure in a work or education environment. For this reason, applicants should treat AI more as an editorial assistant rather than an author who created a completely new text. This will ensure that each sentence reflects a genuine experience that they can elaborate on during interviews.

Reintroduce The Human Element Through Storytelling

Hospitality recruiters who are hiring for different roles often value that narrative originality. More precisely, the ability to easily communicate empathy, service passion, and cross-cultural awareness in a hospitality environment where guest satisfaction is the highest priority. To maintain these qualities in different AI-supported texts, candidates could insert brief personal anecdotes or micro-narratives that demonstrate how they embodied different brand values of the company where they are applying or showcase examples of guest care from their past experience. These concrete examples distinguish human-authored submissions from overly broad, machine-written statements ("I am passionate about excellent guest service") that recruiters frequently cite as red flags (Cui et al., 2025).

Check For Consistency of Voice Across Modes of Communication

One of the points that early career job applicants should be aware of is that the recruiters surveyed in the Les Roches Career Data highlighted the inconsistencies between the articulate written tone of applications and candidates' spoken English during interviews. To avoid this "two voices" problem (Jakesch et al., 2023), applicants should read their intention letters aloud or record short mock interviews using the same content to ensure that their written language matches their oral natural expression in English. This will help students reinforce originality and prepare them for face-to-face or online interview discussions.

Disclose AI Use Where Institutional or Employer Policy Requests It

Transparency builds trust. More and more universities and employers advise students to acknowledge and admit AI assistance when it plays a substantial role in writing professional materials (Wright & Sapkota, 2024). As a result, disclosing and being honest about the use of AI does not penalise candidates involved in a recruitment process. Instead, this practice signals integrity and proves in real time professional ethics. In both academic and recruitment environments, disclosure protects students and applicants from suspicion of plagiarism or misuse of the text.

Prioritize Content Over Linguistic Perfection

Many early-career applicants mistakenly believe that having perfect grammatical flawlessness in a written application equals professionalism. However, hospitality recruiters emphasise that emotional warmth and story telling credibility as stronger predictors of cultural fit inside an organisation (Schmitz-Wilhelmy & Truxillo, 2025). Minor linguistic and grammar imperfections can be forgiven if the application demonstrates genuine motivation and self-awareness. The best practice, therefore, is not to over-edit a text to make it sound and look perfect, but to actually make that personal voice be heard and easily identified by a recruiter.

Recommendations for Employers: Managing AI Fairly and Effectively

Publish Clear Policies on Acceptable AI Use

Hospitality employers and recruiters can easily reduce ambiguity by explicitly stating their expectations in the job postings, during campus presentations or on their own online recruitment portals. For example, a good practice is to specify whether the company permits AI-supported proofreading but discourages AI-generated writing. This can help applicants align more easily with the organisational values of the company on AI use and match expectations. Clear communication reduces perceived unfairness and ensures consistency across recruiters and applicants (OECD, 2021).

Treat AI-Detection Tools as Advisory, not as a Final Decision Maker

Automated AI detectors remain unreliable, with frequent false positives and biased results. Employers who use such tools should interpret their findings as signals for further human review rather than use them as conclusive evidence to reject a candidate. Recruiters' qualitative judgment remains indispensable, particularly in industries like hospitality where personal warmth and soft skills fit cannot be algorithmically scored (Harris-Watson et al., 2023).

Rebalance Selection Criteria Toward Interpersonal Assessment

As written materials become increasingly AI-enhanced, behavioural evaluation methods gain importance in the recruitment process. Structured interviews, role-play exercises, group assessments or situational-judgment questions can allow recruiters to observe the service orientation, empathy, and teamwork that they are looking for in a candidate profile. This shift emphasises the need for identifying observable behaviour over a stylistic polish of an intention letter, which could align the selection processes with the human-centred values of the hospitality sector.

Encourage Equity in Multilingual Recruitment

As discussed in this chapter, insisting on fully unassisted writing may disadvantage non-native English speakers. For these reasons, employers should acknowledge AI's potential as an accessibility tool and differentiate between linguistic assistance and a change in authorship through an AI-generated text. An inclusive approach could involve allowing grammar-support tools such as Grammarly, while discouraging generative rewriting that invents or fabricates experiences.

Promote Recruiter Training in AI Literacy and Bias Awareness

As AI use increases, recruiter education and continuous development become essential. Training could address how to identify AI text, interpret disclosures, and evaluate genuineness without penalising linguistic differences. Workshops co-organised with hospitality schools, Such as Les Roches, could also help recruiters understand the current generational perspectives on technology use to reduce the misunderstanding between employers and applicants.

Shared Responsibilities: Building a Transparent AI Culture

Both employers and applicants share the common responsibility for redefining genuineness in the age of AI. Three collaborative strategies emerge from recent studies and industry practice:

Implement Joint Disclosure Norms

Universities, employers and hospitality associations could adopt shared guidelines, similar to academic citation norms and the responsible use of AI, on how to acknowledge and use AI assistance in job applications and any written materials required for it. Such a practice would ensure transparency and remove the "elephant in the room" responsible for the AI use

Develop Shared AI Literacy Modules

Educational higher education institutions such as Les Roches could create and integrate short workshops or micro-credentials in "Responsible AI Communication" co-designed with global hotel chains. Such training would support students to use

AI ethically in their job applications and help recruiters interpret AI-influenced writing more fairly when encountered in early career applications.

Create And Encourage a Culture of Trust and Conversation

AI's presence in recruitment should not be treated as a race between applicants and recruiters to always identify new ways of using AI to trick the system or to identify those using it. This could rather be an open dialogue about tool usage that can reinforce mutual understanding and focus the evaluation of the candidate based on the qualities that truly matter, such as integrity, interpersonal skills, and commitment to guest experience.

Future-Oriented Implications for Recruitment Digitalisation

Looking ahead, the ongoing digitalisation of recruitment driven by generative AI and broader HR technologies, is likely to reshape how hospitality employers identify, assess, and engage talent, with important implications for both efficiency and human judgement. Research on AI's impact in hiring shows that generative AI is affecting nearly every stage of the recruitment funnel, from role definition and candidate sorting to selection outcomes, and has raised important questions about how organisational practices will adapt to these changes (Bersin, 2025). Within hospitality specifically, industry reports indicate that AI tools can dramatically accelerate search processes, reduce time-to-hire, and expand candidate pools by producing structured evaluation frameworks and richer benchmarking data that align talent with organisational values and strategic goals. As these technologies mature, recruiters are likely to shift away from manual screening toward more strategic, data-informed decision-making, using AI-generated insights to highlight candidate strengths while reserving human evaluation for areas where nuance matters most. Academic work on digital tools in recruitment further suggests that techniques such as gamified assessments, online interactive tasks, and asynchronous video interviews can improve the candidate experience, enhance cultural alignment, and provide additional behavioural signals beyond written text that are important in service-oriented roles (Kuppuswamy et al., 2025). However, as integration deepens, ethical and implementation challenges remain salient: AI systems must be governed to ensure fairness, transparency, and accountability, because bias, privacy concerns, and opaque decision criteria can undermine trust among both recruiters and applicants. For hospitality, where assessments of empathy, interpersonal skills, and brand fit have traditionally depended on human interaction, the future will likely involve hybrid models of recruitment that combine the efficiency and analytical power of AI with intentional, human-centred evaluation methods (Mandić et al., 2025). This means equipping HR professionals with AI literacy and ethical oversight capabilities, designing recruitment processes that balance algorithmic speed with interpretive depth, and adopting digital tools that complement rather than replace human interaction. As broader HR literature suggests, success in this new landscape will depend not just on technological adoption but on strategic integration that preserves the human values at the core of hospitality service, ultimately reinforcing rather than diluting recruiters' ability to identify genuinely authentic and capable talent.

Implications for Global Hospitality Higher Education

The increasing use of generative AI in early-career job applications has significant implications for global hospitality higher education institutions because of the significant curriculum focus on experiential learning, professional identity, and development on human-centred service values. As written job applications become increasingly written by AI, higher education institutions are required to move beyond traditional positions of either prohibiting or fully accepting the use of AI. Instead, they need to integrate AI literacy as a core skill required for the employability of their students. This involves teaching students how to use generative tools responsibly, by making them aware of the differences between linguistic support and authorship. In addition, being able to preserve the natural individual narrative credibility, and at the same time ensure consistency between written and oral communication. Embedding the development of such skills, helps align student practices with recruiter expectations for any future job or internship application.

At a practical level, hospitality universities can operationalise this shift through targeted workshops on responsible AI use in professional writing, mock Applicant Tracking System screenings that reveal how keyword optimisation and automation affect candidate visibility, and recruiter-led panels focused on real-world expectations around AI-assisted applications. Career Services departments can further reinforce these norms through AI disclosure guidelines, simulated interviews comparing written and spoken performance, and reflective exercises that prioritise storytelling and behavioural evidence over linguistic polish. By embedding these practices into career preparation modules, hospitality education institutions can position themselves as active shapers of ethical recruitment norms, ensuring their graduates remain credible, employable, and aligned with the relational values at the core of hospitality work.

CONCLUSION: RECLAIMING AUTHENTICITY IN A HYBRID FUTURE

Generative AI is reshaping early-career recruitment in hospitality by redefining what counts as authentic communication in an early-career job application. Yet, as the evidence from the Les Roches Career Day 2025 survey suggests, the decisive factor in hiring remains human, remains the recruiter. The recruiter's ability to read between the lines, passion, and relational warmth behind the words. Applicants who use AI transparently and enhance its efficiency with personal true stories will likely gain an advantage with their application rather than risk suspicion and be rejected. Likewise, employers who establish clear guidelines on AI use in job applications and invest in continuous training for the staff can preserve fairness while embracing innovation.

Ultimately, the future of hospitality recruitment will depend not on avoiding AI, but on humanising its use and learning how to work together. This can ensure that technology amplifies and improves hospitality job applications, rather than replacing the voices of those who create and ensure genuine guest care.

REFERENCES

Act, A. I. (EU) Regulation 2024/1689 of the European Parliament and of the Council of 13 June 2024 laying down harmonised rules on artificial intelligence (European Union, 2024). *Official Journal of the European Union*, L 168, 1–131. https://eur-lex.europa.eu/eli/reg/2024/1689/oj

Aljabr, F. S., & Al-Ahdal, A. A. M. H. (2024). Ethical and pedagogical implications of AI in language education: An empirical study at Ha'il University. *Acta Psychologica, 251*, 104605. DOI: 10.1016/j.actpsy.2024.104605 PMID: 39549599

Auer, M., Edlinger, G., & Mölk, A. (2021). How do Potential Applicants Make Sense of Employer Brands? *Schmalenbach Journal of Business Research, 73*(1), 47–73. DOI: 10.1007/s41471-021-00107-7

Bárány, A. (2023, June 23). From Humans to Machines: Can Artificial Intelligence Outsmart Human Job Applications? *Erasmus School of Economics*.

Barriball, L., Bremner, J., Buchan, J., Craveiro, I., Dieleman, M., Dix, O., Dussault, G., Jansen, C., Kroezen, M., Rafferty, A. M., & Sermeus, W. (2015). *Recruitment and retention of the health workforce in Europe* (Final Report). European Commission, Directorate-General for Health and Food Safety. https://health.ec.europa.eu/system/files/2016-11/2015_healthworkforce_recruitment_retention_frep_en_0.pdf

Bersin, J. (2024, December 21). *A tumultuous year behind: A challenging, important 2025*. Josh Bersin. https://joshbersin.com/2024/12/a-tumultuous-year-leads-to-a-new-challenging-exciting-2025/

Brannigan, C., Amaral, S., Thorpe, C., Levin, S., Figg, H., Neiva, R., Morgan-Price, S., Troncoso Ferrer, M., García Fernández, C., Moya Izquierdo, S., Castillo, L., Tallos, J., & Molina, C. (2019). *Study on employment and working conditions of aircrews in the EU internal aviation market* (Final Report). European Commission, Directorate-General for Mobility and Transport. https://www.eurocockpit.eu/sites/default/files/2019-04/Study%20on%20employment%20and%20working%20conditions%20of%20aircrew,%20EU%20Commission%202019.pdf

Bui, T. T. U., & Tong, T. V. A. (2025). The Impact of AI Writing Tools on Academic Integrity: Unveiling English-Majored Students' Perceptions and Practical Solutions. *AsiaCALL Online Journal, 16*(1), 83–110. DOI: 10.54855/acoj.251615

Caira, R. (2024, July 9). *CEO Omer Acar leads Raffles and Fairmont Hotels & Resorts into a new era of growth* [Interview]. https://www.hoteliermagazine.com/ceo-omer-acar-leads-raffles-and-fairmont-hotels-resorts-into-a-new-era-of-growth/

Collins, C. J., & Martinez-Moreno, J. E. (2022). Recruitment brand equity for unknown employers: Examining the effects of recruitment message claim verifiability and credibility on job pursuit intentions. *Human Resource Management, 61*(5), 585–597. DOI: 10.1002/hrm.22089

Cui, J., Dias, G., & Ye, J. (2025). *Signaling in the Age of AI: Evidence from Cover Letters* arXiv. https://doi.org//arXiv.2509.25054DOI: 10.48550

Delgado, E. (2023, October 30). *Interview with Emilia Delgado, head of the mandarin oriental hotel group's move ahead programme* [Interview]. https://www.journaldespalaces.com/en/article-68627-interview-with-emilia-delgado-head-of-the-move-ahead-programme.html

Dimanche, F., & Lo, K. (2022). The Elusive Search for Talent: Skill Gaps in the Canadian Luxury Hotel Sector. *Tourism and Hospitality, 3*(1), 31–46. DOI: 10.3390/tourhosp3010003

Fernandez-Mateo, I. (2025). How generative AI is transforming hiring in organizations: Key issues and research questions. *Journal of Organization Design*. DOI: 10.1007/s41469-025-00197-1

Floridi, L. (2011). *The philosophy of information*. Oxford University Press, DOI: 10.1093/acprof:oso/9780199232383.001.0001

Gillespie, N., Lockey, S., Curtis, C., Pool, J., & Ali Akbari. (2023). Trust in Artificial Intelligence: A global study. The University of Queensland; KPMG Australia. DOI: 10.14264/00d3c94

Goffman, E. (1959). *The presentation of self in everyday life*. Anchor Books.

Grieve, P. (2024, April 3). Over Half of Recently Hired Workers Used AI Like ChatGPT in Their Job Search. Money.Com. https://money.com/ai-tools-job-search/

Hamilton, D. (2024). How To Get Your Résumé Past Artificial Intelligence (AI) Screening. Forbes. https://www.forbes.com/sites/dianehamilton/2024/11/25/how-to-get-your-rsum-past-artificial-intelligence-ai-screening/?

Harris-Watson, A. M., Larson, L. E., Lauharatanahirun, N., DeChurch, L. A., & Contractor, N. S. (2023). Social perception in Human-AI teams: Warmth and competence predict receptivity to AI teammates. *Computers in Human Behavior, 145*, 107765. DOI: 10.1016/j.chb.2023.107765

Heimann, A. L., & Schmitz-Wilhelmy, A. (2025). Observing Interviewees' Inner Self: How Authenticity Cues in Job Interviews Relate to Interview and Job Performance. *Journal of Business and Psychology*, *40*(1), 237–256. DOI: 10.1007/s10869-024-09949-4

Hogan, B. (2010). The presentation of self in the age of social media: Distinguishing performances and exhibitions online. *Bulletin of Science, Technology & Society*, *30*(6), 377–386. DOI: 10.1177/0270467610385893

Introna, L. (2016). Algorithms, governance, and governmentality: On governing academic writing. *Science, Technology & Human Values*, *41*(1), 17–49. DOI: 10.1177/0162243915587360

Jakesch, M., Hancock, J. T., & Naaman, M. (2023). Human heuristics for AI-generated language are flawed. *Proceedings of the National Academy of Sciences of the United States of America*, *120*(11), e2208839120. DOI: 10.1073/pnas.2208839120 PMID: 36881628

Kilson, G. A. (2025). Optimizing Employee Attraction and Retention in Hospitality and Tourism: A Systematic Review of Employer Branding Research. *Administrative Sciences*, *15*(5), 153. DOI: 10.3390/admsci15050153

Kumawat, E., Datta, A., Prentice, C., & Leung, R. (2025). Artificial intelligence through the lens of hospitality employees: A systematic review. *International Journal of Hospitality Management*, *124*, 103986. DOI: 10.1016/j.ijhm.2024.103986

Kuppuswamy, D., Challapally, A., Sunanda, K., & Shravani, B., Shilpa, Roy P., & Dayini, V. (2025). Gamificationin recruitment a strategy for engaging millennial and gen z talent. *Academy of Marketing Studies Journal*, *29*(5), 1–10.

https://www.abacademies.org/articles/gamification-in-recruitment-a-strategy-for-engaging-millennial-and-gen-z-talent.pdf

Lee, K.-J., & Choi, S.-Y. (2022). Effects of Organizational Culture on Employer Attractiveness of Hotel Firms: Topic Modeling Approach. *Complexity*, *2022*(1), 4402673. DOI: 10.1155/2022/4402673

Lim, J. S., Shin, D., Lee, C., Kim, J., & Zhang, J. (2025). The Role of User Empowerment, AI Hallucination, and Privacy Concerns in Continued Use and Premium Subscription Intentions: An Extended Technology Acceptance Model for Generative AI. *Journal of Broadcasting & Electronic Media*, *69*(3), 183–199. DOI: 10.1080/08838151.2025.2487679

Lin, L., & Parker, K. (2025). U.S. Workers Are More Worried Than Hopeful About Future AI Use in the Workplace. Pew Research Center. https://www.pewresearch.org/wp-content/uploads/sites/20/2025/02/ST_2025.2.25_AI-Workers_REPORT.pdf

LinkedIn. (2024). The Future of Recruiting 2024. https://business.linkedin.com/content/dam/me/business/en-us/talent-solutions/resources/pdfs/future-of-recruiting-2024.pdf

Mandić, D., Ječmenica, D., & Stanišić, N. (2025). The future of HR in hospitality: Technology-driven HRM practices. The European Journal of Applied Economics, *22*(2), 11–26. DOI: 10.5937/EJAE22-56949

McDowell, E. E. (1987). Perceptions of the Ideal Cover Letter and Ideal Resume. *Journal of Technical Writing and Communication*, *17*(2), 179–191. DOI: 10.2190/BK23-74U3-333Q-0T86

Mekheimer, M. (2025). Generative AI-assisted feedback and EFL writing: A study on proficiency, revision frequency and writing quality. *Discover Education*, *4*(1), 170. DOI: 10.1007/s44217-025-00602-7

Morhart, F. M., Malär, L., Guèvremont, A., Girardin, F., & Grohmann, B. (2015). Brand authenticity: An integrative framework and measurement scale. *Journal of Consumer Psychology*, *25*(2), 200–218. DOI: 10.1016/j.jcps.2014.11.006

New Federal Act on Data Protection (nFADP) (Switzerland, 2023). https://www.kmu.admin.ch/kmu/en/home/facts-and-trends/digitization/data-protection/new-federal-act-on-data-protection-nfadp.html

Nickson, D., Price, R., Baxter-Reid, H., & Hurrell, S. A. (2017). Skill requirements in retail work: The case of high-end fashion retailing. *Work, Employment and Society*, *31*(4), 692–708. DOI: 10.1177/0950017016672791

O'Halloran, R. M., Agena, J., & Froehlich, H. (2018). E-recruitment: Does it assess a candidate's skills? *Journal of Hospitality & Tourism Cases*, *6*(3), 17–23.

OECD. (2021). AI and the Future of Skills, Volume 1: Capabilities and Assessments. OECD. DOI: 10.1787/5ee71f34-en

Paster, J. (2025). Potentials and Limitations of AI as an Academic Writing Assistant for Non-Native English Speakers: An Assessment Framework for ChatGPT-Generated Texts. City State Journal, 2(1), 43–55. retrieved from https://so16.tci-thaijo.org/index.php/CS_J/article/view/1066

Pinpoint. (2025). How Kempinski Hotels launched a new ATS in less than 30 days. https://www.pinpointhq.com/case-studies/kempinski-hotels/?utm_source=chatgpt.com

Preda, K. (2025, June 30). AI vs. Authenticity: A Recruiter's Guide to Spotting and Vetting Modern Resumes. https://www.vectortechnicalinc.com/blog/ai-vs-authenticity-a-recruiters-guide-to-spotting-and-vetting-modern-resumes/

Rosado-Pinto, F., & Loureiro, S. M. C. (2023). What an amazing experience! The role of authenticity and engagement in upscale hotels. *International Journal of Hospitality Management, 114*, 103573. DOI: 10.1016/j.ijhm.2023.103573

Samuk Carignani, Ş., & Burchi, S. (2022). Preparing for online interviews during Covid-19: The intricacies of technology and online human interaction. *SN Social Sciences, 2*(10), 210. DOI: 10.1007/s43545-022-00498-2 PMID: 36187204

Schlegel, R. J., Hicks, J. A., King, L. A., & Arndt, J. (2011). Feeling like you know who you are: Perceived true self-knowledge and meaning in life. *Personality and Social Psychology Bulletin, 37*(6), 745–756. DOI: 10.1177/0146167211400424 PMID: 21402753

Schmitz-Wilhelmy, A., & Truxillo, D. M. (2025). Reality or illusion: A qualitative study on interviewer job previews and applicant self-presentation. *International Journal of Selection and Assessment, 33*(1), e12495. DOI: 10.1111/ijsa.12495

Seasons, F. (2025). Four Seasons Careers. Careers. https://careers.fourseasons.com/us/en/employee-experience

Shibu, S. (2024, March 11). AI Is Changing How Businesses Recruit for Open Roles—And How Candidates Are Gaming the System. Entrepreneur. https://www.entrepreneur.com/business-news/ai-is-changing-how-companies-recruit-how-candidates-respond/470912

Suchman, L. (2007). *Human-machine reconfigurations: Plans and situated actions* (2nd ed.). Cambridge University Press. DOI: 10.1017/CBO9780511808418

The New York Times. (2025, June 23). Employers Are Buried in A.I.-Generated Résumés. The New York Times. https://www.nytimes.com/2025/06/21/business/dealbook/ai-job-applications.html

Tursunbayeva, A., Fernandez, V., Gallardo-Gallardo, E., & Moschera, L. (2025). Artificial intelligence and digital data in recruitment. Exploring business and engineering candidates' perceptions of organizational attractiveness. *European Management Journal, S0263237325000416*. Advance online publication. DOI: 10.1016/j.emj.2025.03.002

Von Doniken, T. (2024, October 9). UZH Students Embracing AI Tools. University of Zurich. https://www.news.uzh.ch/en/articles/news/2024/survey-ai-use-students.html

Vössing, M., Kühl, N., Lind, M., & Satzger, G. (2022). Designing transparency for effective human–AI collaboration. *Information Systems Frontiers*, *24*, 877–895. DOI: 10.1007/s10796-022-10284-3

Waung, M., McAuslan, P., DiMambro, J. M., & Mięgoć, N. (2017). Impression Management Use in Resumes and Cover Letters. *Journal of Business and Psychology*, *32*(6), 727–746. DOI: 10.1007/s10869-016-9470-9

Weiss, D., Liu, S. X., Mieczkowski, H., & Hancock, J. T. (2022). Effects of Using Artificial Intelligence on Interpersonal Perceptions of Job Applicants. *Cyberpsychology, Behavior, and Social Networking*, *25*(3), 163–168. DOI: 10.1089/cyber.2020.0863 PMID: 35021895

Wright, C., & Sapkota, K. (2024). Developing core communication skills in an AI-dominated world: Staying 'old school.'. *Journal of Research in Business Education*, *64*(1).

Yip, J. (2024, July 22). Hey job seekers — hiring managers are onto your ChatGPT-written applications. Business Insider. https://www.businessinsider.com/employers-can-tell-use-chatgpt-ai-job-application-cover-letter-2024-7?

KEY TERMS AND DEFINITIONS

AI Literacy (in Professional Contexts): The competency to understand, use, and critically evaluate artificial intelligence tools ethically and effectively within a specific field, such as knowing how to employ AI for editing without compromising personal authorship in a job application.

Applicant Tracking System (ATS): Software used by employers to automate the initial recruitment process by electronically collecting, sorting, and ranking job applications based on predefined keywords, skills, and qualifications.

Authenticity (in Hospitality Hiring): The perceived genuineness of a candidate's self-presentation, assessed by recruiters as the alignment between their written or spoken narrative, their underlying motivations, and the observable interpersonal skills required for guest-centric roles.

Generative Artificial Intelligence (Gen-AI): A category of artificial intelligence capable of creating new, coherent text, images, or code based on learned patterns from large datasets, fundamentally transforming how written content for job applications is produced.

Homogenization (of Applicant Voice): The effect whereby widespread use of similar AI writing tools leads to job applications that sound uniform and generic, eroding the individual voice and personal nuance that hospitality recruiters value.

Promise-Performance Gap: The risk that an AI-enhanced application creates expectations of specific interpersonal abilities or technical competencies that a candidate cannot demonstrate in practice, potentially leading to poor job fit and early turnover.

Relational Model of Authenticity: A conceptual framework proposing that in AI-mediated recruitment, authenticity is not a fixed trait but an emergent quality negotiated through the interactions between the candidate, the AI tool, and the interpreting recruiter.

APPENDIX

Recruiter Survey on AI-Assisted Applications: Les Roches Career Day 2025

Methodology and Sample Profile

A self-administered questionnaire was distributed in person to recruiters attending the Les Roches Crans-Montana Career Day in March 2025. The survey received 52 complete responses from HR professionals (response rate ~87% based on 60 questionnaires distributed). Respondents represented leading global hospitality brands across key segments: Hotels & Resorts (73%), Restaurants (13%), Events/Travel (8%), and other related sectors (6%). Geographically, the majority operated in Europe (77%), with significant representation from the Middle East (10%), Asia (8%), and worldwide operations (6%). Over 85% of respondents hired for luxury (5-star) or upper-upscale (4-star) properties. The survey aimed to capture empirical, real-time insights into recruiters' perceptions, detection practices, and primary concerns regarding AI-generated job applications.

The Survey Instrument

Respondents answered the following key questions (presented here in abbreviated form):

1. Company Name: (Open-ended)
2. Industry Segment: (Multiple choice)
3. Company Location: (Open-ended)
4. Hotel/Resort Star Rating (if applicable): (Multiple selection)
5. Are you hiring for: (Multiple selection: Internships, Management Trainee/Graduate Programs, Full-time jobs)
6. Do you specifically assess if a CV or cover letter has been generated using AI? (Single choice: Yes, all the time / Yes, we try / No, we don't check)
7. Do you have an AI detector system or Application Tracking System for CV or Cover Letters? (Single choice: Yes / No)
8. If yes, what is the name of it? (Open-ended)
9. Have you noticed an increase in candidates using AI-generated cover letters and CVs? (Single choice: Yes, frequently / Occasionally / Not sure / No, not at all)

10. Does the use of AI-generated applications affect your perception of a candidate's authenticity? (Single choice: Yes, it makes their application feel less personal / No, as long as the content is relevant and well-written / Not sure)
11. Have you rejected candidates because their CV or cover letter appeared AI-generated? (Single choice: Yes, multiple times / Occasionally / No, it's not a factor in our selection process)
12. What is your biggest concern with AI-generated CVs and cover letters? (Select all that apply)
    - o Lack of originality/personalization
    - o Potential inaccuracies or misleading information
    - o Loss of personal writing skills in candidates
    - o No concerns. AI is a useful tool
13. Would you prefer candidates to disclose if they used AI to create their CV or cover letter? (Single choice: Yes, transparency is important / No, as long as the application is strong / Both)
14. Are there specific AI tools you believe are acceptable for candidates to use? (Single choice with specified options: Yes, grammar-checking & formatting tools (e.g., Grammarly, Canva) / Yes, AI-assisted writing tools (e.g., ChatGPT, Deep Seek) / No, we prefer applications written entirely by the candidate / Other)
15. How does AI-generated content impact your selection process? (Single choice with specified options: It makes it harder to differentiate candidates / It has no significant impact / It improves application quality, making screening easier / Other)

Summary of Key Quantitative Findings (Tables)

Table 2. Core Survey Metrics (N=52)

Metric	Response	Count	Percentage
Perceive Frequent/Occasional AI Use by Candidates	"Yes, frequently" or "Occasionally"	43	**82.7%**
Actively Try to Identify AI-Generated Content	"Yes, all the time" or "Yes, we try"	14	**26.9%**
Use a Dedicated ATS or AI Detection System	"Yes"	6	**11.5%**
Believe AI Makes Applications Feel "Less Personal"	"Yes, it makes their application feel less personal"	19	**36.5%**

continued on following page

Table 2. Continued

Metric	Response	Count	Percentage
Have Rejected/Downgraded a Candidate for Apparent AI Use	"Yes, multiple times" or "Occasionally"	16	**30.8%**
Prefer Candidates Disclose AI Use	"Yes, transparency is important"	22	**42.3%**

*Note: Percentages are based on the total number of respondents (52). Some questions allowed multiple selections or had a few non-responses, explaining variations in base counts for specific concerns below.

Table 3. Hierarchy of Recruiter Concerns (Level of Agreement)

Concern	Strongly Agree	Agree	Neutral	Disagree	Strongly Disagree	Total N	% Agreeing
Loss of personal writing skills	17	20	5	3	0	45	**71.2%**
Lack of originality/ personalization	12	18	10	7	1	48	**57.7%**
Potential inaccuracies	7	18	9	9	2	45	**48.1%**
No concerns. AI is a useful tool	2	15	25	5	2	49	**32.7%**

Note: The "Total N" for each row reflects the number of recruiters who selected a level of agreement for that specific concern. The "% Agreeing" column combines "Strongly Agree" and "Agree" responses.

Chapter 6

Qualitative Research Using ChatGPT: A Step-by-Step Thematic Analysis of Interview Responses in Hospitality Education

José Luis Ximénez de Sandoval
http://orcid.org/0000-0001-9021-355X
Les Roches Global Hospitality Education, Marbella, Spain

ABSTRACT

This chapter examines the potential of AI as a qualitative research assistant in hospitality and tourism education. Using Braun and Clarke's (2006) six-phase Thematic Analysis as a framework, the study shows how ChatGPT can support key stages of qualitative research, including transcription, coding, and theme development, under researcher supervision. The findings indicate that ChatGPT can improve efficiency, transparency, and accessibility, reducing the manual workload associated with qualitative analysis. However, its use also presents ethical and epistemological challenges that require careful validation and critical reflection. The chapter concludes that AI should not replace the qualitative researcher, but rather function as an intelligent collaborator supporting interpretive work. From a practical perspective, the study provides guidance for hospitality educators and academic institutions on the responsible integration of generative AI into research training and curriculum design, fostering innovation while preserving critical thinking and human judgment.

DOI: 10.4018/979-8-3373-5112-4.ch006

INTRODUCTION

In recent years, artificial intelligence (AI) has begun to profoundly transform research practices in the social sciences and, in particular, in the fields of tourism and hospitality management. One of the most influential and simultaneously demanding tasks in qualitative research is *Thematic Analysis*, a systematic method for identifying, organizing, and interpreting patterns of meaning (themes) within a set of textual data (Braun & Clarke, 2006).

Traditionally, this technique has relied on Computer-Assisted Qualitative Data Analysis Software (CAQDAS) such as *ATLAS.ti*, *NVivo*, or *MAXQDA*. These programs allow researchers to manage large volumes of qualitative data, label text segments, and construct thematic maps in a rigorous and transparent manner.

However, the recent emergence of generative language models such as *ChatGPT* introduces a new possibility in this domain: the partial or even complete automation of the stages of thematic analysis, from initial coding to the generation and interpretation of themes. Unlike CAQDAS programs, ChatGPT does not require a predefined coding framework; rather, it can generate codes and themes inductively from the text itself.

This capability raises important methodological questions: *Can an AI-based tool produce a thematic analysis with a level of quality and coherence comparable to that achieved by a human researcher using specialized software such as ATLAS.ti?*

The purpose of this study is to demonstrate that ChatGPT can conduct a complete and systematic qualitative research process, fulfilling the analytical needs of a qualitative researcher. The study also aims to contribute to the emerging debate regarding the role of AI in social research and to provide an empirical perspective on its responsible and ethical use in qualitative data analysis.

The first objective of this chapter is to encourage educators and researchers to approach AI confidently but critically, adopting it as a means of conducting qualitative research responsibly and ethically. If artificial intelligence (AI) is acknowledged as a tool that supports educators, its potential role as an aid to researchers should be equally recognized.

The second objective is to demonstrate that ChatGPT can perform rigorous and meaningful research work, serving, always under the researcher's supervision, as a capable assistant, collaborator, or co-analyst, but never as a replacement for human interpretation.

Quantitative researchers have long delegated complex mathematical computations and statistical analyses to computer programs—from *Excel* to *SPSS*—and have focused their efforts on research design, data collection, and interpretation. Many scholars, however, have been reluctant to engage in qualitative methodologies due to the substantial amount of manual work involved, even when using software such as *ATLAS.ti*. With the support of AI, this study proposes to automate much of the qualitative researcher's work, in a similar manner to how quantitative researchers rely on quantitative analysis software.

A further aim of this work is to familiarize undergraduate and graduate students with qualitative research, particularly those accustomed to highly quantitative approaches. By incorporating ChatGPT as a qualitative analysis tool, students can engage with this methodology, which remains less common in university curricula compared with quantitative data analysis.

Without the need for complex manual procedures or costly software, ChatGPT offers accessible guidance and assistance throughout the process of conducting qualitative analysis. The idea that qualitative research can now be automated, much like quantitative analysis, may seem revolutionary, but current developments suggest that this moment has arrived. Thanks to AI, qualitative analysis can become as efficient and structured as quantitative analysis, allowing researchers to focus, as their quantitative counterparts do, on designing research projects, collecting data, and interpreting results.

LITERATURE REVIEW

ChatGPT was launched in November 2022, and since its release, it has attracted enormous attention due to the wide range of applications it has found in the academic field (Xames & Shefa, 2023).

In simple terms, ChatGPT is a generative language model trained to produce human-like text based on user instructions, or *prompts*. This technology is already having a disruptive impact on the tourism industry, contributing to its reinvention and transformation (Buhalis et al., 2019).

Given the rapid pace at which these changes are occurring, authors such as Bulchand-Gidumal et al., (2024) question how far these transformations will reach within organizations. These authors also point out that, with a few exceptions (Saydam et al., 2022;), there are still few studies explaining how AI can affect specific sectors or types of businesses.

From an educational perspective, AI is increasingly reshaping expectations placed on hospitality graduates. El Hajal and Rowson (2020) and El Hajal (2025) argue that automation and digitalization are transforming traditional hospitality roles, creating growing demand for future-oriented skills that extend beyond operational competence. These include adaptability, emotional intelligence, resilience, and lifelong learning capabilities.

Hospitality education, however, often remains rooted in vocational and operational training models, with limited integration of digital literacy and critical engagement with emerging technologies (Ngoepe & Wakelin-Theron, 2023). This gap reinforces the need to reconsider not only *what* is taught, but *how* research and analytical skills are developed within hospitality programmes.

Evidence from exploratory qualitative work on AI applications in hospitality, especially Virtual Reality/Augmented Reality, also emphasizes transformative potential for training, marketing, and service innovation, while noting that diffusion is constrained by practical barriers such as acceptance, implementation complexity, and cost. Salama (2024) points to the need for organizational investment in workforce training and a culture supportive of experimentation to overcome adoption barriers.

Recent hospitality-focused reviews frame AI adoption as both strategic and operational, highlighting applications that improve customer service, expand operational capabilities, and reduce costs, while also warning about workforce implications and risks related to safety, security, and privacy (Limna, 2023).

Within academia more broadly, teachers, researchers, and students have already incorporated tools such as ChatGPT into both academic and non-academic tasks (Rahman et al., 2023). Empirical and conceptual studies suggest that ChatGPT can support idea generation, drafting academic texts, summarizing literature, and assisting with preliminary analytical processes (Xames & Shefa, 2023). These contributions may significantly enhance research efficiency by reducing time spent on repetitive language-related tasks, thereby allowing scholars to focus on conceptual development and interpretation (Dwivedi et al., 2023).

From a research-use perspective, Zhu et al. (2023) argue that ChatGPT can support academic work through writing improvement, translation, and summarization of lengthy material, and they describe prompt-based strategies (e.g., few-shot prompting) to shape outputs for specific audiences and formats. At the same time, they caution that errors can occur even for simple questions and that researchers should avoid over-reliance; importantly, they also note that publishers do not recognize AI tools as authors and require disclosure when such tools are used for text or image generation.

Xames and Shefa (2023) also acknowledge both the opportunities and challenges associated with the use of ChatGPT in scientific research. They argue that researchers, editors, and reviewers can effectively leverage ChatGPT to make the research and publication process more efficient.

ChatGPT gave access to AI and Machine Learning to the general public by answering unstructured questions in natural language text (Dwivedi et al 2023). In this paper, in which more than 70 prestigious authors collaborate, the advantages and disadvantages of using ChatGPT in research are presented. For example, several authors have highlighted its capacity to improve research efficiency by automating language-related tasks such as drafting abstracts, summarizing large amounts of information, and generating preliminary reports or conference papers. These functionalities allow researchers to focus more on creative and analytical work rather than repetitive textual production.

Moreover, ChatGPT contributes to the *democratization of knowledge*, making scientific findings more accessible to the general public by transforming complex research concepts into clear, reader-friendly narratives. Another advantage stated in this paper is its collaborative potential. ChatGPT facilitates interdisciplinary dialogue and co-creation, helping researchers from different domains to exchange ideas and accelerate innovation. Some scholars also emphasize the possibility of *human–AI complementarity*, suggesting that the best results may emerge when AI-generated content is critically reviewed and refined by human expertise rather than used as a stand-alone product.

Regarding the limitations or disadvantages of ChatGPT this paper underscores several important limitations and ethical concerns. The most recurrent critique involves the *accuracy and reliability* of AI-generated content. ChatGPT's outputs, while often coherent and stylistically polished, may contain factual inaccuracies, fabricated references, or incomplete citations. This "illusion of authority" can mislead researchers and readers alike, producing texts that sound convincing but are logically incorrect or unsupported by real data. Consequently, scholars warn that uncritical use of ChatGPT could distort scientific facts, promote plagiarism, or spread misinformation within academia (Dwivedi et al 2023).

Ethical issues surrounding authorship and accountability are equally pressing. Since ChatGPT cannot assume responsibility for its outputs, most journal editors agree that AI systems do not meet the criteria for authorship. Their use raises questions about transparency, intellectual ownership, and the integrity of academic publishing (Dwivedi et al 2023). Furthermore, researchers have drawn attention to the potential *bias reinforcement* within AI models, as these systems learn from data that reflect existing social and institutional inequalities. Consequently, AI-generated texts may unintentionally perpetuate biased or exclusionary narratives (Dwivedi et al 2023).

Despite these limitations, scholars increasingly advocate for a model of human–AI complementarity rather than replacement. ChatGPT may function effectively as a cognitive and methodological assistant when its outputs are continuously reviewed, interpreted, and validated by the human researcher. This perspective aligns with broader debates in hospitality education, which emphasize the irreplaceable value of human judgment, empathy, and critical thinking in technologically mediated environments (El Hajal, 2025).

METHODOLOGY

From a methodological standpoint, thematic analysis has been widely recognized as a flexible and accessible qualitative method, particularly suitable for learning and teaching contexts (Maguire & Delahunt, 2017).

Braun and Clarke's (2006) six-phase framework provides a clear and systematic structure for identifying patterns of meaning within qualitative data, while allowing interpretive depth beyond mere description. Importantly, thematic analysis is a method rather than a methodology, meaning it can be applied across diverse epistemological positions, making it especially appropriate for exploratory research and pedagogical applications.

This work forms part of a broader research project that analyzes 50 semi-structured interviews across four groups representing the educational and professional ecosystem of tourism:

1. University professors of tourism and hotel management
2. University students in tourism and hospitality
3. Tourism industry professionals
4. Customers/guests

Participants were selected through purposive sampling, seeking diversity in age, professional experience, and level of exposure to artificial intelligence.

The interviews were conducted in October 2025, in person, by telephone, and online.

In these pages, our aim is not to present the results of our research, but rather to explain the complete process of developing a qualitative research project using ChatGPT.

To this end, a random sample of six interviews was selected from the full set conducted, and real data were used to illustrate the process step by step.

The study is therefore situated within qualitative research, specifically employing an inductive thematic analysis in which codes and themes emerge during the analysis of the texts. The six-step framework proposed by Braun and Clarke (2006) is adopted as the seminal approach to Thematic Analysis. The methodological novelty lies in the use of ChatGPT, rather than ATLAS.ti or similar software, as the tool for conducting the thematic analysis.

Semi-structured interviews constitute the backbone of many qualitative studies in the social sciences (Campbell et al., 2013). Once the interview transcripts are prepared, the coding process is initiated. When assigning codes to data, the researcher must examine each sentence and paragraph and make a judgment about its meaning. Simply reading the text as if it were a book risks overlooking relevant data (Skjott-

Linneberg & Korsgaard, 2019). The coding process may be conducted using either a deductive or an inductive approach; in this case, an inductive model is adopted. The objectives of an inductive approach in qualitative analysis are:

1. to condense large amounts of textual data,
2. to link the research objective with the findings derived from the data, and
3. to develop a model or theory based on the analyzed texts (Thomas, 2003).

Many studies in the social sciences use coding processes based on the transcription of in-depth semi-structured interviews (Campbell et al., 2013). For these authors, a key concern in qualitative research is the reliability of the coding process when a single researcher performs the task. This problem is common among researchers with limited budgets who cannot form a research team and—due to resource constraints—work as the sole investigator.

In this study, a 10-item questionnaire was designed and administered to all interviewees—professors, students, and professionals—inviting participants to provide brief and concise responses. As noted by Campbell et al. (2013), this format often yields a single code per response, thereby facilitating the coding process. This type of question design also aims to ensure the discriminant capacity of the code set, that is, to minimize ambiguity in the categorization of textual data (Fahy, 2001).

Because this chapter uses Braun and Clarke's (2006) framework as a procedural backbone, it is useful to link it to applied guidance that clarifies how to conduct a rigorous thematic analysis. Maguire and Delahunt (2017) provide a practical, step-by-step guide explicitly grounded in Braun and Clarke's six phases and emphasize that thematic analysis goes beyond summarization: it involves identifying meaningful patterns across the dataset and developing an interpretive account, rather than simply organizing responses by interview questions.

To support students and researchers interested in AI-assisted qualitative inquiry, this chapter also explains the full process step by step, from transcribing interviews to producing the final report. The key distinction is that ChatGPT is used to support the completion of Braun and Clarke's six phases under the researcher's supervision.

RESULTS

As indicated above, the methodology proposed by Braun and Clarke (2006) is followed on a phase-by-phase basis.

Phase 1: Familiarization with the data

The first phase, "Familiarization with the data," involves reading the data carefully and developing a thorough understanding of it. This is, of course, the researcher's task and requires dedicating time to read each interview. ChatGPT can assist the researcher in this phase by transcribing the interviews. Moreover, to facilitate the subsequent coding process, it is advisable to instruct ChatGPT to transcribe the interview with each sentence on a separate line. In this way, both the coding performed by ChatGPT and the subsequent review process are streamlined.

For the interviews, a template with 10 questions was prepared in advance. All groups answered the same 10 semi-open questions.

Table 1 shows the 10 questions answered by all interviewees, regardless of group:

Table 1. Questionnaire

Question 1:	What AI tools do you use?
Question 2:	What do you use AI for?
Question 3:	What advantages does using AI have for you?
Question 4:	To what extent do you trust AI?
Question 5:	Have you received AI training in the last two years?
Question 6:	Do you need AI training?
Question 7:	What prevents you from using AI more frequently or intensively?
Question 8:	What new things will you do with AI in two or three years?
Question 9:	What things will you stop doing because AI will do them for you in 2–3 years?
Question 10:	What dangers does AI have?
Additional comments:	

Although the questions were open-ended, they were designed so that responses would be brief and leave little room for misinterpretation. For this reason, it was not necessary to record the interviews; the researcher took notes of the typically short answers.

Subsequently, as a triangulation step, once the responses were transcribed they were sent back to the interviewees for checking and verification.

The transcription process was carried out using ChatGPT. The researcher read the questions and the interviewee's responses aloud. To perform this task, ChatGPT was instructed to transcribe the content so that each sentence appeared on a separate line, thereby facilitating the subsequent coding process.

PROMPT 1 (TRANSCRIPTION)

> *I am going to read a qualitative interview.*
> *Please transcribe exactly what I say, without summarizing or correcting anything.*
> *Put each sentence or meaning unit on a separate line, separated by a line break (Enter).*
> *Do not add numbers, dashes, or comments—just one line per sentence.*
> *The goal is to prepare the text for line-by-line open coding in a thematic analysis.*
> *Ready?*

Once the transcriptions were completed, they were copied into an Excel sheet (see Table 2).

Table 2. Transcription (excerpt)

Professor 1
Age: 40–50 years
Role: Professor
Date: 21/10/2025
Question 1: What AI tools do you use?
Answer 1: Paid ChatGPT and Copilot.
Question 2: What do you use AI for?
Answer 2: As a professor, for creating exercises and searching for content.
On a personal level, for translating texts and planning trips.
I've also used it to compare products, identify pros and cons, and it provided information that the seller hadn't given me.
Question 3: What advantages does using AI have for you?
Answer 3: It saves time and allows me to reach information that I can't find through traditional Google searches.
Question 4: To what extent do you trust AI?
Answer 4: About 75%.
I have detected some errors.
I once asked about an actor in a movie, and it told me that another actor appeared in it, which was false.
I usually go to the source myself. I always double-check what ChatGPT tells me.
Question 5: Have you received any AI training in the last two years?
Answer 5: Yes, the one provided by the university.
And also, by watching videos on my own on the Internet.

Now the researcher's task is to read the interviews carefully and become familiar with the information provided by the interviewees.

In this way, with the assistance of ChatGPT, all interviews were transcribed and subsequently transferred into an Excel file containing the corresponding transcripts.

Phase 2: Generating Initial Codes

Coding consists of summarizing the content of a sentence or a segment of text in one or several words. This task, which, even in sophisticated programs such as ATLAS.ti, must be carried out manually by the researcher, can be automated with a good prompt so that ChatGPT performs the coding process. In any case, it is the researcher who will validate and accept the codes proposed by ChatGPT or modify them according to their expertise and judgment.

As with any assistant, ChatGPT must be given very clear instructions about what it should do and how it should do it. The following prompt contains the instructions for coding an interview. We will repeat the process for each interview.

It is important to include the concept of temperature in the prompt. Temperature refers to the degree of freedom we allow ChatGPT when performing its task.

The "temperature" is a parameter that controls the model's level of randomness or creativity:

- Low temperature (0–0.2): more consistent, literal, and reproducible responses. *This setting is used in this study for qualitative research, coding, and textual analysis.*
- Medium temperature (≈0.5): more variation; useful when seeking new ideas or exploratory interpretations.
- High temperature (0.8–1.0): greater creativity and unpredictability, which introduces bias and inconsistency across runs.

In this study, the aim is to minimize the model's creativity and subjectivity.

For this reason, it is advisable to state the temperature explicitly in the protocol. Although ChatGPT (standard interface) does not allow this parameter to be set manually, it can be specified within the prompt as an instruction to guide the response style.

PROMPT for CODING

You are a qualitative researcher specializing in tourism and hospitality management. Apply a Thematic Analysis following the methodology of Braun and Clarke

(2006). Respond in an analytical and precise style, as if the model temperature were low (≈0.2), to ensure consistency and reproducibility.

I will provide you with an interview transcript. Analyze the text line by line and perform an initial open coding following these guidelines:

1. *Identify relevant ideas or meanings about the use of artificial intelligence (AI) in tourism and hospitality.*
2. *Create a list of codes, each with:*
   - o *a short and clear name (2-5 words),*
   - o *an operational definition, and*
   - o *a brief textual quotation (max. 2 lines).*
3. *Do not infer or interpret beyond what the text states.*
4. *Do not summarize or generate themes yet; only code.*
5. *Return the information in a Markdown table with the columns:*
   - o *Code*
   - o *Operational definition*
   - o *Textual quotation (example)*

Interview text: (Paste the verbatim transcript here)

This prompt is used to complete the coding phase, with each interview pasted into it.

What ChatGPT returns is a set of codes associated with segments and sentences from each interview.

This task, which is performed manually in ATLAS.ti, can be automated with ChatGPT by using a well-crafted prompt with very specific instructions. In terms of time savings, the gain is substantial; the researcher's subsequent oversight and review remain essential.

The full codebook (Interview 1) is shown in Table 3

Table 3. Codebook (excerpt)

Code	Operational Definition	Textual Quote (Example)
Professional use of AI	Use of AI to create teaching materials and search for educational content	"As a professor, for creating exercises and searching for content."
Personal use: translation and travel	Use of AI for translating texts and planning personal trips	"On a personal level, for translating texts and planning trips."
Advantage: time saving	Considering AI as a tool for completing tasks more quickly	"Time saving."

continued on following page

Table 3. Continued

Code	Operational Definition	Textual Quote (Example)
Advantage: going beyond traditional search	Appreciation of AI for allowing access to information beyond what traditional search engines offer	"To reach where I can't with traditional Google searches."
Partial trust in AI	Level of trust around 75%, accompanied by caution or verification of results	"About 75%."
Expectation: enhancing creativity	Anticipation that AI will help generate new or creative ideas	"Improve creativity."

This procedure was applied to each of the interviews.

Phase 3: Searching for Themes

In this phase, the codes generated in the previous stage are grouped into clusters, families, categories, or themes.

In this case, the prompt to give ChatGPT is very simple:

PROMPT for THEMES

Group the following codes into coherent themes and subthemes, define each theme in 1–2 sentences, and list the associated codes. Then we attach the codebook prepared in the previous phase.

What ChatGPT returns appears in Table 4:

Table 4. Preliminary theme codebook (excerpt)

Theme	Brief Description	Associated Codes
1. AI Adoption and Tools	Which tools are used and how often; differences between paid/free and across sectors.	ChatGPT, Copilot, Gemini, DeepSeek, Perplexity, multiple accounts, Barrier: cost
2. Uses of AI	Concrete applications in teaching, work, and everyday life.	Draft reports, structure ideas, translate, plan trips, organize tasks, write emails, hotel marketing, chatbot, audits
3. Training and Learning	Training experiences and perceived future needs.	Institutional training, no training received, self-learning, peer learning, theoretical need, workplace need, no training needed
4. Perceived Benefits	Cognitive and operational advantages.	Time saving, convenience, idea generation, planning, self-directed learning, AI as companion/tool
5. Trust and Control	Reliability levels and verification mechanisms.	Moderate trust, distrust of data, result review, humanization

From this point on, there is no need to create any new prompts. ChatGPT already knows the six phases of Braun & Clarke (2006) and, once one phase is completed, it then prompts whether to proceed to the next phase.

Phase 4: Reviewing Themes (Decisions to Make)

In this new phase, ChatGPT reviews the themes, establishes categories for each theme, and proposes a set of decisions to be made (see Table 5).

Table 5. Themes and decisions (excerpt)

Preliminary Theme	Evaluation	Decision	Justification
T1: AI Adoption and Tools	Coherent	Keep	Defines the ecosystem (tools, paid/free versions, accounts).
T2: Uses of AI	Coherent	Keep (add "personalization/ marketing")	Integrates "data-based personalization," "chatbot," and "banners" as professional uses.
T3: Training and Learning	Coherent	Keep	Clearly distinguishes between formal training, self-learning, and training needs.
T4: Perceived Benefits	Coherent	Keep	Efficiency/creativity/access. "AI as a companion" remains here.
T5: Trust and Control	Coherent	Keep	Includes verification and "humanization."

In the Evaluation column, ChatGPT classifies each theme and suggests possible decisions. Let's look at the different evaluation categories that appear in our table:

Coherent: The theme is internally consistent; the quotes and codes it contains share a clear conceptual connection. The theme has a well-defined and specific meaning, without including data that belongs to another theme. This category implies that all quotes within the theme relate to a single central idea, the subthemes or categories are complementary, not contradictory and the theme can be summarized clearly in one concise sentence.

Partially Overlapping: This means the theme partially overlaps with another one, there are codes or quotes that could belong to more than one theme, or the conceptual boundaries are unclear. In this case, two themes may address very similar aspects (e.g., "efficiency" and "automation"). Here, the researcher should review the boundaries between themes or consider merging them. Sometimes, a subtheme may simply be misplaced and should be moved.

Incomplete: This label means that the theme is not yet well developed or clearly defined. The data may be insufficient, the quotes do not clearly support the central idea or the theme is too broad or vague. In this case, the theme lacks internal coherence or conceptual density. A possible solution is to subdivide the theme or merge it with another one. Sometimes it simply requires more data or refinement of meaning.

Phase 5: Defining and Naming Themes

In this phase, a theme codebook is provided with definitions, associated codes, and textual quotes from the interviews.

ChatGPT, after evaluating the themes, made a series of changes on its own initiative and presented us with the final theme table (Table 6). In this instance, the changes were found to be appropriate and no objections were raised.

However, it should be noted that a discussion can be initiated at any point to either challenge the proposed changes or request clarification regarding the modifications made to the themes.

As table 6 shows, for each theme, the Theme Codebook includes a definition (2-4 lines), key codes, and 1-2 quotes (from different participant profiles).

Table 6. Themes and definitions (excerpt)

Theme Title	Definition	Codes	Quotes
T1. AI Adoption and Tools	Overview of tools and access modes (ChatGPT, Copilot, Gemini, DeepSeek, Perplexity), distinguishing between personal/professional use and paid/free plans, including strategies like multiple accounts to bypass limits.	Paid/free ChatGPT; Copilot; Gemini/DeepSeek/Perplexity; multiple accounts.	"Paid ChatGPT and Copilot." (Professor) · "Paid ChatGPT, 24 euros per month." (Student)
T2. AI Uses (academic, professional, and daily life)	Specific tasks in study and work (structuring ideas, reports, audits, translation/ writing), as well as in daily life (travel, calendars, diet, remedies). Includes commercial uses: chatbots, banners, and data-driven personalization.	Structuring ideas/texts; reports/ audits; multilingual translation; travel organization; smart calendar; chatbot; banners; personalization.	"To prepare hotel reports... ChatGPT helps me structure them." (Professional) · "I use it to organize trips." (Professional)
T3. Benefits and Accessibility	Perceived advantages: time saving, convenience, creativity support, self-learning, and democratization of access (lower cost for learning or practice).	Time saving; convenience; ideas/creativity; learning; AI as "companion"; saving money.	"Time saving... reaching where I can't get with Google." (Professor) · "It saves you money, for example, on French lessons." (Student)
T4. Trust, Quality, and Verification	Moderate trust (60–80%) varying by task type (higher for simple tasks, lower for data). Control strategies include source verification and humanizing outputs.	Trust 60–80%; distrust in data/updates; verification; humanization.	"About 75%... I always double-check what ChatGPT tells me." (Professor) · "I don't trust it for anything data-related." (Student)
T5. Training and Learning	Mixed trajectories: university training, self-learning (practice and peers), and selective needs (AI theory, programming/ work application). Some respondents see no need for further training for their current use.	Institutional training; no training; self-learning; peer learning; theoretical need; job-related need; no need.	"I've learned by myself, through practice, writing prompts." (Student) · "I need training on the theoretical part of AI." (Professor)

Phase 6: Writing the Report

The thematic analysis concludes with the preparation of the final report.

Although it is recommended that the researcher personally produce the report, there is no reason why artificial intelligence cannot be asked to generate a preliminary version of the analysis, which the researcher may subsequently revise and refine as deemed appropriate.

The researcher must ensure transparency in the connection between the data and the conclusions drawn, allowing the reader to understand both the role played by the researcher and the analytical process followed (Skjott-Linneberg & Korsgaard, 2019). As these authors indicate, interpretation will always remain an integral part of the researcher's work. In the present study, AI was employed to support the data interpretation process.

To complete all phases of this AI-assisted thematic analysis, ChatGPT was also asked to generate the analytical report in order to assess its quality and compare it with a report produced by a human researcher.

An excerpt from the report generated directly by the AI is presented below.

Final Report

1. AI Adoption and Tools

Participants use a variety of AI tools, with ChatGPT being the most frequently mentioned. The free version is the most common, although some users, mainly students and professors, rely on the paid version to access more features or avoid limitations. Other tools mentioned include Copilot, Gemini, Perplexity, and DeepSeek, the latter praised for its technical performance.

A recurring pattern is the use of multiple accounts to bypass usage restrictions, reflecting both high dependency and a lack of institutional infrastructure.

"I don't use the paid version of ChatGPT. I have many different accounts." (Student)

"DeepSeek is free and has no limits." (Professor)

2. AI Uses (Academic, Professional, and Everyday)

AI applications are wide-ranging and functional, covering academic and professional tasks as well as daily life activities.

Among professors, AI is used to structure ideas, write reports, review texts, and translate documents.

"ChatGPT helps me structure hotel reports." (Professional)

Students use AI to write, translate, create routines, or plan trips, and to generate ideas or content for academic work:

> *"I use it to make a smart schedule; I tell it what I have to do, and it gives me a timetable." (Student)*

In the hotel industry, AI also appears in communication and marketing processes, such as corporate chatbots **or** promotional banners, as well as in audit report design. Some professionals recognize the potential of AI for personalizing guest experiences, though they admit "it's not yet used in small hotels."

3. Benefits and Accessibility

The main benefit is time saving, followed by convenience and idea generation. Participants perceive AI as a cognitive support tool that enhances learning and productivity rather than as a replacement.

> *"Time saving, and it lets me reach where I can't through traditional Google searches." (Professor)*

They also highlight the democratization of knowledge access, as it enables learning languages or acquiring new skills without paying for classes or tutors:

> *"It saves you money, for example, on French lessons." (Student)*

AI is perceived as a "work companion" or an extension of human thought, rather than a substitute.

4. Trust, Quality, and Verification

Levels of trust are moderate (60–80%). Interviewees tend to trust AI for simple or structured tasks, but not for factual data, which they always verify.

> *"I don't trust it for anything data-related. For general concepts, yes." (Student)*

Professionals emphasize the need to "humanize" AI-generated content to maintain quality in communication, especially in customer service or institutional contexts:

> *"You always have to review it and humanize it." (Professional)*

This pattern suggests a critical and mature relationship with AI: users value it as a useful tool but recognize its limitations in accuracy, recency, and human tone.

5. Training and Learning

Most participants have not received formal AI training in recent years, although professors mention short courses organized by their universities. Self-learning predominates, through practice, trial-and-error, and observing other users.

> *"I've learned on my own, through practice, writing prompts." (Student)*

Training needs vary: some wish to deepen their theoretical understanding ("how AI is trained"), while others seek applied skills in HR or programming. However, several —especially younger participants— feel that further training is unnecessary for basic everyday use.

"For teaching, I don't need it — maybe a short talk or recommendation." (Professor)

Additional Resources

In addition to conducting the thematic analysis following the six phases proposed by Braun and Clarke (2006), artificial intelligence provides additional functionalities that support the completion of the study. Specifically, it offers various frameworks, theme frequency matrix, thematic maps, and visual representations that facilitate the interpretation and presentation of the findings.

Theme Frequency Matrix

The frequency matrix provides an overview of how themes are distributed across participants. It indicates the presence (1) or absence (0) of each theme within each interview, allowing the researcher to identify patterns of thematic coverage across different participant groups.

Rather than measuring the intensity or importance of themes, the matrix serves a descriptive purpose, supporting transparency and comparison in the thematic analysis process.

Table 7 shows the Theme/Frequency Matrix of this study.

Table 7. Participant/Theme matrix

Participant	T1 Adoption & Tools	T2 Uses (acad/pro/ daily)	T3 Benefits & Accessibility	T4 Trust, Quality & Verification	T5 Training & Learning	T6 Barriers & Limitations	T7 Task Transformation	T8 Customer Experience & Humanization	T9 Future Visions & Sectoral Impact
Lecturer1	1	1	1	1	1	1	0	0	0
Student1	1	1	1	1	1	1	1	1	1
Professor2	1	1	1	1	1	1	1	1	1
Student2	1	1	1	1	1	0	1	0	1
Professional1	1	1	1	1	1	1	1	1	1
Professional2	1	1	1	1	1	0	1	1	1
Totals (n=6)	6	6	6	6	6	4	5	4	5

Thematic Framework

The Thematic framework created by ChatGPT consists of a list of themes with their associated codes presented in bullet-point format. An excerpt from the research Thematic framework is presented below.

Theme 1. AI Adoption and Tools
- ChatGPT (free / paid versions)
- Copilot, Gemini, DeepSeek, Perplexity
- Multiple accounts / parallel use
- Insufficient institutional infrastructure

Theme 2. Uses of AI (academic, professional, and everyday)
- Creation of teaching materials
- Text revision and translation
- Personal organization (travel, routines, schedules)
- Customer communication (chatbots, banners, reports)
- Planning / audits / marketing

Theme 3. Benefits and Accessibility
- Time and effort savings
- Convenience and speed
- Democratized access to knowledge
- Cost savings (self-directed learning)
- Cognitive support ("work companion")

Theme 4. Trust, Quality, and Verification
- Moderate trust levels (60–80%)
- Manual verification of data
- Task-dependent reliability
- Need to "humanize" outputs
- Use of external sources

Theme 5. Training and Learning
- Lack of formal training
- Self-directed and practice-based learning
- Demand for theoretical training (how AI works)
- Demand for applied training (programming, HR, marketing)
- Perceived sufficiency for basic uses

Structural interpretation

ChatGPT also provides mind map–type diagrams that visually summarize the topics addressed. Likewise, it carries out a brief analysis and interpretation of the relationships between the themes identified in the research.

The interpretation for the case under study is presented below.

- The themes are grouped into three macro-domains:

  1. Adoption and Tools → How AI is introduced into practice.
  2. Uses and Benefits → What people do with AI and what they gain from it.
  3. Perceptions and Future → How they assess quality, ethics, training, and future impact.

- Themes 1–3 reflect the functional dimension.
- Themes 4–6 capture the critical and reflective dimension.
- Themes 7–9 project the transformative and ethical dimension.

DISCUSSION

The work produced by ChatGPT confirms the claims made by several authors who have previously analyzed the use of this tool in scientific research (Biswas, 2023; Rahman et al., 2023; Xames & Shefa, 2023). With well-designed and clearly structured prompts, ChatGPT can successfully perform tasks that were traditionally executed manually by researchers.

In this way, qualitative analysis is undergoing a transformation similar to that of quantitative research decades ago, when mathematical and statistical calculations became automated through the use of analytical software such as SPSS or R. As a result, researchers can now dedicate greater effort to the conceptual and interpretative dimensions of their work—focusing on the design of the study, data collection, and interpretation of results—rather than on repetitive or mechanical processes.

In the context of Thematic Analysis (Braun & Clarke, 2006), one of the most time-consuming stages has always been the process of coding and the identification of categories and overarching themes. The findings of this study demonstrate that, with adequate methodological guidance, ChatGPT is capable of performing much of this process, covering all six phases proposed by Braun and Clarke, with results that are both coherent and reproducible. The automation of these phases does not imply replacing the qualitative researcher; rather, it positions ChatGPT as a cognitive assistant that facilitates data management, pattern recognition, and thematic synthesis while preserving the interpretive authority of the human analyst.

Moreover, the study supports the growing body of literature arguing that AI tools can enhance transparency and replicability in qualitative research. By storing prompts, responses, and generated codes, ChatGPT provides a form of audit trail that allows researchers to document and justify each analytic decision (Kiger & Varpio, 2020). This feature addresses one of the traditional criticisms of qualitative methods—limited replicability—and opens new possibilities for mixed-method integration, where AI-assisted coding could complement human interpretation.

Nevertheless, the integration of ChatGPT into the qualitative research workflow is not exempt from challenges and ethical dilemmas. AI-generated content may occasionally contain inaccuracies, inconsistencies, or fabricated elements, which makes the researcher's supervision essential. The risk of automation bias, the tendency to overtrust machine outputs, must be carefully managed to prevent uncritical acceptance of the model's interpretations. Similarly, ethical issues such as data confidentiality, authorship, and the epistemic validity of AI-generated insights need to be addressed through clear research protocols and transparency in reporting (Skjott-Linneberg & Korsgaard, 2019).

From a pedagogical perspective, this study also contributes to hospitality education by demonstrating that AI-assisted qualitative research can lower the entry barriers for students and early-career researchers. Those who might otherwise avoid qualitative methods due to their complexity or time demands can now explore them through structured, AI-guided processes. This democratization of qualitative research aligns with the broader movement toward accessible and technology-supported higher education in tourism and hospitality management (El Hajal & Yeoman, 2025).

In summary, this discussion highlights that ChatGPT represents not a replacement but an augmentation of human research capacity. When used responsibly, it can strengthen the rigor, efficiency, and inclusiveness of qualitative inquiry. However, its use requires ongoing critical engagement, reflexivity, and methodological transparency. The future of qualitative research in hospitality and tourism may therefore depend less on whether AI is used, and more on how researchers integrate it ethically and thoughtfully into their interpretative practice.

PRACTICAL IMPLICATIONS

The findings of this study offer several practical implications for hospitality education, academic research, and institutional management, particularly in a context where artificial intelligence is becoming increasingly embedded in teaching, learning, and knowledge production processes.

Implications for hospitality educators

For faculty members in tourism and hospitality programs, ChatGPT can function as a valuable pedagogical support tool in both teaching and research-related activities. The results suggest that AI-assisted qualitative analysis may lower the perceived complexity of qualitative methodologies, which are often avoided in hospitality curricula in favor of quantitative approaches.

By integrating AI-supported thematic analysis into research methods courses, educators can help students better understand coding logic, theme development, and analytical reasoning without becoming overwhelmed by manual procedures. This may foster greater methodological balance in hospitality education and encourage students to engage with interpretive research traditions.

Furthermore, ChatGPT can support instructors in supervising student dissertations by assisting with preliminary coding, thematic structuring, and clarity checks—while final interpretation and academic judgment remain firmly under human control.

Implications for students and early-career researchers

For undergraduate and postgraduate students, particularly those with limited prior exposure to qualitative analysis, ChatGPT may serve as a cognitive scaffold that facilitates learning-by-doing. Rather than replacing analytical thinking, AI can help students visualize the research process step by step, thereby increasing confidence and methodological understanding.

This is particularly relevant in hospitality education, where students often demonstrate strong applied and managerial skills but limited familiarity with qualitative inquiry. AI-assisted tools may therefore contribute to democratizing access to qualitative research and reducing anxiety associated with open-ended data analysis.

Implications for academic research practice

From a research perspective, the study highlights how ChatGPT can be strategically employed to automate labor-intensive phases of qualitative analysis, such as transcription formatting, initial coding, and theme organization. This efficiency gain allows researchers to dedicate more time to higher-level analytical work, including theory building, interpretation, and integration with existing literature.

Importantly, this approach may be especially valuable for researchers working under constrained resources, limited funding, or individual research conditions-situations common in hospitality and tourism scholarship.

However, institutions should promote clear protocols regarding transparency, documentation of AI use, and ethical responsibility to ensure academic integrity and reproducibility.

Implications for institutional policy and research governance

Universities and hospitality schools may benefit from developing formal guidelines for the responsible use of generative AI in research. Rather than banning AI tools, policies should focus on regulated integration, methodological literacy, and explicit disclosure practices.

Training workshops for faculty and doctoral students could focus not only on how to use AI tools, but also on when and why they should be used, reinforcing critical evaluation rather than technological dependency.

Implications for the hospitality sector

Although this study focuses on education and research, its findings also resonate with industry practice. The ability of AI systems to support analytical reasoning, pattern recognition, and synthesis mirrors challenges faced in hospitality management, particularly in areas such as customer feedback analysis, service evaluation, and organizational learning.

The results suggest that future hospitality professionals trained in AI-assisted qualitative reasoning may be better equipped to interpret customer narratives, employee feedback, and experiential data—skills increasingly valuable in experience-driven service environments.

CONCLUSION

Just as academics and students already rely heavily on tools such as ChatGPT in their daily activities, whether for preparing exercises, developing teaching materials, drafting essays, or grading examinations, university professors and researchers should approach its use in qualitative inquiry with confidence and methodological awareness. The parallel with quantitative research is striking.

Decades ago, statistical analysis became standardized through digital tools such as Excel, SPSS, or R, which automated complex calculations and allowed scholars to focus on interpretation and theory-building. A similar process is now unfolding in qualitative research, where ChatGPT enables a new level of efficiency, accessibility, and transparency in the thematic analysis of textual data.

The findings of this work demonstrate that ChatGPT can assist in all six phases of the *Thematic Analysis* process described by Braun and Clarke (2006), from data familiarization to report writing. While human judgment remains indispensable for interpretation, AI support substantially reduces the mechanical workload of coding, clustering, and theme refinement.

This evolution does not diminish the value of human expertise; rather, it amplifies it, allowing researchers to dedicate more time to critical reflection, conceptual depth, and theoretical contribution. The combination of human insight and machine efficiency thus represents a new hybrid paradigm for qualitative research in the social sciences.

In the field of hospitality and tourism education, this transformation holds particular promise. The integration of AI-driven tools like ChatGPT can democratize access to qualitative methodologies for students who might otherwise perceive them as labor-intensive or overly subjective.

By simplifying data handling and pattern identification, these technologies can foster deeper engagement with reflective and interpretive analysis—skills essential for future hospitality managers, educators, and researchers. Furthermore, embedding AI literacy into research training can equip students with a competitive advantage in a sector increasingly shaped by digitalization and data-driven decision-making.

Nevertheless, the responsible use of ChatGPT demands ongoing critical reflection. Researchers must maintain full authorship accountability, validate AI-generated outputs, and ensure transparency in reporting their methodological processes. ChatGPT should be regarded not as an autonomous agent but as a *cognitive partner*—a tool that augments human inquiry while remaining under human ethical and intellectual control. Misuse, overreliance, or lack of verification could compromise the rigor of qualitative research and distort its interpretive integrity.

Ultimately, the future of qualitative research does not rest on whether AI is adopted, but on how it is integrated into academic practice. When used thoughtfully, ChatGPT has the potential to become an invaluable ally for scholars, enhancing methodological precision, reducing entry barriers for novice researchers, and fostering a more inclusive and innovative research culture. We therefore encourage the academic community, particularly within tourism and hospitality studies, to embrace this emerging paradigm, combining human creativity with artificial intelligence to expand the frontiers of scientific understanding.

REFERENCES

Biswas, S. S. (2023). ChatGPT for research and publication: A step-by-step guide. *The Journal of Pediatric Pharmacology and Therapeutics : JPPT : the Official Journal of PPAG, 28*(6), 576–584. DOI: 10.5863/1551-6776-28.6.576 PMID: 38130350

Braun, V., & Clarke, V. (2006). Using thematic analysis in psychology. *Qualitative Research in Psychology, 3*(2), 77–101. DOI: 10.1191/1478088706qp063oa

Buhalis, D., Harwood, T., Bogicevic, V., Viglia, G., Beldona, S., & Hofacker, C. (2019). Technological disruptions in services: Lessons from tourism and hospitality. *Journal of Service Management, 30*(4), 484–506. DOI: 10.1108/JOSM-12-2018-0398

Bulchand-Gidumal, J., William Secin, E., O'Connor, P., & Buhalis, D. (2024). Artificial Intelligence's impact on hospitality and tourism marketing: Exploring key themes and addressing challenges. *Current Issues in Tourism, 27*(14), 2345–2362. DOI: 10.1080/13683500.2023.2229480

Campbell, J. L., Quincy, C., Osserman, J., & Pedersen, O. K. (2013). Coding in-depth semistructured interviews: Problems of unitization and intercoder reliability and agreement. *Sociological Methods & Research, 42*(3), 294–320. DOI: 10.1177/0049124113500475

Dwivedi, Y. K., Kshetri, N., Hughes, L., Slade, E. L., Jeyaraj, A., Kar, A. K., Baabdullah, A. M., Koohang, A., Raghavan, V., Ahuja, M., Albanna, H., Albashrawi, M. A., Al-Busaidi, A. S., Balakrishnan, J., Barlette, Y., Basu, S., Bose, I., Brooks, L., Buhalis, D., & Wright, R. (2023). Opinion Paper:"So what if ChatGPT wrote it?" Multidisciplinary perspectives on opportunities, challenges and implications of generative conversational AI for research, practice and policy. *International Journal of Information Management, 71*, 102642. DOI: 10.1016/j.ijinfomgt.2023.102642

El Hajal, G. (2025). Transitions into the futures: AI disruption and resilience in hospitality graduates. *Research in Hospitality Management, 15*(1), 20–22. DOI: 10.1080/22243534.2024.2438709

El Hajal, G., & Rowson, B. (2020). The future of hospitality jobs. *Research in Hospitality Management, 10*(1), 55–61. DOI: 10.1080/22243534.2020.1790210

El Hajal, G., & Yeoman, I. (2025). AI and the future of talent management in tourism and hospitality. *Current Issues in Tourism*, 1–18. https://doi.org/10.1080/13683500.2024.2439395

Fahy, P. J. (2001). Addressing some common problems in transcript analysis. *International Review of Research in Open and Distance Learning*, *1*(2). Advance online publication. DOI: 10.19173/irrodl.v1i2.321

Kiger, M. E., & Varpio, L. (2020). Thematic analysis of qualitative data: AMEE Guide No. 131. *Medical Teacher*, *42*(8), 846–854. DOI: 10.1080/0142159X.2020.1755030 PMID: 32356468

Limna, P. (2023). Artificial Intelligence (AI) in the hospitality industry: A review article. *International Journal of Computing Sciences Research*, *7*, 1306–1317. DOI: 10.25147/ijcsr.2017.001.1.103

Maguire, M., & Delahunt, B. (2017). Doing a thematic analysis: A practical, step-by-step guide for learning and teaching scholars. *All Ireland journal of higher education, 9*(3).

Ngoepe, L. L., & Wakelin-Theron, N. (2023). Factors that contribute towards the-employability of hospitality graduates. *African Journal of Hospitality, Tourism and Leisure*, *12*(4), 1495–1511.

Rahman, M. M., Terano, H. J., Rahman, M. N., Salamzadeh, A., & Rahaman, M. S. (2023). ChatGPT and academic research: A review and recommendations based on practical examples. *Journal of Education. Management and Development Studies*, *3*(1), 1–12.

Salama, A. F. (2024). The Impact of AI Applications (Virtual Reality and Augmented Reality) in the Hospitality Industry: Opportunities and Challenges. *Journal of Association of Arab Universities for Tourism and Hospitality*, *27*(1), 109–124. DOI: 10.21608/jaauth.2024.300010.1586

Saydam, M. B., Arici, H. E., & Koseoglu, M. A. (2022). How does the tourism and hospitality industry use artificial intelligence? A review of empirical studies and future research agenda. *Journal of Hospitality Marketing & Management*, *31*(8), 908–936. DOI: 10.1080/19368623.2022.2118923

Skjott Linneberg, M., & Korsgaard, S. (2019). Coding qualitative data: A synthesis guiding the novice. *Qualitative Research Journal*, *19*(3), 259–270. DOI: 10.1108/QRJ-12-2018-0012

Thomas, D. R. (2003). *A general inductive approach for qualitative data analysis*. School of Population Health University of Auckland.

Xames, M. D., & Shefa, J. (2023). ChatGPT for research and publication: Opportunities and challenges. *SSRN*, *6*(1), 390–395. DOI: 10.2139/ssrn.4381803

Zhu, J. J., Jiang, J., Yang, M., & Ren, Z. J. (2023). ChatGPT and environmental research. *Environmental Science & Technology*, *57*(46), 17667–17670. DOI: 10.1021/acs.est.3c01818 PMID: 36943179

Section 2
Pedagogical Approaches

Chapter 7
Innovating Hospitality Finance Education Through Revenue Strategies and Technology

Albian Albrahimi
http://orcid.org/0000-0001-6237-4874
Les Roches Global Hospitality Education, Crans-Montana, Switzerland

ABSTRACT

This chapter explores how advances in technology are reshaping the way finance and revenue management are taught in hospitality education. It highlights how tools like data analytics, forecasting models, and real-time market insights are being integrated into classroom learning, case studies, and professional development. By sharing practical examples and teaching approaches, the chapter shows how hospitality programs can prepare students to think strategically, adapt to changing market dynamics, and apply innovative solutions in real-world setting.

INTRODUCTION

Hospitality education is undergoing a paradigm shift as artificial intelligence (AI) and digital technologies transform industry practices. Nowhere is this more evident than in the teaching of finance and revenue management in hospitality programs. As hotels embrace data analytics, machine learning models, and real-time market intelligence to optimize revenues, educators face the challenge of updating

DOI: 10.4018/979-8-3373-5112-4.ch007

curricula to mirror these innovations. The goal is to prepare graduates who are not only fluent in financial principles but also adept at leveraging cutting-edge tools to make strategic decisions. This chapter explores how advances in technology are reshaping hospitality finance education. It discusses the integration of data analytics platforms, forecasting models, and real-time market data into classroom learning and professional development, illustrating these changes through practical examples and contemporary teaching approaches. By sharing insights from several executive-level courses and related industry cases, the chapter shows how hospitality programs can equip students to think strategically, adapt to dynamic market conditions, and apply innovative revenue solutions in real-world settings. The chapter is structured as follows: first, it reviews the background literature on digital transformation in hospitality and its implications for education. It then proposes a curriculum architecture for AI-infused revenue and finance education, describes the technology stack and data workflows used in teaching labs, and illustrates methods for linking revenue management with financial outcomes. Subsequent sections discuss case-based learning and academic integrity in the age of AI. The chapter concludes with an implementation roadmap and future directions.

This chapter is written as a proposed, adaptable framework for embedding AI into hospitality finance and revenue-management teaching. It does not document one institution's existing syllabus; rather, it translates contemporary industry practice and executive-education experience into a scaffolded curriculum model that other educators can adapt. Throughout the chapter, AI is treated as decision support that must be interrogated and governed (human-in-the-loop), so that students learn the strategic logic of revenue and finance before they learn the technological process.

BACKGROUND & LITERATURE REVIEW

This section reviews rapid advances in hotel revenue management and digital transformation, from foundational yield management (Kimes, 1989) and forecasting accuracy (Weatherford & Kimes, 2003) to strategy-led digital change and customer-centric revenue practices (Cross et al, 2009; Kane et al., 2015; Verhoef et al., 2021).

The imperative to modernize hospitality finance education stems from rapid digital transformation in the industry. In recent years, hotels worldwide have widely adopted technologies such as AI-driven pricing, customer analytics, and automation, fundamentally altering how revenue management and financial decisions are made. To and Yu (2025) report that AI applications in hospitality have grown significantly in the last few years, with large hotel chains leading the adoption of tools like chatbots, predictive personalization, and dynamic pricing engines. Reviews of automation and AI in the sector confirm this trajectory, noting accelerating deployment across both front-of-house and operational functions (Jabeen et al., 2022). This surge reflects a broader trend: hospitality organizations recognize that data and technology can yield competitive advantage in enhancing customer experiences and optimizing revenues. However, research cautions that technology alone is not a solution and that strategic vision and organizational alignment are critical. Kane et al. (2015) famously argued that "strategy, not technology, drives digital transformation," emphasizing that true digital maturity comes from top-led strategic agendas and the ability to articulate how technology creates value for the organization's future. In other words, digital fluency in management means understanding the business value of tech tools, not just their technical features. This perspective informs education: hospitality programs must teach not only technical tool usage but also strategic thinking to leverage those tools effectively.

Despite recognition of these needs, studies have found a gap between industry practice and academic preparation in revenue management (RM) and finance. Cetin et al. (2016) surveyed industry professionals and concluded that "*formal hospitality...education and training programs concerning pricing and RM are far from providing the maximum level of competency*" needed for today's revenue management careers. The study identified persistent challenges in the field such as difficulty finding qualified RM talent and pressures from owners for quick financial results, and urged that curriculum enhancements are necessary to address these gaps. In the same vein, only a minority of hospitality organizations currently excel at data-driven personalization. Busulwa et al. (2022) found that management support and an innovative culture were stronger predictors of digital transformation success than sheer technology spending, underlining that human and strategic factors remain paramount. These findings suggest that hospitality education must evolve to produce graduates who combine analytical skills with strategic acumen and change leadership abilities. Research into the current readiness of hospitality curricula for this shift indicates that many programs still have significant ground to cover (Busulwa et al., 2022).

There is encouraging movement in this direction. Pioneering hospitality programs have begun integrating technology-oriented content and experiential learning. For instance, leading hospitality education institutions have introduced simulation-based teaching in revenue management over a decade ago, linking theoretical concepts with practical decision-making in a competitive, data-rich environment. Industry-academic collaborations are also emerging: the Hospitality Sales and Marketing Association International (HSMAI) offers certification courses in revenue optimization, and companies provide educational licenses for revenue management systems (RMS) and business intelligence dashboards. Moreover, literature on hospitality education emphasizes balancing technical and human skills. Skills like communication, cultural intelligence, and empathy remain "the keystone of extraordinary guest experiences".

Thus, educators face a dual mandate: infuse curricula with cutting-edge analytical and technological content while reinforcing the service mindset and ethical reasoning that define the hospitality profession.

The background literature points to a clear need for innovative hospitality finance education. Strategy must lead technology adoption, and curricula should develop both analytical prowess and strategic, human-centric thinking. The following sections build on these insights to propose concrete ways of redesigning hospitality finance and revenue management education for the AI age.

CURRICULUM ARCHITECTURE FOR AI-INFUSED REVENUE & FINANCE EDUCATION

This section presents a proposed, adaptable curriculum architecture for AI-infused revenue and finance education. It aligns with evidence on revenue-management education needs and a total-hotel profit orientation, integrating analytics, pricing, and distribution with strategic leadership (Anderson & Xie, 2010; Cetin et al., 2016; Queenan et al., 2011). The modules and examples are illustrative templates: they show where AI can be embedded, why it improves learning, and which safeguards keep the focus on strategic reasoning rather than tool operation.

The proposed architecture aligns with evidence on RM education needs and total-hotel profit orientation, integrating analytics, pricing, and distribution with strategic leadership (Anderson & Xie, 2010; Cetin et al., 2016; Queenan et al., 2011).

Table 1. AI-Infused Revenue & Finance Curriculum Map.

Module	Core Learning Outcomes	Primary Tools	Assessment Examples
Foundations: Digital Strategy in Hospitality	Explain digital disruption Analyze business models Articulate strategy-technology fit	Business Model Canvas Digital maturity frameworks Case analysis tools	Case brief Strategy memo
Core RM & Finance	Forecast demand Design pricing/channel controls Link to profit & budgets	Excel/RMS PMS data STR benchmarking datasets	Forecast workbook Channel-mix ROI analysis
Integrative: AI & Total Revenue	Apply ML-enhanced segmentation Scenario planning Owner-ROI narrative	Intro Machine Learning BI dashboards What-if tools	Capstone simulation
Electives / Workshops	Deepen analytics or fintech complete certifications	Power BI / Tableau Vendor sandboxes	Certification Analytics mini-project

Designing a curriculum that integrates AI, analytics, and modern revenue strategies requires a structured architecture that builds competencies in a logical progression. This chapter proposes an architecture of interlocking modules spanning foundational theory, technology application, strategic integration, and experiential learning. The design is informed by several executive-level courses that serve as cornerstones from Les Roches Global Hospitality. Framed within a larger educational design, these courses show how each component contributes to producing graduates proficient in both finance and innovation.

Foundational Module: Digital Transformation in Hospitality

The first part of the curriculum establishes a broad understanding of how technology is reshaping hospitality business models and operations. This module covers theoretical frameworks such as the Business Model Canvas, digital maturity models, and change management theories (e.g., Kotter's stages for implementing change). Students learn the *Strategy vs. Technology* paradigm, internalizing that digital initiatives must serve strategic ends. Key topics include the impact of emerging technologies (AI, Internet of Things, big data) on service delivery and customer behavior, as well as organizational enablers of innovation (leadership vision, culture, dynamic capabilities).

Hospitality cases such as the rise of platform business models like Airbnb versus traditional hotels are analyzed to highlight strategic inflection points. Learning outcomes at this stage emphasize analysis and understanding: students should be able to articulate how digital trends (like mobile check-in, AI chatbots, or platform distribution) affect hospitality financial performance and competitiveness. They also begin developing "digital fluency," i.e. the ability to discuss technology's value in business terms, rather than just its features. This foundational module sets the stage for more technical and applied learning by ensuring everyone grasps why technology matters for revenue and finance. AI is introduced here only as an object of strategic analysis (e.g., mapping where AI creates value, risk, or governance demands), not as a substitute for conceptual understanding.

Core Module: Hospitality Revenue Management and Finance

Building on that strategic foundation, the core of the curriculum delves into revenue management techniques and financial analysis, augmented with data-driven tools. This forces strategic justification and keeps human judgment in the loop. This module covers traditional revenue management concepts such as demand forecasting, dynamic pricing, distribution channel management, market segmentation, and key performance metrics (ADR, RevPAR, etc.). Students learn forecasting not only as a theoretical exercise but by using contemporary tools: they might apply time-series forecasting models in Excel or a specialized RMS, leveraging historical data sets to project demand. Chapters from standard RM textbooks (e.g., on forecasting and overbooking) are complemented by hands-on practice with technology. The curriculum introduces an array of hospitality systems: Property Management Systems (PMS) for handling reservations and transactions, Revenue Management Systems for optimizing rates, Customer Relationship Management (CRM) platforms for tracking guest data, and business intelligence software for visualization of trends. Students get exposure to how these systems interconnect in industry practice, for example, how PMS booking data feeds into an RMS which then suggests rate changes, and how those decisions flow into financial forecasts and budgeting. To mirror industry complexity, the course employs real-world datasets such as STR (Smith Travel Research) reports (anonymized) and competitive benchmarking data. An important design principle here is linking revenue tactics to financial outcomes. Thus, when covering pricing strategies, the curriculum also covers profitability analysis: students examine how a high-occupancy/low-rate strategy vs. a low-occupancy/high-rate strategy impacts not just RevPAR but also gross operating profit. Concepts like GOPPAR (Gross Operating Profit per Available Room) are introduced to underscore the finance-revenue linkage. By the end of this core module, students are expected to do more than recall concepts. They should be able to build a basic demand forecast, recommend a pricing strategy based on data, and evaluate the financial implications of revenue decisions. To make AI explicit without turning the course into software training, students first build a baseline forecast and pricing logic manually, then compare it against an AI-enabled forecast/recommendation (from an RMS or a simple model) and must explain any overrides in writing.

Integrative Module: Strategic Revenue Leadership and AI Applications

The next layer of the curriculum architecture integrates the insights from the first two modules, pushing students to synthesize strategic thinking with analytical skills. In this module, advanced topics are explored: AI and machine learning applications in revenue management (e.g., algorithms for personalized pricing or upselling), total revenue management across departments (rooms, F&B, ancillary services), and scenario planning for market disruptions. Pedagogically, this is achieved through case studies and simulation exercises that require cross-functional decision-making. For example, a capstone simulation might present students with a virtual hotel environment where they must adjust pricing and marketing spend in real time in response to competitor moves and demand shocks (some programs use simulations like Cesim or bespoke games to emulate this competitive environment). Additionally, this module addresses strategic topics such as distribution strategy (balancing direct bookings vs. online travel agencies), channel analytics, and emerging phenomena like sharing economy impact on hotel revenues. A distinctive feature is the inclusion of AI-based tools: students might use a simple machine learning model to segment customers by booking behavior or evaluate an "AI recommendation engine" for cross-selling hotel services. Notably, they learn to critically assess these technologies such as understanding issues of data quality, bias, or the risk of relying purely on black-box algorithms. The learning outcomes focus on higher-order capabilities: strategic decision-making, leadership, and innovation. Students practice justifying their revenue strategies to stakeholders (e.g., writing a memo to an owner explaining why investing in a new RMS yields long-term ROI despite short-term costs). This integrative module solidifies the curriculum's aim to produce strategic technologists: hospitality finance professionals who can wield advanced tools while maintaining a big-picture strategic perspective. Short, stackable electives (e.g., analytics dashboards or fintech) can deepen skills as resources allow.

Capstone or Integrated Project

A required capstone element is an AI use statement documenting which AI tools were used, what inputs were provided, what outputs were accepted or rejected, and how human judgment determined the final recommendation. This disclosure reinforces academic integrity and mirrors governance practices increasingly expected in analytics-driven revenue teams.

The curriculum culminates in an experiential capstone that integrates revenue strategy, financial justification, and technology-enabled execution. Students develop a comprehensive revenue strategy plan for a hypothetical or real hospitality business. Typical tasks include market research, such as comp set analysis, forecasting demand and revenues, designing pricing and distribution tactics, and presenting a financial plan with ROI estimates for proposed technology investments. One representative assignment is a twelve month digital transformation roadmap for a mid sized hotel, including phased deployments, resource budgeting, and a KPI dashboard. Students work in teams to apply the TOE Technology Organization Environment framework to assess readiness, use the Business Model Canvas to articulate value creation, and incorporate financial metrics to evaluate feasibility and expected impact. The intent is to simulate the work graduates will perform as revenue managers, finance analysts, and digital transformation leads.

AI integration can fail when students learn the tool sequence without understanding the strategic rationale. To avoid adopting technology for technology's sake, the curriculum should be scaffolded so that conceptual finance logic precedes automation and so that AI supported outputs are treated as hypotheses to test rather than answers to copy. The recommended design is therefore strategy first. Students learn the revenue finance decision logic, then use AI to generate structured alternatives, and finally apply professional judgment to validate, override, and communicate decisions. This mirrors practice in revenue teams, where algorithms accelerate analysis but leaders remain accountable for outcomes, fairness, and owner value.

A practical strategy first scaffold is a four stage learning progression. Stage A conceptual foundation requires students to complete forecasting, displacement, and profitability decisions without AI, using transparent methods and stated assumptions. Stage B AI as generator introduces AI to produce baseline forecasts, scenario narratives, or segmentation hypotheses, while students document inputs and identify what the tool cannot observe. Stage C critique and governance asks students to stress test outputs for plausibility, bias, and data quality, compare results to benchmarks such as STR trends or known market drivers, and record overrides in a structured override log. Stage D strategic communication culminates in an owner ready memo that links the chosen revenue action to profit, risk, and ethics, supported by a reproducible calculation trail.

Assessment should measure strategic thinking, not tool speed. A practical design combines a quantitative workbook covering forecasting, displacement, Net RevPAR, and GOPPAR impacts, a concise owner or GM decision memo that justifies the strategy and the role of AI, and a short viva style check to confirm students can defend assumptions and overrides. Where generative AI is permitted, instructors can require prompt and output appendices or the AI use statement to formalize disclosure and reduce ambiguity around acceptable use, consistent with emerging national policy guidance on generative AI in higher education (Higher Education Authority, 2025).

Faculty capability and resourcing should be treated as design variables. Faculty development can remain lightweight but intentional, with short sessions on analytical prompting, common failure modes, and assessment redesign, supported by shared case packs and datasets. Resource planning should prioritize a minimal viable lab, including dataset access, spreadsheet models, and one BI dashboard, before investing in vendor systems. Course policy should make the human in the loop principle explicit, requiring students to demonstrate what they learned, how they validated AI outputs, and how they would govern AI use in practice. This emphasis on human oversight reflects growing scholarly attention to the role of human judgment in AI-assisted learning environments (Memarian & Doleck, 2024).

To operationalize the scaffold within an existing revenue management or hospitality finance course, educators can implement a short three week micro unit. Week 1 establishes a baseline forecast without AI and computes profit implications with transparent assumptions. Week 2 introduces AI for alternative scenario generation and candidate actions, with students documenting inputs, identifying missing information, benchmarking against baseline and external signals, and completing an override log. Week 3 produces an owner ready decision memo quantifying expected revenue and profit effects and explaining governance choices, supported by a brief oral check. To prevent superficial use, constrain AI to bounded purposes, require evidence for any AI generated claim that influences a decision, and grade accountability through override logs and disclosure. Used in this way, AI increases the volume and diversity of practice while preserving standards for reasoning, evidence, and professional judgment.

TECHNOLOGY LAB STACK & DATA WORKFLOWS

Hands-on training with PMS, RMS, and BI dashboards reflects industry best practices linking forecasting, optimization, and performance monitoring (El Gayar et al., 2011; Noone et al., 2011; Weatherford & Kimes, 2003). To make AI tangible, students treat RMS recommendations as model outputs to be challenged: they inspect drivers, test sensitivity, and document when and why they override the algorithm.

AI features (such as anomaly detection or auto-generated insight summaries) can accelerate sensemaking, but students are assessed on the narrative logic that links dashboard signals to revenue and profit actions.

Table 2. Teaching Lab: Technology Stack and Data Workflow.

Component	Purpose	Student Tasks	Example Platforms
PMS (training)	Transactions & reservations Segment/rate code data	Post bookings Extract OTB, pickup, ADR/RevPAR	Opera training Cloud PMS
RMS (simulated)	Forecast & price recommendations	Run forecasts Evaluate elasticity & overbooking	Excel model IDeaS/Duetto (edu)
BI Dashboard	KPI visualization & monitoring	Build RM dashboards Variance/budget tracking	Power BI Tableau
External Feeds	Market intelligence & comp-set benchmarking	Compute indices Rate-shop analysis	STR samples OTA rate data

Industry / RM trend	AI capability used in class	Student task	Learning outcome assessed	Safeguards (human-in-the-loop)

continued on following page

Table 2. Continued

Real-time pricing pressure	AI-supported demand forecasting and price recommendation	Compare manual forecast to AI forecast; justify overrides for high-impact dates	Forecast reasoning; pricing rationale; profit linkage	Written override log; oral defense spot-checks
Market volatility / shocks	Scenario generation and stress testing	Generate scenarios with AI; revise using external signals (events, macro)	Scenario thinking; sensitivity analysis	Require non-AI evidence citations; explain revisions
Channel-cost complexity	AI-assisted channel mix optimization	Compute Net RevPAR and contribution by channel; propose rules	Profit orientation; distribution strategy	Calculations must be student-built; dataset appendix
Personalization vs fairness	Segmentation and offer design	Design offers; evaluate fairness and privacy trade-offs	Ethical judgment; compliance awareness	Fairness checklist; peer review; instructor audit
Data quality issues	Anomaly detection and cleaning hints	Identify data errors; document cleaning; show impact on forecast	Data literacy; governance	Reproducible steps; version control of files
Owner ROI expectations	AI-supported narrative drafting	Draft investment case; refine with ROI model and risks	Financial justification; narrative coherence	ROI model must be original; disclose AI assistance
Operational constraints	Constraint-aware optimization prompts	Explain how staffing/ space constraints alter RM actions	Cross-functional thinking	Rubric rewards trade-off articulation
Academic integrity risks	AI transparency protocols	Submit AI use statement and reflective memo	Metacognition; integrity	Mandatory disclosure; short viva-style check

When AI is used to synthesize external signals (events, rate-shopping, macro indicators), students must cite the original sources and explain how each signal changes the forecast or pricing decision.

To bring an AI-infused hospitality finance curriculum to life, institutions must create a technology lab stack, a suite of software tools and data resources that students can use for hands-on learning. Equally important is designing data workflows that mimic real-world processes, from data collection to analysis to decision output. This section outlines the key components of a hospitality revenue management lab, describes how data flows through these components, and highlights how each element contributes to learning outcomes. The overarching goal is to provide students with an authentic environment to practice using technology in revenue strategy, thereby bridging the gap between classroom theory and industry practice.

Core Systems in the Lab Stack

A realistic hospitality revenue lab includes several integrated systems reflective of those used in hotel companies:

- Property Management System (PMS): The PMS is the transactional heart of hotel operations, recording reservations, guest profiles, room availability, check-in/check-out, and revenue postings. In the lab, an educational version of a PMS (or a simulated interface) allows students to see how bookings are entered and how data like occupancy, ADR (Average Daily Rate), and revenues are generated day by day. For example, students might use a training version of OPERA PMS or a cloud-based academic PMS to input sample reservations and observe how the system tracks different market segments and rate codes. AI can be layered on top of PMS exports to classify demand patterns (e.g., pace anomalies or segment shifts) and to generate hypotheses that students must validate with the underlying booking records.
- Revenue Management System (RMS): A specialized RMS is the analytical engine of the stack. In industry, platforms (e.g., IDeaS, Duetto, SAS) forecast demand and recommend price/yield actions. Teaching labs can simulate these functions with spreadsheet models or lightweight tools that ingest historical bookings, pickup, and competitor rates to produce daily or segment-level recommendations. Where possible, vendor-provided educational access exposes students to real interfaces and dashboards. Through RMS work, students practice booking-pace analysis, unconstrained vs. constrained demand, overbooking logic, price elasticity, and model evaluation. To make AI tangible, students treat RMS recommendations as model outputs to be challenged: they inspect drivers, test sensitivity, and document when and why they override the algorithm.
- Business Intelligence (BI) & KPI Dashboards: Decision-making requires consolidated, visualized data. A BI layer (e.g., Tableau, Power BI, or a custom dashboard) aggregates PMS/RMS outputs plus external signals to track occupancy, ADR, RevPAR, channel mix, pickup by segment, and forward on-the-books (OTB) vs. last year/budget. In the lab, dashboards surface exception-based views (needles, spikes, gaps), link revenue actions to profit KPIs (Net RevPAR, flow-through), and support quick "what-if" checks. This builds data-storytelling skills and reinforces how digital metrics connect to financial outcomes without relying on vendor-specific cases. AI features (such

as anomaly detection or auto-generated insight summaries) can accelerate sensemaking, but students are assessed on the narrative logic that links dashboard signals to revenue and profit actions.

- External Data Feeds (Market Intelligence): Real-world revenue management relies on external market data such as competitor pricing, market occupancy trends, economic indicators, etc. Thus, the lab includes data feeds or datasets that provide real-time market insights. An example is STR reports (Smith Travel Research), which give benchmarking data on a hotel's competitive set (e.g., average occupancy, ADR, and RevPAR of similar hotels in the market). Anonymized STR sample reports are incorporated into exercises so students practice calculating index metrics (e.g., a hotel's market Penetration Index, which is its share of market occupancy). Another source is rate shopping data; some tools can be used to scrape competitors' room rates from online travel agencies. Additionally, economic and event data (like citywide event calendars, school holidays, airline capacity data) are introduced qualitatively or via cases to simulate the environment in which revenue managers operate. By working with external data, students learn to adjust forecasts and strategies based on broader market dynamics, preparing them to respond to real-world demand drivers. When AI is used to synthesize external signals (events, rate-shopping, macro indicators), students must cite the original sources and explain how each signal changes the forecast or pricing decision.

Data Workflows and Integration

With these components in place, a key learning for students is how data flows through the hospitality tech ecosystem and informs decisions. A simplified workflow might be:

1. **Data Generation & Collection:** Transactions occur in the PMS (reservations, check-ins, financial postings). At the same time, external data (market stats, competitor rates) is collected. In class, this could mean the instructor provides a daily feed or dataset update.
2. **Data Processing & Forecasting:** The RMS component pulls relevant data (historical bookings, current pickup trends, maybe web traffic data if available as a proxy for demand) and processes it using forecasting models. Students might manually run this by updating a forecast spreadsheet or using an RMS tool that can be configured with the latest data. The output could be a forecast for the next 90 days of occupancy and a recommended optimal price for each day.

3. **Decision Analysis:** The BI/dashboard then aggregates both the internal data and external insights. For example, after forecasting, students examine a dashboard showing future dates where demand is projected high or low. They also see competitor pricing for those dates and perhaps an event calendar. With all this, they perform analysis: Should we yield higher (increase rates) or stimulate demand with a promotion? What is the likely financial outcome (revenue and profit) of those decisions?
4. **Strategy Implementation:** Based on analysis, decisions are fed back, e.g., students might "apply" new prices or inventory controls (like closing a discount rate) in the simulated RMS or PMS. In a live setting, this would mean the revenue manager updates rate plans in the system, which then distribute to sales channels. In the lab, the implementation might be simulated by recording the decision and then seeing its effect when the next "day" of operations is run (as in a simulation game, where after decisions, the program advances and shows new booking results).
5. **Monitoring & Feedback:** Finally, the subsequent data is monitored via the dashboard. Students observe how their decisions affected pickup, revenue, and possibly guest metrics. For example, did a price increase for a high-demand date maximize revenue without harming occupancy? Did closing a cheap channel push business to higher-paying channels, and what was the net effect on RevPAR and profit? This closes the loop, teaching students to continuously monitor and adjust.

This cyclical workflow is practiced repeatedly through various scenarios (high season vs. low season, group business vs. transient mix changes, etc.), reinforcing understanding. It demonstrates that revenue strategy is an iterative, data-driven process.

Integration of AI and Automation

A modern lab should also expose students to AI and automation within these workflows. For example, it can illustrate how machine learning might automate parts of forecasting or price optimization. An exercise may involve using a simple predictive model (e.g., a regression that predicts bookings from search engine query trends or a classification model to flag which days are "special events" based on data patterns). Instruction should emphasize that AI is increasingly embedded in commercial RMS and CRM systems, such as algorithms that adjust prices multiple times a day or personalize offers in real time. However, the pedagogy must also emphasize caution: students discuss scenarios in which algorithmic pricing goes wrong (including well-documented hospitality or airline failures) to underscore why human oversight remains crucial. Ethical use of guest data should be highlighted as well; for instance, if CRM data are used to set rates dynamically for different customers (personalized pricing), what are the privacy and fairness considerations? These discussions link the lab work to broader lessons on responsible technology use.

The technology lab stack and data workflows provide the means for students to practice what the curriculum advocates. By working with PMS, RMS, dashboards, and real datasets, students gain concrete skills in using contemporary hospitality technology. More importantly, they learn how information flows through a hotel's systems to inform revenue and finance decisions. This experiential learning demystifies advanced tools and prepares students to enter the workforce confident in handling the technology that underpins modern revenue strategy. It addresses the widely cited skills gap. By graduation, students can demonstrate experience with the same types of reports, systems, and analyses they will encounter as analysts or managers, thereby increasing their employability and effectiveness from day one.

TEACHING REVENUE STRATEGIES WITH FINANCE LINKAGES

One of the central aims of innovating hospitality finance education is to break down silos between *revenue management* and *traditional finance/accounting* teachings. In practice, revenue strategies (like pricing, distribution, and demand stimulation) directly influence financial outcomes (revenues, profits, and even asset values). Therefore, a modern curriculum emphasizes the explicit linkage between revenue management decisions and financial performance, ensuring that students adopt a holistic view of a "revenue strategy" as not just maximizing top-line income, but optimizing sustainable profitability and value creation. This section discusses pedagogical approaches to integrate finance concepts into revenue management teaching (and vice versa), highlighting key content areas where these linkages are critical, and providing examples of classroom techniques to reinforce them.

Integrating Profitability Metrics into Revenue Management

Traditional hospitality programs have often taught revenue management with a focus on top-line metrics like Occupancy, ADR, and RevPAR (Revenue per Available Room). While these remain essential, an innovative curriculum links them to bottom-line considerations. For instance, when discussing pricing strategy, students are taught to consider contribution margin and costs of distribution. An example exercise may present two scenarios: selling a room via an online travel agency (OTA) at $100 with a 20% commission, versus selling direct on the hotel website at $95 with minimal commission. Students calculate that the net revenue (after commission) is $80 in the first scenario and $95 in the second, highlighting that the lower rate direct sale is actually financially preferable due to cost differences. This introduces the concept of Net RevPAR (net revenue per available room, after distribution costs) and encourages strategic channel management for profit, not just revenue. GOPPAR (Gross Operating Profit per Available Room) can be introduced as a metric to evaluate strategies. For a given revenue strategy, students examine expense implications: e.g., aggressively courting weekend leisure guests might boost occupancy and revenues, but if it entails higher variable costs (breakfast included, or higher utility usage), the net profit must be assessed. By analyzing simplified income statements under different revenue scenarios, students learn to align revenue goals with overall financial health.

Forecasting and Budgeting

Another critical linkage connects revenue management forecasts to financial budgets. In teaching demand forecasting (a core RM skill), instruction should extend to cash-flow and budgeting implications. Students can be tasked with translating a rooms-revenue forecast into a full departmental budget. For example, if next month's rooms revenue is projected at $500,000 (based on expected occupancy and ADR), what does that imply for total hotel revenue (adding food & beverage and ancillary spend) and for variable expenses that scale with volume (labor, cost of goods, utilities)? Such exercises reinforce financial accounting concepts such as fixed vs. variable costs and operating leverage. After covering forecasting techniques (e.g., regression, pickup methods), the course can require teams to produce a mini profit-and-loss projection for a hotel under multiple demand scenarios. This practice underscores that revenue management feeds directly into finance: accurate forecasts are essential for budgeting, and strategic choices must fit financial constraints (for instance, using the forecast to justify additional staffing or a renovation schedule). The approach also mirrors industry realities, where revenue leaders increasingly participate in budget planning and are held accountable not only for revenue targets but also for profitability metrics such as flow-through (the share of incremental revenue that converts to profit).

Teaching Total Revenue Management

Traditionally, hotel revenue management focused on the rooms department. A modern curriculum broadens the scope to total-hotel revenue management, integrating ancillary revenue streams and even customer lifetime value. That shift naturally brings finance considerations to the fore, since departments carry distinct cost structures and margins. For example, coursework can examine yielding banquet space or dynamically pricing restaurant menus and then trace how those tactics affect overall profitability. Students are encouraged to think in terms of profit optimization rather than pure top-line maximization. A case study might contrast two groups: a large tour group seeking a steep room discount but likely to spend heavily on banquets versus a smaller corporate group paying higher room rates with minimal ancillary spend. Students analyze which business is more profitable once total revenue and variable costs are netted out. The takeaway is clear: the "highest revenue" option is not always the best for the bottom line.

Finance-Driven KPIs and Analysis

Revenue management education should explicitly integrate finance-driven metrics. A core example is return on investment (ROI) for marketing or distribution initiatives. When a hotel considers investing in a new revenue management system or a metasearch campaign, students evaluate ROI by comparing initial cost with the expected revenue uplift or cost reduction. In an industry with tight margins, management will demand ROI evidence for any technology or strategy. Assignments can require students to build a concise ROI model for projects such as mobile check-in or a loyalty app, factoring in technology costs, expected increases in direct bookings or on-property spend, and payback period. This discipline of quantifying benefits against costs trains students to justify innovations with sound financial reasoning, consistent with the principle that strategy, not technology, should drive adoption.

Another essential tool is breakeven and displacement analysis for group-sales decisions. Students learn to calculate the breakeven rate for a discounted group and determine the room rate at which accepting the group, while displacing transient demand and incurring F&B or other variable costs, still makes financial sense. The calculation uses contribution margins and displacement cost, bridging revenue management with cost accounting.

By systematically linking revenue tactics to financial outcomes, the curriculum equips students to be strategic revenue optimizers, not mere revenue maximizers. Graduates learn to avoid common pitfalls (e.g., prioritizing short-term top-line gains that erode profit or brand) and to focus on sustainable performance aligned with owner expectations. In practice, concise decision memos that compare net revenue, flow-through, and displacement across alternatives (e.g., flash sale vs. hold Best Available Rate) keep the finance linkage front and center.

CASELETS, ASSIGNMENTS & CLASSROOM PRACTICE

Experiential learning via STR analytics, simulations, and live cases is consistent with RM pedagogy that builds decision quality under uncertainty (Noone et al., 2011;

Wang et al., 2015). To translate theoretical knowledge and technology skills into managerial competence, an effective hospitality finance curriculum relies heavily on *experiential learning* such as case studies, practical assignments, simulations, and interactive classroom activities. This section describes various pedagogical techniques and examples of coursework that bring revenue strategy and technology to life. These range from brief "caselets" used in class discussions, to full-length case studies, to hands-on projects and simulations. Each is designed to reinforce concepts, encourage critical thinking, and give students practice in applying what they've learned to realistic scenarios. By immersing students in quasi real-world problems, these methods help bridge the gap between academic learning and professional practice.

Industry Case Studies

Case studies are a staple in business education, and this curriculum selects or develops cases specific to hospitality revenue and finance innovation. Ideal cases blend qualitative and quantitative challenges. For example, a hotel deciding on a new pricing approach or implementing a tech system with sufficient data for analysis. One case chronicles *Marriott International's mobile app ecosystem* redesign aimed at a "frictionless guest journey" from booking to checkout. Reported outcomes included significant growth in mobile check-in adoption and higher on-property spend among app users. Students analyze how Marriott integrated digital tools (mobile check-in, chat, mobile key) and how those initiatives translated into both improved customer experience and increased revenue per guest. Discussion emphasizes critical success factors such as pairing technology changes with staff training and process redesign, underscoring that revenue-tech initiatives require holistic change management.

Another case examines *Accor's "ALL" (Accor Live Limitless) platform*, which unified more than 40 brands into a digital lifestyle loyalty ecosystem spanning accommodation, dining, and entertainment. Students evaluate the shift from a traditional loyalty program to a platform model and its revenue implications, greater direct bookings and higher member spend balanced against substantial investment and partnership requirements. Juxtaposing the Marriott and Accor cases highlights contrasting digital strategies: enhancing operations and guest experience versus creating new revenue streams and brand loyalty. These real-world initiatives prepare students to lead similar projects and to critically evaluate tech-driven strategies encountered in practice.

Experiential Methods

To reinforce decision quality under uncertainty, the course blends rapid caselets, a brief simulation run, a guest talk, and a structured reflection loop into one experiential arc. Students first tackle 10-15 minute, data-light caselets (e.g., OTB spike + rumored citywide event + comp-set rates) to practice fast judgment; they then complete a short simulation round (pricing, overbooking, channel controls) to observe immediate consequences. Next, an industry practitioner delivers a focused live case (e.g., preparing for a major event or post-implementation RMS lessons) with Q&A that grounds classroom learning in current practice. Finally, students submit a reflective memo connecting choices and outcomes to theory (forecasting, displacement, price fairness) and proposing one improvement for the next cycle. This compact sequence operationalizes Kolb's cycle (experience → reflection → concepts → experimentation), deepens transfer from tools to strategy, and keeps workload tight while preserving pedagogical impact (Anderson & Xie, 2010; Noone et al., 2011; Wang et al., 2015).

Group Projects and Assignments

The course includes substantial group projects that often serve as capstones. One signature project tasks teams with developing a digital transformation and revenue enhancement plan for a hypothetical hotel. The brief requires teams to present a refined Business Model Canvas, an implementation roadmap with phases and resources, and 3-5 KPIs to evaluate success, all tailored to a chosen innovation concept. Deliverables must reference course frameworks (e.g., the Technology-Organization-Environment model for context analysis, dynamic capabilities, and change-management principles), specify implementation steps and costs, and define measurement plans. Requiring both a Business Model Canvas visual and a roadmap diagram builds clear, concise communication. These projects foster teamwork and mirror professional scenarios in which multidisciplinary teams craft executive-ready proposals. Presentations delivered to the class or a panel including industry guests develop students' ability to articulate and "sell" strategy, a key skill for future managers advancing new initiatives.

Another regular assignment is analysis of *STR reports* and external benchmarking data. STR reports are given for anonymized hotels (which includes occupancy, ADR, RevPAR and index vs. comp set for a month or year). Students must interpret the numbers: e.g., "Hotel X has a RevPAR Index of 105, ADR Index 110, Occupancy Index 95. What does that tell you about its performance and strategy?" The ideal answer would note that the hotel's ADR is higher than competitors but occupancy lower, implying a high-rate strategy that might be sacrificing some volume, then discuss whether that's optimal or if adjustments are needed. Incorporating such industry reports trains students in a bread-and-butter task of revenue managers: benchmarking and identifying weaknesses or strengths in performance. All property data are anonymized (e.g., "an upscale hotel in City Y") to maintain confidentiality and keep attention on analysis.

By leveraging these various case-based and experiential methods, the curriculum ensures that theory is continually married to practice. Students do not simply memorize formulas for forecasting or list the advantages of a tech tool, they *use* them in context, make decisions, see outcomes, and discuss them. This approach resonates with Kolb's experiential learning cycle: concrete experience (doing a simulation or case), reflective observation (class discussion and write-up), abstract conceptualization (connecting back to theory), and active experimentation (applying insights in the next scenario). The result is deeper learning and higher retention of skills. Graduates from such a program have essentially "rehearsed" their future jobs: they have analyzed real data, solved realistic problems, worked in teams, and defended their recommendations. As hospitality businesses increasingly seek talent who can hit the ground running amidst rapid digital change, these practice-oriented pedagogies give students and innovative programs a competitive edge.

ETHICS, POLICY, AND ACADEMIC INTEGRITY

Fairness perceptions in dynamic pricing and responsible use of guest data require managers to complement algorithmic tools with ethical judgment (Heo & Lee, 2011; Mattila & Choi, 2005). Operational safeguards, transparent classroom use of AI, and professional norms, ensure integrity from classroom to practice. Managers should maintain explicit AI-pricing override rules, periodic bias reviews, and plain-language guest communications on price fairness.

As hospitality finance education increasingly incorporates AI and digital tools, it encounters a complex landscape of ethical and policy considerations. This section addresses those challenges on two levels: (1) the ethical and policy issues related to using AI and data in hospitality business practice, which educators must instill in students; and (2) the academic integrity and ethical use of technology within the educational process itself. In weaving these discussions into the curriculum, the goal is to develop not only skilled but also responsible professionals who can navigate the moral and regulatory facets of revenue management innovation.

Ethical Use of Data and AI in Hospitality

Modern revenue management relies heavily on customer data such as purchase history, demographics, and online behavior, and on AI algorithms that inform decisions. This reliance raises important ethical questions related to privacy, consent, fairness, and transparency. Instruction covers major data privacy regulations, including the General Data Protection Regulation in the European Union, which imposes strict rules on the storage and processing of personal data. For example, when a hotel's revenue strategy uses guest profiles to set personalized prices or to offer tailored packages, the regulation requires clear consent from guests for that use of their data.

Scenarios involving personalized pricing, where online retailers displayed different prices to users based on browsing history or device and provoked public backlash, can be examined in detail. In a hospitality context, a guiding question is whether it is ethical for a loyalty program to offer different room rates to members based on past spending. Students analyze the line between personalization that adds value to the customer and discrimination that treats customers unfairly. The concept of algorithmic bias is introduced: if an AI pricing model unintentionally produces higher prices for guests from certain locations or booking channels that correlate with protected characteristics, the outcome may be discriminatory. Students are trained to scrutinize automated recommendations and, when appropriate, to override them, which underscores the continued importance of human judgment. At the policy level, organizations should formalize procedures for auditing AI outcomes and ensuring fairness.

Another ethical dimension concerns pricing during crises, sometimes called price gouging. A typical exercise presents a case in which a natural disaster creates a surge in demand for lodging and the revenue system recommends tripling rates. Although some jurisdictions enforce anti-gouging statutes, hotels must weigh obligations to the community and the brand. Class discussion considers how to balance revenue opportunities with social responsibility, often concluding that short term profit is not worth long-term damage to trust and reputation. Alternatives include setting reasonable rate caps, allocating inventory to relief efforts, and communicating the rationale clearly.

Integrity and Equity in the Classroom Innovation

Curriculum innovation should keep equity explicitly in view. Advanced digital tools must not disadvantage students who lack devices, reliable internet, or assistive technologies. When an online simulation performs best with high-speed connectivity, provide campus access, loaner equipment, and downloadable or low-bandwidth alternatives. Apply universal design principles to all materials, ensure compatibility with screen readers and captioning, and offer multiple ways to demonstrate learning. Address representation directly by selecting cases, data sets, and guest speakers that reflect a diversity of roles, identities, and geographies; this helps counter long-standing gender and cultural imbalances in revenue management and finance and signals that talent is welcome from many backgrounds.

Ethics and integrity should run through both what is taught about AI-enabled revenue strategy and how it is taught. Graduates should leave with current technical skills and a clear moral compass that guides the use of those skills. The industry benefits when professionals protect guest trust, follow the law, and act fairly while pursuing revenue and profit. Educational institutions sustain credibility by upholding the same standards in the classroom, so that honesty, fairness, inclusion, and respect remain nonnegotiable even as new tools are adopted.

IMPLEMENTATION ROADMAP (FOR EDUCATORS)

Successful curriculum transformation mirrors hotel digital programs: top-led, iterative, cross-functional, and metrics-driven (Kane et al., 2015; Wang et al., 2015).

Translating the vision of an AI-enhanced, strategically integrated hospitality finance curriculum into reality requires a clear implementation roadmap. This section outlines a step-by-step plan that academic institutions can follow to design and roll out such a curriculum. This roadmap considers resource requirements, stakeholder involvement, and staged development to manage change effectively. It is informed by program development experience as well as best practices gleaned from literature on curriculum design and digital transformation initiatives. Notably, this roadmap echoes the phased approach taught to students for implementing technology in hotels, underscoring that schools themselves must undergo a transformation process.

Adopting the proposed curriculum can follow a lean, four-move path.

1. Align and assess: in 4-6 weeks, confirm graduate competencies with an industry mini-panel (hotel, vendor, association) and run a light digital-maturity pulse to identify quick wins (e.g., STR case pack, Excel pickup model).
2. Build the minimal viable lab stack: assemble a PMS training dataset, a spreadsheet RMS (forecast + overbooking logic), and one BI dashboard. Embed ethics and data governance touchpoints.
3. Pilot and iterate: test the forecasting and pricing module with one cohort. Track forecast MAPE, RevPAR to GOPPAR linkage rubrics, and student experience. Fix the top three frictions and publish a one-page quick-start guide.

4. Evaluate and refresh annually: use an advisory review to rotate one new dataset or case each year, align to CHIA (Certification in Hotel Industry Analytics), HSMAI (Hospitality Sales & Marketing Association International) credentials, and plan faculty upskilling (8-12 hours/year).

By following this implementation roadmap, an institution can navigate the change systematically. It addresses common pitfalls: faculty resistance is mitigated by involving them early and providing training, student unease is reduced by piloting and support, and resource issues are handled by planning and leadership backing. Much like a hotel implementing a new system, the keys are top-management support, phased implementation, cross-functional collaboration, and clear metrics for success.

FUTURE DIRECTIONS

Next-generation RM will integrate deeper data science, total revenue optimization, and data storytelling while preserving human-centric service (Anderson & Xie, 2010; Noone, 2016; Wang et al., 2015).

The next wave of curriculum innovation will embed core data-science competencies within revenue management rather than treating them as electives. Students should be able to clean and model hospitality data, code basic forecasting and optimization routines (e.g., pickup-based time series, regularized regression, gradient-boosting for demand), and evaluate model performance with decision-relevant metrics (accuracy metrics for forecasts, uplift for promotions, profit-based loss functions). Capstones can require students to prototype a lightweight recommendation engine for ancillary upselling or to cluster guests by booking behavior and price sensitivity, then translate findings into pricing fences and distribution rules (Kane et al., 2015; Verhoef et al., 2021; Wang et al., 2015).

Revenue education will increasingly integrate environmental and social performance into financial decision-making. Alongside RevPAR and GOPPAR, students should work with Net RevPAR after distribution costs, Flow-through, and GOPPAR-S (GOPPAR adjusted for material sustainability investments or carbon price assumptions). Framing sustainability as revenue-relevant (premium willingness to pay, channel preferences, loyalty effects) prepares graduates to articulate owner value under evolving disclosure regimes while avoiding green-premium myths through careful testing and attribution (Aksoy et al., 2022; Sigala, 2020).

As RMS/BI systems automate forecasting and price recommendations, competitive advantage will hinge on interpretation, narrative, and ethical judgment. Curricula should therefore scaffold: (a) data storytelling, turning dashboards into owner-ready memos that link RevPAR actions to GOP and cash flow; (b) cross-functional facilitation, running a revenue meeting that balances marketing, operations, and finance trade-offs; and (c) AI governance such as spotting algorithmic bias, setting override rules, and communicating fair-pricing policies to guests. Assessment should move beyond right-answer numeric to board-style pitches that defend strategy under uncertainty and fairness constraints (Anderson & Xie, 2010; Heo & Lee, 2011; Noone et al., 2011).

By anticipating these directions now, educators can lay groundwork to build flexible curriculum frameworks that can absorb new content, fostering faculty development in data-science, and establishing partnerships that enable resource sharing. The hospitality leaders of the future will likely work in environments where change is the only constant, and our education must therefore instill adaptability, curiosity, and an innovation mindset, alongside technical know-how. The journey of curriculum evolution will continue, as dynamic as the industry it serves.

CONCLUSION

The hospitality industry stands at the crossroads of technological innovation and traditional service excellence. This chapter examined how advances in AI, data analytics, and digital tools are reshaping the teaching of finance and revenue management in hospitality education. The review grounded the discussion in current literature and practice, noting that while technology is transforming operations and guest experiences, strategic vision and human factors ultimately determine the success of digital transformation. This dual perspective underpins the core argument: hospitality finance education must integrate cutting-edge revenue strategies and technology without losing sight of strategic, ethical, and human-centric competencies.

The chapter outlined a modern curriculum architecture that interweaves digital strategy, revenue analytics, and strategic leadership. Students move from understanding disruptive forces to mastering optimization tools and, finally, to synthesizing technology and finance into innovative strategy. The technology lab stack section detailed how hands-on work with PMS, RMS, dashboards, and real hospitality data bridges theory and practice, preparing graduates for hotel revenue workflows. The discussion further linked revenue choices to financial outcomes, urging a shift beyond RevPAR toward profitability, ROI, and asset value. Ethics and policy considerations emphasized privacy, fairness, and honesty in data and AI use, alongside clear guidance for academic integrity in the classroom.

Looking ahead, the chapter anticipated deeper integration of data science, more personalized lifelong learning pathways, AR/VR-enhanced teaching, a stronger emphasis on sustainability, and a continual blending of human insight with AI capabilities. By fostering adaptability and continuous innovation, hospitality education can graduate strategists who harness AI for insight while exercising creativity, ethical judgment, and leadership.

In conclusion, "innovating hospitality finance education through revenue strategies and technology" is both an exciting opportunity and a pressing imperative. The synergy of advanced tools and strategic pedagogy can produce a generation of hospitality professionals who are as comfortable with algorithms and dashboards as they are with balance sheets and customer relationships. These individuals will be capable of driving performance in their organizations by making informed, agile decisions and by continually adapting to change. Education is where this capability is cultivated. By redesigning our curricula and teaching practices as outlined in this chapter, hospitality programs can truly prepare students to *think strategically, adapt to changing market dynamics, and apply innovative solutions in real-world settings*, fulfilling the promise stated in our introduction. The impact will be far-reaching, benefiting not just students and universities, but also the hospitality industry and its customers, who ultimately gain from the infusion of fresh, well-equipped talent ready to redefine excellence in hospitality finance and revenue management.

REFERENCES

Aksoy, L., Choi, S., Doğru, T., Keiningham, T., Lorenz, M., Rubin, D., & Tracey, J. B. (2022). Global trends in hospitality. *Journal of Business Research, 142*, 957–973.10.1016/j.jbusres.2021.12.068_ PMID: 36540755

Anderson, C. K., & Xie, X. (2010). Improving hospitality industry sales: Twenty-five years of Revenue Management. *Cornell Hospitality Quarterly, 51*(1), 53–67. 10.1177/1938965509354697

Busulwa, R., Pickering, M., & Mao, I. (2022). Digital transformation and hospitality management competencies: Toward an integrative framework. *International Journal of Hospitality Management, 102*, 103–132. 10.1016/j.ijhm.2021.103132

Cetin, G., Demirciftci, T., & Bilgihan, A. (2016). Meeting revenue management challenges: Knowledge, skills, and abilities. *International Journal of Hospitality Management, 57*, 132–142. DOI: 10.1016/j.ijhm.2016.06.008

Cross, R. G., Higbie, J. A., & Cross, Z. N. (2009). Revenue management's renaissance: A rebirth of the art and science of profitable revenue generation. *Cornell Hospitality Quarterly, 50*(1), 56–81. 10.1177/1938965508328716

El Gayar, N., Saleh, M., Atiya, A. F., El-Shishiny, H., Zakhary, A., & Habib, H. A. (2011). An integrated framework for advanced hotel RM. *International Journal of Contemporary Hospitality Management, 23*(1), 84–102. 10.1108/09596111111101689

Heo, C. Y., & Lee, S. (2011). Influences of consumer characteristics on fairness perceptions of revenue management pricing in the hotel industry. [DOI:]. *International Journal of Hospitality Management, 30*(2), 243–251. 10.1016/j.ijhm.2010.07.002

Higher Education Authority. (2025). *Generative AI in Higher Education Teaching & Learning: Policy Framework (Version 1.0)*. Higher Education Authority.

Jabeen, F., Al Zaidi, S., & Al Dhaheri, M. H. (2022). Automation and AI in hospitality and tourism: A review. *Tourism Review, 77*(4), 1043–1061. 10.1108/TR-09-2019-0360

Kane, G. C., Palmer, D., Phillips, A. N., Kiron, D., & Buckley, N. (2015). *Strategy, not technology, drives digital transformation*. MIT Sloan Management Review and Deloitte University Press.

Kimes, S. E. (1989). Yield management: A tool for capacity-constrained service firms. *Journal of Operations Management, 8*(4), 348–363. 10.1016/0272-6963(89)90035-1

Mattila, A. S., & Choi, S. (2005). The impact of hotel pricing policies on perceived fairness and satisfaction with the reservation process. *Journal of Hospitality & Leisure Marketing*, *13*(1), 25–39. 10.1300/J150v13n01_03

Memarian, B., & Doleck, T. (2024). Human-in-the-loop in artificial intelligence in education: A review and entity-relationship (ER) analysis. *Computers in Human Behavior: Artificial Humans*, *2*(1), 1–11. 10.1016/j.chbah.2024.100053

Noone, B. (2016). Pricing for hotel revenue management: Evolution in an era of price transparency. *Journal of Revenue and Pricing Management*, *15*, 264–269. 10.1057/rpm.2016.8

Noone, B. M., McGuire, K. A., & Rohlfs, K. V. (2011). Social media meets hotel revenue management: Opportunities, issues and unanswered questions. *Journal of Revenue and Pricing Management*, *10*(4), 293–305. 10.1057/rpm.2011.12

Queenan, C. C., Ferguson, M. E., & Stratman, J. K. (2011). Revenue management performance drivers: An exploratory analysis within the hotel industry. *Journal of Revenue and Pricing Management*, *10*(2), 172–188. 10.1057/rpm.2009.31

Sigala, M. (2020). Tourism and COVID-19: Impacts and implications for advancing and resetting industry and research. *Journal of Business Research*, *117*, 312–321. 10.1016/j.jbusres.2020.06.015 PMID: 32546875

To, W. M., & Yu, B. T. W. (2025). Artificial intelligence research in tourism and hospitality journals: Trends, emerging themes, and the rise of generative AI. *Tourism and Hospitality*, *6*(2), 63–89. 10.3390/tourhosp6020063

Verhoef, P. C., Broekhuizen, T., Bart, Y., Bhattacharya, A., Qi Dong, J., Fabian, N., & Haenlein, M. (2021). Digital transformation: A multidisciplinary reflection and research agenda. *Journal of Business Research*, *122*, 889–901. 10.1016/j.jbusres.2019.09.022

Wang, X. L., Li, X., & Liang, S. (2015). Revenue management: Progress, challenges, and prospects. *Journal of Travel & Tourism Marketing*, *32*(7), 797–811. 10.1080/10548408.2015.1063798

Weatherford, L. R., & Kimes, S. E. (2003). A comparison of forecasting methods for hotel revenue management. *International Journal of Forecasting*, *19*(3), 401–415. 10.1016/S0169-2070(02)00011-0

ADDITIONAL READINGS

Anderson, C. K., Kimes, S. E., & Carroll, B. (2009). Teaching revenue management at the Cornell University School of Hotel Administration. *Transactions on Education*, *9*(3), 109–116. 10.1287/ited.1090.0024

Hayes, D., & Miller, A. (2011). *Revenue management for the hospitality industry* (2nd ed.). Wiley.

Ivanov, S., & Webster, C. (2019). *Robots, artificial intelligence, and service automation in travel, tourism and hospitality*. Emerald Publishing. 10.1108/9781787566873

Ka, X., Ying, T., & Tang, J. (2023). A conceptual model for developing digital maturity in hospitality micro and small enterprises. *Journal of Theoretical and Applied Electronic Commerce Research*, *18*(3), 1511–1528. 10.3390/jtaer18030076

Kimes, S. E. (2010). Successful tactics for surviving an economic downturn: Results from an international study. *Cornell Hospitality Report*, *10*(7), 6–11.

Chapter 8
Using AI to Enhance Wine Education in Fine Dining Operations

Sarah Jane Elisabeth Belanger
http://orcid.org/0009-0005-8052-1600
Abu Dhabi Hospitality Academy-Les Roches Global Hospitality Education, Abu Dhabi, UAE

Leonardo Roman Carbajal
Abu Dhabi Hospitality Academy-Les Roches Global Hospitality Education, Abu Dhabi, UAE

Abdul Rehimane Musthafa
Abu Dhabi Hospitality Academy-Les Roches Global Hospitality Education, Abu Dhabi, UAE

Edmund Goh
Abu Dhabi Hospitality Academy-Les Roches Global Hospitality Education, Abu Dhabi, UAE

ABSTRACT

This chapter presents a UAE-appropriate approach to using artificial intelligence as added support—not a substitute for judgement—in teaching food-and-wine pairing for fine-dining service. We address a practical constraint: universities typically do not serve alcohol on campus, yet graduates must analyse dishes, justify pairings, and speak confidently to guests in licensed venues. Drawing on sensory-science principles and hospitality pedagogy, we describe a student-first routine in which learners construct their own tasting notes, rationales, and concise guest-facing lines, then use clearly instructed AI to compare and refine their work. The approach

DOI: 10.4018/979-8-3373-5112-4.ch008

increases practice density, makes reasoning visible, and keeps instructors focused on coaching. We outline classroom applications across service, culinary, teaching, student learning, operations, and cross-cultural communication, and discuss benefits and limitations in the UAE context. Overall, the chapter offers a transferable method that makes pairing logic explicit, repeatable, and assessable.

INTRODUCTION

Graduates need the confidence and tools to explain food-and-wine pairing clearly, connect dish structure to guest preferences, and recommend matches that elevate the meal.

In most international restaurants, that sentence still points toward wine. Food-and-wine pairing remains a recognised part of gastronomic culture and a durable part of the dining experience—more than a passing trend (Eschevins et al., 2019). As one large consumer survey put it, "Most (87%) French consumers consider wine to be the most important element to match with food," and the ritual of the food–wine match sits within UNESCO's listing of the French gastronomic meal (as cited in Eschevins et al., 2019). Whether or not wine sales grow every year, the practice holds its place in guest expectations at the premium end of the market.

The UAE adds a distinctive backdrop. As a tourism economy, the country continues to elevate its luxury dining profile, drawing international guests who bring global expectations about pairing and service language to licensed venues. That trajectory is visible in high-end restaurant recognition and in official tourism priorities that put service excellence at the centre of competitiveness (United Arab Emirates Ministry of Economy and Tourism, 2024). In parallel, spend by international travellers has reached record projections, reinforcing the broader commercial importance of high-quality hospitality communication in premium dining contexts (World Travel & Tourism Council, 2025). For graduates stepping into those roles, pairing fluency and guest-centric phrasing are not extras; they are part of basic credibility.

At the same time, universities in the UAE operate under a clear legal and cultural framework. Alcohol consumption is lawful only in licensed venues and remains bounded by federal and emirate-level rules; on campus, alcohol is typically not served. That shapes classroom practice and limits how often students can calibrate their tasting vocabulary through side-by-side work with alcoholic samples (United Arab Emirates Ministry of Justice, 2020). The constraint is practical, not philosophical: hospitality schools still carry the responsibility to prepare students for international service standards, yet they must do so in ways that respect local norms. The result is a familiar teaching tension. Without regular tasting in class, novices can find it harder to stabilise a shared structure for aroma and mouthfeel, and to translate technical analysis into a short, confident guest line.

This chapter addresses that tension head-on. Our aim is to show how artificial intelligence can be used as added support—not a replacement for judgement or palate training—to make the rules and language of pairing explicit, repeatable, and assessable in the UAE context. The argument is simple. If we separate reasoning (which can be practised lawfully using non-alcoholic analogues, aroma resources, and clear frameworks) from alcoholic service (which remains the domain of licensed venues and internships), then we can increase the density of meaningful practice without compromising norms. AI helps by enforcing structure and accelerating feedback, so students can cycle through note → rationale → guest line many times in a single session. In this design, the student always goes first; the model serves as a comparator that follows fixed instructions (headings, word limits, neutral tone) and never as the authority.

Two foundations make this workable. First, we lean on sensory-science logic that is both teachable and defensible: intensity matching, congruency or contrast, and overall harmony/off-flavour checks. Students apply these rules to dishes described by simple variables—fat, acid, heat, sweetness, texture, and key aromatics—then commit to a pairing and defend it. This moves them away from vague "rules of thumb" and toward transparent reasoning (Eschevins et al., 2019). Second, we prioritise service language. It is not enough to be right; graduates must be clear. The target is a ≤25-word, guest-facing sentence that names one concrete sensory hook and reduces choice anxiety at the point of selection. That same discipline applies to non-alcoholic recommendations, which are built from the same rules and phrased with the same care.

The value of AI here is pragmatic. When used with very clear instructions, ChatGPT can reformat tasting notes into a shared template, surface weak vocabulary, and produce a counter-proposal that tags which rule justifies each choice. Students then compare, keep what is precise, fix what is generic, and—crucially—finish with a cold-start task without any AI. This raises practice density in the same contact time and keeps the instructor's coaching focused on reasoning and phrasing. Evidence from online and hybrid hospitality teaching suggests that well-designed, short, interactive tasks can sustain engagement in practical subjects, which supports this approach in settings where in-person tasting must be limited (Orlowski et al., 2021).

The context outside the classroom matters, too. Dubai's fine-dining visibility and the growth of premium properties increase the premium placed on precise, respectful beverage communication in licensed venues. Recognition at the highest levels reinforces what guests will expect to hear when they ask for a recommendation at the table (Michelin Guide, 2025). Students who can analyse a dish, justify a pairing with clear rules, and speak in a tone aligned with local values will be better prepared to meet that moment—whether the recommendation points to a grand cru, a by-the-glass option, or a carefully constructed non-alcoholic drink.

Purpose of this chapter. We present a practical, UAE-appropriate teaching model in which AI serves as an assistive tool to (1) stabilise tasting vocabulary and structure, (2) drill pairing logic through many short cycles, and (3) refine guest-facing language for both wine and non-alcoholic options. The model respects legal and cultural parameters while preparing students for international service standards in licensed venues. Our stance throughout is conservative about claims: AI is a scaffold that speeds practice and makes expectations visible; palate calibration and professional judgement remain human.

Structure of the chapter. Section 2 reviews the literature across five themes: hospitality pedagogy, global wine education practices, the UAE context, tourism development, and AI in hospitality teaching. Section 3 outlines our methods and scope, emphasising student-first tasks, clear instruction blocks for AI comparison, and cold-start assessment. Section 4 describes current practices and challenges in the UAE, including cultural/legal constraints, limited tasting exposure, and market signals that raise expectations. Section 5 details the applications of AI across six perspectives—service, culinary, teaching, student learning, operational, and cross-cultural—with simple classroom tools. Section 6 offers three ready-to-run scenarios that translate the approach into practice. Section 7 discusses benefits and limits, broader implications for hospitality education, and ethics in the UAE context. Sections 8 and 9 conclude with a brief synthesis and targeted recommendations for educators, institutions, students, and industry.

Taken together, the chapter argues for a practical middle path: use AI to multiply good practice, not to replace it. Teach the rules, train the language, respect the context—and let technology do what it does best: organise, compare, and accelerate feedback while the craft remains firmly in human hands.

LITERATURE REVIEW

This review synthesizes scholarship on hospitality pedagogy, global wine-service practice, the UAE regulatory and market context, tourism development, and AI-enabled learning to derive design principles for the model used in this chapter.

Hospitality Education and Pedagogy (F&B)

Hospitality programmes typically combine theory with applied, experiential learning to help students translate concepts into service behaviours (Li et al., 2024). In food and beverage subjects, this structure supports the connection between tasting frameworks, pairing knowledge, and service language in more realistic service situations (Orlowski et al., 2021).

Game-based tasks have been shown to increase engagement and support more confident learning of wine-related vocabulary, particularly among beginners (Poole et al., 2022). Younger cohorts also respond well to practical, multisensory activities that move beyond rote tasting lexicons and encourage active participation (LaTour et al., 2021).

Online and hybrid delivery can sustain skills engagement in practical F&B courses when teaching presence is strong and activities are carefully structured (Orlowski et al., 2021). Virtual field experiences broaden access and can support some skills outcomes, while in-person visits more consistently generate emotional connection and reports of deep learning. Together, this evidence points to a complementary blend rather than a direct replacement (Nimri et al., 2024).

Two design implications follow for wine education in fine-dining contexts. First, learners benefit from a shared tasting vocabulary and repeated, low-stakes rehearsal that supports the translation of analysis into concise, guest-facing pairing suggestions at the point of choice (Terrier & Jaquinet, 2016). Second, when practical exposure is constrained, well-scaffolded digital experiences—such as videos, simulations, prerecorded tastings, and guided discussions—can help maintain learning momentum while preserving space for instructor feedback and support (Orlowski et al., 2021).

Wine Education Globally: Standard Practices in Fine-Dining Operations

From a sensory-science perspective, food–beverage pairing can be organised around three broad perceptual principles. Intensity refers to balancing overall flavour weight between dish and beverage; congruency and contrast describe whether shared or opposing sensory attributes are foregrounded; and harmony captures whether the pairing avoids off-flavours or clashes across aroma, taste, and texture (Eschevins et al., 2019). Together, these principles provide a stable analytical scaffold that can be taught, rehearsed, and assessed independent of specific products.

Global wine education for restaurant service reflects this structure and typically converges on three pillars: structured tasting, pairing logic, and guest-centric communication. Programmes and professional credentials emphasise calibrated sensory description (nose–palate–finish; acid–tannin–body), varietal and regional typicity, and table-side protocols, creating a shared language across markets. External certifications are widely used by employers as signals of competence and as scaffolds for training. While such credentials can increase knowledge and confidence, learning gains do not automatically translate into service or sales outcomes without deliberate coaching for transfer (Rinck & Taylor, 2025; Orlowski, 2022).

To engage newer cohorts, wine educators are encouraged to adopt more accessible narratives that reduce reliance on dense technical jargon and lower barriers to participation (LaTour et al., 2021). Complementing this approach, game-based and interactive learning activities can strengthen engagement and interest in wine-related vocabulary, particularly among novice learners (Poole et al., 2022).

Within beverage curricula, specialist certification providers—notably the Wine & Spirit Education Trust (WSET) and the Court of Master Sommeliers (CMS)—had already shifted many introductory courses online prior to the pandemic, indicating earlier acceptance of digital delivery than in many academic programmes (as cited in Orlowski et al., 2021). This certification-led shift complements campus teaching: standardised content can be accessed at scale, while local programmes concentrate on contextualised service practice.

Food–beverage pairing is increasingly explained through generalisable sensory principles rather than fixed pairing lists. By reasoning from dish variables such as fat, acid, heat, and texture, learners can apply principles of intensity, congruency or contrast, and harmony rather than memorising fixed pairings (Eschevins et al., 2019). In service contexts, communication at the point of choice is as important as analytical accuracy. Empirical studies show that concise pairing notes on menus can reduce perceived risk and increase wine-by-the-glass sales, while richer descriptors heighten attention and support more deliberate selection (Terrier & Jaquinet, 2016; Reynolds, 2024).

Technology as augmentation. Socially constructed and immersive tools expand access to scenarios such as cellar tours and service rehearsals and can increase short-term engagement. At the same time, because wine education has traditionally relied on social interaction and group learning, the findings support a complementary rather than purely substitutive model in advanced programmes (Moonen et al., 2024). In consumer-facing contexts, multisensory and digital layers increasingly personalise the wine journey, offering capabilities that may also be adapted for educational practice and assessment (Velasco et al., 2024)

The UAE Context: Religious and Cultural Limits, Legality, and Market Signals

The United Arab Emirates is a Muslim-majority country that operates within a legal and sociocultural framework shaping how wine is discussed, taught, and served. Alcohol consumption is lawful only in permitted venues and remains bounded by federal and emirate-level rules; within this context, hospitality programmes need to approach wine education with sensitivity to local norms, guest choice, and non-alcoholic alternatives (United Arab Emirates Ministry of Justice, 2020; Martín, 2021). Regulatory adjustments have also altered access: in Dubai, the 30% municipality tax on alcohol was removed and individual liquor-license fees were waived, reducing barriers and changing price signals within licensed ecosystems (Caterer Middle East, 2023). Abu Dhabi has likewise simplified access within its licensing framework, while the emergence of the first craft brewery illustrates broader hospitality-driven diversification (Mansuri, 2024).

Parallel market indicators point to a maturing fine-dining scene with rising expectations for beverage professionalism. Media and guidebooks document curated wine lists and sommelier-led initiatives, including a dedicated Dubai Sommelier Award and, in 2025, the emirate's first three-star MICHELIN recognition—public signals that elevate pairing discourse at the table (Fellows, 2024; Michelin Guide, 2025; Prideaux, 2025). These developments are embedded in a national tourism trajectory: travel and tourism's contribution to GDP and employment remains substantial, and international visitor spend is projected to reach record levels—dynamics that likely intensify demand for premium dining and beverage experiences in the UAE hospitality sector (World Travel & Tourism Council, 2024, 2025). Policy priorities under the UAE Tourism Strategy 2031 further position service excellence as a competitiveness lever, aligning hospitality training with visitor satisfaction and spend (UAE Ministry of Economy & Emirates Tourism Council, 2024).

For educators, the implication is that wine education in the UAE must be designed with sensitivity to the legal limits on alcohol service and to the wider sociocultural context in which hospitality is practiced. This includes preparing students for licensed service environments while ensuring that learning remains inclusive, lawful, and culturally respectful for those who abstain (Martín, 2021; United Arab Emirates Ministry of Justice, 2020). The next subsection examines how tourism growth amplifies these requirements.

Tourism Development in the UAE: Implications for Wine Knowledge in Fine Dining

Building on the regulatory and market context outlined in Section 2.3, this subsection focuses on how tourism growth translates into concrete skill demands for fine-dining beverage service.

Tourism is a strategic pillar of the UAE economy and continues to expand in spend and visibility. Sector analyses report that international traveller spend is projected to reach a record AED 228 billion, reinforcing premium dining demand in licensed venues (World Travel & Tourism Council, 2025). The prior year's outlook likewise framed travel and tourism as reaching "new heights," signalling sustained momentum in visitor flows and hospitality revenues (World Travel & Tourism Council, 2024). At policy level, the UAE Tourism Strategy 2031 prioritizes competitiveness and service excellence, linking workforce upskilling directly to the nation's tourism goals (UAE Ministry of Economy & Emirates Tourism Council, 2024). As part of this diversification, large integrated-resort projects—such as the announced Wynn Al Marjan Island in Ras Al Khaimah—are adding new luxury hospitality capacity with dining, entertainment, and a gaming area, further supporting demand for high-standard beverage service in licensed venues. (Wynn Resorts, 2025)

These macro signals translate to the restaurant floor. Guidebooks and media have amplified the country's fine-dining profile—sommelier awards and, in 2025, Dubai's first three-star MICHELIN recognition—raising guest expectations for pairing fluency and polished, guest-centric service language (Fellows, 2024; Michelin Guide, 2025; Prideaux, 2025). In practice, this means staff must navigate varietal typicity, explain pairing rationales succinctly, and offer alcohol-free pathways with equal confidence for diverse guest segments.

Workforce dynamics further reinforce the need for flexible training. Emiratization and destination-branding priorities place increasing value on UAE nationals in front-of-house roles, where context-appropriate guest communication supports authentic visitor experiences and destination representation (Michael et al., 2024). In parallel, specialized hospitality capacity in higher education remains relatively constrained and student preferences can tilt away from some front-facing hospitality roles, so programs benefit from high-impact, scalable pedagogy—industry partnerships, micro-credentials, and digitally supported practice—that can build transferable service and communication skills in more flexible ways (Rutledge, 2024; Goh et al., 2025).

AI in Education and Hospitality: Teaching, Training, and Operations

AI in education is increasingly associated with systems that support feedback, guidance, and assessment, particularly where these tools are used to extend teaching rather than replace it (Holmes et al., 2023). In hospitality, smart technologies have been associated with more responsive and personalised forms of service through the aggregation and real-time coordination of information (Neuhofer et al., 2015). Together, these developments highlight AI as more than a technical tool: they position it as a mechanism that may shape learning, service, and decision-making, while also raising important pedagogical and ethical questions.

Learner-side affordances. Online and virtual formats can sustain engagement and learner satisfaction in practical F&B courses when they are designed with strong social presence, with instructors actively facilitating meaningful interaction (Orlowski et al., 2021). Comparative studies of virtual and on-site winery field trips suggest complementary strengths. Virtual formats broaden access and increase skills engagement, while in-person visits more reliably generate emotional engagement and reports of deep learning (Nimri et al., 2024). For wine education in regulated environments, this evidence supports blended pathways in which AI-supported tools provide rehearsal and feedback, alongside calibrated exposure through industry partners.

Wine-specific applications. In both consumer and training contexts, multisensory and digital layers are increasingly used to personalise the wine journey before, during, and after consumption (Velasco et al., 2024). Case evidence highlights AI-enabled recommendation systems that learn from chemical and sensory data and translate these patterns into human-readable preference prompts. In educational settings, this logic may be adapted for classroom drills focused on pairing reasoning and sensory vocabulary (Feller, 2022). Startup trajectories further illustrate how AI, user-centred design, and iterative development can transform consumer pairing applications into scalable B2B tools. In educational contexts, such models may also inform the design of instructional simulations and applied learning activities (Choi & Serrato, 2024). In parallel, commercial wine-education platforms are expanding subscription-based digital resources, including maps, guides, pairing tools, and other structured study materials for wine learners. (Wine Folly, 2024).

Teaching and assessment. For instructors, conversational AI can function as a tutoring and viva-style tool that normalises tasting-note structure (e.g., nose–palate–finish; acid–tannin–body) and supports supervised dialogue with "guest archetypes." Early adoption research in hospitality and tourism education indicates generally favourable attitudes toward such tools, which is important for uptake; however, learning impact remains dependent on instructional design and facilitation rather than the technology alone (Abou-Shouk et al., 2025).

Importantly, much of the hospitality literature cited here examines AI primarily through the lens of user acceptance and intention rather than measured learning outcomes. This reinforces the need for pedagogical designs that foreground reasoning, structure, and assessment alignment over tool adoption alone. Immersive environments may heighten presence and short-term recall in sommelier learning, but social co-presence and coached practice remain critical for interactional finesse, underscoring a model of augmentation rather than replacement (Moonen et al., 2024). Ethical guidance from the broader education literature further cautions against overreliance, emphasises transparency with learners, and highlights the need to validate AI outputs against trusted frameworks (Dave & Patel, 2023).

Operational decision-making. In hospitality operations, smart systems can aggregate information and coordinate interactions in real time, supporting more responsive and personalised service processes (Neuhofer et al., 2015). In restaurant settings, this logic can extend to menu engineering, cellar rotation, and attach-rate analysis, which students can practise through sandbox-style exercises (Choi & Serrato, 2024). As learners simulate service scenarios, AI can expose them to a wider range of guest preferences and constraints, such as budget, sweetness tolerance, or non-alcoholic preference. This accelerates the development of transferable heuristics for pairing and communication. Importantly, these tools complement rather than substitute human judgement about context, culture, and hospitality style (Velasco et al., 2024).

Practical implications. For fine-dining wine education in the UAE, AI-enabled systems are most effective when they (a) normalise vocabulary and pairing logic against recognised structures, (b) provide deliberate practice through supervised simulation, (c) personalise tasks to learner goals and constraints, including alcohol-free pathways, and (d) return reliable analytics to instructors for targeted coaching. The following subsection reviews sensory-science foundations and pairing models that can be codified within these tools.

Synthesis (Design Principles)

Taken together, the literature indicates that effective wine-pairing education rests on a shared tasting lexicon with a fixed note structure; a rule-based approach that reasons from dish variables (fat, acid, heat, texture) rather than memorised lists; and iterative, low-stakes practice with structured instructor feedback. Analytic competence must be coupled to guest-facing communication by requiring concise menu lines and table-side phrasing. Where direct tasting is constrained, learning can be sustained through aroma resources, non-alcoholic analogues, and well-scaffolded virtual activities, with tasting-led calibration pursued via licensed partners. External certifications and digital tools help standardise content and extend practice, while local programmes supply contextualisation and cultural fit. In the UAE context—amid growing premium dining and tourism expectations—these principles together provide a lawful, inclusive, and industry-aligned pathway to pairing fluency.

METHODOLOGY / APPROACH

This chapter reports how AI is introduced to support food-and-wine pairing education in a UAE university setting and why these choices are pedagogically sound. It is presented as a teaching report rather than a controlled experiment. The aim is to describe a workable approach that supports pairing as a reasoned, sensory-science-based task, while indicating how the work will continue as an exploratory case within the programme.

The methodological design is informed by a focused review of four areas: hospitality and F&B education and experiential learning; online and virtual formats for practical subjects; sensory-science models of food–beverage pairing; and guest decision aids at the point of choice. From this literature, several practices were adopted that translate directly into classroom design. First, tasting-note structure was standardised to stabilise sensory language across students (Orlowski et al., 2021). Second, pairing was taught through dish variables—fat, acid, heat, sweetness, and texture—rather than memorised lists, aligning instruction with rule-based reasoning (Eschevins et al., 2019). Third, short, guest-facing pairing statements were embedded to develop service communication at the point of choice (Reynolds, 2024).

Collectively, these design choices are intended to achieve three learning outcomes: (1) accurate use of a shared sensory vocabulary, (2) reasoned food–beverage pairing based on intensity, congruency/contrast, and harmony, and (3) concise, guest-appropriate service communication for both wine and non-alcoholic options.

Teaching takes place at Abu Dhabi Hospitality Academy I Les Roches, where alcohol is not served on campus. Despite this constraint, students must still develop the competencies required for fine-dining roles after graduation. To support vocabulary development and structural understanding, non-alcoholic wines are used alongside aroma resources and visual supports to practise descriptors (nose–palate–finish) and to assess acidity, body, texture, and balance. Pairing activities are introduced through curated dish briefs that specify key variables, enabling students to reason from the plate to the beverage and to articulate their choices clearly.

AI is positioned as an assistive study tool and, crucially, as a guided comparator rather than an authority. Holmes et al. (2023) caution against forms of AI in education that automate or supplant teaching and learning rather than augmenting them in ways that support human guidance and understanding. In response to this risk, AI use in the present model is deliberately constrained: students must decide first, articulate their reasoning explicitly, and use AI output only as a structured basis for comparison and critique. Only after this student-first stage is the same dish brief processed through a tightly instructed ChatGPT prompt that applies identical pairing rules—intensity matching, congruency or contrast, and overall harmony—and requires justification against those rules (Eschevins et al., 2019). Students then compare their work with the AI-generated output using an analytic rubric focused on vocabulary precision, alignment with pairing principles, clarity of service language, and inclusion of a non-alcoholic option (Orlowski et al., 2021). The pedagogical value lies in this gap analysis, where divergences in judgement or rationale render the underlying rules explicit and coachable.

The design accommodates substantial variation in prior exposure to wine. For students with limited familiarity, structured tasting templates, dish-variable reasoning, and non-alcoholic analogues provide a low-risk entry point that foregrounds shared vocabulary and analytical logic rather than prior product knowledge. For students with greater international or industry experience, the same framework supports deeper calibration by requiring intuitive judgements to be made explicit and defended through shared rules and precise service language. This differentiated use of a common structure reflects principles of constructive alignment, enabling students to engage with the same intended learning outcomes through appropriately varied tasks (Biggs & Tang, 2011). Although developed within a UAE university context, the approach is therefore transferable to other settings where alcohol access is limited or regulated, including alcohol-free campuses and institutions operating in Muslim-majority destinations.

To make this pedagogical sequence explicit, Box 1 summarises the full "student-first + AI as comparator" cycle that underpins the teaching approach.

Box 1. The "Student-First + AI as Comparator" Teaching Cycle

1. Student-First Task
Students independently complete a tasting note and pairing rationale using shared sensory vocabulary and rule-based principles.
2. AI as Comparator (Constrained)
After submission, AI generates an alternative response using the same pairing rules (intensity, congruency/contrast, harmony).
3. Comparison & Reflection
Students compare outputs using an analytic rubric to identify alignment, gaps, and imprecision.
4. Refinement & Feedback
Students revise their work with instructor feedback, strengthening judgement and service language.

↺ The cycle repeats across scenarios, increasing complexity and independence

Throughout the module, classroom activities maintain a strong connection to service communication. Students repeatedly translate technical analysis into concise pairing statements suitable for menus or table-side dialogue, as dish-level cues reduce perceived risk and support more confident selections (Terrier & Jaquinet, 2016). Brief menu-copy drills further prioritise clarity and a single concrete sensory hook, keeping phrasing neutral and guest-centred (Reynolds, 2024).

The approach generates illustrative teaching artefacts—including before-and-after tasting notes, concise pairing rationales, and example menu lines—which are used to refine instruction and calibrate marking. To strengthen the contribution of this teaching report, evaluation focuses on descriptive and formative indicators rather than experimental comparison. The primary aim is to monitor feasibility, consistency, and instructional value as the model is implemented across cohorts, without making causal claims about learning outcomes.

Evaluation draws on several complementary sources. Analytic rubric distributions are reviewed across cohorts to examine patterns in vocabulary precision, alignment with pairing principles, clarity of service language, and inclusion of non-alcoholic options. Short student reflections collected at key points in the module are used to identify perceived challenges, moments of conceptual clarity, and the role of AI comparison in supporting reasoning. Where possible, informal feedback from internship hosts and industry supervisors provides an external perspective on students' ability to articulate pairing decisions in real service contexts.

As the work proceeds, cohorts are treated as an exploratory case, allowing the teaching model to be refined through iterative implementation. The intention is to document feasibility and instructional value while maintaining a clear focus on principled, sensory-science-based reasoning in food-and-wine pairing. By foregrounding structure, comparison, and service communication rather than product exposure, the approach remains adaptable for hospitality programmes operating under regulatory, cultural, or institutional constraints where direct tasting may be limited.

CURRENT PRACTICES AND CHALLENGES

Traditional Delivery of F&B Education

Hospitality programmes typically blend concise theory with practical activities—labs, service drills, role-play, and field visits—to convert conceptual knowledge into repeatable service behaviours through coached feedback (Li et al., 2024). Within this model, wine instruction combines theory and tasting with food-pairing principles and wine-service practices relevant to restaurant settings (Orlowski, 2022). For novice learners, game-based and socially constructed tasks are used to build vocabulary and confidence (Poole et al., 2022). Since the pandemic, well-designed online and hybrid formats have sustained engagement and satisfaction in practical subjects (Orlowski et al., 2021). In wine-specific contexts, virtual field experiences can deliver skills engagement on some dimensions, while on-site exposure more reliably elicits emotional connection—suggesting a complementary blend (Nimri et al., 2024).

Challenges in the UAE

Cultural and legal frame. Alcohol consumption is lawful only in licensed venues and is regulated at federal and emirate levels; universities typically do not serve alcohol on campus, which shapes classroom practice (United Arab Emirates Ministry of Justice, 2020). Cultural scholarship underscores the need to align food and service with local identity and values (Martín, 2021).

Limited tasting exposure. Because alcoholic tastings are restricted on campus, students have fewer repetitions to develop a shared vocabulary for aroma and structure; programmes therefore employ virtual tools, aroma kits, non-alcoholic wines, and visual scaffolds to create structured practice without alcoholic service (Orlowski et al., 2021).

Curriculum time and uneven industry exposure. F&B modules compete with other requirements, and internships provide variable contact with beverage service, limiting the density of coached repetitions needed for pairing analysis and service phrasing (Goh et al., 2025). Students often encounter pairing during internships, but exposure can be informal and inconsistent, creating a gap between what industry expects and what has been practised in a structured way (Rutledge, 2024).

Common knowledge gaps. Novices frequently rely on brand names or broad adjectives instead of sensory descriptors, use inconsistent tasting-note structures, and default to rule-of-thumb pairings rather than reasoned analysis; translating technical assessment into brief, guest-friendly language is a recurring challenge (LaTour et al., 2021).

Market signals that raise expectations. As outlined in Sections 2.3 and 2.4, the UAE's expanding tourism economy, international fine-dining recognition, and growth in integrated resort developments have elevated expectations for beverage knowledge and service fluency in licensed venues. Within this context, the challenge for education lies not in articulating these market signals, but in preparing students to meet heightened pairing and communication expectations despite limited on-campus tasting opportunities and uneven industry exposure. This gap between industry standards and structured practice places additional pressure on programmes to deliver efficient, scalable pedagogy that supports both alcoholic and non-alcoholic service contexts.

Implications for Skill Development and Employability

These conditions define a clear capability set for graduates. Vocabulary precision within a shared structure allows novice staff to describe aroma, acidity, tannin, body, and balance consistently (Rinck & Taylor, 2025). Reasoned pairing analysis—intensity matching, congruency or contrast, and harmony—should replace memorised lists, with learners also able to articulate non-alcoholic equivalents when appropriate (Eschevins et al., 2019). Concise service language at the point of choice (menu lines and table-side phrasing) reduces perceived risk and supports better selections (Terrier & Jaquinet, 2016). Given limited contact hours and uneven industry exposure, programmes should increase practice density and feedback via well-designed virtual components while seeking calibrated in-venue experiences where feasible (Nimri et al., 2024). Finally, contextual and cultural fluency—a working understanding of the UAE's framework and guest expectations—is essential for respectful, effective communication across properties and segments (United Arab Emirates Ministry of Justice, 2020).

As a hospitality university operating in the UAE, we recognise the practical constraint that alcohol is not served on campus; nevertheless, our objective is to deliver an educational experience that aligns with industry requirements for fine dining. Within that aim, AI is an added support—a means to structure tasting language, rehearse pairing logic systematically, and accelerate feedback—while judgement and palate training remain with the instructor and the student.

AI APPLICATIONS IN WINE EDUCATION

We use AI as added support to structure vocabulary, make pairing logic explicit, and accelerate feedback. Judgement and palate training remain with the instructor and the student.

Service Perspective: Menu Psychology, Upselling, and Guest Recommendations

Guests decide faster and with more confidence when menus include brief, dish-level pairing suggestions, and this can lift by-the-glass sales (Terrier & Jaquinet, 2016). Richer wine descriptors also increase attention and help diners meet their selection goals (Reynolds, 2024). In class, AI functions as a guided comparator: students first write their own tasting note, pairing rationale, and one-sentence guest line; only then do they generate an AI output constrained to the same rules and format. Comparing both against a rubric exposes gaps in precision, logic, and clarity (Orlowski et al., 2021). To demystify industry practice, we also show how algorithmic recommenders translate structured inputs into pairings, purely as context for students' human-led decisions (Feller, 2022).

Teaching deliverables: a bank of menu lines written by students, refined with AI for brevity and tone, then validated in class dialogue (Terrier & Jaquinet, 2016).

Culinary Perspective: AI and Food Pairing

Culinary training is grounded in hands-on technique and authorial judgement, and AI is most valuable when it reveals structure–flavour relationships rather than replacing creative decision-making. Sensory science explains why food and beverage combinations may contrast, balance, or harmonise—through mechanisms such as mixture suppression, hyper-additivity, and texture interactions and thus provides a rule-based foundation for pairing logic (Schifferstein et al., 2022). Within this frame,

AI can encode principles of intensity, congruency or contrast, and harmony, allowing learners to test how changes in fat, acid, heat, or texture shift pairing outcomes.

As a forward-looking extension, emerging kitchen technologies suggest how these principles may be rehearsed in future learning environments. AI-assisted 3D/4D printing and related automation enable precise manipulation of texture and mouthfeel, which could offer controlled ways to explore pairing-relevant effects (Ng, 2026; Seol et al., 2026). In educational settings, such tools may allow students to iterate acidity, crunch, or viscosity, compare their decisions against a rule-based AI counter-proposal, and then exercise chef-led judgement about what best communicates the dish's narrative on the plate. While these developments extend beyond the immediate scope of AI-supported wine education, they point to future contexts in which structured reasoning, sensory literacy, and human judgement remain central to food-and-beverage pedagogy (Mohanty et al., 2024).

Culinary application in education: In culinary education, students can iteratively adjust elements such as acidity, texture, and contrast, compare these choices with rule-based digital suggestions, and—under chef-led guidance—decide which option creates the most balanced and coherent dish (Schifferstein et al., 2022).

Teaching Perspective: Tutoring Systems, Simulations, and VR

AI scales formative feedback without diluting teaching presence. A tasting-note normalizer nudges learners into a common structure—nose, palate, finish; acid, tannin, body—so instructors can mark consistently (Orlowski et al., 2021). For experiential breadth, virtual winery visits can sustain skills engagement when in-person tasting experiences are limited, while in-person visits tend to generate stronger emotional engagement; each format can therefore be used for what it does best (Nimri et al., 2024). Where deeper immersion is needed, VR environments can increase recall in sommelier or cellar simulations if the task fits the medium (Moonen et al., 2024).

Teaching deliverables: Structured, instructor-facilitated interactive tasks, followed by feedback and debrief, can help sustain engagement and teaching presence in online culinary and beverage learning environments (Orlowski et al., 2021).

Student Learning Perspective: Personalization, Mobile Practice, and Inclusive Pathways

Students may benefit from personalised AI-supported practice that delivers customised exercises, provides adaptive guidance when they encounter difficulty, and supports clearer written responses through automatic feedback (Zawacki-Richter et al., 2019). Because universities in the UAE do not serve alcohol on campus, learners also need credible non-alcoholic equivalents generated by the same rules used for wine, so that reasoning—not the beverage—does the pedagogical work (Velasco et al., 2024). Acceptance of AI as a study aid is also promising in hospitality contexts, with early evidence showing positive user intentions toward ChatGPT-style tools (Abou-Shouk et al., 2025).

Student deliverables: paired outputs (wine and NA) with rule tags—intensity match, congruency/contrast, harmony—so learners can defend either option clearly (Velasco et al., 2024).

Operational Perspective: Analytics for Menu Engineering and Cellar Logic

To build commercial awareness, learners explore sandboxed scenarios—where to place pairing lines on a menu, how copy length affects readability, and how by-the-glass suggestions might influence attach rate—without claiming real revenue effects (Reynolds, 2024). Case work on digital pairing platforms shows how inputs, feedback loops, and product constraints shape recommendations, which helps students link service language to inventory realities (Choi & Serrato, 2024).

Operational deliverables: short "what-if" briefs—change one dish variable or one menu placement and justify how the pairing line must change—marked for clarity and feasibility (Choi & Serrato, 2024).

Cross-Cultural Perspective: Global Service, Local Constraints

Graduates in the UAE may go on to work in licensed hospitality settings while serving guests within a wider legal and sociocultural framework. Alcohol service is bounded by federal and emirate-level regulation, while hospitality practice also reflects local identity, heritage, and norms of cultural representation (United Arab Emirates Ministry of Justice, 2020; Martín, 2021). For educators, this means preparing students to communicate beverage options with sensitivity and professionalism, including credible non-alcoholic alternatives where appropriate.

Cross-cultural deliverables: paired service lines—one for a wine-seeking guest, one for an NA-seeking guest—each limited to 25 words and grounded in the same rule-based rationale (Martín, 2021).

Table 1 summarises how these cross-cultural service principles are embedded within the broader student-first teaching cycle, including the production and assessment of paired wine and non-alcoholic service outputs.

Table 1. The Student-First + AI-as-Comparator Teaching Cycle for Food–Wine and Non-Alcoholic Pairing

Phase	Student task (student-first)	AI step (constrained)	Output artefact	How it's checked
1. Tasting language	Write a short tasting note for the (NA) sample: nose → palate → finish; note acidity, tannin/body, texture.	Reformat to your template; flag vague words for replacement.	Clean tasting note (house format).	Vocabulary precision; structure followed.
2. Pairing logic	From dish variables (fat/acid/heat/ texture), propose one wine and one NA pairing; justify each using intensity, congruency/contrast, harmony.	Generate a counter-proposal that uses the same three rules and labels the rule(s) for each choice.	Short rationale (≤120 words) with rule tags.	Rule alignment; defensibility of choices.
3. Service phrasing	Distil the analysis to one guest-facing sentence (≤25 words) for wine and one for NA.	Compress to ≤25 words; neutral tone; check readability.	Two one-sentence lines (wine + NA).	Clarity; brevity; neutrality; sensory hook present.
4. Compare & reflect	Place student version and AI version side by side; annotate where they differ and why (e.g., chili heat, sweetness, sauce reduction).	Provide a brief "risks & mitigations" line (e.g., "watch tannin with chili").	Annotated comparison sheet.	Metacognitive insight; correct identification of trade-offs.
5. Cold-start practice	Repeat without AI; update pairings if one dish variable changes (e.g., add heat or acid).	(No AI in this step.)	Final unaided note + pairing + guest line.	Same rubric; performance without scaffolds.

CASE STUDIES / SCENARIOS

The following scenarios illustrate how this cycle is enacted in practice across tasting, pairing, menu-copy development, and table-side communication. All activities follow one rule: students decide first, then they may use ChatGPT with very clear instructions (specifying format, rules, word limits, and tone) to compare and tighten their work. On campus, tasting uses non-alcoholic analogues, aroma kits, and visual scaffolds; alcoholic service is reserved for licensed venues.

Scenario A: "Main Grape Varietal Drill" (pairing choice from dish variables)

Aim: Help beginners practise matching a dish to one of eight core grape varieties using three simple rules: intensity match, congruency or contrast, and overall harmony.

Eight varieties (house set). Sauvignon Blanc • Chardonnay • Riesling • Pinot Grigio/Gris • Pinot Noir • Merlot • Cabernet Sauvignon • Syrah/Shiraz

Materials: Aroma kit or non-alcoholic wine analogues; dish cards listing fat / acid / heat / sweetness / texture / key aromatics; one worksheet per student.

Student-first (25–30 min)

- Choose one grape for the assigned dish.
- Write a 120-word rationale using the three rules.
- Optionally, propose one non-alcoholic drink pairing (tea, botanical, fermented, or de-alcoholised) justified by the same rules.

ChatGPT compare (6–8 min)

Students paste the dish card only into ChatGPT with clear instructions like:

- "Use exactly these headings: intensity match; congruency/contrast; harmony/off-flavour checks."
- "Pick one grape from the list and justify in ≤100 words."
- "Give one non-alcoholic pairing justified by the same rules in ≤60 words."
- "Add one line labelled 'Risks & Mitigations' (e.g., chili heat vs. tannin)."
- "Neutral tone. No brand names."

Compare & annotate (8–10 min). Side-by-side, mark where your choice agrees or differs and why (e.g., you weighted heat higher).

What's collected. Your 120-word rationale, the ChatGPT rationale, and a three-bullet reflection: what I'd keep / change / watch out for.

Outcome: Students commit to a grape, defend it with the rules, and learn to critique a model's answer without treating it as the authority.

Scenario B: Menu-Copy Studio (turn analysis into guest-facing lines)

Aim: Convert technical analysis into two ≤25-word menu sentences: one for the wine, one for the non-alcoholic drink, both grounded in the same logic.

Student-first (15–20 min)

Using your dish and grape from Scenario A:

- Write one menu line (wine, ≤25 words).
- Write one menu line (non-alcoholic, ≤25 words).

- Both should be neutral in tone and include one specific sensory hook (e.g., "citrus-zest grip," not "refreshing").

ChatGPT polish (5–6 min)

Paste your two sentences with clear instructions such as:

- "Return exactly two lines: (1) Wine, (2) Non-alcoholic."
- "Keep each line ≤25 words."
- "Neutral tone; one concrete sensory detail; no hype."
- "Do not change the recommendation—only improve clarity and brevity."

Read-aloud check (5 min). Pairs read lines aloud; replace vague adjectives with precise hooks.

What's collected: Your original two lines and your final two lines.

Outcome: Students practise precise, guest-friendly language at the point of choice and see how the same rules support both wine and non-alcoholic options.

Scenario C: Table-Side Role-Play (verbal recommendation)

Aim: Deliver the pairing verbally to different guest types, adapting tone and emphasis while staying concise.

Materials: Dish cards; guest archetype cards (Time-pressed; Budget-aware; Sweetness-sensitive; Non-alcoholic only; Adventurous); the two menu lines from Scenario B.

Student-first (15–18 min)

Triads rotate roles (server/guest/observer). Each round:

- Server opens with one clean sentence (choose wine or non-alcoholic first, based on the guest card).
- Guest asks one follow-up (e.g., "I'm sensitive to heat; will this taste too sharp?").
- Server adapts with one sentence that keeps the rule logic visible.

Optional ChatGPT tone check (3–4 min)

Paste your spoken sentence with clear instructions like:

- "Check for neutral, respectful tone and clarity."
- "Suggest one small improvement (≤12 words) without changing the recommendation."
- "Keep it ≤25 words."

What's collected: One observer card per round (ticks for clarity, respectful tone, specific sensory hook) and each student's final personal line set (wine + non-alcoholic).

Outcome: Confidence, speed, and culturally aware phrasing under time pressure.

What Students Gain

- Knowledge: A practical map of the eight core grapes linked to fat/acid/heat/sweetness/texture.
- Reasoning: Habit of citing intensity, congruency/contrast, harmony—not vague "rules of thumb."
- Communication: Two ≤25-word lines (wine + non-alcoholic) that are neutral, concrete, and usable on a menu or table-side.
- Judgement: Ability to use ChatGPT as a second opinion—keeping precise ideas, fixing generic ones—while staying in charge.
- Transfer: Verbal delivery and quick adaptation when one dish variable changes.

DISCUSSION

Traditional vs. AI-enhanced methods

Traditional F&B teaching builds tacit know-how through short theory inputs, practice drills, role-play, and field experiences; it relies on coached repetition to stabilise service behaviours (Orlowski et al., 2021). In the UAE, the main constraint is that universities typically do not serve alcohol on campus, which limits repeated tasting and shared calibration (United Arab Emirates Ministry of Justice, 2020).

AI-enhanced practice adds speed and structure without replacing judgement: students write first, then use ChatGPT with very clear instructions (fixed headings, word limits, neutral tone) to compare and tighten their work—raising practice density in the same teaching time (Orlowski et al., 2021).

What AI adds—and what it does not

AI makes reasoning visible by forcing students to cite intensity, congruency/contrast, and harmony rather than vague "rules of thumb" (Eschevins et al., 2019). It also helps compress technical analysis into guest-facing lines that reduce choice risk at the point of selection (Terrier & Jaquinet, 2016).

AI does not create palate skill; mouthfeel and balance must still be calibrated through carefully designed experiences where feasible (Nimri et al., 2024).

Implications for hospitality management education

This learner-centred, clearly scaffolded approach may also be adaptable beyond wine to other beverage and food categories, provided the focus remains on engaging, meaningful, and accessible interpretation rather than dense technical language (LaTour et al., 2021). In settings where tastings are limited, virtual preparation can sustain engagement while targeted industry exposure provides affect and authenticity (Orlowski et al., 2021). External credentials remain important as hiring signals; classroom AI should accelerate readiness for those standards, not replace them (Rinck & Taylor, 2025).

Ethics and culture in the UAE

On campus, activities rely on non-alcoholic analogues and aroma resources; alcoholic service belongs in licensed venues (United Arab Emirates Ministry of Justice, 2020). Language should remain respectful and neutral, aligning with local values in how food and drink are discussed (Martín, 2021). Early evidence of positive user intentions toward AI in tourism and hospitality suggests that supervised use of such tools may be acceptable to learners, provided they are framed as support tools rather than replacements for human judgement (Abou-Shouk et al., 2025).

CONCLUSION

This chapter presented a practical, UAE-appropriate way to use AI as added support in wine education. The challenge is structural: universities do not serve alcohol on campus, yet graduates must communicate credibly about wine and also propose non-alcoholic alternatives in licensed venues (United Arab Emirates Ministry of Justice, 2020). The response is to centre learning on explicit sensory-science rules—intensity, congruency or contrast, and harmony—and to require students to convert that reasoning into concise guest-facing pairing lines of no more than 25 words (Eschevins et al., 2019).

AI's role is to enforce structure and accelerate feedback: students write first, compare against a tightly instructed ChatGPT output, and then improve. Culinary studios extend the same logic to texture and recipe decisions; operational sandboxes build commercial awareness of menu copy and attach-rate without claiming revenue effects (Reynolds, 2024).

In a destination where luxury hospitality is expanding and service quality is positioned as a strategic priority, these capabilities carry clear professional relevance. UAE tourism policy identifies hospitality as a pillar of national competitiveness and stresses the importance of education and training in equipping students and nationals for the evolving needs of the sector (UAE Ministry of Economy, 2024). In this context, the proposed model helps connect classroom learning to industry expectations by developing transferable pairing reasoning, guest-facing communication, and service judgement without depending exclusively on direct alcohol service in university settings. Although designed within a UAE university context, the model is potentially applicable in other environments where alcohol access is limited or regulated, including alcohol-free campuses and institutions operating in Muslim-majority destinations. By prioritizing sensory reasoning, rule-based pairing logic, and AI-supported comparison over product exposure alone, programmes can remain responsive to fine-dining expectations while respecting local norms and institutional constraints.

RECOMMENDATIONS

For educators

Educators are encouraged to adopt a *student-first, then compare* approach when integrating AI into wine and non-alcoholic pairing education. Students should first produce tasting notes, pairing rationales, and concise menu lines independently, before using ChatGPT under tightly constrained prompts with fixed headings, word limits, and tone. To reinforce learning integrity, summative assessment should include a cold-start task completed without AI support (Orlowski et al., 2021). Pairing defences should be anchored consistently to three sensory-science principles—intensity, congruency or contrast, and harmony or off-flavour risk—so that justification remains analytical rather than intuitive (Eschevins et al., 2019). To manage cognitive load and build early confidence, instruction should begin with a stable, limited set of core grape varieties before expanding scope (LaTour et al., 2021). In parallel, educators should require a non-alcoholic pairing for each dish, justified using the same rules, to normalise inclusive beverage practice and ensure transferability across service contexts (Velasco et al., 2024).

For institutions

At an institutional level, effective implementation depends on appropriate resourcing and policy clarity. Programmes should invest in aroma kits, calibrated non-alcoholic beverage analogues, and visual tasting scaffolds to support lawful, on-campus sensory training where alcohol service is restricted (Le Nez du Vin, n.d.). Institutions are also encouraged to support hybrid experiential models that combine virtual winery or restaurant experiences for skills engagement with industry placements that allow calibrated tasting and service exposure in licensed venues (Nimri et al., 2024). Clear institutional guidance on AI use is essential, particularly policies that prioritise student-first work, transparent AI assistance, and unaided assessment components to protect academic integrity (Orlowski et al., 2021). Finally, alignment with external credentials—through recognition or co-designed micro-credentials—can help standardise expectations and strengthen industry relevance (Rinck & Taylor, 2025).

For students

Students should be encouraged to lead consistently with their own reasoning and to treat ChatGPT as a second opinion rather than an authority. The core skill to be developed is the ability to defend a pairing choice using explicit sensory rules rather than relying on brand recognition or generic descriptors (Eschevins et al., 2019). Particular emphasis should be placed on practising concise, guest-appropriate service language, with recommendations limited to approximately 25 words, neutral in tone, and grounded in a single concrete sensory hook (Terrier & Jaquinet, 2016). Students should also actively build a repertoire of non-alcoholic pairings—including tea-based, botanical, fermented, and de-alcoholised options—that map coherently to the same analytical principles used for wine (Velasco et al., 2024).

For industry

Industry partners play a critical role in reinforcing structured pairing education during internships and early career stages. Employers are encouraged to provide interns with clear dish briefs that specify key variables and service tone, and to require one wine and one non-alcoholic pairing line per dish to support consistent reasoning and communication (Reynolds, 2024). The use of short, dish-level pairing cues on menus can further reduce perceived risk for guests and support confident selection in fine-dining contexts (Terrier & Jaquinet, 2016). Where direct tastings are not feasible for trainees, industry partners can offer parallel learning experiences—such as aroma sets or non-alcoholic tasting flights—that mirror the logic and structure of the wine programme, ensuring continuity of learning (Le Nez du Vin, n.d.).

REFERENCES

Abou-Shouk, M., Abdelhakim, A. S., Elgarhy, S. D., Rabea, A., & Abdulmawla, M. (2025). ChatGPT usage intention for tourism and hospitality customers. *Tourism Recreation Research*. Advance online publication. DOI: 10.1080/02508281.2025.2465962

Biggs, J., & Tang, C. (2011). *Teaching for quality learning at university* (4th ed.). Open University Press.

Caterer Middle East. (2023). Alcohol licenses now free in Dubai and 30% tax removed in all MMI stores. Caterer Middle East. https://www.caterermiddleeast.com/news/alcohol-licenses-now-free-in-dubai-and-30-percent-tax-removed-in-all-mmi-stores

Choi, B.-J., & Serrato, C. (2024). PairAnything's tech-forward approach to revolutionize wine selection. Journal of Information Technology Teaching Cases. Advance online publication. DOI: 10.1177/20438869241258234

Dave, M., & Patel, N. (2023). Artificial intelligence in healthcare and education. *British Dental Journal, 234*(10), 761–764. https://doi.org/10.1038/s41415-023-5845-2

Eschevins, A., Giboreau, A., Julien, P., & Dacremont, C. (2019). From expert knowledge and sensory science to a general model of food and beverage pairing with wine and beer. *International Journal of Gastronomy and Food Science*, *17*, 100144. DOI: 10.1016/j.ijgfs.2019.100144

Feller, G. (2022, May 17). Predicting palates: Can artificial intelligence improve wine buying? Wine Industry Advisor. https://wineindustryadvisor.com/2022/05/17/predicting-palates-can-artificial-intelligence-change-wine-tasting/

Fellows, R. (2024, December 9). *The winners of Star Wine List of the Year UAE 2024/'25 make it "almost impossible to get a bad bottle of wine". Star Wine List.* https://starwinelist.com/wine-story/the-winners-of-star-wine-list-of-the-year-uae-2024-25-make-it-almost-impossible-to-get-a-bad-bottle-of-wine

Goh, E., Richardson, S., & Thomas, N. (2025). Opportunities, challenges, and future prospects of establishing a hospitality institution in the UAE: A case study of the Abu Dhabi Hospitality Academy, Les Roches. *Journal of Teaching in Travel & Tourism*. Advance online publication. DOI: 10.1080/15313220.2025.2517607

Holmes, W., Bialik, M., & Fadel, C. (2023). Artificial intelligence in education. In *Data ethics: Building trust* (pp. 622–653). Globethics Publications. https://doi.org/10.58863/20.500.12424/4276068

LaTour, K. A., Joy, A., & Noujeim, R. (2021). Developing wine appreciation for new generations of consumers. *Cornell Hospitality Quarterly*, *62*(3), 337–345. DOI: 10.1177/1938965520978382

Le Nez du Vin. (n.d.). Wine aroma kits: Master Kit (54 aromas). Le Nez du Vin. https://www.lenez.com/en/aroma-kits/wine/

Li, F., Wong, C. U. I., Zhang, H., & Chen, X. (2024). *A bibliometric analysis of pedagogies adopted in tourism and hospitality education.* Tourism Critiques: Practice and Theory. Advance online publication. https://doi.org/10.1108/TRC-12-2023-0033

Mansuri, M. (2024). How UAE's first brewery plans to redefine the region's F&B scene. *Caterer Middle East*. https://www.caterermiddleeast.com/people/how-uaes-first-brewery-plans-to-redefine-the-regions-fb-scene-community-sustainability-experiences

Martín, E. (2021). Nation building and social change in the United Arab Emirates through the invention of Emirati cuisine. *The Sociological Review*, *69*(3), 538–559. DOI: 10.1177/0038026121 1009090

Michael, N., Fotiadis, A. K., & Michael, I. (2024). Emiratization and hospitality sector destination branding of Dubai: An impact analysis. *Journal of Human Resources in Hospitality & Tourism*, *23*(2), 171–193. DOI: 10.1080/15332845.2024.2282197

Michelin Guide. (2025, July 3). *Two restaurants awarded three MICHELIN stars for the first time in Dubai*. https://guide.michelin.com/ae-du/en/article/michelin-guide-ceremony/three-michelin-stars-dubai-2025

Mohanty, P. P., Tiwari, S., & Nair, B. B. (2024). Analysing food innovation drivers: Chefs' perspectives. *Journal of Culinary Science & Technology*, *22*(1), 178–195. DOI: 10.1080/15428052.2022.2036661

Moonen, N., Heller, J., Hilken, T., Han, D.-I. D., & Mahr, D. (2024). Immersion or social presence? Investigating the effect of virtual reality immersive environments on sommelier learning experiences. *Journal of Wine Research*, *35*(2), 101–118. DOI: 10.1080/09571264.2024.2310297

Neuhofer, B., Buhalis, D., & Ladkin, A. (2015). Smart technologies for personalized experiences: A case study in the hospitality domain. *Electronic Markets*, *25*(3), 243–254. DOI: 10.1007/s12525-015-0182-1

Ng, J. K. W. (2026). AI-driven 3D and 4D food printing: Innovations for sustainability, personalization, and global applications. *Food Reviews International*. *42*(2), 773–801. https://doi.org/10.1080/87559129.2025.2502438

Nimri, R., Yang, M. J. H., Yang, E. C. L., & Arcodia, C. (2024). Investigating student engagement of online experiential learning: A comparison of virtual and in-person winery field trips. *Journal of Teaching in Travel & Tourism, 24*(4), 405–425. DOI: 10.1080/15313220.2024.2402987

Orlowski, , M. (2022). *External wine education and certification for restaurant service staff: A mixed-methods evaluation of training effectiveness. International Hospitality Review, 36*(2), 258–277. https://doi.org/10.1108/IHR-03-2021-0023

Orlowski, M., Mejia, C., Back, R., & Fridrich, J. (2021). Transition to online culinary and beverage labs: Determining student engagement and satisfaction during COVID-19. *Journal of Hospitality & Tourism Education, 33*(3), 163–175. DOI: 10.1080/10963758.2021.1907193

Poole, S. M., Maier, T. A., Wiss, B., & Smith, S. (2022). Game-based learning in wine education. *Journal of Hospitality & Tourism Education. 34*(3), 210–215. https://doi.org/10.1080/10963758.2020.1868310

Prideaux, S. (2025, May 22). Michelin star restaurants in Dubai: The 2025 guide. *Condé Nast Traveller Middle East.* https://www.cntravellerme.com/story/michelin-star-restaurants-dubai

Reynolds, D. (2024). Wine-menu design: An investigation using brain–computer interface technology. *Journal of Foodservice Business Research, 27*(1), 26–39. DOI: 10.1080/15378020.2022.2063631

Rinck, K., & Taylor, D. C. (2025). What role do wine certifications play in the modern restaurant? *Journal of Human Resources in Hospitality & Tourism, 24*(3), 517–535. DOI: 10.1080/15332845.2025.2484955

Rutledge, E. J. (2024). The tour guide profession: An attractive option for UAE nationals majoring in tourism? *Tourism and Hospitality Research.* Advance online publication. DOI: 10.1177/14673584241278451

Schifferstein, H. N. J., Kudrowitz, B. M., & Breuer, C. (2022). Food perception and aesthetics—Linking sensory science to culinary practice. *Journal of Culinary Science & Technology, 20*(4), 293–335. DOI: 10.1080/15428052.2020.1824833

Seol, J., Kim, J., Hong, Y., Cha, M., Park, S., Jang, K.-J., Kim, S.-J., & Son, H. I. (2026). Toward intelligent 3D food printing: A review on the perspective of materials, fabrication, monitoring, and control. *Critical Reviews in Food Science and Nutrition. 66*(5). https://doi.org/10.1080/10408398.2025.2538546

Terrier, L., & Jaquinet, A. L. (2016). Food–wine pairing suggestions as a risk reduction strategy: Reducing risk and increasing wine by the glass sales in the context of a Swiss restaurant. *Psychological Reports, 119*(1), 174–180. https://doi.org/10.1177/0033294116659113

United Arab Emirates Ministry of Economy & Emirates Tourism Council. (2024, April 25). *Hospitality advisory committee reviews initiatives outlined in UAE Tourism Strategy 2031 and their role in boosting the national hospitality sector's competitiveness*. https://www.moet.gov.ae/en/-/hospitality-advisory-committee-reviews-initiatives-outlined-in-uae-tourism-strategy-2031-and-their-role-in-boosting-the-national-hospitality-sector-s-competitiveness

United Arab Emirates Ministry of Justice. (2020). Federal Decree Law No. (15) of 2020 concerning the Penal Code [PDF]. https://www.moj.gov.ae/assets/2021/

Velasco, C., Vargas, J., & Petit, O. (2024). Multisensory experiences and technology in the context of wine experiences. *Journal of Wine Research, 35*(2), 85–100. DOI: 10.1080/09571264.2024.2310304

Wine Folly. (2024, December 16). *Wine Folly expands its wine education offerings with the launch of Wine Folly+ subscription. Wine Business*. https://www.winebusiness.com/news/article/296230

World Travel & Tourism Council. (2024). Travel and tourism in the UAE reaches new heights, reveals WTTC. https://wttc.org/news/travel-and-tourism-in-the-uae-reaches-new-heights-reveals-wttc

World Travel & Tourism Council. (2025). International traveller spend in the UAE to reach a record AED 228bn. https://wttc.org/news/international-traveller-spend-uae-to-reach-a-record-aed-228bn

Wynn Resorts. (2025, July 2). Wynn Al Marjan Island debuts Enclave: A destination within a destination [Press release]. https://www.newsroom.wynnresorts.com/en/wynnalmarjan/wynn-al-marjan-island-debuts-enclave-a-destination-within-a-destination/

Zawacki-Richter, O., Marín, V. I., Bond, M., & Gouverneur, F. (2019). Systematic review of research on artificial intelligence applications in higher education – where are the educators? *International Journal of Educational Technology in Higher Education, 16*, 39. https://doi.org/10.1186/s41239-019-0171-0

Chapter 9
Using Student Perceptions of AI to Inform Academic Policy and Assessment Practices

Rachel Germanier
http://orcid.org/0000-0002-5629-0882
Les Roches Global Hospitality Education, Crans-Montana, Switzerland

ABSTRACT

Generative AI is transforming higher education by enabling accessible text creation, information retrieval, and academic support. This chapter reports on a mixed-methods study of bachelor students' engagement with an AI-integrated assessment and their views on AI in education, exploring how academic policy and assessment should adapt. A quantitative phase examined how students' perceptions of AI influenced perceived learning, followed by qualitative interviews on attitudes and practices. Data from mid-2025 showed affective attitudes toward AI were the strongest predictors of perceived learning. Thematic analysis revealed strategic use of AI for academic support, ethical boundaries, and a desire for institutional guidance. AI also offered emotional support, boosting confidence. Recommendations include a roadmap for designing assignments according to a 2-lane model and focusing on assessing learning and critical thinking in an ethical and supportive manner.

INTRODUCTION

Since its widespread adoption in early 2023, the use of generative AI is challenging the previously held assumptions in higher education. In parallel, AI is

DOI: 10.4018/979-8-3373-5112-4.ch009

revolutionizing the workplace with not only repetitive tasks being automated but creative work being outsourced to AI rather than being crafted by human employees. New skills in the realm of digital literacy which were unheard of a decade ago will be heavily in demand by the remaining workforce who will be working in an ever more efficient and productive workplace. In the hospitality industry, which is already facing a recruitment challenge, this problem is particularly acute raising the issue of how hospitality education needs to adapt to this radical change. Through a mixed-methods approach, this research examined the current perceptions of AI among future professionals and leaders in the hospitality industry who are studying at a private international university of applied sciences in Switzerland. Such an exploration contributes to filling the gap identified by the author that the student voice was often absent from the discussion about GenAI use in assessments and lacking in existing AI policy literature. The first prong of the study explored how perceptions of AI affect students' perceived learning outcomes while the second probed into more detail regarding their use and attitude to AI in their studies. Reflection on the two data sets enables a suggestion for consequential policy changes and assessment practices bearing in mind the omnipresence of generative AI in the educational and professional spheres.

REVIEW OF THE LITERATURE

AI in the Hospitality Workspace

The phenomenal impact of AI on the workplace in general and in hospitality in particular is undeniable. McKinsey Global Institute (2024) states that up to 30% of business activity could be automatable by 2030 and as many as 12 million "occupational transitions" might be required in Europe. The effects on the hospitality industry are likely to be just as considerable. While AI cannot replace the human touch for which the industry is renowned, it can readily undertake tasks such as menu planning, inventory, ordering and chat/email composition (Marr, 2025). Indeed, its impact is already being seen in areas dependent on the industry such as Los Angeles where it is replacing lower level jobs (Fourrage, 2025). The scale of AI immersion in processes is evident as demonstrated in Deloitte's recent report stating, "hotels are leaning on technology to help teams work smarter, with 81% of hoteliers prioritizing increasing employee productivity and 49% listing integrating AI-powered solutions as priority tech initiatives," (Deloitte US, 2026).

Recent literature indicates that AI can assist managers in making evidence-based decision-making (HSMAI Foundation, 2025) but in a particularly honest post on LinkedIn, Matt Welle, CEO of the hospitality software company Mews, exposed his disappointment at AI's ability to successfully select suitable candidates when recruiting (Welle, 2025) demonstrating an example of the current limits of AI's capacity to out-perform humans in some tasks. Despite this example, recent research indicates that skills like resilience, agility and analytical thinking are going to be more and more in demand for roles which integrate AI (Mäkelä & Stephany, 2025) than in those which do not.

AI in Education

One year ago, 86% of students were using AI (Digital Education Council, 2024) and this number is clearly on the rise. Developing the ability to think critically, show resilience and act in an agile manner while faced with generative AI, a tool which can undertake the highest level of Bloom's taxonomy of educational goals, creating, is therefore the challenge faced by the educators of the next generation of employees (Digital Education Council, 2025). Mogavi et al. (2024) note that many educators fear that use of generative AI fosters superficial learning and undermines the development of social and critical thinking skills. Indeed, the term cognitive debt was coined to explain the effect of using generative AI in an academic task (Kosmyna et al., 2025) adding to the negative perception of the tool.

AI and Assessments

As one of the tasks of educators is to assess their students' learning, it is valid to ask how they perceive this is possible when faced with such a potent tool at students' disposal. Acknowledging the presence of generative AI, Perkins and Furze et al. (2024) provide 5-level model of AI use in assessment, ranging from 1 where no AI is allowed to be used, to level 5 where AI and the student co-create the work to be assessed, in a collaborative manner, perhaps reflecting the expectations of the workplace. There is an argument that the scale could be modified to add a level of 0 where no AI is supposed to be used in the assessment, but students circumvent these restrictions and use generative AI nevertheless. Perkins and Furze et al.'s model is typical of the "traffic light" approach to AI in assessment (Hanken School of Economics, 2025; University of Leeds, 2026) which prescribe levels of permissible AI use and rely, to differing extents, on student declarations of such use. AI detection tools are available to many educators but they are unreliable (Perkins, Furze, et al., 2024; Perkins, Roe, et al., 2024) and, as Foltýnek and Newton (2026) explain, there are countless ways available to students to bypass them without AI-written work being detected as such exposing the futility of even attempting to determine AI use. While banning the use of AI in assessments is one avenue, it is not one which is seen to prepare the future entrants to the workplace (Digital Education Council,

2025). Indeed, lacking in Perkins and Furze et al.'s (2024) model is integration of critical thinking in relation to AI use in assessment. As mentioned above, literature has shown that this is a skill which employers are looking for and which we as educators are therefore beholden to develop in our classwork and assess formally as part of our assessment strategy.

AI Use in Hospitality Education

An early paper in this field was written two years ago (Ivanov & Soliman, 2023) and accurately predicted an "AI tsunami". More recently, Dogru et al.'s (2024) insightful paper aligned with Ivanov and Soliman's (2023) work in seeing generative AI as a disruptive technology. Supporting the perspective explored earlier, they state that teaching environments need to specifically prepare future hospitality managers for how to deal with blended teams consisting of both humans and generative-AI-driven platforms. For that to happen, they advocate for generative AI to be integrated across all subjects and while there is a sub-text of critical thinking needing to be applied, it is not mentioned explicitly.

Dogru et al. (2024) acknowledge the challenges relating to authorship in this new era, expose the difficulties outlined in Foltýnek and Newton (2026) and call for clear policies regarding the use of generative AI tools in academic writing. They close their article with ten questions to stimulate discussion on generative AI use in the academy which include reflection on critical thinking and academic integrity. The mixed-methods study at the heart of this chapter is a response to this impetus, gaining insight from students to inform policy decisions regarding assessment in the era of Generative AI.

Current Policies

Many papers have called for clear institutional policies on generative AI use in academic contexts. Dogru et al. (2024), Mhlanga (2023) and Dwivedi et al. (2024) suggest institutions make explicit acceptable and prohibited use of AI while Ivanov and Soliman (2023) and Dogru et al. (2024) call for policies which require transparency and disclosure of AI use in all academic work. A strong call is made for staff and students to receive training in ethical and critical use of AI (Dogru et al., 2024; Mhlanga, 2023; Zhai, 2022) and for AI ethics and AI literacy to be embedded into curriculum design and assessment (Dogru et al., 2024; Ivanov & Soliman, 2023).

Student Perspectives

Students, whose voices had not been adequately considered in the context of AI in education previously (Tierney et al., 2025), are now beginning to be heard. Increasingly, research, including this study, is turning to students to foreground their perspectives. Echoing the sentiments presented above, students have been shown to want clear policies (Barus et al., 2025; Singer-Freeman et al., 2025) and training in appropriate and ethical AI use (Barus et al., 2025; O'Donnell et al., 2025). They claim to use generative AI for brainstorming (Habib, 2024), for language help and editing (Johnston et al., 2024), for tutoring (Keshtkar et al., 2024) and, finally, for outsourcing cognitive effort (Gogh & Kovari, 2025), linking to the cognitive debt mentioned previously.

Hypothesis Development

In this section, the rationale for the hypothesis in the quantitative part of the study will be presented. The hypothesis was: Students' perceptions of AI in education - across affective, behavioural and cognitive facets - will positively predict their overall perceived learning in an AI-supported assessment. Bation and Pudan's (2024) work underpinned this hypothesis with their findings indicating there existed "a significant relationship between students' attitudes toward AI and their learning outcomes" and that exploring this relationship would lead to "fostering a positive and constructive environment for AI integration in education" (p. 1243).

Independent Variable

The items used to measure the independent variable, attitude to AI, came from the ATTARI-WHE scale (Gnambs et al., 2025). The domains of work, healthcare and education were each broken down into three facets: cognitive, affective and behavioural leading to a 9-item scale which was chosen for its pertinence and brevity. Only the results for education are detailed in this chapter.

Dependent Variable

The dependent variable, perception of learning about using AI, was measured with a novel 11-item scale. As no appropriate existing scale was identified, based on the premise of Seymour et al.'s (2000) work on Student Assessment of Learning Gains, five dimensions were explored as shown below in Table 1 with the relevant literature sources for each.

Research Question Development

The second, qualitative, part of the study addressed the following research question: How do students reflect on the ethics, usefulness, limitations and trustworthiness of generative AI tools in their academic work? The four areas under exploration for this part came from the following sources: usefulness was first mentioned in relation to technology in the Technology Acceptance Model (Davis, 1989); trustworthiness derived from McKnight et al.'s (2002) work; Ethics in AI was discussed at length in the AI4People ethical framework (Floridi et al., 2018) and the limitations overlapped with critical digital literacy taken from the work of Selwyn (2016) and the Open University (2025).

Research Gaps Being Addressed

Despite growing calls for clearer AI policies and stronger integration of critical thinking in assessment, the student voice remains largely absent from current scholarship. At the same time, existing research suggests that students' perceptions of AI may meaningfully shape their learning, yet this relationship is underexplored. These gaps make a mixed-methods design essential: quantitative data can illuminate broad patterns in attitudes and learning, while qualitative insights reveal the nuances of students' experiences. Together, they offer the evidence needed to inform policy decisions and effective, future-ready assessments.

METHODS AND RESULTS

The study followed an explanatory sequential design (Plano-Clark et al., 2008) whereby in stage one, quantitative data, in this case a combination of questionnaire data using predominantly a 1-5 Likert scale and exam results from a critical assessment of an assignment focused on critical engagement with generative AI were combined from 82 students taught by the researcher in a private international higher education institution in Switzerland specialized in hospitality management. In the subsequent second stage, 107 interviews were undertaken by and of students, including those from stage one. More detail on each stage and the results follow.

Methods and Results for Stage 1

A cross-sectional quantitative analysis was conducted using survey data collected via Microsoft Forms over one week in May 2025. Students' exam scores were collected in June 2025. The sample comprised 82 students from a population of 107 enrolled in Methods of Research Inquiry across four fifth-semester classes taught by the author. As this course contained one assessment which required the use and critical reflection of GenAI, the students following it were deemed an appropriate population from which participants could self-select. A minimum of 80 participants was required to ensure a 95% confidence level, which was achieved. Responses were linked to participants' identities to enable cross-tabulation with grades, making informed consent essential. Ethical clearance was obtained in advance and the questionnaire was reviewed by an experienced quantitative researcher who suggested minor edits to ensure active consent provision. The study's purpose and ethical considerations were explained verbally before students accessed the survey in class via a link or QR code.

The questionnaire contained three sections. The first captured demographics (age, nationality, gender). The second used the above-mentioned ATTARI-WHE scale (Gnambs et al., 2025) to explore perceptions of AI. This brief scale is well suited to web-based surveys. Although nine items spanned three domains: work, healthcare and education, each assessed through cognitive, affective and behavioural facets using a five-point Likert scale, only the education domain results are presented here. The education-related items were: "AI is helpful for learning and teaching," "I have positive feelings when I think about how AI is used in education and training," and "If I wanted to learn something new, I would choose a learning programme with AI rather than one without." These three facets showed low reliability ($\alpha = .55$), so they were analysed separately.

The third section assessed students' perceived learning from an assignment requiring critical engagement with generative AI. Although the Cognitive, Affective, and Psychomotor Perceived Learning Scale (Rovai et al., 2009) was initially considered, it did not align well with the learning dimensions outlined in Perkins and Furze et al.'s (2024) model. As a result, a novel five-dimensional scale was developed, exploring cognitive understanding (CU), technical proficiency (TP), critical evaluation (CE), ethical awareness (EA) and metacognitive reflection (MR). This was underpinned by Seymour et al.'s (2000) work on self-assessed learning gains (SALG). All statements used a five-point Likert scale (1 = strongly disagree to 5 = strongly agree). The literature underpinning these items is shown in Table 1 below.

Table 1. Sources of dimensions of perception of learning

Dimensions	Questions	Literature source
Cognitive understanding	q1, q2, q3	Zawacki-Richter et al. (2019)
Technical proficiency	q4, q5, q6	Carretero et al. (2017)
Critical evaluation	q7, q8	Zawacki-Richter et al. (2019)

continued on following page

Table 1. Continued

Dimensions	Questions	Literature source
Ethics awareness	q9	Zawacki-Richter et al. (2019)
Metacognitive reflection	q10, q11	Pintrich (2002)

Internal consistency was analysed for the three multi-item domains: cognitive understanding ($\alpha = .86$), technical proficiency ($\alpha = .67$) and critical evaluation ($\alpha = .75$). The overall perceived-learning index showed high reliability ($\alpha = .92$). The questionnaire concluded with an optional open-ended question: "Any other comments on your perception of AI as a result of your first MoRI [Methods of Research Inquiry] assignment?" Data were analysed using SPSS.

The mean age of participants was 21, with students from 38 nationalities. Perceived learning outcomes were generally high (Ms = 3.45–4.32). The highest ratings for perception of learning were for critical evaluation skills, including identifying AI errors (CE2; M = 4.32, SD = 0.84) and distinguishing appropriate use (CU2; M = 4.17, SD = 0.89). Lower scores were observed for behavioural intentions to AI (EDU BEH; M = 3.45, SD = 1.07) and metacognitive reflection as perceived learning (MR1; M = 3.68, SD = 1.15).

Regression analyses supported the hypothesis that students' perceptions of AI in education (but not in the other domains) predicted their overall perceived learning, explaining 18% of the variance, $R^2 = .18$, $F(3, 78) = 5.52$, $p = .002$. The affective facet was the only significant predictor ($\beta = 0.25$, SE = 0.10, $p = .014$), indicating that students with more positive feelings toward AI reported higher perceived learning. Behavioural and cognitive perceptions were not significant ($ps \geq .22$).

When analysing the five learning subdomains separately, model fit was significant for cognitive understanding ($R^2 = .19$, $p < .001$) and critical evaluation ($R^2 = .19$, $p < .001$), marginal for technical proficiency ($R^2 = .09$, $p = .064$) and non-significant for ethical awareness and metacognitive reflection. In all significant models, the affective facet consistently predicted perceived learning: cognitive understanding ($\beta = 0.27$, $p = .018$), critical evaluation ($\beta = 0.24$, $p = .018$) and technical proficiency ($\beta = 0.30$, $p = .014$). Behavioural and cognitive facets were not significant in any model.

These findings suggest that students' emotional responses to AI more strongly influenced their perceived learning than behavioural intentions or cognitive evaluations. Subsequently, qualitative comments in the questionnaire were compared to exam results, revealing that students with the highest grades valued the assignment's emphasis on critical thinking and acknowledged AI's limitations. In contrast, students who failed the assignment gave more varied responses, including confusion about its purpose and uncertainty about how to engage critically with AI.

Methods and Results for Stage Two

The second stage followed the structure outlined by Plano-Clark et al. (2008) in which qualitative data are used to elaborate and contextualize quantitative findings. This phase was designed to provide greater interpretive depth and nuance to the statistical results generated in the first stage.

The same participant cohort was retained for this stage as well as some students who had not filled in the questionnaire resulting in 107 interviews. Each participant engaged in a one-to-one interview conducted in English, using a peer-interview format with the aim of obtaining richer data by using a repeated insider approach. To ensure consistency across the dataset all interviewees used as a guide the same interview schedule covering the four themes of students' reflections on their use, perceived trustworthiness, ethics and limitations of generative AI in their academic work. As is appropriate for semi-structured interviews, interviewers were free to probe further to gain meaningful insights where relevant. Interviews were conducted in June 2025, with informed consent obtained from all participants prior to data collection.

Interviews were audio-recorded and transcribed using AI transcription tools chosen by each interviewer. Transcripts were anonymized to preserve confidentiality and subsequently subjected to thematic analysis using ChatGPT with the researcher using MAXQDA to search for relevant quotes for the themes identified. This combined approach played to generative AI's strength of being able to analyse a relatively large corpus while maintaining researcher oversight.

Analysis of the interview data revealed five themes which will be addressed in turn: AI as a tutor; trust, verification and prompt literacy; ethical reasoning; role of the teacher and the institution and, finally, equitable access to AI tools.

AI as a Tutor

Students consistently described AI as a scaffold for academic development, particularly in the early stages of task engagement and to comprehend challenging material. Its utility was most pronounced in concept clarification, summarisation and structural support. One student noted, "I use it to help understand finance and sustainability - things that feel too abstract at first," highlighting AI's role in demystifying complex or unfamiliar domains. Beyond comprehension, AI was also valued for its capacity to support ideation and writing. As another participant explained, "It helps me generate ideas or structure my argument when I'm stuck," suggesting that AI functions as a cognitive catalyst during moments of academic inertia.

Importantly, students emphasized the non-judgmental nature of AI. "It doesn't judge you like people do. It's like a private tutor," one student reflected, positioning

AI as a safe and supportive interlocutor. AI was also seen as a confidence builder, sometimes at the beginning of an assignment or "by making learning easier." This framing underscores the emotional dimension of AI use, where, as per the psychological safety model (Edmondson, 1999), psychological safety enhances learning engagement.

Trust, Verification and Prompt Literacy

While students acknowledged AI's benefits, they demonstrated a critical awareness of its limitations. Trust in AI outputs was not assumed; rather, it was claimed to be actively negotiated through repeated prompting and cross-verification. "I refine the question until the AI gives me what I want," one student explained, illustrating the emergence of prompt literacy as a key skill. One student described the Research Methods course, which included the literature review assignment examined in stage one of this study, as a key moment in their learning: "It's like having a study assistant, but the responsibility to learn and think still belongs to us. Especially thanks to what we learned in our current MORI course, I feel more confident when I use AI because I know how to use it properly and understand both its strengths and limits." Students also differentiated between tools based on perceived reliability. "ChatGPT is good for writing, but Perplexity gives better sources," noted one participant, indicating a strategic use of platforms aligned with task-specific needs. Verification practices were common, with students claiming to routinely triangulate AI outputs against institutional platforms and search engines. As one student stated, "I always compare it with Moodle or Google before I use anything," reinforcing the importance of critical digital literacy in AI-supported learning.

One participant reflected honestly that they did not engage with this level of critical analysis: "So...if I'm using it for schoolwork to tell me the assessment outline and summarize it for me, it's probably going to get some things wrong, but I just choose to blindly trust it because it's easier at that time than not." A classmate reflected that the literature review assignment had potentially shown "a lot of people who use AI in our classes firsthand that it's wrong or can't do an assignment well," demonstrating that learning about AI was perceived in others through this assessment.

Ethical Reasoning

Ethical considerations were central to student discourse, with clear distinctions drawn between support and substitution. "If AI supports your thinking, it's fine. If it replaces it, it's cheating," one student asserted, articulating a normative boundary that aligns with academic integrity. Another commented, "If you use AI to do, to write your whole work or to provide something that is not yours, then it is completely wrong and unethical," demonstrating a clear ethical positioning and unwillingness to avoid cognitively challenging tasks.

However, an existence of pressures that complicate ethical decision-making was revealed. "Sometimes I know it's borderline, but it's the only way I can manage," admitted one participant, pointing to a submission to pressure while acknowledging the troublesome ethical situation.

Inconsistent institutional guidance exacerbated these tensions. "We need proper guidelines. Some teachers say don't use it, others tell us to," one student observed, highlighting the need for coherent and transparent policies. This ambiguity not only undermines ethical clarity but also places the burden of interpretation on students, who may lack the resources to navigate such complexity independently.

Teacher and Institutional Role

Students expressed a strong desire for educators and institutions to take an active role in shaping AI use. The absence of consistent expectations across courses was a source of frustration. "Every class has different rules. It's confusing," one student remarked, underscoring the pedagogical dissonance that arises from fragmented approaches. There was also a call for formal education on AI literacy. "We should have classes on how to use AI responsibly - like prompt design," suggested one participant, indicating that technical proficiency and ethical awareness should be embedded within curricula.

Rather than viewing AI as a threat to traditional pedagogy, students advocated for its integration alongside human instruction. "AI shouldn't replace teachers. It should be used with teachers," one student emphasized, reflecting a vision of AI as a complementary tool rather than a substitute.

The tension between students' digital realities and institutional expectations is captured in one student's blunt observation: "And no matter, like, even if the teachers say, oh, you can't use AI, you can't use this, it's going to happen anyway. It's going to happen regardless," highlighting the disconnect between educators and learners when it comes to generative AI use.

Equitable Access and Peer Pressure

Finally, students highlighted the socio-economic and cultural dimensions of AI use. Access to premium tools was uneven, raising concerns about digital inequality. "Some students pay for better AI - that's unfair," one student noted, pointing to subscription models as a barrier to equitable participation, even in the elite private educational environment studied. Another student alluded to initially receiving "wrong information" with the free version before paying for an upgrade which "will be good, it will give you the right answer sometimes," showing confidence that paid-for content is likely to provide a more satisfactory response.

Social norms also shaped engagement, with AI use described as a form of peer conformity. "It's like social media. Everyone uses it so you kind of have to," remarked one participant, suggesting that usage is often driven by collective expectation rather than individual choice.

For non-native speakers, AI offered linguistic support that enhanced academic expression. "As a non-native speaker, it helps me express myself more clearly," one student shared, illustrating how AI can mitigate language-based disadvantage and foster inclusion.

DISCUSSION

This study explored student perceptions of generative AI in education through a mixed-methods design, revealing nuanced insights into how AI is currently shaping the student learning experience. The findings underscore the urgent need for higher education institutions to adapt academic policy and assessment practices to align with the realities of student use of generative AI tools.

Emotional Orientation and Perceived Learning

The quantitative first stage of the study demonstrated that students' affective attitudes toward AI were the strongest predictors of perceived learning, particularly in domains such as cognitive understanding, technical proficiency and critical evaluation. This aligns with Bation and Pudan's (2024) assertion that positive attitudes toward AI correlate with improved learning outcomes. The affective dimension - students' emotional responses to AI - emerged as more influential than cognitive or behavioural facets, suggesting that emotional safety and confidence play a pivotal role in shaping meaningful engagement with AI tools highlighting the importance of these elements for teaching practice.

Analysis of the qualitative data from stage two reinforced this finding. Students described AI as a "non-judgmental tutor," emphasizing its role in building confidence and reducing anxiety during academic tasks. This emotional support was particularly valuable in the early stages of assignment engagement, where AI helped clarify abstract concepts and scaffold initial thinking. The perception of AI as a safe and supportive interlocutor suggests that its integration into learning environments may enhance student agency and reduce barriers to participation, especially for those who experience academic insecurity or language-related challenges, particularly relevant in the international setting of this chapter's research. Explicit recommendations from educators for students to use AI in their courses in addition to discussions about the students' interactions with AI and their critical engagement with it will legitimise and destigmatise its use from the student perspective in the future. Such reinforcement of the validity of using GenAI echoes the professional landscape and better prepares the students for the new workplace.

Strategic Use and Prompt Literacy

Students demonstrated a high level of strategic engagement with AI, using it for ideation, summarization and structural support. Many did not blindly trust AI outputs; instead, they claimed to engage in iterative prompting and cross-verification, indicating emerging prompt literacy and critical digital competence. This behaviour reflects the principles of the Technology Acceptance Model (Davis, 1989), where perceived usefulness and ease of use influence adoption, but also suggests a shift toward more sophisticated user practices. Others admitted to outsourcing tasks requiring cognitive engagement onto generative AI for an easy ride, aligning with the findings of Gogh and Kovari (2025).

Students' ability to differentiate between platforms, for example using ChatGPT for writing and Perplexity for sourcing, illustrates an ability to align tools with task-specific needs. This strategic engagement supports the findings of Keshtkar et al (2024) who noted that students expect AI tutors to be reliable, adaptable and context aware. However, the behaviour of some students "blindly trusting" AI due to its convenience highlights the risk of intellectual outsourcing and the accumulation of cognitive debt (Kosmyna et al., 2025). These findings underscore the challenges facing the academy. Some students readily turn to a tool to do their work for them, accumulate a reduced ability to engage with difficulties and potentially therefore learn very little. The requirement for students to use AI responsibly and reflectively needs to be accompanied by them learning critical AI literacy.

Such emerging prompt literacy is highly relevant for the hospitality industry, where AI is rapidly reshaping operational roles and demanding a workforce capable of critical evaluation and collaboration with intelligent systems and able to apply advanced digital judgement rather than passive technological dependence.

Ethical Reasoning and Institutional Ambiguity

Ethical reasoning was a prominent theme in student discourse. Participants consistently distinguished between AI as a support tool and AI as a substitute for original thought. The boundary between ethical and unethical use was clearly articulated: using AI to scaffold thinking was acceptable while using it to replace cognitive effort was considered cheating. This demonstrates that these students' perspectives align with the ethical frameworks proposed by Floridi et al. (2018) and the calls for ethical instruction in AI use by Dogru et al. (2024) and Mhlanga (2023).

However, students also revealed the pressures that complicate ethical decision-making, including time constraints and inconsistent guidance from faculty. The lack of coherent institutional policy was a source of frustration and inconsistent requirements across the faculty body regarding the permitted use of AI provoked sentiments of annoyance. Such ambiguity and inconsistency place the burden of interpretation on students, undermining the very confidence required of them to do well.

The findings echo calls in the literature for clear, transparent and enforceable policies on AI use in academic contexts (Dogru et al., 2024; Dwivedi et al., 2024; Ivanov & Soliman, 2023). Students expect institutions to define acceptable and prohibited uses of AI, require disclosure of AI use in academic work and provide training in ethical reasoning. Without such policies, students are left to negotiate ethical boundaries in isolation, increasing the risk of misuse and undermining academic integrity.

Assessment Design in the AI Era

Currently, detection tools are not fit for purpose (Foltýnek & Newton, 2026; Perkins, Roe, et al., 2024) and students are already using AI in assessments, regardless of institutional prohibitions. The University of Newcastle in Australia's (Holmes, 2025) novel 2-lane model which removes ambiguity regarding AI use in assessments is a pragmatic solution to this problem. It puts forward a model in which students are assessed in both secure supervised assessments which "facilitate observable attainment of program/course learning outcomes, verifying that students demonstrated the required knowledge and skills" as well as open assessments which are based on the assumption that students ***may*** engage with GenAI to compete the task. The author suggests taking this further, assuming that students ***will*** engage with GenAI in any non-supervised assessment. Once this assumption is made, educators then step back and focus on ensuring that their assessments actually assess the students' learning as per the course learning objectives. Such a step-change requires a shift from enforcement to engagement. Institutions must design assessments that acknowledge AI's presence and leverage its capabilities to foster deeper learning. This includes tasks that require students to critique AI-generated content, compare multiple AI outputs and reflect on their own cognitive processes, just as they will be required to do in the workplace.

The practices demonstrated by students in this study – including prompt literacy, ethical reasoning, and critical evaluation – align with the collaborative intent of level 5 in Perkins and Furze et al.'s (2024) AI assessment scale. However, the findings also reveal that co-creation with AI is pedagogically meaningful only when paired with critical thinking. Students who interrogated AI outputs, triangulated sources, and reflected on ethical boundaries reported higher perceived learning and performed better. In contrast, those who relied on AI uncritically struggled to meet assessment expectations. These results confirm the researcher's suggestion in the literature review that level 5 of Perkins and Furze et al.'s (2024) model be extended to explicitly include critical engagement with AI, thereby aligning assessment design with both academic goals and the demands of AI-integrated professional environments.

Pedagogical Implications and Faculty Development

Students in this study expressed a strong desire for educators to take an active role in shaping AI use. The absence of consistent expectations across courses was a source of confusion and frustration. Participants called for formal education on AI literacy, including prompt design, verification strategies and ethical reasoning. This aligns with the recommendations of Zhai (2022), Dogru et al. (2024) and the Open University (2025), who advocate for embedding AI literacy into curriculum design and teaching practice.

Rather than viewing AI as a threat to traditional pedagogy, students envisioned it as a complementary tool. Such a perspective supports the integration of AI into blended learning environments, where human instruction and AI support coexist to enhance learning outcomes. Faculty development programs must therefore equip educators with the skills to design AI-integrated assignments, facilitate critical discussions about AI use and model ethical engagement with AI tools. The mammoth nature of this task has been highlighted eloquently by Foltýnek and Newton (2026) and is not to be underestimated, but is necessary if, as educators, we want to assess our students' learning in this age of ready access to generative AI.

This study also highlights the importance of emotional intelligence in teaching. Students valued AI for its non-judgmental nature, but also recognized the irreplaceable role of human educators in providing mentorship, feedback and ethical guidance. Faculty must be prepared to navigate the emotional dimensions of AI use, including student anxiety, overreliance and ethical uncertainty. This requires a shift in pedagogical mindset - from gatekeeping to guiding, or, as one commentator described, from building fences to watering the plants (Digital Education Council, 2025) and a commitment to fostering trust, transparency and critical engagement.

Equity and Access

Equitable access to AI tools emerged as a concern in the data, even within a private educational environment. Students noted that subscription models to Large Language Models create disparities, with some gaining access to more reliable or advanced AI platforms than others. This digital inequality risks exacerbating existing educational disparities and undermining the principle of fair education and assessment. Institutions must consider how to provide equitable access to AI tools, whether through institutional subscriptions, partnerships with AI providers, or integration of free and open-source platforms into learning environments.

Language support was another equity-related theme. Non-native speakers described AI as a valuable tool for enhancing academic expression and overcoming linguistic barriers. This suggests that AI can foster inclusion and support diverse learners, but only if access is universal and guidance is provided. Institutions must ensure that AI use does not become a privilege reserved for those with financial means or technical expertise.

Readiness for the Professional World

The findings of this study suggest that students are beginning to develop foundational competencies that align with the evolving demands of AI-integrated professional environments, especially in hospitality. Their emerging prompt literacy, strategic tool selection, and ethical reasoning reflect a readiness to engage with AI not merely as a support tool but as a collaborative partner. This aligns with Dogru et al.'s (2024) call for hospitality education to prepare students for blended teams composed of humans and AI-driven platforms. The ability to refine prompts, verify outputs, and articulate ethical boundaries indicates that students are acquiring the agility and discernment required to operate in such contexts. Moreover, the emphasis on emotional safety and confidence-building through AI use resonates with Mäkelä and Stephany's (2025) argument that human skills like resilience and analytical thinking are increasingly valuable in AI-mediated roles. However, the variability in students' depth of engagement – from strategic use to blind trust – underscores the need for structured instruction in AI literacy and ethics, as advocated by Zhai (2022) and the Open University (2025), to ensure consistent professional readiness across cohorts and to bridge the gap between academic practice and workplace expectations.

RECOMMENDATIONS

The recommendations from this study are two-fold, firstly on an institutional policy level, and secondly at an educator level.

Recommendations for Institutional Policy

Based on the findings of this mixed-methods study which foregrounded the perception of students in a private, international higher education hospitality education context, the first institutional policy recommendation is for the development of clear, enforceable, and consistently communicated policies regarding AI use in assessments. The recommendation is that rather than trying to prohibit or limit AI use (Dogru et al., 2024; Mhlanga, 2023) with its associated challenges, even to student and faculty wellbeing (Corbin et al., 2025), there be a focus on assessing student learning while taking as read that AI will be used in any and all unsupervised assessments. The 2-lane approach implemented by Newcastle University seems an appropriate, feasible and understandable model which requires a certain percentage of a course grade to be achieved in a "secure" setting while the remainder of the grade assumes or even assesses critical use of GenAI. Tasks could involve students comparing AI-generated material with their own work, assessing AI-generated work with specific criteria, or being encouraged to find a workable solution to a problem with the help of AI. Such a recommendation not only answers the clamour from students for clarity regarding GenAI in assessments but relieves the burden from educators to identify inappropriate use of GenAI tools. However, such a change in policy requires the second recommendation, that institutions embed ethical and critical AI literacy into curricula through workshops, modules or courses focused on prompt design, verification strategies, and critical evaluation (Zhai, 2022; Open University, 2025). Thirdly, equitable access to AI tools should be prioritized by securing institutional licenses for premium platforms or ensuring availability of reliable free alternatives to all students, independent of financial means. Additionally, faculty development programs must equip educators to integrate AI into teaching and assessment, lead critical discussions and model ethical use, while offering practical guidance on assignment design, AI literacy and emotional support strategies while recognizing that such programmes require continual updating to keep pace with evolving technologies.

Roadmap for Redesigning Assessments

Based on the policy above specific to assessments, a four-step roadmap can be envisaged as indicated in Figure 1.

Figure 1. A 4-step roadmap for AI-ready assessments

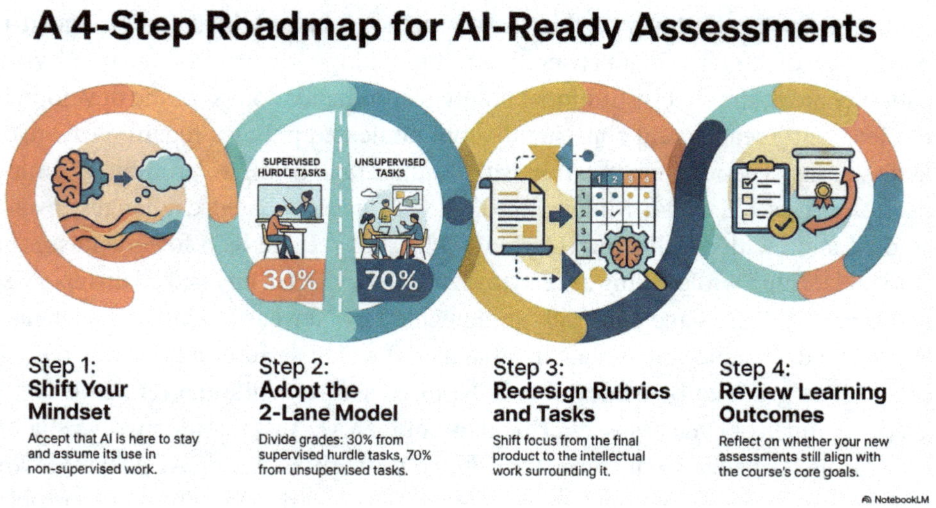

In detail, Step 1 entails faculty recognising that "it is not feasible nor desirable to restrict, limit, or ban generative AI" in assessments (Liu & Bates, 2025, p. 12) and changing the mindset to assume or expect the use of in all non-supervised assessments. Step 2 requires dividing assessments as per the Newcastle 2-lane model – supervised and non-supervised assessments. 30% of the grade is assessed in a supervised environment. This is a hurdle assessment and must be passed to pass the course. The remaining 70% of the grade can be achieved in an unsupervised environment. Step 3 involves redesigning rubrics and tasks to shift the focus from the product being assessed (the old "create" from Bloom's taxonomy) to the intellectual work surrounding it. This includes students' ability to appraise AI outputs, reflect on their own thinking, and demonstrate original contribution (Digital Education Council, 2025; Perkins, Furze, et al., 2024). Finally, step 4 demands educators' reflection on whether the learning outcomes are being assessed or whether they need modifying. This roadmap will not be implementable overnight but will enable educators to move beyond the futile practice of estimating how much AI contributed to a student's work to focusing instead on assessing students' criticality toward AI and the extent of their learning.

Students need to know how to use AI proficiently in order to be prepared for a hospitality industry which is at the forefront of AI use in many of its sectors. The recommendations laid out above contribute to ensuring the hospitality education of the future prepares them well for this reality.

Limitations and Recommendations for Further Research

The scope of this study was small and the willingness and ability of the author to generalise is limited. Although the research was mixed methods in nature, the author suggests that readers focus on the transferability of findings to other contexts (Lincoln & Guba, 1985) as is common in qualitative work within a constrained setting rather than generalisability which is the fundamental aim of quantitative work.

While the chapter advocates for the implementation of a 2-lane model of assessing, it acknowledges the "enormous" scale of redesigning assignments (Foltýnek & Newton, 2026).

Stage two of the data collection was conducted by students, with interview pairings selected by the author. This approach offered several advantages: notably, the absence of a hierarchical power dynamic between interviewer and interviewee potentially contributed to richer, more candid responses. Additionally, the delegation of interviewing to over 100 students enabled a significantly larger dataset than would have been feasible had the author conducted all the interviews personally. However, this method also introduced certain limitations as control over the data gathering process was inherently limited. Variability in interviewing styles, levels of probing and adherence to the interview protocol may have affected the consistency and depth of the data collected. There was also potential for bias to be introduced by peer relationships, which could have influenced both the content and tone of responses. Furthermore, the lack of direct oversight during interviews may have impacted the reliability and comparability of the data across participants. Despite these limitations, the work presents a rich picture of student perspectives on generative AI use in academic work in 2025.

Areas of future research in this field should continue to interrogate the perspective of the student, the educator, the policy makers and the future employers. As students inevitably rely more and more heavily and consistently on generative AI, research needs to be undertaken to explore the effect of the cognitive debt (Kosmyna et al., 2025), the consequences of outsourcing of challenging tasks and the potential reduction in critical thinking students may experience. Voice needs to be given to educators faced with the enormous challenges posed by the AI tsunami. Policy makers should be interrogated regarding the feasibility of implementing secure assessments. Finally, employers – in this case in the hospitality sector but potentially more widely - must be interrogated to determine their requirements in this rapidly evolving era and to ascertain to what extent the education being provided is achieving this end.

REFERENCES

Barus, O. P., Hidayanto, A. N., Handri, E. Y., Sensuse, D. I., & Yaiprasert, C. (2025). Shaping generative AI governance in higher education: Insights from student perception. *International Journal of Educational Research Open*, *8*, 100452. DOI: 10.1016/j.ijedro.2025.100452

Bation, N. D., & Pudan, J. C. (2024). Exploring the correlation between students' attitudes towards AI and their learning outcomes. *International Journal of Social Science and Human Research*, *07*(02), 1243–1247. DOI: 10.47191/ijsshr/v7-i02-45

Carretero, S., Vuorikari, R., & Punie, Y. (2017). *DigComp 2.1: The Digital Competence Framework for Citizens with eight proficiency levels and examples of use*. Publications Office of the European Union / JRC., DOI: 10.2760/38842

Corbin, T., Dawson, P., Nicola-Richmond, K., & Partridge, H. (2025). 'Where's the line? It's an absurd line': Towards a framework for acceptable uses of AI in assessment. *Assessment & Evaluation in Higher Education*, *50*(5), 705–717. DOI: 10.1080/02602938.2025.2456207

Davis, F. D. (1989). Perceived usefulness, perceived ease of use, and user acceptance of information technology. *Management Information Systems Quarterly*, *13*(3), 319–340. DOI: 10.2307/249008

Deloitte, U. S. (2026). *Future of Hospitality: AI-Driven Industry Trends*. https://www.deloitte.com/us/en/Industries/consumer/articles/future-of-hospitality-ai-innovation.html

Digital Education Council. (2024, February 8). *Digital Education Council global AI student survey 2024*. Digital Education Council. https://www.digitaleducationcouncil.com/post/digital-education-council-global-ai-student-survey-2024

Digital Education Council. (2025, July 7). *"Watering the plants, not just building fences": Rethinking assessment in the AI era*. Digital Education Council. https://www.digitaleducationcouncil.com/post/watering-the-plants-not-just-building-fences-rethinking-assessment-in-the-ai-era

Dogru, T., Line, N., Hanks, L., Acikgoz, F., Abbott, J., Bakir, S., Berbekova, A., Bilgihan, A., Iskender, A., Kizildag, M., Lee, M., Lee, W., McGinley, S., Mody, M., Onder, I., Ozdemir, O., & Suess, C. (2024). The implications of generative artificial intelligence in academic research and higher education in tourism and hospitality. *Tourism Economics*, *30*(5), 1083–1094. DOI: 10.1177/13548166231204065

Dwivedi, Y. K., Pandey, N., Currie, W., & Micu, A. (2024). Leveraging ChatGPT and other generative artificial intelligence (AI)-based applications in the hospitality and tourism industry: Practices, challenges and research agenda. *International Journal of Contemporary Hospitality Management*, *36*(1), 1–12. DOI: 10.1108/IJCHM-05-2023-0686

Edmondson, A. (1999). Psychological safety and learning behavior in work teams. *Administrative Science Quarterly*, *44*(2), 350–383. DOI: 10.2307/2666999

Floridi, L., Cowls, J., Beltrametti, M., Chatila, R., Chazerand, P., Dignum, V., Luetge, C., Madelin, R., Pagallo, U., Rossi, F., Schafer, B., Valcke, P., & Vayena, E. (2018). AI4People—An ethical framework for a good AI society: Opportunities, risks, principles, and recommendations. *Minds and Machines*, *28*(4), 689–707. DOI: 10.1007/s11023-018-9482-5 PMID: 30930541

Foltýnek, T., & Newton, P. M. (2026). What does YouTube advise students about bypassing AI-text detection tools? A pragmatic analysis. *Journal of Academic Ethics*, *24*(8), 8. Advance online publication. DOI: 10.1007/s10805-025-09675-3

Fourrage, L. (2025, August 22). *Top 5 jobs in hospitality that are most at risk from AI in Los Angeles-and how to adapt*. Nucamp. https://www.nucamp.co/blog/coding-bootcamp-los-angeles-ca-hospitality-top-5-jobs-in-hospitality-that-are-most-at-risk-from-ai-in-los-angeles--and-how-to-adapt

Gnambs, T., Stein, J.-P., Appel, M., Griese, F., & Zinn, S. (2025). An economical measure of attitudes towards artificial intelligence in work, healthcare, and education (ATTARI-WHE). *Computers in Human Behavior: Artificial Humans*, *3*, 100106. DOI: 10.1016/j.chbah.2024.100106

Gogh, E., & Kovari, A. (2025). Homework in the AI era: Cheating, challenge, or change? *Frontiers in Education*, *10*, 1609518. Advance online publication. DOI: 10.3389/feduc.2025.1609518

Habib, S. (2024, May 2). *AI can help – and hurt – student creativity*. University of South Carolina. https://www.sc.edu/uofsc/posts/2024/02/conversation-ai-help.php

Hanken School of Economics. (2025, August). *Hanken traffic light model for the use of GenAI & report templates*. Hanken School of Economics. https://www.hanken.fi/sites/default/files/2025-08/hanken_traffic_light_model_for_the_use_of_genai_student_presentation_0.pdf

Holmes, M. (2025, November 13). *University of Newcastle Assessment Framework.* The University of Newcastle, Australia. https://www.newcastle.edu.au/current-staff/teaching-and-research/teaching-resources/ldti/ldti-teaching-resources/resources/university-of-newcastle-assessment-framework

HSMAI Foundation. (2025). *The state of generative AI in talent management, sales, marketing and revenue management* (AI-Powered Workforce: Hospitality's next Evolution). HSMAI Foundation. https://global.hsmai.org/wp-content/uploads/2025/11/GenAI-Research-Case-Study-2-Recruitment.pdf

Ivanov, S., & Soliman, M. (2023). Game of algorithms: ChatGPT implications for the future of tourism education and research. *Journal of Tourism Futures, 9*(2), 214–221. DOI: 10.1108/JTF-02-2023-0038

Johnston, H., Wells, R. F., Shanks, E. M., Boey, T., & Parsons, B. N. (2024). Student perspectives on the use of generative artificial intelligence technologies in higher education. *International Journal for Educational Integrity, 20*(1), 1–21. DOI: 10.1007/s40979-024-00149-4

Keshtkar, F., Rastogi, N., Chalarca, S., & Bukhari, S. A. C. (2024). AI tutor: Student's perceptions and expectations of AI-driven tutoring systems: A survey-based investigation. *The International FLAIRS Conference Proceedings,* 37. DOI: 10.32473/flairs.37.1.135314

Kosmyna, N., Hauptmann, E., Yuan, Y. T., Situ, J., Liao, X.-H., Beresnitzky, A. V., Braunstein, I., & Maes, P. (2025). *Your brain on ChatGPT: Accumulation of cognitive debt when using an AI assistant for essay writing task* (No. arXiv:2506.08872; Version 1). arXiv. https://doi.org//arXiv.2506.08872DOI: 10.48550

Lincoln, Y. S., & Guba, E. G. (1985). *Naturalistic inquiry.* SAGE Publications. DOI: 10.1016/0147-1767(85)90062-8

Liu, D. Y. T., & Bates, S. (2025). *A whitepaper from the 'Generative AI in Education: Opportunities, Challenges and Future Directions in Asia and the Pacific' project.* Asia Pacific Rim Universities.

Mäkelä, E., & Stephany, F. (2025). *Complement or substitute? How AI increases the demand for human skills* (No. arXiv:2412.19754). arXiv. https://doi.org//arXiv.2412.19754DOI: 10.48550

Marr, B. (2025, May 13). *How generative AI will affect jobs in restaurants and hospitality.* Forbes. https://www.forbes.com/sites/bernardmarr/2025/05/13/how-generative-ai-will-affect-jobs-in-restaurants-and-hospitality

McKinsey Global Institute. (2024). *The race to deploy generative AI and raise skills*. McKinsey & Company. https://www.mckinsey.com/mgi/our-research/a-new-future-of-work-the-race-to-deploy-ai-and-raise-skills-in-europe-and-beyond?

McKnight, D. H., Choudhury, V., & Kacmar, C. (2002). Developing and validating trust measures for e-commerce: An integrative typology. *Information Systems Research*, *13*(3), 334–359. DOI: 10.1287/isre.13.3.334.81

Mhlanga, D. (2023). *Open AI in education, the responsible and ethical use of ChatGPT towards lifelong learning* (SSRN Scholarly Paper No. 4354422). Social Science Research Network. DOI: 10.1007/978-3-031-37776-1_17

Mogavi, R. H., Deng, C., Juho Kim, J., Zhou, P., Kwon, Y. D., Metwally, A. H. S. M., Tlili, A., Bassanelli, S., Bucchiarone, A., Gujar, S., Nacke, L. E., & Hui, P. (2024). ChatGPT in education: A blessing or a curse? A qualitative study exploring early adopters' utilization and perceptions. *Computers in Human Behavior: Artificial Humans*, *2*(1), 100027. DOI: 10.1016/j.chbah.2023.100027

O'Donnell, F., Porter, M., & Fitzgerald, S. (2025). The role of artificial intelligence in higher education: Higher education students use of AI in academic assignments *Irish Journal of Technology Enhanced Learning*, *8*(1). Advance online publication. DOI: 10.22554/szwjfy54

Open University. (2025). *A framework for the learning and teaching of critical AI literacy skills*. Open University. https://www.open.ac.uk/blogs/learning-design/wp-content/uploads/2025/01/OU-Critical-AI-Literacy-framework-2025-external-sharing.pdf

Perkins, M., Furze, L., Roe, J., & MacVaugh, J. (2024). The AI assessment scale (AIAS): A framework for ethical integration of generative AI in educational assessment. *Journal of University Teaching & Learning Practice*, *21*(06). Advance online publication. DOI: 10.53761/q3azde36

Perkins, M., Roe, J., Vu, B. H., Postma, D., Hickerson, D., McGaughran, J., & Khuat, H. Q. (2024). GenAI detection tools, adversarial techniques and implications for inclusivity in higher education. *International Journal of Educational Technology in Higher Education*, *21*(1), 53. DOI: 10.1186/s41239-024-00487-w

Pintrich, P. R. (2002). The role of metacognitive knowledge in learning, teaching, and assessing. *Theory into Practice*, *41*(4), 219–225. DOI: 10.1207/s15430421tip4104_3

Plano-Clark, V., Huddleston-Casas, C., Churchill, S., Green, N., & Garrett, A. (2008). Mixed methods approaches in family science research. *Journal of Family Issues*, *29*(11), 1543–1566. Advance online publication. DOI: 10.1177/0192513X08318251

Rovai, A. P., Wighting, M. J., Baker, J. D., & Grooms, L. D. (2009). Development of an instrument to measure perceived cognitive, affective, and psychomotor learning in traditional and virtual classroom higher education settings. *The Internet and Higher Education*, *12*(1), 7–13. DOI: 10.1016/j.iheduc.2008.10.002

Selwyn, N. (2016). *Is technology good for education?* Polity Press. https://www.scribd.com/document/835694093/Is-Technology-Good-for-Education-Neil-Selwyn

Seymour, E., Wiese, D., Hunter, A.-B., & Daffinrud, S. (2000, March 27). *Creating a better mousetrap: On-line student assessment of their learning gains*. National Meetings of the American Chemical Society Symposium, San Francisco.

Singer-Freeman, K., Verbeke, K., & Barre, B. (2025). Generative AI usage among university students depends on academic level and task. *Higher Learning Research Communications*, *15*(2), 1–25. DOI: 10.18870/hlrc.v15i2.1616

Tierney, A., Peasey, P., & Gould, J. (2025). Student perceptions on the impact of AI on their teaching and learning experiences in higher education. *Research and Practice in Technology Enhanced Learning, 20*, 005–005. DOI: 10.58459/rptel.2025.20005

University of Leeds. (2026). *Categories of assessments*. Generative AI. https://generative-ai.leeds.ac.uk/ai-and-assessments/categories-of-assessments/

Welle, M. (2025, October 10). Our AI recruitment experiment failed [Post]. *LinkedIn*. https://www.linkedin.com/posts/matthijswelle_our-ai-recruitment-experiment-failed-activity-7382314919452594176-DSbP/

Zawacki-Richter, O., Marín, V. I., Bond, M., & Gouverneur, F. (2019). Systematic review of research on artificial intelligence applications in higher education – where are the educators? *International Journal of Educational Technology in Higher Education*, *16*(1), 39. DOI: 10.1186/s41239-019-0171-0

Zhai, X. (2022). *ChatGPT user experience: Implications for education* (SSRN Scholarly Paper No. 4312418). Social Science Research Network. DOI: 10.2139/ssrn.4312418

Chapter 10

Teaching in the Virtual Worlds: Integrating Immersive and AI Technologies in Hospitality Education

Nansy Kouroupi
http://orcid.org/0000-0001-8065-8520
Les Roches Global Hospitality Education, Crans-Montana, Switzerland

ABSTRACT

Immersive and AI technologies are reshaping how hospitality competence is taught, rehearsed and assessed, but their value depends less on novelty than on design discipline and governance. This chapter presents a conceptually grounded narrative review of extended reality (VR, AR and social VR) and AI-enabled systems (conversational agents and learning analytics), interpreted through experiential and socio-constructivist lenses and the Cognitive Affective Model of Immersive Learning. Synthesising evidence across four application clusters, it shows where these tools strengthen operational fluency, service recovery, safety and hygiene, communication and data-informed judgement, and where they raise vulnerabilities around generative AI, assessment integrity, privacy and data governance, cost and equity. Drawing on hospitality-industry cases and international policy guidance, it provides evidence-strength signposting and a five-pillar implementation architecture with a constraint-led risk register to support accountable adoption.

DOI: 10.4018/979-8-3373-5112-4.ch010

INTRODUCTION

Hospitality education is at a practical crossroads. Operations are increasingly data-inflected and automated, yet the work remains irreducibly human. Service work is mediated by data, automation, and AI-driven or synthetic media, but it is still profoundly human in its demands for composure, empathy, and sound judgement under pressure (European Commission, 2022a; Huang & Rust, 2018; Kouroupi, 2025; UN Tourism, 2025; Wirtz et al., 2018; World Bank, 2019).

XR is reaching a point where it can do more than 'show' hospitality; it can let students rehearse it. With virtual reality (VR), augmented reality (AR), and mixed reality (MR) now more stable and accessible, and with AI increasingly able to scaffold feedback and role-play, classrooms can stage complex service situations without exposing guests, staff, or brands to real-world risk. The value here is not spectacle but controlled pressure, as a late-night service recovery that escalates, a food-safety check with time constraints, the choreography of a dining room at peak load, or rapid revenue choices when demand shifts mid-shift. Still, the evidence base cautions against treating immersion as a pedagogy in its own right, as learning gains appear to depend on instructional design, alignment with outcomes, and how performance is assessed (Garzón & Acevedo, 2019; Radianti et al., 2020;.

Hospitality-specific studies enhance this point. For example, experimental work on VR game training for frontline contexts suggests that VR may shape affective outcomes differently from knowledge retention (Leung et al., 2022), which matters if we are designing training for both attitude and procedure rather than assuming one will automatically follow the other.

Policy signals also push the conversation forward. The European Commission's Transition Pathway for Tourism frames digital skills and responsible technology uptake as structural requirements for competitiveness and resilience, explicitly implicating education and training ecosystems in that shift (European Commission, 2022a). In that sense, the question is already moving from whether immersive and AI tools will enter hospitality curricula to where they belong, how they should be taught, and what forms of learning evidence should justify their place (Córdova-Esparza, 2025).

XR, AI and Experiential Learning

This topic matters because hospitality education has long relied on experiential learning, doing, reflecting, abstracting, and re-testing in authentic or near-authentic conditions. Traditional methods (role-play, live labs, internships) are powerful, but they can be logistically costly, uneven in exposure, and difficult or risky to stage at full intensity. XR extends this tradition by making complex service moments repeatable, observable, and safely debriefable, while AI extends it further by offering immediate, criterion-referenced feedback and adaptive challenge at scale. The result is a credible pathway to expand deliberate practice around the competencies that hospitality actually rewards, such as procedural fluency, situational awareness, and emotionally intelligent communication.

Hospitality programmes already rely on a distinctive training mix, including production labs (e.g., kitchens, service labs, front-office simulations), role-play and case methods for service recovery and emotional labour, and work-integrated learning through internships and placements. Immersive and AI-enabled environments should be framed as additions to this portfolio rather than replacements. The comparative advantage of XR tends to be highest where physical access is constrained (capacity limits, safety, cost, seasonality) or where repeated exposure to rare but consequential scenarios is pedagogically desirable (such as, complaint escalation, emergency procedures, multi-table prioritisation). In parallel, AI tools can augment coaching and feedback loops, but should be designed to preserve learner agency and educator oversight, aligning with international guidance that emphasises human-centred use, teacher agency, and the need for governance and evidence before scaling (OECD, 2021a; OECD & Education International, 2023).

Systematic review of immersive VR in higher education strengthens the evidence base by identifying design features that reliably support learning, such as well-defined instructional goals, calibrated fidelity, explicit guidance, and structured debriefing (Radianti et al., 2020; Rojas-Sánchez et al., 2023). Over more than a decade of research, meta-analytic evidence indicates that augmented reality yields moderate positive effects on conceptual understanding and visual-spatial reasoning, with larger gains when feedback is embedded in authentic activities and cognitive load is managed (Buchner et al., 2022; Chang et al., 2022b).

Parallel work on AI-driven conversational agent systems, when guided by clear educational frameworks and human supervision, suggests they can enhance human tutoring (Córdova-Esparza, 2025; Kulik & Fletcher, 2016), particularly in language instruction settings (Dai & Wu, 2025). The evidence specific to hospitality remains scarce, so these applications are best treated as hopeful yet tentative. This pattern aligns with the Cognitive Affective Model of Immersive Learning (CAMIL), which argues that heightened feelings of presence and agency can boost motivation, interest, and self-efficacy, leading to enhanced learning when extraneous load is minimised (Makransky & Petersen, 2021). Presence, agency, and emotionally engaging narratives appear to support both conceptual understanding and procedural performance, provided that unnecessary distractions are kept to a minimum. When immersive media and AI are thoughtfully incorporated into organised teaching strategies crafted by humans, they have the potential to strengthen the practical basis of hospitality education rather than displace it.

Problem Statement and Gap

Despite this momentum, a dilemma persists. Pilot projects and proof-of-concepts multiply, yet pedagogical implications and integration strategies for immersive and AI tools in hospitality remain under-specified. Four interrelated gaps shape the problem space.

Across immersive learning research, the recurring message is not that higher fidelity automatically produces stronger learning, but that instructional design and alignment to outcomes shape the effect. Systematic syntheses in VR and AR education show benefits, yet also highlight uneven evaluation quality and frequent emphasis on usability over learning outcomes (Chang et al., 2022b; Radianti et al., 2020). This matters in hospitality modules where 'performance' is behavioural, time-pressured, and interpersonal and therefore the pedagogy must be engineered as deliberately as the simulation.

First, alignment and design discipline. The strongest results occur when technologies serve a clearly defined task sequence, not when fidelity or novelty drives the lesson. Meta-analyses and reviews underline that benefits concentrate when cognitive load is managed, guidance is present, and debriefs help learners consolidate rules and exceptions (Buchner et al., 2022; Chang et al., 2022b; Radianti et al., 2020). Without such scaffolding, high fidelity can distract novices, inflating extraneous processing. For hospitality, where cognitive and affective demands are coupled, the risk of 'spectacle over substance' is real.

Second, social learning and coordination. Multi-user environments elevate both opportunities and risks. Reviews of collaborative VR emphasise the need for explicit roles, visible artefacts (for example shared checklists and dashboards), and facilitation to prevent cognitive and social overload (Petersen et al., 2023; van der Meer et al., 2023). Hospitality tasks (such as front-desk escalations, event coordination, back-of-house synchronisation) are precisely the kinds of joint activity that could benefit from such design, but they also expose how fragile poorly orchestrated virtual teamwork can be.

Third, equity and access. Immersive adoption could widen achievement gaps if device access, bandwidth, or tolerance for head-mounted displays varies across student cohorts. Without deliberate inclusion strategies (like loaner equipment, desktop modes for social VR, comfort-first session design, and equivalent non-VR pathways with aligned assessment) XR risks becoming another vector of inequality rather than a tool for widening participation.

Fourth, governance, assessment integrity, and data protection. AI-powered conversational agents and learning-analytics systems generate granular interaction data (Córdova-Esparza, 2025; Dai & Wu, 2025). Ethical and privacy principles (such as transparency, purpose limitation, proportionality, and learner agency) are well established in the learning-analytics literature but must be operationalised in concrete classroom and programme-level protocols if trust is to be maintained (Liu & Khalil, 2023; Pardo & Siemens, 2014). The arrival of generative AI intensifies these concerns since boundary lines between legitimate formative assistance and inappropriate outsourcing of judgement become blurred, and assessment designs, audit trails, and integrity policies need to evolve in tandem.

These gaps do not weaken the case for XR and GenAI; they sharpen it. For hospitality schools, the central challenge is not acquiring headsets and chatbots, but integrating immersive and AI tools into curricula, assessment, and governance in ways that are educationally principled, feasible, and trustworthy. That integration challenge motivates an evidence-led set of questions about effectiveness, boundary conditions, and governance requirements for curriculum adoption.

Aim and Research Questions

Against this backdrop, the chapter treats XR and GenAI as components of an instructional system rather than educational ends. The analytical centre of gravity is pedagogical: what works, for whom, under what conditions, and at what cost (including the costs to academic integrity, learner trust, and governance capacity).

This chapter investigates how immersive and AI-driven tools and environments can be integrated into hospitality curricula to enhance experiential learning, and examines the benefits, challenges, and conditions for responsible implementation. Specifically, it asks:

a. Which uses of XR (VR/AR/MR) and AI show the strongest evidence of improving learning that is directly relevant to hospitality-operational routines, service recovery, safety and hygiene, interpersonal communication, and data-informed decision-making?
b. Which instructional features (for example pre-training, guidance, pacing, debriefing) and institutional supports (such as staff capability, infrastructure, governance) are associated with successful outcomes?
c. What ethical, financial, and operational risks must programmes address to ensure trustworthy, inclusive, and sustainable integration, particularly in relation to assessment integrity and data governance?

The contribution is threefold. First, it transposes patterns from the wider XR/AI education literature into hospitality's emotionally demanding, team-based contexts, where evidence remains relatively sparse (Boon et al., 2024; Calisto & Sarkar, 2024; Leung et al., 2022; Liu & Goel, 2022; van der Meulen & de Vries, 2023; Yadav, 2025). Second, it foregrounds governance, integrity, and equity as core design constraints rather than afterthoughts, drawing explicitly on learning-analytics and AI-ethics scholarship and tourism-sector policy. Third, it offers a pragmatic roadmap for 'teaching in the virtual worlds' that connects classroom design, assessment practice, and institutional strategy to the realities of hospitality work.

This chapter first positions XR and GenAI within hospitality's competency-intensive learning needs, then explains the narrative review approach used to synthesise the evidence. It subsequently develops an evidence-led argument about where immersive and AI-supported approaches can add value (and where they may not), before translating that synthesis into a staged adoption roadmap and a set of governance-facing recommendations for curriculum design, assessment integrity, data protection, and staff development (Makransky & Petersen, 2021; Pardo & Siemens, 2014; Radianti et al., 2020).

METHODS

Narrative Literature Review

This chapter adopts a narrative literature review (NLR) to synthesise evidence on integrating immersive and AI tools (XR plus AI tutoring and analytics) in hospitality education. The approach privileges transparency and relevance over exhaustiveness, while applying explicit scope, selection, and synthesis procedures to support credibility and replicability (Snyder, 2019; Baethge et al., 2019).

NLR is particularly suited to this study because, as Baumeister and Leary (1997) argue, it can provide a coherent overview of the available literature while integrating findings from multiple fields. In contrast to strictly systematic reviews, a narrative review allows greater flexibility in interpreting complex and rapidly evolving topics (Green et al., 2006), such as the convergence of AI, XR, and metaverse-style environments in hospitality education. This methodological choice acknowledges that the evidence base is heterogeneous, cross-disciplinary, and developing at speed, and that understanding conditions for effectiveness and governance is more useful for practitioners than a narrow focus on pooled effect sizes.

Search Strategy, Databases, and Inclusion Criteria

Eligibility included peer-reviewed empirical or review articles published between 2010 and 2025, conducted in higher-education or professional training contexts relevant to hospitality, and reporting learning-relevant outcomes (for example engagement, knowledge or skills, retention, or teamwork) for VR/AR/AI deployments. Foundational pre-2010 works were included where theoretically essential. Exclusions comprised non-educational deployments, purely technical papers without learning outcomes, and opinion pieces without evaluative data. English-language sources were prioritised.

Searches were conducted across Scopus, Web of Science, ERIC, and Google Scholar using controlled combinations of keywords and Boolean operators such as:

a. "hospitality education" OR "tourism education"
b. AND "virtual reality" OR "augmented reality" OR "XR" OR "metaverse"
c. AND "artificial intelligence" OR "AI-powered conversational agents" OR "AI tutors" OR "learning analytics"
d. AND "learning outcomes" OR "skills" OR "assessment".

Reference chaining (backwards and forwards) from anchor reviews (for example Chasokela, 2025; Garzón et al., 2019; Merchant et al., 2014; Radianti et al., 2020) identified additional studies germane to design features and outcome patterns. Titles and abstracts were screened against eligibility criteria, followed by full-text review for fit. For included studies, we recorded design, sample, intervention, outcomes, and key moderators such as guidance, fidelity, and debrief. To mitigate selection bias in this narrative review, we privileged meta-analyses and systematic reviews where available and triangulated their findings with education, and hospitality-specific empirical studies. A light-touch appraisal (clarity of outcomes, obvious validity threats, and transferability to hospitality-relevant tasks) informed confidence statements in the synthesis rather than formal scoring.

As a narrative synthesis, the review remains vulnerable to selection and publication bias and to evidence drift in fast-moving domains. Effect estimates vary widely across contexts and designs. Accordingly, conclusions emphasise conditions for effectiveness and boundary conditions rather than universal prescriptions.

Policy and Industry Documents

To situate educational practices within broader sectoral developments and governance debates, the review also incorporated high-level policy and industry documents. These included, for example, the European Commission's Transition Pathway for Tourism and related digital-skills initiatives, OECD and UNESCO recommendations on AI and data governance, and UN Tourism publications on digital transformation and workforce skills in tourism and hospitality.

Unlike the database search for academic articles, these documents were purposefully sampled based on their relevance to tourism ecosystems, higher education, digital skills, and AI ethics. Selection focused on landmark reports and recommendations from reputable organisations (European Commission, 2022a; OECD, 2021b, 2024;

UNESCO, 2021; UN Tourism, 2025) and on policy texts that are already shaping institutional expectations around data protection, governance, and responsible AI use. Including these sources makes the evidentiary base for claims about governance, assessment integrity, and institutional strategy more transparent, addressing concerns about how policy-oriented publications were identified and integrated.

Analytical Lenses

Interpretation was guided by constructivist learning traditions. Experiential Learning Theory, with its cycle of concrete experience, reflection, abstraction, and experimentation, was used to frame XR as structured practice with debrief (Kolb & Kolb, 2005). Socio-cultural perspectives following Vygotsky (1978) were used to situate collaborative, scaffolded performance in shared virtual spaces and AI-mediated guidance, highlighting learning as a social process of joint problem-solving with shared artefacts and roles.

In parallel, the Cognitive Affective Model of Immersive Learning (CAMIL) provides a theoretical lens to understand how presence, agency, and emotional engagement affect motivation, cognitive load, and learning outcomes in immersive environments (Makransky & Petersen, 2021). CAMIL helps to explain why high-fidelity immersive scenes can both support and hinder learning: presence and agency can increase interest and self-efficacy, yet poorly aligned designs risk inflating extraneous load. This is directly relevant to hospitality scenarios that are affectively charged and procedurally complex.

Together, these lenses anchor claims about why immersion and adaptive feedback may yield gains beyond novelty effects, and they support a consistent focus on design discipline, assessment alignment, and governance. They also provide a structured way to discuss conditions under which XR and AI might undermine learning (for example by eroding assessment integrity, amplifying inequities, or normalising opaque data-collection practices) and how institutional and programme-level safeguards can mitigate these risks.

CONCEPTUAL FOUNDATIONS

Experiential and Socio-Constructivist Learning in Hospitality

The conceptual starting point is not technology but practice. Hospitality education has long been grounded in experiential learning, where students cycle through doing, reflecting, abstracting, and re-testing in environments that approximate real service settings. In practice-heavy programmes, competence grows when learners repeatedly encounter concrete situations, make decisions, and then step back to make sense of why particular responses worked better than others. XR and AI are best understood as additional instruments in this cycle rather than as a separate pedagogical paradigm (Kolb & Kolb, 2005).

Experiential Learning Theory (ELT) articulates this logic as a sequence of concrete experience, reflective observation, abstract conceptualisation, and active experimentation (Kolb & Kolb, 2005). In hospitality contexts, augmented reality (AR) can make tacit constraints visible in situ (for instance, overlaying hygiene standards on kitchen workstations or visualising guest-flow lines in a restaurant) while virtual reality (VR) enables near-authentic but consequence-free rehearsal of complex encounters such as service recovery at peak load. When these experiences are followed by structured debriefs, whether human-led or supported by AI-generated prompts, they can be translated into shared rules of thumb and principles that transfer to the workplace (Chang et al., 2022b; Radianti et al., 2020).

A socio-constructivist lens adds the social texture that is characteristic of hospitality work. Following Vygotsky (1978), learning can be viewed as a social process of joint problem-solving with shared artefacts, roles, and mediated facilitation. Multi-user virtual environments (often framed as social VR or 'metaverse classrooms') allow teams of students to coordinate front-desk escalation scenarios, cross-department event planning, or crisis simulations while working around common artefacts such as checklists, dashboards, and spatial layouts. Systematic reviews of social VR and collaborative learning environments indicate that, when designed with clear objectives, artefact-centred tasks, and guided debrief, such environments can support 'deep and meaningful' e-learning, including stronger team processes and shared products (Mystakidis et al., 2021; Paulsen et al., 2024; Rojas-Sánchez et al., 2023).

These theoretical strands matter for what follows because they sharpen the distinction between using XR/AI and designing with them. They frame immersive and AI-enabled tools as components of an experiential, socially grounded system that must still answer basic questions like: What experiences are being staged? What forms of reflection are scaffolded? How are individual and group performances made visible and assessable? They also connect directly to concerns about governance and assessment integrity by foregrounding the central role of artefacts, feedback, and data in how learners' performances are captured, interpreted, and judged (Pardo & Siemens, 2014).

Presence, Cognitive Load, and Immersive Learning

Presence and cognitive load provide a second, more fine-grained layer to this conceptual foundation. Presence -the subjective sense of 'being there' in a mediated environment- is frequently cited as a signature strength of immersive media. Experimental and meta-analytic work shows that immersive VR can generate higher presence than equivalent desktop simulations, often accompanied by increased motivation, interest, and self-efficacy (Makransky & Petersen, 2021; Merchant et al., 2014). Meta-analyses of VR-based instruction report small-to-moderate gains in learning, particularly for spatial and procedural tasks where being able to 'stand inside' the environment matters (Merchant et al., 2014; Radianti et al., 2020).

However, more presence is not automatically more learning. Research in multimedia and immersive learning has repeatedly documented that strongly immersive versions of a learning task can increase presence yet decrease performance when they impose high extraneous cognitive load; for example, through unnecessary visual detail, distracting interactions, or complex controls. Makransky et al. (2019) famously show that adding fully immersive VR to an already effective science lab simulation produced 'more presence but less learning' when design choices did not minimise unnecessary processing.

Cognitive load theory distinguishes between intrinsic load (inherent to the task), extraneous load (imposed by the way information is presented), and germane load (mental effort that contributes to learning). In hospitality scenarios, intrinsic load is already substantial: students must juggle procedures, emotional tone, spatial constraints, and real-time decision-making in often noisy, time-pressured situations. XR can help by making some relationships easier to see (such as the layout and sequencing of a housekeeping routine or the choreography of a dining room) but it can also add extraneous load if visual and interactional richness is not carefully constrained (Buchner et al., 2022; Chang et al., 2022b; Radianti et al., 2020).

Syntheses of VR and AR in education converge on a set of design conditions under which immersive tools are most effective. Effects tend to be strongest when instructional goals are explicit, fidelity is calibrated to the task rather than maximised for its own sake, guidance and prompts are embedded in the experience, and debriefs help learners connect concrete events to abstract principles (Chang et al., 2022b; Garzón & Acevedo, 2019; Merchant et al., 2014).

These principles map directly onto hospitality practice. For example, a VR service-recovery scenario that prioritises photorealistic décor over clear conversational affordances risks misallocating cognitive resources. Similarly, AR overlays that flood a kitchen view with icons and text can obscure rather than clarify safety and sequencing standards. By contrast, designs that scaffold attention (like using role cards, checklists, temporal 'chunks,' and pause-and-coach moments) tend to support both immediate performance and later recall (Mystakidis et al., 2021; Paulsen et al., 2024).

The same logic underpins concerns about assessment integrity and governance. Highly immersive assessments that are not transparently structured can make it harder for learners and staff to trace how judgements were formed; cognitive overload can obscure criteria and encourage reliance on opaque automated scoring (Buchner et al., 2022). Insights from learning-analytics and data-ethics work underscore that assessment designs in such environments need to be legible, auditable, and proportionate-for example, through clear rubrics, recorded artefacts for moderation, explicit consent processes, and transparent rules about when and how AI assistance is permitted (Pardo & Siemens, 2014).

The Cognitive Affective Model of Immersive Learning (CAMIL) and its Limits

The Cognitive Affective Model of Immersive Learning (CAMIL) integrates these strands by linking technological features (immersion and interactivity), psychological responses (presence, agency, emotional engagement), and learning outcomes via motivational and cognitive pathways (Makransky & Petersen, 2021). In CAMIL, immersive environments are expected to enhance learning when they (a) increase presence and agency in ways that boost interest, intrinsic motivation, and self-efficacy, and (b) channel that heightened engagement into germane processing rather than extraneous load (Makransky & Petersen, 2021).

CAMIL is especially useful here because it forces a mechanism-level explanation: immersion and agency can increase presence, which in turn shapes motivation, affect, and cognitive load. The implication is practical, if cognitive load is poorly managed, an emotionally intense service-recovery simulation may generate arousal without learning. A mechanism-first approach therefore supports design choices such as graduated difficulty, guided reflection, and feedback pacing (Makransky & Petersen, 2021).

Across the studies summarised in current reviews, this logic is visible. The strongest outcomes in VR and AR implementations tend to occur when immersion serves a clearly defined task, fidelity is calibrated, and activities are framed within a sequence such as 'AR primer - VR rehearsal - guided reflection.' Under these conditions, presence and agency appear to support deeper conceptual understanding and more robust procedural performance in tasks that are directly relevant to hospitality (ranging from hotel check-in sequences to frontline service training) particularly when coupled with explicit feedback and structured debrief (Chang et al., 2022b; Garzón & Acevedo, 2019; Merchant et al., 2014; Radianti et al., 2020).

At the same time, CAMIL (and its evidentiary base) has limits that matter for a realistic hospitality narrative.

First, the model is primarily built from studies in science, technology, and related domains. Hospitality tasks are more socially and emotionally saturated, as tone, empathy, and service recovery are not peripheral but central outcomes. Presence can amplify emotional responses, which may be beneficial for engagement but also risks overwhelming novices in high-stakes scenes if support is thin. CAMIL's emphasis on balancing affect and load remains relevant, but the contexts in which it has been validated caution against assuming that every hospitality use case will manifest similar effect sizes or dynamics (Makransky & Petersen, 2021; Makransky et al., 2019).

Second, the model is largely agnostic about assessment and data governance. CAMIL helps to diagnose when a design might be 'all spectacle and no learning' but it says little about how performance is captured, stored, and interpreted. In immersive hospitality assessments, this becomes critical. A VR scenario may be motivationally powerful yet educationally problematic if the data trails it produces are opaque, if AI-based scoring cannot be explained to students or exam boards, or if generative tools can covertly assist during what is meant to be an individual judgement task. Integrating CAMIL with insights from learning-analytics ethics and AI governance (such as principles of purpose limitation, data minimisation, and learner agency) therefore becomes essential (Pardo & Siemens, 2014).

Third, CAMIL focuses mainly on individual learners, whereas hospitality education frequently assesses team performance, coordination, and role flexibility. Social-VR research extends this picture by showing that collaborative gains in immersive environments occur when shared artefacts, clear phases, and facilitation keep social and cognitive load manageable (Mystakidis et al., 2021; Paulsen et al., 2024), without such structuring, presence in a busy virtual restaurant or hotel lobby can quickly become overwhelming. This suggests that CAMIL-informed design in hospitality needs to be complemented by socio-constructivist principles when immersive tasks are inherently collaborative and service-oriented.

Taken together, CAMIL offers a useful diagnostic lens rather than a recipe. For the purposes of this chapter, it serves three roles. It underlines that immersive and AI-enabled designs should be judged less by their novelty and more by how they manage presence, motivation, and load in relation to clear learning goals. It provides a vocabulary for explaining why some hospitality-oriented XR pilots deliver strong gains while others disappoint. And it makes visible a set of boundary conditions (such as emotional intensity, social complexity, data governance, and assessment integrity) that are taken up explicitly in later sections when examining implementation, institutional readiness, and hospitality-specific cases.

EVIDENCE SYNTHESIS AND ADOPTION CONSTRAINS

From Novelty to Competence-Based Design

Across the literature, a consistent point of convergence is that XR and AI become educationally defensible in hospitality only when they are treated as instruments for specific competencies, not as generic 'innovation'. Hospitality work is irreducibly experiential as it involves time-pressured judgement, embodied routines, and the management of service encounters where technical execution and relational labour co-exist. That character of work is exactly what makes immersive rehearsal and structured digital feedback attractive, but it is also what exposes weak designs. In other words, the question is rarely whether these tools can be engaging; it is whether they can produce assessable, transferable performance under conditions that resemble practice (Kolb & Kolb, 2005; Makransky & Petersen, 2021; Radianti et al., 2020). The service literature reinforces the same implication from a different angle; as AI reshapes frontline work and decision support becomes normalised, graduates will need not only procedural fluency but also the ability to interrogate automated outputs and maintain accountability in human-facing contexts (Huang & Rust, 2018; Wirtz et al., 2018).

A useful way to organise the evidence is therefore not by technologies as such, but by the learning problems they plausibly solve and the governance conditions required for their use. Not all 'virtual worlds' require head-mounted displays. A Marriott case-study describes the development of a virtual onboarding environment ('Voyage') designed to replace paper-based onboarding distributed across brands and geographies (ON24, n.d.). The case highlights features aligned with social learning and programme oversight, such as a collaborative environment blending social learning tools with learning management functions, access in 22 languages, and manager-facing usage statistics used to identify when a new hire is not engaging with relevant learning resources. In the initial implementation, the programme was used with 65 new hires, with anticipation of global scaling (ON24, n.d.). For hospitality educators, this example is useful because it foregrounds organisational learning architecture (including coaching roles, participation monitoring, and community building) rather than novelty. It also offers a practical bridge between campus-based cohorts and distributed work-integrated learning models.

Four application clusters dominate: a. immersive simulation for procedural/spatial performance; b. augmented overlays for in-situ micro-scaffolding; c. conversational AI for practice volume and feedback; and d. collaborative virtual environments for team-based coordination. Across all four, two cross-cutting issues recur, assessment integrity (what counts as legitimate performance when AI assistance is available) and institutional governance (what data are collected, how decisions are audited, and who is accountable) (Cotton et al., 2024; Kofinas et al., 2025; Liu & Khalil, 2023; Pardo & Siemens, 2014).

Evidence Strength Signposting

To help readers distinguish what is relatively established from what remains emergent, the synthesis uses confidence tags that reflect the type, consistency, and domain relevance of the evidence (meta-analyses/systematic reviews; hospitality-specific studies; and the extent to which outcomes are performance-based rather than attitudinal). These tags are interpretive rather than statistical, and they are intended to support curriculum decision-making rather than to rank technologies.

Confidence Guide

High: multiple high-quality syntheses with broadly consistent findings, and clear transfer to hospitality-relevant tasks.

Moderate: convincing evidence in adjacent fields plus some relevant hospitality studies, but outcomes are design-contingent or context-sensitive.

Low: promising but limited evidence, heavy reliance on small samples, short-term studies, or non-independent reports.

Indicative Confidence by Application Cluster

Immersive VR simulation for procedural/spatial performance: Moderate (strong cross-domain syntheses; hospitality evidence growing but still uneven).

Augmented overlays for in-situ micro-scaffolding: Moderate (multiple meta-analyses; hospitality-specific evaluation is still limited).

Conversational AI for practice volume and feedback: Moderate for learning support; Low-to-Moderate for integrity, bias, and behavioural impacts in hospitality-specific assessment contexts.

Collaborative virtual environments for team-based coordination: Low-to-Moderate (systematic reviews suggest potential, but rigorous outcome evidence and hospitality transfer remain comparatively sparse).

Immersive Simulation for Procedural and Spatial Performance

The most mature evidence base concerns immersive virtual reality (IVR) simulations. Meta-analytic work across educational settings suggests that VR can yield small-to-moderate learning gains relative to traditional instruction, with stronger effects where tasks are spatially complex, procedurally sequenced, and assessed through performance rather than satisfaction (Merchant et al., 2014). Systematic reviews add an important nuance as the 'VR effect' is neither uniform nor automatic. Outcomes depend heavily on instructional design choices, including explicit learning goals, scaffolding, and structured debriefing that turns experience into conceptual understanding and re-application (Craig & Kay, 2023; Radianti et al., 2020).

Hospitality-specific studies echo these boundary conditions rather than contradict them. When VR is used to stage operational encounters (for example, front-office sequences) under situated cognitive assumptions, learners can gain traction on task sequencing and environmental constraints that are difficult to teach through description alone (Liu & Goel, 2022). Longitudinal evidence from hospitality employee training similarly points to advantages in retention and attitudes for VR game-based formats, although the durability of these advantages is not guaranteed across contexts and designs (Leung et al., 2022). Reviews focused on tourism and hospitality adopt a sober stance, where VR appears most defensible when fidelity is calibrated to the learning goal and embedded in a structured learning sequence, not when it is used as spectacle or a one-off 'experience' (Calisto & Sarkar, 2024; van der Meulen & de Vries, 2023).

Hilton's Oculus for Business case illustrates a concrete hospitality deployment that links immersive design to operational understanding (Kover, 2020; Oculus for Business, n.d.). In the case-study description, corporate team members complete VR modules simulating operational tasks (e.g., preparing multiple room-service trays under time constraints, practising selected steps from room-cleaning procedures, and rehearsing guest check-in and loyalty-benefit delivery). The stated rationale is to build empathy for frontline work so that corporate decisions do not inadvertently add friction to hotel operations. The same case document also reports VR scenarios designed for hotel team members, including role-taking and role-play with virtual guests across touchpoints (front desk, breakfast service, departures), explicitly targeting the affective and interactional demands of guest service (Oculus for Business, n.d.; Meta, 2025). Given that VR's effects on empathy are mixed and domain-dependent in the wider literature, it is appropriate to treat the case as illustrative of design intent and organisational learning strategy rather than as a definitive effectiveness evaluation (Ventura et al., 2020). For curriculum planning, such cases are best treated as practice-facing design patterns (what was built, for which task constraints, and with what implementation logic) that require local educational evaluation (learning outcomes, usability, equity effects, and assessment integrity) before they can be treated as evidence of effectiveness.

Published industry cases from Lufthansa, Air France-KLM and LATAM Airlines describe VR training solutions for cabin-crew on various aspects, including safety exercises, hospitality services et al., using virtual reality and 3D aircraft models (Lufthansa Aviation Training, n.d.; Meta, n.d.; NTT DATA, n.d.). The LATAM case reports a reduction in time required to complete critical safety exercises (90 minutes instead of 4 hours) and indicates that the first VR-enabled course achieved a 100% success rate (NTT DATA, n.d.). The LATAM case (NTT DATA, n.d.) also notes scalability advantages; where training was previously conducted individually, more than 30 trainees can now complete the exercises simultaneously, with claimed longer-run cost reductions through reduced reliance on grounded aircraft for practical exercises (NTT DATA, n.d.). For hospitality education, the key takeaway is not the aviation specifics but the operational logic. Immersive environments can reduce bottlenecks, increase repetitions without consuming scarce real-world facilities, and support structured performance tracking, provided that programme teams have the capacity to maintain devices, scenarios, and evaluation dashboards.

CAMIL helps explain why these patterns recur. Presence and agency can increase motivation and self-efficacy, yet they translate into learning only when extraneous cognitive load is constrained and learners are guided towards relevant cues and decisions (Makransky & Petersen, 2021). Experimental evidence is particularly instructive here, as adding immersive VR can increase presence while decreasing learning when cognitive demands are poorly managed, reminding us that 'more immersion' is not a pedagogical principle (Makransky et al., 2019). Related work in immersive learning points in the same direction indicate that VR can support learning when cognitive and affective processes are aligned with task structure, not merely when environments look realistic (Makransky & Mayer, 2022; Parong & Mayer, 2021).

For hospitality curricula, this evidence supports a clear assessment implication. VR is most convincing when it is used for observable, performance-based tasks (such as service recovery moves, adherence to SOPs, sequencing under time pressure, and hazard recognition) assessed with explicit rubrics and artefact trails (such as screen recordings, decision logs, and structured reflection). This does two things at once, first it anchors VR in competence demonstration rather than experience consumption, and second, it strengthens integrity because the assessment focuses on situated reasoning and behaviour rather than polished text products that can be easily outsourced to generative AI (Cotton et al., 2024; Kofinas et al., 2025; Perkins, 2023). Taken together, VR is most defensible in hospitality education when it is positioned as assessable rehearsal of observable performance (plus debrief), not as an immersive 'experience' separated from competence claims.

Augmented Overlays for In-Situ Micro-Scaffolding and Standards Visibility

Augmented reality (AR) occupies a different instructional niche. Where VR substitutes the environment, AR preserves real settings and adds targeted cues. That makes AR particularly suitable for short, repeated micro-practice in labs and simulated workplaces, as it can externalise invisible standards (layout rules, safety checks, mise-en-place flows) and support feedback at the moment of action. Meta-analytic evidence over the last decade indicates that AR produces moderate positive effects on learning, particularly for conceptual understanding and visuospatial reasoning, while also showing that outcomes depend on task scope and information density (Chang et al., 2022b; Garzón & Acevedo, 2019; Garzón et al., 2019). A systematic review focused on cognitive load (Buchner et al., 2022) offers an additional caution that AR can support performance, but cognitive load effects are mixed and appear contingent on learner expertise and design quality (Buchner et al., 2022).

Taken together, these findings suggest a constructive role for AR in hospitality education that is distinct from VR. AR is well suited to preparing learners for performance by making standards visible and reducing avoidable errors early in training. Used well, it can function as a scaffold that is gradually withdrawn as learners internalise routines and build judgement. Used poorly, it can become a crutch that produces procedural compliance without discretionary decision-making. This matters for assessment integrity, as an overlay that prescribes every step can inflate performance while masking independence. In assessment terms, AR activities therefore benefit from 'fading' designs and criteria that reward both procedural correctness and the rationale for deviations in context, with clear documentation of how AR content is curated and updated (Buchner et al., 2022; Chang et al., 2022b).

Conversational AI and Intelligent Tutoring: Practice Volume, Feedback, and Integrity

AI-powered conversational agents and tutoring systems address a different bottleneck, the need for high-frequency practice and timely feedback at scale. The broader tutoring literature suggests that intelligent tutoring systems can improve learning outcomes, with meta-analytic evidence indicating substantial effects in well-structured domains (Kulik & Fletcher, 2016; VanLehn, 2011). More recent meta-analyses focused specifically on AI chatbots report positive learning effects across educational contexts, although effects vary by discipline, task structure, and implementation (Wu & Yu, 2024; Wu & Li, 2024). The implication for hospitality education is not that chatbots should replace teaching, but that they can expand practice opportunities in domains where repetition matters, such as language and intercultural communication, complaint handling, upselling dialogues, and procedural reasoning around safety checks and service standards.

The tourism and hospitality literature is now beginning to map this terrain more explicitly. Work on generative AI in tourism and hospitality outlines opportunities for personalised learning and content generation while emphasising the need to clarify disciplinary judgement and boundaries of acceptable use (Fouad et al., 2024; Zhu & Yu, 2025). In hospitality and tourism education specifically, ChatGPT is being positioned for role-play, feedback, and scenario exploration, but the educational value is contingent on how programmes manage integrity, authorship, and critical engagement (Perkins, 2023; Zhang et al., 2024). Evidence from adjacent professional domains supports the same conditional stance, that chatbots can strengthen self-directed learning when aligned with clear standards and human oversight, but they are not inherently educative (Chang et al., 2022a; Han et al., 2025).

This is where assessment integrity becomes central rather than decorative. The academic integrity literature is converging on the point that detection-only approaches are brittle, and that generative AI is now capable of producing plausible outputs across many task types, including those once assumed 'authentic' (Balalle & Pannilage, 2025; Cotton et al., 2024; Kofinas et al., 2025). A second, subtler risk concerns cognitive dependency, when dialogue systems become default 'thinking partners', learners may practise less originality and judgement. Systematic review evidence flags over-reliance as a plausible concern, even if the evidence base remains emergent and heterogeneous (Zhai et al., 2024). For hospitality curricula, the design response is to treat AI literacy and integrity as explicit outcomes embedded in assessment. Students document prompts and interactions, critique AI outputs, justify acceptance or rejection, and demonstrate reasoning through oral or performative components where appropriate (Cotton et al., 2024; Evangelista, 2025; Francis et al., 2025; Perkins, 2023). In this framing, AI does not 'solve' feedback scarcity; it increases the need for clear standards, auditable processes, and discipline-specific definitions of legitimate assistance.

Collaborative Virtual Environments: Team Coordination, Distributed Judgement, and Social Load

The final application cluster concerns multi-user virtual environments and social VR. These environments extend the logic of immersive simulation from individual rehearsal to collaborative, role-based learning, that is precisely the kind of learning hospitality requires when students must coordinate front and back-of-house decisions, manage events, or negotiate service failures as teams. Systematic reviews of social VR and collaborative learning suggest that such environments can support meaningful learning when tasks are genuinely collaborative, artefact-centred, and facilitated, rather than loosely co-present (Mystakidis et al., 2021; Paulsen et al., 2024; van der Meer et al., 2023). Experimental evidence strengthens this conclusion as collaborative generative activities in immersive VR (co-creating external artefacts such as checklists or decision maps) can increase learning when goals are clear and reflective pauses are built into the activity structure (Petersen et al., 2023).

For hospitality education, these findings matter because they specify what prevents multi-user environments from becoming chaotic. Multi-user presence raises both cognitive and social load; without role clarity, time-boxed phases, visible artefacts, and facilitation, coordination tasks can quickly degenerate into noise rather than learning (Paulsen et al., 2024; van der Meer et al., 2023). The assessment challenge is also distinctive as collaborative immersive work inherits familiar group-work problems (uneven contribution, hidden labour) and adds issues of identity, logging, and accessibility. Assessment designs that combine process evidence (system logs, artefacts, peer/self-assessment) with outcome criteria are more defensible than designs that rely on final products alone, particularly in AI-rich contexts (Cotton et al., 2024; Liu & Khalil, 2023; Pardo & Siemens, 2014).

Institutional Governance and Real-World Adoption: The Conditions That Make Pedagogy Scalable

A weakness in much technology-enhanced learning discourse is the assumption that good pedagogy alone guarantees sustainable adoption. The implementation literature on immersive VR in higher education suggests otherwise. Longitudinal evaluation of VR teaching laboratories shows that even when student experiences are positive, adoption can remain patchy when maintenance demands, staffing, and curricular integration are not built into the operating model (Marks & Thomas, 2022). Reviews of immersive VR in higher education echo this pattern, with many projects remain pilot-bound, dependent on local champions, and weakly diffused across programmes (Craig & Kay, 2023; Radianti et al., 2020; Rojas-Sánchez et al., 2023; Stracke et al., 2025). In hospitality education, where curricula are often tied to accreditation and industry expectations, these organisational realities become part of the pedagogical problem. If staff capability, support structures, and assessment governance cannot be sustained, learning designs will not scale reliably.

Governance is equally central because XR and AI generate data-rich learning environments. Student perspectives research in learning analytics shows unease about opaque data collection and secondary uses, even where benefits are acknowledged (Jones et al., 2020). Systematic review work on privacy and data protection in learning analytics reinforces the need for purpose limitation, transparency, and learner agency as design and policy requirements (Liu & Khalil, 2023). Ethical and privacy principles proposed for learning analytics provide a practical foundation for institutional governance in XR/AI teaching, and proportionality, accountability, and legitimacy of data use are not optional if programmes expect learners to trust feedback systems or AI-supported judgement (Pardo & Siemens, 2014). These governance concerns are not merely administrative; they shape assessment credibility and thus what learning outcomes can be defended, particularly when AI assistance is available and when behavioural logs are used for evaluation (Cotton et al., 2024; Kofinas et al., 2025).

Equity and wellbeing further constrain adoption. Digital equity research documents persistent gaps in access, connectivity, and digital support, reminding us that 'effectiveness' claims are often setting-dependent (Amjad et al., 2024; Drljić et al., 2025). For XR specifically, cybersickness and fatigue are not edge cases; they affect a non-trivial minority, with implications for participation and evaluation bias if not planned for (Stanney et al., 2020). These factors are not add-ons to the evidence synthesis; they delimit what a programme can legitimately require and what a study can credibly generalise.

Synthesis: What the Evidence Supports, and What It Does Not

A coherent reading of the literature is neither celebratory nor dismissive. XR and AI can extend the experiential strengths of hospitality education, but only under conditions that are increasingly explicit across reviews and empirical studies, such as that these tools must be matched to clearly articulated outcomes; the designs must manage cognitive load and provide guidance and debriefing; and the assessments must privilege process visibility and professional judgement rather than polished outputs alone (Makransky & Petersen, 2021; Merchant et al., 2014; Radianti et al., 2020). At the same time, the same evidence base makes it difficult to defend unqualified claims of effectiveness, because outcomes are heterogeneous and adoption is constrained by governance capacity, operational sustainability, equity, and integrity requirements (Craig & Kay, 2023; Liu & Khalil, 2023; Marks & Thomas, 2022). The practical implication for hospitality curricula is blunt as XR/AI should be designed as an instructional system (including competencies, assessments, staff capability, governance, and operating model) because that is where the evidence says learning is won or lost.

RECOMMENDATIONS FOR RESPONSIBLE INTEGRATION OF IMMERSIVE AND AI TECHNOLOGIES IN HOSPITALITY EDUCATION

From Industry Diffusion to Curriculum Responsibility

XR and AI are no longer peripheral to hospitality practice. The sector's operational core is increasingly shaped by datafied decision-making, automated service interfaces, and human–machine teaming, with implications for how service work is designed, supervised, and evaluated (Doborjeh et al., 2022; Huang & Rust, 2018; Wirtz et al., 2018). Empirical and review evidence in hospitality and tourism documents a widening application portfolio (such as forecasting and revenue optimisation, customer-service chatbots, recommendation engines, robotics, and immersive environments for training and experience design), alongside persistent concerns about data quality, transparency, and workforce readiness (Cozzio et al., 2025; Doborjeh et al., 2022; Sousa et al., 2024). For education, the significance is not simply that graduates should be 'digitally fluent'. It is that these technologies reshape professional accountability, such as what counts as competent judgement, how decisions are justified, and how trust is maintained when systems mediate service encounters and organisational learning.

Recent sector frameworks converge on a similar stance. UN Tourism positions AI adoption as contingent on transparency, human oversight, inclusion, and governance capacity, precisely because trust and legitimacy are core to tourism systems (UN Tourism, 2025). The World Tourism Organization's future-of-work policy paper and the OECD's tourism workforce analysis both frame digitalisation as a skill transition rather than a technology upgrade, implying that education providers must integrate digital, ethical, and socio-emotional competences into mainstream curricula (OECD, 2021a, 2021b; World Tourism Organization, 2019). European strategies similarly link competitiveness and resilience to digital capability, responsible adoption, and skills development, creating a clear policy signal that hospitality schools will be judged not only on adoption, but on the quality and integrity of that adoption (Council of the European Union, 2022; European Commission, 2022a).

Recommendation 1: Design From Competencies and Assessment, Then Select the Minimum Technology

A defensible design principle is to begin with competence claims and assessment logic, then choose the least complex technology that enables credible demonstration of those competencies. Across educational meta-analyses and systematic reviews, XR effects are consistently context-dependent, as benefits are more likely for spatially and procedurally complex tasks, and designs fail when guidance is weak or cognitive demands are poorly managed (Merchant et al., 2014; Radianti et al., 2020; Stracke et al., 2025). CAMIL clarifies that presence and agency can support motivation and self-efficacy, yet learning suffers when extraneous cognitive load is high or when immersive activity is insufficiently structured (Makransky & Petersen, 2021; Makransky et al., 2019).

In hospitality education, this points towards a differentiated portfolio rather than 'XR everywhere'. VR is most defensible for high-stakes rehearsal where repeatability and observation matter (such as in service recovery under pressure, crisis procedures, or operational sequencing) provided pre-briefing, scaffolding, and debriefing are built in (Leung et al., 2022; Liu & Goel, 2022; Radianti et al., 2020). AR, by contrast, is better treated as in-situ micro-scaffolding that makes standards visible while preserving real-world cues. Meta-analytic work suggests AR can support conceptual and visuospatial learning, but cognitive load outcomes are mixed and strongly design-contingent, so AR tasks should be tightly scoped, with information density controlled and scaffolds faded over time to protect independent judgement (Buchner et al., 2022; Chang et al., 2022b; Garzón & Acevedo, 2019).

Recommendation 2: Rebuild Assessment for AI-Saturated Learning, Not for Detection

Generative AI changes the assessment problem space. Systematic review evidence on AI and academic integrity highlights that detection-only responses are fragile and can create inequities, while even 'authentic' tasks may be vulnerable when students can outsource reasoning to dialogue systems (Balalle & Pannilage, 2025; Cotton et al., 2024; Kofinas et al., 2025). A separate, emerging concern is cognitive dependency, when over-reliance on AI dialogue systems may be associated with reduced originality and critical engagement, although the evidence remains heterogeneous and developing (Zhai et al., 2024). In hospitality, where professional judgement and relational competence are central, this is not a marginal issue. It bears directly on what schools can credibly claim graduates are able to do.

A more defensible assessment posture foregrounds process visibility and discipline-specific accountability. The literature converges on practical moves, such as multi-stage tasks, annotated drafts, oral components, in-class reasoning checks, and reflective accounts of how AI was used (or not used), with criteria that reward justification and judgement rather than surface polish (Cotton et al., 2024; Evangelista, 2025; Francis et al., 2025). Here XR can be used strategically, as performance-based assessments in VR or collaborative environments can be scored against observable behaviours and decision rationales, supported by artefact trails and structured reflection. This does not make assessment 'AI-proof', but it makes competence claims more defensible because the evidence of learning is behavioural and interpretive rather than purely textual (Makransky & Petersen, 2021; Perkins, 2023).

Recommendation 3: Treat Governance and Data Protection as Pedagogical Infrastructure

XR and AI in education are data-intensive. Learning analytics research shows students often accept potential benefits while remaining uneasy about opaque data collection, secondary uses, and profiling, which can erode trust even in otherwise well-designed interventions (Jones et al., 2020; Liu & Khalil, 2023). Foundational principles for learning analytics ethics emphasise proportionality, legitimacy of data use, transparency, and accountable governance—principles that become more, not less, important when immersive platforms capture granular behavioural traces (Pardo & Siemens, 2014).

Policy guidance aligns with this evidence. UNESCO's Recommendation on the Ethics of AI and its generative AI guidance emphasise human-centred governance, transparency, and participatory approaches, while the European Commission's educator-facing AI guidelines stress accountability, critical AI literacy, and institutional support for safe experimentation (European Commission, 2022b; UNESCO, 2021; 2023). OECD work on AI and equity in education adds that governance must protect vulnerable learners while enabling innovation, implying that ethics and inclusion cannot be bolted on after adoption (OECD, 2024).

For hospitality schools, the practical implication is to formalise governance as part of programme design, with risk-tiered approval for XR/AI activities, data protection impact assessment where data capture is non-trivial, clear purpose statements, consent mechanisms that are intelligible and meaningful, minimised retention, and auditable oversight for AI-enabled feedback or scoring. These measures are not administrative overhead. They are preconditions for legitimate use, especially when assessment claims are attached to the outputs of these systems (Liu & Khalil, 2023; Pardo & Siemens, 2014).

Recommendation 4: Plan for Implementation Feasibility as a Condition of Educational Quality

A persistent lesson from higher education VR implementations is that pedagogical promise does not translate into sustained adoption without an operating model. Evaluations of purpose-built VR labs show that rich learning experiences can co-exist with patchy institutional uptake when maintenance, staffing, and curricular integration are under-resourced (Marks & Thomas, 2022). Reviews similarly report that immersive initiatives often remain pilot-bound, dependent on local champions, and fragile when support capacity is limited (Craig & Kay, 2023; Radianti et al., 2020; Rojas-Sánchez et al., 2023; Stracke et al., 2025).

Cost should therefore be treated as an explicit outcome variable rather than a background constraint. Evidence from simulation research outside hospitality has shown that cost is frequently under-measured despite being central to scalability; the same critique applies to XR/AI adoption decisions in education (Zendejas et al., 2013). A pragmatic response is staged scaling, by beginning with a limited number of high-enrolment, high-impact competencies, evaluate learning outcomes and total cost of ownership in parallel, and expand only when staff capability and support models are demonstrably stable (Marks & Thomas, 2022; Radianti et al., 2020). This aligns with policy calls to move beyond isolated pilots towards strategic facilities and cross-institutional capacity-building (European Commission, 2022a; OECD, 2021b).

Recommendation 5: Build Equity, Accessibility, and Wellbeing Into the Design Brief

Digital equity research in higher education shows that access, connectivity, and digital-literacy supports remain uneven; without safeguards, technology-enhanced designs risk widening participation gaps (Amjad et al., 2024; Drljić et al., 2025). OECD analysis warns that AI may exacerbate inequities if adopted without explicit inclusion strategies and transparency (OECD, 2024). For XR, wellbeing is not a soft concern. Cybersickness and fatigue affect a non-trivial minority and can introduce participation bias if alternatives are not planned (Stanney et al., 2020). Evidence from immersive learning research also suggests that cognitive and affective load can undermine learning when experiences are not carefully structured, reinforcing the need for comfort-first configurations, breaks, and option pathways (Makransky et al., 2019; Parong & Mayer, 2021).

A credible inclusion strategy therefore includes: loan or shared-access models, desktop alternatives for immersive tasks, flexible scheduling, explicit accommodation pathways, and assessment designs that allow equivalent demonstration of competence without penalising learners who cannot participate in head-mounted VR (Amjad et al., 2024; Stanney et al., 2020). In hospitality, this has sectoral resonance, as European and global tourism strategies repeatedly position inclusion and accessibility as core to sustainable tourism futures, which curricula should reflect not only as content but as practice (Council of the European Union, 2022; European Commission, 2022a; World Tourism Organization, 2019).

Integrated Takeaway: Instruction Leads, Governance Keeps Pace

Taken together, the evidence and policy signals support a disciplined bottom line. XR and AI can strengthen hospitality education when they are embedded in competence-based curricula, assessed through process-visible performance and judgement, and governed through transparent, proportionate data and integrity frameworks (Cotton et al., 2024; Liu & Khalil, 2023; Makransky & Petersen, 2021; Radianti et al., 2020). The technologies do not reduce the need for teaching; they raise the stakes for design, institutional capability, and accountability. For programmes that treat implementation feasibility, equity, and governance as part of educational design rather than operational afterthoughts, XR and AI become less a 'digital add-on' and more a coherent response to the workforce and service transformation already under way (OECD, 2021a, 2021b; UN Tourism, 2025; World Tourism Organization, 2019).

Practical Implications: Translating Evidence into an Implementation Architecture

In institutional settings, the feasibility of XR/AI integration is often determined less by the pedagogical concept and more by the cost and workload profile across the lifecycle. A realistic planning view includes: hardware procurement and refresh cycles; content creation or licensing; device management (updates, storage, charging, hygiene protocols); accessibility accommodations and alternative pathways; staff development for educators and technicians; data governance and vendor management; and evaluation capacity for learning outcomes and learner wellbeing. International policy guidance on AI in education consistently stresses that scaling depends on infrastructure, teacher professional learning, and governance arrangements that protect equity and agency, rather than treating adoption as a purely technical upgrade (OECD, 2021b; OECD & Education International, 2023). For hospitality education specifically, where cohorts often include high proportions of working students and placements are central, implementation plans should explicitly address timetable fit, supervision load, and how immersive/AI activities will be assessed without undermining academic integrity.

A FIVE-PILLAR IMPLEMENTATION STRATEGY FOR HOSPITALITY EDUCATION

Figure 1 is intended as an implementation architecture rather than a checklist. It is built on a recurring empirical pattern across immersive learning and AI-in-education research, where learning gains and credible assessment depend less on 'immersion' or 'automation' in the abstract, and more on: a. tight alignment between competencies, task design, and assessment, and b. governance conditions that sustain trust over time (Liu & Khalil, 2023; Makransky & Petersen, 2021; Pardo & Siemens, 2014; Radianti et al., 2020). For hospitality programmes, those conditions matter significantly because education sits close to practice, accreditation expectations, and employer scrutiny; if XR/AI is adopted without assessment integrity and data governance, the reputational downside can exceed any pedagogical gain (Cotton et al., 2024; Kofinas et al., 2025; UN Tourism, 2025).

The five pillars are: 1. strategic alignment and partnerships; 2. outcomes-first curriculum and assessment design; 3. faculty capability and workload realism; 4. equity, inclusion, and learner wellbeing; and 5. trustworthy data practices and assessment integrity. The pillars are mutually reinforcing, as weaknesses in one pillar (for example, fragile infrastructure or ambiguous AI-use rules) routinely reappear elsewhere as 'learning' problems or integrity disputes (Cotton et al., 2024; Craig & Kay, 2023; Marks & Thomas, 2022).

Figure 1. A five-pillar implementation architecture for immersive and AI technologies in hospitality education

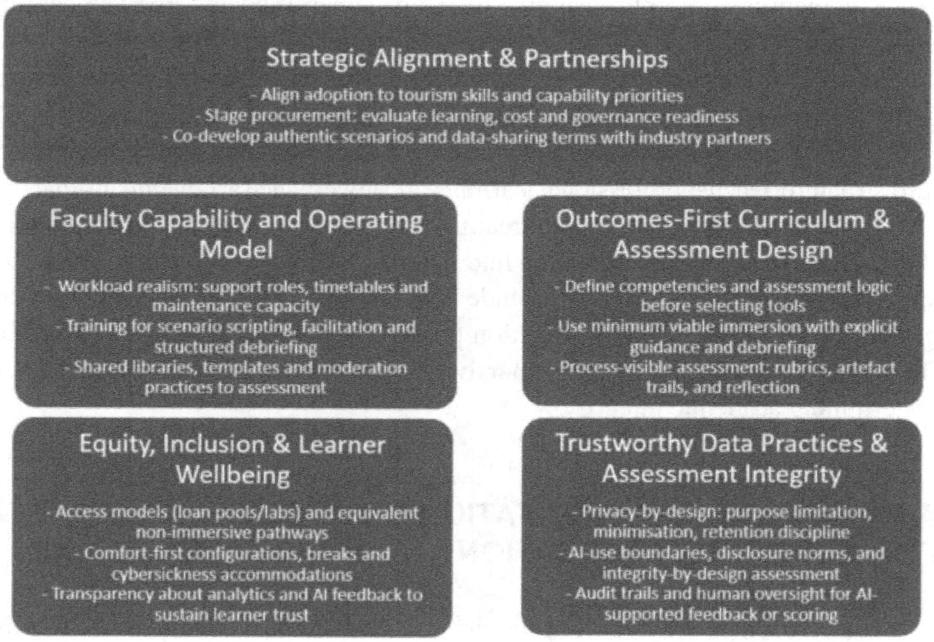

Pillar 1. Strategic Alignment and Partnerships: From Pilots to Workforce Relevance

A credible XR/AI strategy begins with alignment to sector skill and capability priorities rather than opportunistic experimentation. Tourism policy guidance frames digital upskilling, responsible technology adoption, and capacity building as structural needs for competitiveness and resilience, with implications for education and training providers (European Commission, 2022a; OECD, 2021b; World Tourism Organization, 2019; World Economic Forum, 2025). At the same time, tourism-facing AI reports stress transparency, human oversight, and inclusion as practical adoption principles, signalling that governance should be treated as a professional requirement, not merely an institutional compliance function (OECD, 2024; UN Tourism, 2025; UNESCO, 2021).

Operationally, this pillar has three immediate implications for hospitality schools. First, procurement should be staged and evaluative. For instance, to start with bounded, high-value use cases, define success criteria, and scale only when learning outcomes, costs, and governance procedures are stable (Radianti et al., 2020; van der Meulen & de Vries, 2023; Zendejas et al., 2013). Second, partnerships with hotels, restaurants, and destinations should be framed around content co-development and authenticity, not only placements. The best educational rationale for immersive rehearsal is the ability to make complex practice repeatable (for instance, service recovery or front-office sequences) and then connect rehearsal back to workplace performance expectations (Leung et al., 2022; Liu & Goel, 2022;). Third, industry adoption research suggests that perceptions of AI's risks and benefits vary across hierarchical levels, with recurring concerns around data quality, transparency, vendor dependence, and workforce readiness, that are exactly the issues hospitality curricula should teach students to diagnose and govern (Cozzio et al., 2025; Doborjeh et al., 2022).

Pillar 2. Outcomes-First Curriculum and Assessment Design: 'Minimum Viable Immersion'

The design rule is blunt, to begin with competencies and assessment, then select the minimum technology that makes performance visible, repeatable, and feedback-rich. Meta-analytic and review evidence suggests that VR tends to be most defensible for spatially and procedurally complex tasks when guidance and debriefing are explicit, while AR effects are positive but design-sensitive, particularly around information density and cognitive load (Buchner et al., 2022; Chang et al., 2022b; Merchant et al., 2014; Radianti et al., 2020). CAMIL strengthens the same conclusion theoretically, as presence and agency can support motivation and self-efficacy, but learning benefits are conditional on constraining extraneous cognitive load and aligning activities tightly to learning goals (Makransky & Petersen, 2021; Makransky et al., 2019).

For hospitality programmes, this logic supports a curriculum sequence that resembles a staged competence pipeline rather than a technology showcase. A defensible pattern is to use AR micro-scaffolds for standards visibility and error reduction, VR rehearsal for high-stakes scenarios, and structured debrief/reflection (which may include AI-mediated feedback when governed) to connect performance to principles and re-application. The sequencing matters because it shifts XR from 'experience' to deliberately supported practice (Chang et al., 2022b; Makransky & Petersen, 2021; Radianti et al., 2020). Where hospitality-specific evidence is available, it reinforces the value of situated sequencing, as VR training aligned to operational task structure has been linked to improved learning effectiveness in hospitality contexts, and VR game-based training has shown longitudinal advantages for employee learning and attitudes relative to traditional formats (Leung et al., 2022; Liu & Goel, 2022).

Assessment integrity must be designed into this pillar, not appended later. The generative AI literature is converging on two points that matter for hospitality education: detection-only responses are brittle, and even 'authentic' assessments can be compromised if they rely primarily on polished products rather than visible reasoning (Balalle & Pannilage, 2025; Cotton et al., 2024; Kofinas et al., 2025). The practical implication is a shift towards process-visible assessment design, with rubric-scored performance tasks in immersive scenarios; with required artefact trails (decision logs, recordings, drafts); and with structured reflection that makes AI use auditable and professionally justifiable. This stance aligns integrity with hospitality's professional norms of accountability and transparency rather than treating it as punitive rule enforcement (Cotton et al., 2024; Kofinas et al., 2025; Perkins, 2023).

Pillar 3. Faculty Capability and Workload Realism: Designing the Operating Model

A recurring reason XR initiatives stall is not student resistance but institutional underestimation of staff workload, technical support, and curriculum integration effort. Longitudinal evidence from higher education VR labs shows that even when experiences are positive, adoption can remain patchy when maintenance, staffing, and integration are not normalised into routine teaching (Marks & Thomas, 2022). Reviews likewise note that many implementations remain pilot-bound, dependent on individual champions, and weakly diffused across programmes (Craig & Kay, 2023; Radianti et al., 2020; Stracke et al., 2025).

This pillar therefore requires a deliberate 'design support' layer, with scenario scripting, facilitation and debriefing skills, cognitive-load management, and assessment rubric calibration. CAMIL is useful here as a shared design language for staff, as it makes clear that presence is not the goal; the goal is structured activity that converts affect and attention into learning (Makransky & Petersen, 2021). In multi-user environments, workload realism also includes facilitation competence, as collaborative immersive learning benefits depend on role clarity, artefact-centred tasks, and structured phases; none of which happen reliably without trained facilitation (Paulsen et al., 2024; Petersen et al., 2023; van der Meer et al., 2023). A practical institutional response is to treat XR/AI teaching as a supported studio model (templates, shared scenario libraries, moderation practices), not as an individual lecturer's hobby.

Pillar 4. Equity, Inclusion, and Learner Wellbeing: Access is Part of Validity

Equity is not an ethical 'extra'; it is a validity condition. Digital equity research continues to document gaps in access, support, and readiness that shape who can participate and who benefits (Amjad et al., 2024; Drljić et al., 2025). OECD work warns that AI can widen inequities if deployed without explicit inclusion safeguards, reinforcing the need to treat distributional effects as part of evaluation rather than an afterthought (OECD, 2024). For XR specifically, cybersickness and fatigue affect a non-trivial minority, and unmanaged discomfort can distort participation and introduce bias into both learning outcomes and assessment fairness (Stanney et al., 2020).

A credible implementation posture can include for instance: device-loan pools or on-campus access, desktop modes where appropriate, scheduled breaks and comfort-first configurations for VR, and equivalent non-VR pathways with aligned assessment criteria. The point is not to dilute learning challenge, but to prevent technology from becoming a hidden participation filter (Amjad et al., 2024; Stanney et al., 2020). Where learning analytics and AI feedback are used, equity-by-design also means transparency about what is collected and how it is used, because surveillance perceptions can undermine trust and engagement, particularly among vulnerable learner groups (Jones et al., 2020; Liu & Khalil, 2023).

Pillar 5. Trustworthy Data Practices and Assessment Integrity: Governance as Pedagogy

XR/AI teaching is unavoidably data-intensive. Learning analytics research shows that students can be uneasy about opaque collection, secondary uses, and profiling, even when they acknowledge benefits (Jones et al., 2020). Systematic review evidence on privacy and data protection in learning analytics emphasises purpose limitation, transparency, and learner agency as recurring requirements for trustworthy practice (Liu & Khalil, 2023). Foundational ethical principles for learning analytics reinforce the same governance logic, where proportionality, accountability, and legitimacy of data use should be designed into systems, not negotiated after controversy arises (Pardo & Siemens, 2014).

This pillar therefore requires explicit, auditable governance with clear purpose statements; consent flows and opt-out routes where feasible; minimised logging and proportional retention; and accessible explanations of AI-supported feedback or scoring. It also requires assessment governance in the AI era, such as explicit boundaries for acceptable AI use, mechanisms for disclosure, and moderation practices that treat integrity as a learning outcome and a professional norm (Cotton et al., 2024; European Commission, 2022b; OECD, 2024; UNESCO, 2021). In hospitality education, the pedagogical opportunity is to make this visible, and students to be assessed not only on operational performance, but on whether they can justify tool use responsibly in ways consistent with service accountability and trust (Cotton et al., 2024; UN Tourism, 2025).

Application Risks and Mitigations: A Constraint-Led Risk Register Mapped to the Pillars

The five pillars also function as a risk management map. When adoption fails, it typically fails in predictable ways, for instance, when governance is under-specified, costs and workload are underestimated, access is uneven, infrastructure is brittle, or immersion is substituted for learning design. The literature and policy guidance broadly agree that mitigation is most effective when these constraints are anticipated and continuously evaluated rather than retrofitted (European Commission, 2022b; Marks & Thomas, 2022; OECD, 2024; UNESCO, 2021; van der Meulen & de Vries, 2023).

Ethical Risk: Privacy, Transparency, and Bias (Pillars 1 and 5)

XR/AI environments generate behavioural traces that can feel surveillance-like if purposes and boundaries are opaque, undermining learner trust and legitimate use (Jones et al., 2020; Pardo & Siemens, 2014). Mitigation starts with governance, such as, purpose limitation, data minimisation, retention schedules, and access controls, supported by intelligible consent and learner agency (Liu & Khalil, 2023; Pardo & Siemens, 2014). Where AI recommendations or feedback are used, the institution needs accountability measures such as impact assessment practices and auditable decision pathways, consistent with UNESCO's ethics recommendation and OECD guidance on equity and inclusion (OECD, 2024; UNESCO, 2021). The standard here is not perfection; it is reviewability and proportionality.

Financial Risk: Cost, Sustainability, and Opportunity Cost (Pillars 1 and 3)

XR/AI costs are not only hardware. Maintenance, staff time, content development, and support structures often determine whether pilots mature into curriculum infrastructure (Craig & Kay, 2023; Marks & Thomas, 2022; van der Meulen & de Vries, 2023). A robust mitigation is to treat cost as an outcome variable, and track total cost of ownership alongside learning outcomes, and report workload and support requirements transparently (van der Meulen & de Vries, 2023; Zendejas et al., 2013). Scale-up should be staged and justified by comparative value, and invest first where immersive rehearsal plausibly outperforms lower-cost modalities for the same competency (Merchant et al., 2014; Radianti et al., 2020).

Operational Risk: Infrastructure Fragility and Interoperability (Pillars 1 and 3)

Operational fragility—downtime, fragmented systems, and limited support—erodes instructional time and discourages staff adoption, even when pedagogy is sound (Marks & Thomas, 2022; van der Meulen & de Vries, 2023). Mitigation is organisational as much as technical, with the need to centralise device management, standardise onboarding and troubleshooting workflows, and embed support capacity close to teaching teams. Interoperability and exportability (particularly for assessment artefacts and analytics) reduce vendor lock-in and make evaluation feasible (Craig & Kay, 2023; van der Meulen & de Vries, 2023).

Inclusion Risk: Access Gaps, Accommodation Needs, and Participation Bias (Pillar 4)

Uneven access, digital readiness gaps, and disability-related needs can widen participation gaps if not designed for. Digital equity evidence supports access packages and targeted support as core mitigation measures, not student 'responsibility' (Amjad et al., 2024; Drljić et al., 2025). For XR, cybersickness mitigation and equivalent pathways are essential to fairness; otherwise, discomfort becomes a hidden selection mechanism (Stanney et al., 2020). Equity safeguards should be evaluated explicitly, consistent with OECD concerns about AI amplifying existing inequalities (OECD, 2024).

Pedagogical Risk: 'Presence Without Learning' and Poor Transfer (Pillar 2)

Immersion can raise engagement yet depress learning when cognitive load is poorly managed or reflection is absent. Experimental evidence shows that adding immersive VR can increase presence while reducing learning under certain conditions, underscoring that design discipline is not optional (Makransky et al., 2019). Mitigation requires explicit competencies, scaffolding, structured prompts, and debriefing that converts experience into abstraction and re-application—i.e., design discipline rather than immersion as an end in itself and reinforced by reviews of immersive VR in higher education (Makransky & Petersen, 2021; Parong & Mayer, 2021; Radianti et al., 2020). Where learning goals are largely declarative, programmes should ask whether the immersive premium is educationally justified relative to simpler modalities (Merchant et al., 2014; Radianti et al., 2020).

Mitigation Summary: What 'Good Practice' Looks Like in One Sentence

A defensible XR/AI adoption posture in hospitality education combines auditable governance, staged scaling anchored in high-impact competencies, operational readiness and staff capability, equity-by-design and wellbeing protections, and routine evaluation that tracks learning outcomes, usability, and cost together (European Commission, 2022b; Lewis, 2019; Marks & Thomas, 2022; OECD, 2024; Zendejas et al., 2013). Usability measures are useful but insufficient; they need to sit alongside performance evidence and assessment artefacts that make reasoning and AI use reviewable (Cotton et al., 2024; Kofinas et al., 2025; Lewis, 2019).

LIMITATIONS AND CAVEATS

This chapter offers a narrative synthesis rather than a formal systematic review, so its contribution lies in integrative argumentation and conceptual framing, not in estimating a single pooled effect size (Baethge et al., 2019; Baumeister & Leary, 1997; Snyder, 2019). The evidence base it draws on is dominated by higher-education studies and adjacent professional-training contexts; reported effects are heterogeneous and likely moderated by task demands, learner characteristics, institutional infrastructure, and instructional design choices (Craig & Kay, 2023; Radianti et al., 2020; Stracke et al., 2025).

Study Scale and Outcome Heterogeneity

A recurring constraint is that many XR studies remain small-scale, exploratory, or methodologically diverse, with substantial variation in comparison conditions, outcome measures, and follow-up periods (Craig & Kay, 2023; Radianti et al., 2020; Stracke et al., 2025). This matter because average effects can conceal dispersion, as in immersive settings, learning gains tend to concentrate where task design is explicitly scaffolded, extraneous cognitive load is actively constrained, and debriefing links experience to abstraction and re-application (Makransky & Petersen, 2021; Makransky et al., 2019; Merchant et al., 2014). In practical terms, the field needs more multi-site, hospitality-relevant trials with transparent design descriptions and comparable outcome metrics, so that external validity improves and 'what works' can be specified with greater precision (Radianti et al., 2020; Stracke et al., 2025).

Hospitality-Domain Generalisability

Evidence for AR's educational potential is well developed across disciplines, including meta-analytic work, yet hospitality-specific AR studies remain relatively sparse compared with VR and related immersive formats (Buchner et al., 2022; Chang et al., 2022b; Garzón & Acevedo, 2019; Garzón et al., 2019). This asymmetry makes it risky to assume that effect sizes, mechanisms, or implementation burdens will translate evenly across hospitality subdomains. Culinary training, front-office operations, and revenue management differ in their cognitive structure, feedback cycles, and performance visibility; these differences may shape what 'augmentation' can realistically improve and how it should be assessed (Chang et al., 2022b; Radianti et al., 2020).

Cybersickness, Ergonomics, and Participation Bias

Cybersickness and fatigue are not marginal inconveniences; they can affect participation, attention, and equity, particularly when head-mounted displays are used intensively or without careful comfort-first configuration (Stanney et al., 2020). Even where average tolerance is acceptable, a non-trivial minority may experience discomfort that changes attendance patterns and introduces selection effects into both learning and evaluation (Stanney et al., 2020). Programmes therefore need planned accommodations and equivalent non-VR pathways, not as an afterthought but as part of the learning design's validity conditions (Amjad et al., 2024; Stanney et al., 2020).

Equity and Access

Equity is a boundary condition for interpreting the evidence base, not a secondary implementation detail. Many studies are conducted in well-resourced settings, and the feasibility of XR/AI-enabled learning is sensitive to device access, bandwidth, support staffing, and digital-literacy scaffolds (Amjad et al., 2024; Drljić et al., 2025; Radianti et al., 2020). The implication is straightforward, that claims about learning effectiveness should be contextualised, and adoption strategies need to be evaluated not only for average gains but also for distributional effects across learner groups (OECD, 2024; Radianti et al., 2020).

Privacy, Data Protection, and Integrity

AI-enabled tutoring, analytics, and immersive platforms can generate granular interaction data and create new 'visibility' into learners' behaviour. Without clear purpose limitation, data minimisation, transparency, and learner agency, these practices risk undermining trust and normalising surveillance-like dynamics in educational settings (Jones et al., 2020; Liu & Khalil, 2023; Pardo & Siemens, 2014). In parallel, generative AI expands the grey zone between legitimate support and inappropriate outsourcing of judgement, which means assessment design and governance need to be treated as part of learning quality, not merely compliance (Cotton et al., 2024; Kofinas et al., 2025; Perkins, 2023). Where these safeguards are weak, the chapter's pedagogical claims should be read cautiously, because integrity and trust are not externalities; they shape what can be credibly assessed and what learning outcomes can be defended.

CONCLUSION AND FUTURE DIRECTIONS

The chapter argues that immersive and AI technologies extend, rather than overturn, hospitality's longstanding commitment to experiential, practice-based learning. When designed as part of an experiential cycle (structured exposure, guided reflection, abstraction, and re-testing) XR can make complex, high-stakes encounters repeatable and observable, while AI can contribute scalable, criterion-referenced feedback (Chang et al., 2022a; Fouad et al., 2024; Kolb & Kolb, 2005; Radianti et al., 2020; Wu & Yu, 2024). Evidence from higher education and emerging hospitality trials suggests that the clearest gains are most plausible for spatially and procedurally complex tasks, provided fidelity is calibrated, guidance is explicit, and debriefing is systematic (Calisto & Sarkar, 2024; Leung et al., 2022; Liu & Goel, 2022; Merchant et al., 2014; van der Meulen & de Vries, 2023).

Conceptually, the Cognitive Affective Model of Immersive Learning (CAMIL) has been used to make sense of these patterns, where presence and agency can boost motivation and self-efficacy, but only contribute to learning when extraneous cognitive load is constrained and activities are tightly aligned with clear learning goals (Makransky & Petersen, 2021; Makransky et al., 2019). Across the four application domains reviewed (VR simulations, AR overlays, AI-powered conversational agents, and multi-user virtual environments), the chapter foregrounds both pedagogical promise and shared vulnerabilities (assessment integrity, governance capacity, cost, and equity) that determine what can be claimed at scale (Cotton et al., 2024; Liu & Khalil, 2023; Pardo & Siemens, 2014).

Finally, by juxtaposing educational evidence with sectoral developments and policy signals, the analysis has treated XR/AI adoption as part of tourism's broader digital transition rather than a purely classroom-level innovation (European Commission, 2022a, 2022b; UN Tourism, 2025; World Tourism Organization, 2019).

Concluding Implications for Educators, Institutions, and Policymakers

These implications should be read alongside the preceding risk-mitigation guidance, which operationalises governance, inclusion, and integrity requirements for adoption at scale.

For educators, the implication is straightforward but demanding, to start from competencies and assessment, then select the minimum technology needed. XR should be reserved for scenarios where safe, high-fidelity rehearsal genuinely adds value (such as service recovery under pressure, safety and hygiene drills, event operations), while AR micro-overlays and AI-supported practice can handle more contained tasks (Chang et al., 2022b; Liu & Goel, 2022; Radianti et al., 2020). Performance-based assessments in immersive environments should focus on observable behaviours (for example empathy moves, SOP adherence, decision quality), accompanied by artefact trails and reflective commentary that make both learning processes and AI use auditable (Cotton et al., 2024; Makransky & Petersen, 2021; Perkins, 2023).

Institutions, in turn, need to treat faculty capability, infrastructure, and governance as preconditions rather than afterthoughts. The evidence converges on the simple point that learning outcomes follow design discipline and staff capability more reliably than device specification, so investment should prioritise scenario authoring, debriefing practice, cognitive-load management, and oversight of AI-enabled feedback (Boon et al., 2024; Craig & Kay, 2023; Merchant et al., 2014). That investment also needs an access model and privacy-by-design protocols that are operational, auditable, and proportionate to educational purpose, particularly where AI-supported feedback and analytics are involved (Liu & Khalil, 2023; Pardo & Siemens, 2014; Stanney et al., 2020).

For policymakers and sector bodies, the chapter reinforces the logic of recent tourism and AI-ethics initiatives, such as frameworks for responsible innovation that must simultaneously support experimentation, protect learners and workers, and promote inclusion (European Commission, 2022a, 2022b; OECD, 2021b, 2024; UNESCO, 2021; UN Tourism, 2025). Funding models that prioritise shared XR/AI facilities can reduce duplication of content development effort and accelerate evidence accumulation across institutions. Cross-institutional pilots, and industry-academia partnerships around content and data governance would directly support the kinds of staged, evidence-informed adoption advocated here.

Future Research Directions

Priority areas for future research are outlined in Table 1, with emphasis on longitudinal transfer, cost-effectiveness and scalability, equity-by-design, and assessment integrity in contexts where AI assistance is available.

Table 1. Future research directions

Area	Future Exploration Angle
Longitudinal transfer and career impact	Cohort designs should follow learners across placements, internships, and early employment to test whether XR/AR/AI-supported practice predicts observable workplace performance, retention, progression, and safety or service quality outcomes. Where feasible, studies should triangulate self-report with supervisor ratings and behavioural indicators, and explicitly model how transfer varies by task type and support structures (Leung et al., 2022; Liu & Goel, 2022).
Cost-effectiveness and scalability	Comparative evaluations should estimate total cost of ownership and learning return on investment across device classes (per example, mobile AR, standalone head-mounted displays, PC-based VR), content strategies (commercial versus in-house), and cohort sizes. Mixed-methods designs are particularly valuable here because 'hidden costs' (staff time, maintenance, support, content updates) often determine scalability more than purchase price (Radianti et al., 2020; van der Meulen & de Vries, 2023; Zendejas et al., 2013).
Comparative modality effectiveness	Studies should test whether XR produces learning gains beyond well-designed non-immersive simulations for the same competencies, while accounting for opportunity costs, educator workload, and assessment validity. Designs that use comparable instructional time and equivalent scaffolding across conditions would help clarify when immersion is educationally defensible rather than simply engaging (Merchant et al., 2014; Radianti et al., 2020).

continued on following page

Table 1. Continued

Area	Future Exploration Angle
Equity-by-design models	Experimental trials should examine access packages (loan devices, desktop modes, flexible scheduling), comfort-first configurations, and transparency around analytics to identify combinations that reduce participation gaps without diluting challenge. Researchers should report differential effects across learner groups and track whether cybersickness and fatigue systematically exclude specific participants, creating biased estimates of 'effectiveness' (Liu & Khalil, 2023; Stanney et al., 2020).
Assessment integrity with AI assistance	Rubrics and audit trails should be developed and validated to distinguish productive AI-mediated feedback from inappropriate outsourcing of judgement. Work is needed on protocols that preserve integrity while retaining the formative value of automated coaching, including clear disclosure norms, purpose limitation for assessment data, and governance mechanisms that make contested decisions reviewable (Liu & Khalil, 2023; Pardo & Siemens, 2014).

REFERENCES

Amjad, A. I., Aslam, S., Tabassum, U., Sial, Z. A., & Shafqat, F. (2024). Digital equity and accessibility in higher education: Reaching the unreached. *European Journal of Education, 59*(4), e12795. DOI: 10.1111/ejed.12795

Baethge, C., Goldbeck-Wood, S., & Mertens, S. (2019). SANRA-a scale for the quality assessment of narrative review articles. *Research Integrity and Peer Review, 4*(1), 5. DOI: 10.1186/s41073-019-0064-8 PMID: 30962953

Balalle, H., & Pannilage, S. (2025). Reassessing academic integrity in the age of AI: A systematic literature review on AI and academic integrity. *Social Sciences & Humanities Open, 11*, 101299. DOI: 10.1016/j.ssaho.2025.101299

Baumeister, R. F., & Leary, M. R. (1997). Writing narrative literature reviews. *Review of General Psychology, 1*(3), 311–320. DOI: 10.1037/1089-2680.1.3.311

Boon, Q. W., Sulaiman, T., & Razali, F. (2024). Innovative Integration of Experiential Learning in Hospitality and Tourism Management Education: A Systematic Review. In Hamdan, A. (Ed.), *Achieving Sustainable Business Through AI, Technology Education and Computer Science. Studies in Big Data, 159*. Springer. DOI: 10.1007/978-3-031-71213-5_4

Buchner, J., Buntins, K., & Kerres, M. (2022). The impact of augmented reality on cognitive load and performance: A systematic review. *Journal of Computer Assisted Learning, 38*(1), 285–303. DOI: 10.1111/jcal.12617

Calisto, M. de L., & Sarkar, S. (2024). A systematic review of virtual reality in tourism and hospitality: The known and the paths to follow. *International Journal of Hospitality Management, 116*, 103623. DOI: 10.1016/j.ijhm.2023.103623

Chang, C.-Y., Hwang, G.-J., & Gau, M.-L. (2022a). Promoting students' learning achievement and self-efficacy: A mobile chatbot approach for nursing training. *British Journal of Educational Technology, 53*(1), 171–188. DOI: 10.1111/bjet.13158

Chang, H.-Y., Binali, T., Liang, J.-C., Chiou, G.-L., Cheng, K.-H., Lee, S. W.-Y., & Tsai, C.-C. (2022b). Ten years of augmented reality in education: A meta-analysis of (quasi-) experimental studies to investigate the impact. *Computers & Education, 191*, 104641. DOI: 10.1016/j.compedu.2022.104641

Chasokela, D. (2025). Investigating the role of virtual reality to support student engagement, spatial awareness and problem-solving skills in engineering education. *International Journal of Instruction, 18*(3), 613–636. DOI: 10.29333/iji.2025.18332a

Córdova-Esparza, D.-M. (2025). AI-powered educational agents: Opportunities, innovations, and ethical challenges. *Information (Basel)*, *16*(6), 469. DOI: 10.3390/info16060469

Cotton, D. R. E., Cotton, P. A., & Shipway, J. R. (2024). Chatting and cheating: Ensuring academic integrity in the era of ChatGPT. *Innovations in Education and Teaching International*, *61*(2), 228–239. DOI: 10.1080/14703297.2023.2190148

Council of the European Union. (2022). *European Tourism Agenda 2030*. https://data.consilium.europa.eu/doc/document/ST-15441-2022-INIT/en/pdf

Cozzio, C., Santos Arteaga, F. J., & Maurer, O. (2025). *Artificial intelligence adoption in hospitality: Challenges and opportunities across hierarchical levels*. Tourism Review. Vol. ahead-of-print No. ahead-of-print. DOI: 10.1108/TR-10-2024-0913

Craig, C. D., & Kay, R. (2023). A systematic overview of reviews of the use of immersive virtual reality in higher education. *Higher Learning Research Communications*, *13*(2), 42–60. DOI: 10.18870/hlrc.v13i2.1430

Dai, L., & Wu, F. (2025). An AI-powered conversational system for college students learning English as a second language. *Education and Information Technologies*, *30*(16), 23393–23417. DOI: 10.1007/s10639-025-13640-3

Doborjeh, Z., Hemmington, N., Doborjeh, M., & Kasabov, N. (2022). Artificial intelligence: A systematic review of methods and applications in hospitality and tourism. *International Journal of Contemporary Hospitality Management*, *34*(3), 1154–1176. DOI: 10.1108/IJCHM-06-2021-0767

Drljić, K., Čotar Konrad, S., Rutar, S., & Štemberger, T. (2025). Digital equity and sustainability in higher education. *Sustainability (Basel)*, *17*(5), 2011. DOI: 10.3390/su17052011

European Commission. (2022a). *Directorate-General for Education, Youth, Sport and Culture. Ethical guidelines on the use of artificial intelligence (AI) and data in teaching and learning for educators*. Publications Office of the European Union. https://data.europa.eu/doi/10.2766/153756

European Commission. (2022b). *Directorate-General for Internal Market, Industry, Entrepreneurship and SMEs*. Transition pathway for tourism. Publications Office of the European Union. https://ec.europa.eu/docsroom/documents/49498

Evangelista, E. D. L. (2025). Ensuring academic integrity in the age of ChatGPT: Rethinking exam design, assessment strategies, and ethical AI policies in higher education. *Contemporary Educational Technology*, *17*(1), ep559. DOI: 10.30935/cedtech/15775

Fouad, A. M., Salem, I. E., & Fathy, E. A. (2024). Generative AI insights in tourism and hospitality: A comprehensive review and strategic research roadmap. *Tourism and Hospitality Research*, *0*(0), 14673584241293125. Advance online publication. DOI: 10.1177/14673584241293125

Francis, N. J., Jones, S., & Smith, D. P. (2025). Generative AI in higher education: Balancing innovation and integrity. *British Journal of Biomedical Science*, *81*, 14048. DOI: 10.3389/bjbs.2024.14048 PMID: 39850144

Garzón, J., & Acevedo, J. (2019). Meta-analysis of the impact of augmented reality on students' learning gains. *Educational Research Review*, *27*, 244–260. DOI: 10.1016/j.edurev.2019.04.001

Garzón, J., Pavón, J., & Baldiris, S. (2019). Systematic review and meta-analysis of augmented reality in educational settings. *Virtual Reality (Waltham Cross)*, *23*(4), 447–459. DOI: 10.1007/s10055-019-00379-9

Green, B. N., Johnson, C. D., & Adams, A. (2006). Writing narrative literature reviews for peer-reviewed journals: Secrets of the trade. *Journal of Chiropractic Medicine*, *5*(3), 101–117. DOI: 10.1016/S0899-3467(07)60142-6 PMID: 19674681

Han, J.-W., Park, J., & Lee, H. (2025). Development and effects of a chatbot education program for self-directed learning in nursing students. *BMC Medical Education*, *25*(1), 825. Advance online publication. DOI: 10.1186/s12909-025-07316-2 PMID: 40457281

Huang, M.-H., & Rust, R. T. (2018). Artificial intelligence in service. *Journal of Service Research*, *21*(2), 155–172. DOI: 10.1177/1094670517752459

Jones, K. M. L., Asher, A., Goben, A., Perry, M. R., Salo, D., Briney, K. A., & Robertshaw, M. B. (2020). We're being tracked at all times: Student perspectives of their privacy in relation to learning analytics in higher education. *Journal of the Association for Information Science and Technology*, *71*(9), 1044–1059. DOI: 10.1002/asi.24358

Kofinas, A. K., Tsay, H.-H. A., & Pike, D. (2025). The impact of generative AI on academic integrity of authentic assessments within a higher education context. *British Journal of Educational Technology*, *56*(6), 2522–2549. DOI: 10.1111/bjet.13585

Kolb, A. Y., & Kolb, D. A. (2005). Learning styles and learning spaces Enhancing experiential learning in higher education. *Academy of Management Learning & Education*, *4*(2), 193–212. DOI: 10.5465/amle.2005.17268566

Kouroupi, N. (2025). Parallel Universes: A Fresh Perspective in Tourism. In Santos, J. D., Barbosa Sousa, B., & Botelho Pires, P. (Eds.), *Leveraging Digital Marketing for Tourism. Tourism on the Verge*. Springer. DOI: 10.1007/978-3-031-88582-2_9

Kover, A. (2020, March 10). *A new perspective on hospitality: How Hilton uses VR to teach empathy*. Tech at Meta. https://tech.facebook.com/reality-labs/2020/3/a-new- perspective-on-hospitality-how-hilton-uses-vr-to-teach-empathy/

Kulik, J. A., & Fletcher, J. D. (2016). Effectiveness of intelligent tutoring systems: A meta-analytic review. *Review of Educational Research*, *86*(1), 42–78. DOI: 10.3102/0034654315581420

Leung, X. Y., Chen, H., Chang, W., & Mhlanga, L. (2022). Is VR game training more effective for hospitality employees? A longitudinal experiment. *Tourism Management Perspectives*, *44*, 101020. DOI: 10.1016/j.tmp.2022.101020

Lewis, J. R. (2019). Measuring Perceived Usability: SUS, UMUX, and CSUQ Ratings for Four Everyday Products. *International Journal of Human-Computer Interaction*, *35*(15), 1404–1419. DOI: 10.1080/10447318.2018.1533152

Liu, Q., & Khalil, M. (2023). Understanding privacy and data protection issues in learning analytics using a systematic review. *British Journal of Educational Technology*, *54*(6), 1715–1747. DOI: 10.1111/bjet.13388

Liu, T.-W., & Goel, L. (2022). Learning effectiveness of 3D virtual reality in hospitality training: A situated cognitive perspective. *Journal of Hospitality and Tourism Technology*, *13*(3), 441–460. DOI: 10.1108/JHTT-03-2021-0091

Lufthansa Aviation Training. (n.d.). *Hospitality training courses for cabin crews*. Retrieved December 25, 2025, from https://www.lufthansa-aviation-training.com/hospitality-training

Makransky, G., & Mayer, R. E. (2022). Benefits of taking a virtual field trip in immersive virtual reality: Evidence for the immersion principle in multimedia learning. *Educational Psychology Review*, *34*(4), 1771–1798. DOI: 10.1007/s10648-022-09675-4 PMID: 35475019

Makransky, G., & Petersen, G. B. (2021). The Cognitive Affective Model of Immersive Learning (CAMIL): A theoretical, research-based model of learning in immersive virtual reality. *Educational Psychology Review*, *33*(3), 937–958. DOI: 10.1007/s10648-020-09586-2

Makransky, G., Terkildsen, T. S., & Mayer, R. E. (2019). Adding immersive virtual reality to a science lab simulation causes more presence but less learning. *Learning and Instruction*, *60*, 225–236. DOI: 10.1016/j.learninstruc.2017.12.007

Marks, B., & Thomas, J. (2022). Adoption of virtual reality technology in higher education: An evaluation of five teaching semesters in a purpose-designed laboratory. *Education and Information Technologies*, *27*(1), 1287–1305. DOI: 10.1007/s10639-021-10653-6 PMID: 34257511

Merchant, Z., Goetz, E. T., Cifuentes, L., Keeney-Kennicutt, W., & Davis, T. J. (2014). Effectiveness of virtual reality-based instruction on students' learning outcomes in K- 12 and higher education: A meta-analysis. *Computers & Education*, *70*, 29–40. DOI: 10.1016/j.compedu.2013.07.033

Meta (2025). Four benefits of VR in hospitality. Meta for Work. https://forwork.meta.com/blog/four-benefits-of-vr-in-hospitality/

Meta (n.d.). *Air France-KLM: How mixed reality became a training solution across an entire airline* [Case study]. Meta for Work. Retrieved December 25, 2025, from https://forwork.meta.com/case-studies/air-france-klm-mixed-reality-training/

Mystakidis, S., Berki, E., & Valtanen, J.-P. (2021). Deep and meaningful e-learning with social virtual reality environments in higher education a systematic literature review. *Applied Sciences*, *11*(5), 2412. DOI: 10.3390/app11052412

NTT DATA. (n.d.). *LATAM Airlines boosts cabin crew training with immersive experiences* [Case study]. Retrieved December 25, 2025, from https://services.global.ntt/en-us/about-us/case-studies/latam-airlines

ON24. (n.d.). *Marriott virtual onboarding environment* (Case study). https://cdn.featuredcustomers.com/CustomerCaseStudy.document/on24_marriott_26553.pdf

Oculus for Business. (n.d.). *Building empathy to enhance hospitality: How Hilton is elevating learning with Oculus for Business* [Case study]. Retrieved December 31, 2025, from https://securecdn.oculus.com/sr/oculus-business-hilton-case-study

OECD. (2021a). OECD Digital Education Outlook 2021: Pushing the Frontiers with Artificial Intelligence, Blockchain and Robots. OECD Publishing, Paris. DOI: 10.1787/589b283f-en

OECD (2021b). *Preparing the tourism workforce for the digital future* (OECD Tourism Papers, No. 2021/02). OECD Publishing. DOI: 10.1787/23071672

OECD (2024). *The potential impact of artificial intelligence on equity and inclusion in education* (OECD Artificial Intelligence Papers, No. 23). OECD Publishing. DOI: 10.1787/dee339a8-en

OECDEducation International. (2023). *Opportunities, Guidelines and Guardrails on Effective and Equitable Use of AI in Education*. OECD Publishing.

Pardo, A., & Siemens, G. (2014). Ethical and privacy principles for learning analytics. *British Journal of Educational Technology*, *45*(3), 438–450. DOI: 10.1111/bjet.12152

Parong, J., & Mayer, R. E. (2021). Cognitive and affective processes for learning science in immersive virtual reality. *Journal of Computer Assisted Learning*, *37*(1), 226–241. DOI: 10.1111/jcal.12482

Paulsen, L., Dau, S., & Davidsen, J. (2024). Designing for collaborative learning in immersive virtual reality: A systematic literature review. *Virtual Reality (Waltham Cross)*, *28*(1), 63. DOI: 10.1007/s10055-024-00975-4

Perkins, M. (2023). Academic Integrity considerations of AI large language models in the post-pandemic era: ChatGPT and beyond. *Journal of University Teaching & Learning Practice*, *20*(2), 1–24. DOI: 10.53761/1.20.02.07

Petersen, G. B., Stenberdt, V., Mayer, R. E., & Makransky, G. (2023). Collaborative generative learning activities in immersive virtual reality increase learning. *Computers & Education*, *207*, 104931. DOI: 10.1016/j.compedu.2023.104931

Radianti, J., Majchrzak, T. A., Fromm, J., & Wohlgenannt, I. (2020). A systematic review of immersive virtual reality applications for higher education: Design elements, lessons learned, and research agenda. *Computers & Education*, *147*, 103778. DOI: 10.1016/j.compedu.2019.103778

Rojas-Sánchez, M. A., Palos-Sánchez, P. R., & Folgado-Fernández, J. A. (2023). Virtual reality and education: A systematic literature review and bibliometric analysis. *Education and Information Technologies*, *28*(1), 155–192. DOI: 10.1007/s10639-022-11167-5 PMID: 35789766

Snyder, H. (2019). Literature review as a research methodology: An overview and guidelines. *Journal of Business Research*, *104*, 333–339. DOI: 10.1016/j.jbusres.2019.07.039

Sousa, A. E., Cardoso, P., & Dias, F. (2024). The use of artificial intelligence systems in tourism and hospitality: The tourists' perspective. *Administrative Sciences*, *14*(8), 165. DOI: 10.3390/admsci14080165

Stanney, K., Lawson, B. D., Rokers, B., Dennison, M., Fidopiastis, C., Stoffregen, T., Weech, S., & Fulvio, J. M. (2020). Identifying causes of and solutions for cybersickness in immersive technology reformulation of a research and development agenda. *International Journal of Human-Computer Interaction*, *36*(19), 1783–1803. DOI: 10.1080/10447318.2020.1828535

Stracke, C. M., Bothe, P., Adler, S., Heller, E. S., Deuchler, J., Pomino, J., & Wölfel, M. (2025). Immersive virtual reality in higher education: A systematic review of the scientific literature. *Virtual Reality (Waltham Cross)*, *29*(64), 64. Advance online publication. DOI: 10.1007/s10055-025-01136-x

Tourism, U. N. (2025). *Artificial intelligence adoption in tourism - Key considerations for sector stakeholders*. UN Tourism. DOI: 10.18111/9789284426065

UNESCO. (2021). *Recommendation on the ethics of artificial intelligence*. https://unesdoc.unesco.org/ark:/48223/pf0000380455

UNESCO. (2023). Guidance for generative AI in education and research. UNESCO. https://unesdoc.unesco.org/ark:/48223/pf0000386693/PDF/386693eng.pdf.multi

van der Meer, N., van der Werf, V., Brinkman, W.-P., & Specht, M. (2023). Virtual reality and collaborative learning: A systematic literature review. *Frontiers in Virtual Reality*, *4*, 1159905. DOI: 10.3389/frvir.2023.1159905

van der Meulen, F. J., & de Vries, M. (2023). A literature review of implementing virtual reality in hospitality education. *Research in Hospitality Management*, *13*(1), 55–61. DOI: 10.1080/22243534.2023.2239584

VanLehn, K. (2011). The relative effectiveness of human tutoring, intelligent tutoring systems, and other tutoring systems. *Educational Psychologist*, *46*(4), 197–221. DOI: 10.1080/00461520.2011.611369

Ventura, S., Badenes-Ribera, L., Herrero, R., Cebolla, A., Galiana, L., & Baños, R. (2020). Virtual reality as a medium to elicit empathy: A meta-analysis. *Cyberpsychology, Behavior, and Social Networking*, *23*(10), 667–676. DOI: 10.1089/cyber.2019.0681 PMID: 32757952

Vygotsky, L. S. (1978). *Mind in Society: Development of Higher Psychological Processes* (Cole, M., John-Steiner, V., Scribner, S., & Souberman, E., Eds.). Harvard University Press. DOI: 10.2307/j.ctvjf9vz4

Wirtz, J., Patterson, P. G., Kunz, W., Gruber, T., Lu, V. N., Paluch, S., & Martins, A. (2018). Brave new world Service robots in the frontline. *Journal of Service Management*, *29*(5), 907–931. DOI: 10.1108/JOSM-04-2018-0119

World Bank. (2019). *World development report 2019: The changing nature of work*. https://www.worldbank.org/en/publication/wdr2019

World Economic Forum. (2025). *Travel and tourism at a turning point: Principles for transformative growth*. World Economic Forum. https://www.weforum.org/publications/travel-and-tourism-at-a-turning-point- principles-for-transformative-growth/

World Tourism Organization. (2019). *The Future of Work and Skills Development in Tourism - Policy Paper*. UNWTO. DOI: 10.18111/9789284421213

Wu, R., & Yu, Z. (2024). Do AI chatbots improve students' learning outcomes? Evidence from a meta-analysis. *British Journal of Educational Technology*, *55*(1), 10–33. DOI: 10.1111/bjet.13334

Wu, X., & Li, R. (2024). Unravelling effects of AI chatbots on EFL learners' language-skill development: A meta-analysis. *The Asia-Pacific Education Researcher*, *0*(0). Advance online publication. DOI: 10.1007/s40299-024-00853-2

Yadav, S. J. (2025). Virtual reality as a tool for enhancing employee training and development in the hotel industry. In Bildir, K., & Bildir, S. (Eds.), *Revolutionizing hospitality management systems with AI, VR, and machine learning* (pp. 361–384). IGI Global. DOI: 10.4018/979-8-3693-8769-6.ch014

Zendejas, B., Wang, A. T., Brydges, R., Hamstra, S. J., & Cook, D. A. (2013). Cost The missing outcome in simulation-based medical education research: A systematic review. *Surgery*, *153*(2), 160–176. DOI: 10.1016/j.surg.2012.06.025 PMID: 22884087

Zhai, C., Wibowo, S., & Li, L. D. (2024). The effects of over-reliance on AI dialogue systems on students' cognitive abilities: A systematic review. *Smart Learning Environments*, *11*(28), 28. Advance online publication. DOI: 10.1186/s40561-024-00316-7

Zhang, K., Li, X., Ye, H., Lin, K. J., Chen, S., & Law, R. (2024). How can ChatGPT assist hospitality and tourism education? *Journal of Teaching in Travel & Tourism*, *24*(4), 438–448. DOI: 10.1080/15313220.2024.2384743

Zhu, J., & Yu, S. (2025). Generative AI for tourism and hospitality education. *Current Issues in Tourism*, 1–9. DOI: 10.1080/13683500.2025.2500730

Chapter 11 Teaching the Human–AI Balance: Enhancing Technical and Interpersonal Skills in Front Office Education Through AI-Powered Simulation

Zaid Rouby
Abu Dhabi Hospitality Academy-Les Roches Global Hospitality Education, Abu Dhabi, UAE

Christopher Dutt
http://orcid.org/0000-0003-0219-0277
Abu Dhabi Hospitality Academy-Les Roches Global Hospitality Education, Abu Dhabi, UAE

ABSTRACT

The rapid development of Artificial Intelligence (AI) has affected every aspect of life. Educators are wrestling with how to suitably embed AI to improve student learning and understanding while not over-relying on the technology. While there are many industry solutions available that leverage AI, few are focused on training, and rarely are other tools like Virtual Reality (VR) included. This chapter proposes a solution combining AI and VR, which can be used in class to teach students the operational and interpersonal skills needed in the Front Office department. Through careful course scaffolding and maintaining a human-in-the-loop approach, students can be trained very effectively in how to work in the front office, use AI, and carefully evaluate AI responses.

DOI: 10.4018/979-8-3373-5112-4.ch011

FRONT OFFICE TRAINING: OPERATIONAL AND EMOTIONAL COMPETENCIES

A vital component of university education is industry collaboration to ensure that students enter the workforce with industry-ready skills (Abdallah et al., 2024; McCartney & Kwok, 2023; Sufi et al., 2025). How well universities are doing in this regard is debated, with the sentiment remaining that on-the-job training yields more insightful and relevant skills for their career (see Baum & Devine, 2007). Many universities attempt to improve this by providing role plays, simulations, field trips and hands-on experience with the relevant systems (Abdallah et al., 2024).

Hospitality education offers a perfect example of efforts to promote greater industry connections to provide more industry-ready skills, given the wide variety of skill sets required and their applied nature (see Sufi et al., 2025). Technology has a significant role to play by helping students learn, teaching them technological skills, and supporting their learning of industry-ready skills (Sufi et al., 2025). In particular, the development of technologies such as Virtual Reality and Artificial Intelligence offer significant prospects for education sectors to help (Chance, 2025). AI-enhanced simulations offer a unique opportunity to close the gap between academic and industry demands by creating adaptive scenarios based on real industry data, enabling students to practice skills that directly reflect workplace needs.

Within the wide spectrum of courses in a hospitality degree, courses related to front office provide an interesting opportunity. Such courses sit between the more practically orientated Food and Beverage courses and the more academic management classes, providing an interesting testing ground for skill-based technology training for both practical and academic-focused classes. In the front office, there are two broad skill sets that need to be practiced: technical skills, relating to completing job-related tasks and using the relevant systems; and interpersonal skills, to support colleagues and guests (see Hai-yan & Baum, 2006). Front office staff's work is a prime example of emotional labor, requiring employees to manage feelings to create a publicly observable display of service (Hochschild, 2012).

From the technical side, AI has been reported to improve student fluency in core systems like Opera PMS by offering adaptive, real-time feedback and operational decision-making scenarios (Shiohira, 2021). Previous studies have found that AI is effective in technical skill development, reporting up 30% improvement in competency scores, in a shorter period of time than traditional methods (Vadisetty & Polamarasetti, 2024). In terms of interpersonal skills, this becomes a little more challenging. Linguistically, AI has been found helpful in improving students' English skills and knowledge across a range of fields (Shumeiko & Osadcha, 2024; Stamer et al., 2023). However, while AI models have reported success in improving individuals' interpersonal skills, the simulating of and training in the handling of emotions can be more challenging (Lin et al., 2024). When coupled with Virtual Reality (VR), studies have reported success in both outcomes and student experience when teaching interpersonal skills through various simulations grounded in real experiences (Budnarowski et al., 2025).

There is, therefore, good evidence that tools such as AI and VR can be leveraged effectively to develop industry-ready students. This chapter will review the role AI can play in skill development, explore caveats and issues that should be accounted for, consider existing industry and academic users, before presenting a suggested solution and structure to best leverage strengths of such tools.

SKILL DEVELOPMENT

The Role of Artificial Intelligence

AI offers numerous opportunities for individuals to develop their skills (Devi et al., 2024; Vadisetty & Polamarasetti, 2024; Wang et al., 2024). AI has the ability to act as a personalized mentor or coach, providing students with a sufficiently challenging learning environment to help them gain the necessary skills for future employment and career growth (Devi et al., 2024; Vadisetty & Polamarasetti, 2024; Zhai et al., 2021) (See chapter 12: From Fairs to Predictive Paths: Ethical AI Across Generations in Career Development). These learning experiences are customizable, and able to adapt to the user and ensure they understand the content before progressing (Cardona et al., 2023; Wang et al., 2024). Scholars suggest framing AI's pedagogical role in three domains: *AI as a tutor*, providing adaptive guidance; *AI as a peer*, simulating dialogues and emotional encounters; and *AI as an assessor*, delivering analytics on performance (Shumeiko & Osadcha, 2024; Zhai et al., 2021). When used in these three perspectives, AI is able to sufficiently support students' learning by guiding and challenging them to develop their knowledge and critical thinking skills (Zhai et al., 2021). A critical component of this framework is trust calibration. Research shows that learners often either over-trust or under-trust AI systems, leading to misuse or disuse (Glikson & Woolley, 2020). Training programs must, therefore, embed exercises to encourage students to critically reflect on AI's responses to better understand how AI can be used in real-world and industry settings (see Myers et al., 2018).

By incorporating AI in such a fashion, it is expected that educators can leverage the ability of AI to improve students' skills, particularly technical skills, more effectively and efficiently (Pashaie et al., 2024; Vadisetty & Polamarasetti, 2024). Furthermore, when AI is leveraged alongside humans, they are able to offer faster, more efficient, and potentially more accurate services which can improve the customer experience (Leocádio et al., 2024).

Training programs that are developed to incorporate AI, particularly through simulations and possibly in conjunction with other tools such as VR could offer students an effective and insightful learning experience (see Budnarowski et al., 2025; Peters, 2023). Currently, most applied solutions largely focus on managing the guests' experience, while education solutions offer simulations based on limited live and current situations.

However, the key component in both these situations is the *support* from AI or *leveraging* AI. That is, AI and humans are working together to provide training (Pashaie et al., 2024). Studies have reported that when working together, AI and humans can create better quality outputs faster than either can by working alone (Dell'Acqua et al., 2023). Therefore, it is important that any new training system that leverages AI should also ensure students are also trained to use their own judgement to maximize the value of AI.

Caution should, however, be taken to ensure that individuals (students, faculty, and industry) use AI appropriately (Zhai et al., 2021). The overuse of AI can lead to a loss of skill, even among experts, as we forget how to complete tasks without AI, or because AI simplifies tasks, limiting our ability to judge task complexity (Macnamara et al., 2024; Pashaie et al., 2024). Furthermore, the concern of AI hallucinations and the creation of fake or incorrect information requires prudent due diligence (Monteith et al., 2024). In a training sense, this becomes a concern if only AI is used, because it will become difficult for the learner to distinguish between the factual and erroneous information if the skills and knowledge are all grounded in AI-based learning (Macnamara et al., 2024). Therefore, while AI offers unbound opportunities to help develop skills and provide a wealth of different scenarios for learners to experiment with, it must be used with caution to ensure the skill is not lost to AI (Macnamara et al., 2024) and that the simulations and skills being taught are accurate (Monteith et al., 2024).

There are, however, some notable concerns that should be considered when incorporating AI. AI is prone to hallucinations and poor decisions based on erroneous or biased data (Monteith et al., 2024). In fact, as AI learns from AI generated data, there is a danger of compounding biases and errors becoming more obvious and extreme (Mills, 2025). If students are not taught how to interact with AI properly or are only exposed to AI-based trainings, there is a danger of students being underprepared for reality, based on AI hallucinations, and/or an inability to critically assess and question potentially erroneous data.

In a contradiction to AI's ability to develop skills, there is a threat of individuals losing their skills (Liu, 2024) as they rely on AI for 'mundane' or 'monotonous' tasks. If AI is inappropriately prompted or embedded in a class or training, an over-reliance on AI may occur and actually reduce the very skills we are attempting to improve. Of further concern is the threat that individuals may lose the ability to be aware of their skill loss or unable to assess skill quality because of their over-reliance (Macnamara et al., 2024). Such an over-reliance can result in trust issues with AI (Glikson & Woolley, 2020), with students over-trusting or even under-trusting AI. This can then result in the over or under use of AI, disadvantaging the student either way.

The Role of Virtual Reality

Virtual Reality (VR) includes systems which transport users into an alternative, digital, reality, with varying degrees of authenticity and immersion, as reflected in Figure 1.

Figure 1. Reality-virtuality continuum (Skarbez et al., 2021), adapted from Milgram et al., 1995)

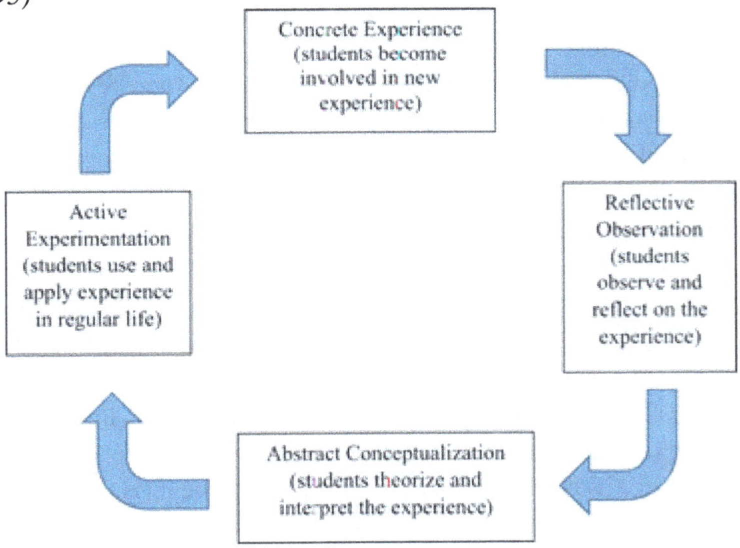

In Augmented Reality, digital images or information are superimposed over images of the real environment, while Augmented Virtuality generates a mostly virtual environment using some elements of the real world (Skarbez et al., 2021). Virtual Reality creates a fully virtual environment, giving users the sensation of being transported to a different world (Baker et al., 2023). Skarbez's Matrix-like virtual environment considers the inclusion of more physical stimuli, such as haptic, through direct brain stimulation (Skarbez et al., 2021). Movement between the virtual and real world has been termed Mixed Reality, with Apple's Vision Pro being probably one of the best known examples of such technology, allowing users to adjust their degree of immersion (Gurman, 2024).

Virtual reality, itself, can be divided into three key types: Non-immersive, semi-immersive, and fully immersive. Non-immersive systems utilize technology like regular computer or TV screens, and show users an alternative environment (Baker et al., 2023; Beck et al., 2019). Semi-immersive technologies project images “onto large screen monitors or the walls, and optional also to the floor of a room, enabling multiuser virtual…experiences” (Beck et al., 2019, p. 593). Fully-immersive systems leverage devices like head-mounted displays to isolate the user from the external environment and fully immerse them in the digital world (Baker et al., 2023; Beck et al., 2019). Non-immersive are the most feasible to implement due to the limited hardware requirements. However, the degree of immersion and impact is notably reduced (Baker et al., 2023). Semi-immersive would be useful in a classroom setting, but given the extensive hardware and software requirements, are likely to be less feasible. The final type of VR, fully-immersive, is likely to be more feasible while also offering more immersive and impactful experiences for users in terms of their enjoyment and learning experience.

Numerous studies have examined and commented on the ability of VR simulations to develop individuals’ skill sets and result in more effective and long-term learning (Xie et al., 2021). However, there are limited practical applications of VR in industry (cf. Roberts, 2024), and few considerations of the intersection between AI and VR (cf. Chance, 2025).

In situations where AI and VR are integrated, users will additionally be exposed to some of the challenges presented by VR. These include issues related to authenticity (Nam et al., 2022)– or fidelity (Hamstra et al., 2014), presence, immersiveness, and, depending on the type of VR system used, headset discomfort, and cybersickness (Baker et al., 2023; Nam et al., 2022, 2023). When using VR in educational contexts, improvements in user skills and knowledge have been reported (Hamstra et al., 2014; Xie et al., 2021) and improve student engagement (Hamstra et al., 2014). However, when the simulation appears unrealistic, encourages an inauthentic experience, does not make users feel as if they are immersed in the simulation, present in the experience, or distracted by low system quality, the discomfort of any head-mounted device, or feel nauseous, their satisfaction (Baker et al., 2023; Nam et al., 2022, 2023) and learning experience can be compromised. Therefore, while there is much to gain from integrating VR in education and training, especially when the simulation is improved with AI input, more factors must be considered to ensure an effective experience.

AI Simulations: Academic and Industry Solutions

AI, and to a lesser extent, VR, has been adopted by both industry and academia to help improve guest experiences and train staff and students more effectively. These vary from more generic chat bots to answer questions, to more detailed and specific systems to offer a more personalized experience. However, most of the solutions adopted by industry are guest-facing solutions, designed to improve the customer experience. There is an opportunity for educational institutions to work with industry to address this gap and provide solutions or evidence for solutions to support staff training through technologies like AI and VR. In the few cases where VR solutions have been developed for trainings, hotels report vast improvements in the number of guest complaints and customer satisfaction (Roberts, 2024). This suggests that there is scope for development and a perfect situation for education institutions to support industry (McCartney & Kwok, 2023; Sufi et al., 2025).

Industry Solutions

Hoteliers have adopted AI for several reasons and in several aspects. Some businesses have created broad incubators, designed to encourage individuals to submit ideas for improvements to the hotels for their consideration and adoption (Marriott, 2025a). Marriott's Travel Brilliantly campaign (Marriott, 2013), while dated, is a good example of this. From this, Marriott, created the RenAI, an AI powered navigator to provide recommendations to tourists (Marriott, 2025b). Other hotels have, likewise, adopted general AIs to support a variety of guest requests. These frequently look at personalizing the guest experiences, such as Virgin Hotels' AI assistant, Lucy, which allows guests to check-in, control technology in their room, order room service, and offer advice on local attractions (Virgin Hotels, 2025), or AI-powered chatbots which allow guests to ask questions or make room or restaurant reservations (Morch, 2024; Nazareth, 2024). Hotels have also adopted narrow AIs which excel at completing specific tasks (Kuusi & Heinonen, 2022). Such tools can help with revenue management, security, fraud detection, predict maintenance (Al-Hyari et al., 2023), reduce food waste (Sigala et al., 2025; Winnow, 2025), marketing content creation (Heitmann, 2024), and room management (Talukder et al., 2024) among numerous other specific tasks. Some hotels have taken the adoption of AI further by including robots in the service; the Henn-na hotel in 2015 in Japan, and the Flyzoo hotel in 2018 in China (Law et al., 2020). While these are not as widespread as other forms of technology, they could become more prevalent as awareness and customer demand increases (Nam et al., 2021). The following table provides a summary of various industry AI tools that either have been adopted or are available.

Table 1. AI industry solutions

Company	Solution
Boom (Boom, 2025)	AI-driven property management system for boutique properties
Winnow (Winnow, 2025)	AI Food waste analysis
TravAI (TravAI, 2025)	Hotel-specific training programmes including hotel features and selling techniques.
Jasper (Jasper, 2025)	Marketing tool to support marketing activities and promote team collaboration.
GoDesk (GoDesk, 2025)	AI Assistant for telephone calls and instant messaging to handle common requests.
Kobby (Kobby, 2025)	AI Assistant to make reservations, answer common requests, and upsell
Seekda (Seekda, n.d.)	AI Assistant to make reservations, answer common requests, and upsell
Supervity (Supervity, 2025)	Dynamic pricing agent
	Digital concierge
	Reservation agent
	Employee HR chatbot
	Marketing & Sales recommendations and reputation management
	Financial agent – reconciliation, dispute resolution
	Procurement analysis or order placement
Marriott's RENAI (Marriott, 2025b)	Digital Navigator/ concierge
Virgin Hotels' Lucy (Virgin Hotels, 2025)	Personal 'comfort' assistant
	Keyless entry
	Room control (lights, thermostat)
	Room service ordering
	Virtual concierge
Henn na Hotel (HIS Hotel Holdings, 2025)	Service robots (dinosaur or humanoid)
	Holographic check-in agents
	Steam closets
Flyzoo Hotel (Alizila, 2019)	Service robots for room service and F&B delivery
	Voice activated virtual assistant
	Keyless entry with biometrics

Note: This list is not comprehensive and only seeks to inform, not recommend or endorse any product or solution.

It is evident that a large number of solutions exist for hotels to adopt or that have already been adopted. However, few offer a comprehensive solution (cf. GoDesk,

2025; Kobby, 2025; Seekda, n.d.; Supervity, 2025) with widely accessible data that is not contained in departmental silos. Furthermore, most are used to enhance staff operational efficiency rather than offering staff training. The one solution from Table 1 which does offer training solutions (TravAI, 2025) appears to generate hypothetical situations. There is scope for such a model to be trained on data from a specific hotel or brand's history to provide a more customized training experience.

Academic Solutions

A plethora of use cases and examples exist addressing the use of AI in education across many disciplines, covering various degrees of adoption (Zhai et al., 2021). The focus here is specifically on AI programs adopted by hotel schools to expose students to real situations.

Some institutions have developed AI chat bots to assist with student learning by answering students' questions (Woltering, 2025), acting as a more targeted and controlled version of models such as ChatGPT. There is also great potential to use AI, especially when coupled with technologies such as VR, to provide service and skill-based training to students (Peters, 2023). While this is largely hypothetical, some institutions have developed and adopted VR simulations for their students to help make their students industry-ready (Roberts, 2024).

Proposed Solutions

The integration between AI and VR is, however, less evident. It appears as if the two solutions are being implemented independently. Together, both can offer effective and powerful solutions to develop skills in novel and memorable ways.

From a solution side, a comprehensive database of consumer complaints, hotel responses, and response accuracy can be compiled, thanks to AI (see Vadisetty & Polamarasetti, 2024) which can analyzed and packaged into a training program more effectively (Peng et al., 2022). For an individual hotel unit, an AI model would be able to be trained on past guest experiences to offer staff similar simulated situations and 'ideal' responses to help staff learn how to handle customer's queries. Such a system would be able to assess and guide participants on both their technical and interpersonal responses. Such a system could be expanded to brand-level, country-level, or even global. Such expansions could benefit regional or multinational brands and educational institutions. In such situations, students could be taught not only how to complete the technical elements of front office, but also the interpersonal elements of handling different customers from around the world, interacting with different brands. While adding costs and development challenges, embedding such an AI-based training system within a VR environment to offer simulated guest encounters can help develop and improve the students' experience and learning.

To ensure the best use of AI while reducing the negatives, students can be provided with the opportunity to work through use an AI-based simulation before discussing the simulation and outcomes with the rest of the class (Myers et al., 2018). This instructor-guided collaborative session (Cardona et al., 2023; Dell'Acqua et al., 2023) would allow students to learn from each other and also explore the appropriateness of different responses in terms of why some would work and others would not.

IMPLEMENTATION CHALLENGES AND RECOMMENDATIONS

The first and conceivably most important recommendation is to promote the human-in-the-loop training, ensuring that humans remain involved. This was identified by the US Department of Education as the most important recommendation in their report on AI use in education (Cardona et al., 2023). The collaboration between human and AI has provided positive results, suggesting better quality and faster outputs than either alone (Dell'Acqua et al., 2023). Beyond the inclusion of the teacher in the development of the class, student involvement, such as through the suggested debrief and discussion, should be encouraged (Myers et al., 2018). This would help to enhance students' critical thinking skills and help to protect against complacency, over-reliance on AI, and potential skill loss (Liu, 2024; Macnamara et al., 2024) by encouraging students to critique their simulations and remain cognitively engaged. A related concern, which will be particularly evident when adopting AI following a human-in-the-loop approach, is educator readiness. Integrating AI into hospitality curricula shifts educators' roles from instructors to facilitators and curators of AI-driven learning experiences. Research in simulation-based education highlights the importance of structured debriefing to promote reflection and transfer (Myers et al., 2018). The manner in which such simulations are adopted also requires careful consideration. A progressive scaffolding approach should be followed, where more technical skills are focused on first, before moving to more complex interpersonal ones. Such an approach would build students' confidence with the topic, the function, and the AI/simulation before confronting them with more variable interpersonal challenges. From a program-perspective, the adoption of such simulations close to any internship could help better prepare students for their internship. A longitudinal feedback period would also help by asking students to comment on the effectiveness of the simulation compared to their internship experience. Therefore, faculty and administrator development programs, communities of practice, and co-design with students can mitigate resistance and enhance implementation success.

Secondly, while the primary motive of the course would be to use AI to teach front office skills, its secondary motive can help prepare students for a career with AI. By experiencing these simulations and then discussing the outcomes, students can learn how to appropriately leverage AI (Zhai et al., 2021) to obtain appropriate outcomes.

Thirdly, careful consideration should be given to the AI model employed to minimize inaccuracies and biases that may affect the quality of the outcome (Cardona et al., 2023; Wang et al., 2024). While educator's choices are likely to be limited to the models which provide the experience necessary, the structure, training, and bias in the model could be considered as part of the post-simulation debrief.

Fourthly, research suggests that learning outcomes in authentic, high-fidelity simulations do not always translate directly to workplace contexts (Doozandeh & Hedayati, 2022; Hamstra et al., 2014; Myers et al., 2018). Therefore, the inclusion of post-simulation debriefs will help students contextualize these into workplace settings. Furthermore, longitudinal measures of performance should be considered and tracked to ensure long-term improvements.

Fifthly, as with any AI model, its solutions will only be as good as the data it is trained upon. If the methods of capturing guest complaints and hotel responses (and their success) are flawed e.g. by asking staff to update manually, the data can be biased, meaning the AI model will offer poor or even wrong suggestions. If this is embedded in training programs and used to create VR simulations, these can teach students completely wrong approaches. Furthermore, if there is a bias in the cultural origin of data sources or language used may mean the model is being trained on only a small potential segment. For example, if US-based hotels are very active in updating their experiences, any model would favor a US-centric approach, potentially ignoring or underplaying the cultural inputs from Europe, the Middle East, and Asia. Therefore, the success of any such training system is dependent upon quality data being collected.

Finally, there are ethical concerns which will need to be addressed to introduce the more advanced and sophisticated solution of a VR simulation based on AI situations trained on live guest and hotel data. These include issues of privacy, consent, and bias which will require educational institutions to adopt appropriate AI and data governance frameworks (Cardona et al., 2023) to protect guests, hotels, students, faculty, and institutions.

CONCLUSION

The hospitality industry is one of the most dynamic and guest-facing sectors, demanding employees with strong technical and interpersonal skills (Hai-yan & Baum, 2006). For higher education institutions, particularly those specializing in hospitality management, the challenge is to prepare students for this reality while simultaneously bridging the gap between academic training and workplace readiness (McCartney & Kwok, 2023; Sufi et al., 2025). As this chapter has demonstrated, AI and VR present powerful opportunities to reimagine front office education and training, ensuring that graduates enter the workforce with both technical and emotional competencies.

AI-enabled learning environments can provide scalable, adaptive, and data-driven training experiences, offering students the opportunity to engage with a wide range of scenarios, including those rarely encountered in internships, thereby expanding their exposure and preparedness. The integration of VR further enhances this by adding immersion, presence, and emotional engagement, creating a simulation that is not only functional but also experientially authentic.

However, technology, particularly AI, must be used with caution. AI systems are susceptible to hallucinations, biases, and over-simplification. Furthermore, overreliance on AI risks both skill loss and a form of "automation complacency" where learners defer too readily to AI outputs. To mitigate this, training must intentionally incorporate opportunities for students to encounter and critically evaluate AI responses through a human-in-the-loop approach. In addition, ethical considerations around privacy, consent, and dataset bias must be addressed if AI-driven simulations are to be trusted and sustainable. Governance frameworks, aligned with guidance from organizations such as the U.S. Department of Education (Cardona et al., 2023), will be essential in balancing innovation with responsibility.

Guest-facing solutions have been frequently adopted by industry, while training solutions are lacking. In education, several solutions exist leveraging VR for industry-based training, or AI to support students in class. This chapter has proposed a merge of the two styles. AI can collect and analyze data on guest complaints and hotel responses before creating scenarios, through text or VR simulations, for students or trainees to practice their responses. To better leverage AI, these scenarios can then be discussed in a class to help students appreciate the support and limitations of AI and promote human-in-the-loop approaches.

Looking forward, the call to action is clear. To help hospitality education remain relevant, AI and VR can be adopted as integral tools for preparing students for a technology-mediated workplace. Universities should invest in developing cross-institutional repositories of training simulations, collaborate with industry to co-create authentic datasets, and adopt governance frameworks that safeguard ethical use.

Industry, for its part, must recognize the untapped potential of AI for staff training and partner more actively with academia in piloting and scaling these solutions.

REFERENCES

Abdallah, A., Dutt, C. S., & Pijls-Hoekstra, R. (2024). Sustaining the experience: Students' perceptions of online field trips. *Journal of Teaching in Travel & Tourism*, *24*(3), 298–323. DOI: 10.1080/15313220.2023.2299031

Al-Hyari, H. S., Al-Smadi, H. M., & Weshah, S. R. (2023). The impact of Artificial Intelligence (AI) on guest satisfaction in hotel management: An empirical study of luxury hotels. *Geo Journal of Tourism and Geosites*, *48*(2, supplement), 810–819. DOI: 10.30892/gtg.482spl15-1081

Alizila. (2019, March 10). Introducing Alibaba's FlyZoo Future Hotel [Corporate]. Alizila. https://www.alizila.com/introducing-alibabas-flyzoo-future-hotel/

Baker, J., Nam, K., & Dutt, C. S. (2023). A user experience perspective on heritage tourism in the metaverse: Empirical evidence and design dilemmas for VR. *Information Technology & Tourism*, *25*(3), 265–306. DOI: 10.1007/s40558-023-00256-x

Baum, T., & Devine, F. (2007). Skills and training in the hotel sector: The case of front office employment in Northern Ireland. *Tourism and Hospitality Research*, *7*(3–4), 269–280. DOI: 10.1057/palgrave.thr.6050046

Beck, J., Rainoldi, M., & Egger, R. (2019). Virtual reality in tourism: A state-of-the-art review. *Tourism Review*, *74*(3), 586–612. DOI: 10.1108/TR-03-2017-0049

Boom. (2025). AI property management software for short-term rentals [Corporate]. Boom. https://www.boomnow.com/

Budnarowski, D., Jereczek, D., Detka, K., & Wieczorek, I. (2025). Application of artificial intelligence and virtual reality in soft skills training with modeled personality. *Applied Sciences (Basel, Switzerland)*, *15*(16), 9067. DOI: 10.3390/app15169067

Cardona, M. A., Rodríguez, R. J., & Ishmael, K. (2023). Artificial intelligence and the future of teaching and learning. U.S. Department of Education. https://tech.ed.gov/

Chance, E. A. (2025). The combined impact of AI and VR on interdisciplinary learning and patient safety in healthcare education: A narrative review. *BMC Medical Education*, *25*(1), 1039. DOI: 10.1186/s12909-025-07589-7

Dell'Acqua, F., McFowland, E., Mollick, E. R., Lifshitz-Assaf, H., Kellogg, K., Rajendran, S., Krayer, L., Candelon, F., & Lakhani, K. R. (2023). Navigating the jagged technological frontier: Field experimental evidence of the effects of AI on knowledge worker productivity and quality. SSRN Electronic Journal. DOI: 10.2139/ssrn.4573321

Devi, L. S., Das, S., Gayathri Kumar, A. R., Keerthana, A. H., Sai Ram, P. C., & Rakesh, K. (2024). Influence of artificial intelligence-based skill development training on employability. *International Journal of Educational Reform, 10567879241238366*. Advance online publication. DOI: 10.1177/10567879241238366

Doozandeh, P., & Hedayati, S. (2022). The effect of simulation fidelity on transfer of training for troubleshooting professionals: A meta-analysis. *IISE Transactions on Occupational Ergonomics and Human Factors, 10*(3), 117–134. DOI: 10.1080/24725838.2022.2099483

Glikson, E., & Woolley, A. W. (2020). Human trust in artificial intelligence: Review of empirical research. *The Academy of Management Annals, 14*(2), 627–660. DOI: 10.5465/annals.2018.0057

GoDesk. (2025). GoDesk [Corporate]. GoDesk. https://www.godesk.ai/home.html

Gurman, M. (2024, February 18). Why some of Apple's biggest fans are returning their vision pros. Bloomberg. https://www.bloomberg.com/news/newsletters/2024-02-18/apple-vision-pro-returning-3-500-device-over-comfort-lack-of-apps-and-price-lsrk88mq

Hai-yan, K., & Baum, T. (2006). Skills and work in the hospitality sector: The case of hotel front office employees in China. *International Journal of Contemporary Hospitality Management, 18*(6), 509–518. DOI: 10.1108/09596110610681548

Hamstra, S. J., Brydges, R., Hatala, R., Zendejas, B., & Cook, D. A. (2014). Reconsidering fidelity in simulation-based training. *Academic Medicine, 89*(3), 387–392. DOI: 10.1097/ACM.0000000000000130

Heitmann, M. (2024). Generative AI for marketing content creation: New rules for an old game. *NIM Marketing Intelligence Review, 16*(1), 10–17. DOI: 10.2478/nimmir-2024-0002

Hotel Holdings, H. I. S. (2025). Henn na Hotel [Corporate]. Henn-Na Hotel. https://group.hennnahotel.com/

Hochschild, A. R. (2012). The managed heart: Commercialization of human feeling (Updated ed). University of California Press.

Jasper. (2025). Jasper [Corporate]. Jasper. https://www.jasper.ai

Kobby. (2025). Kobby: AI Assistant for Hotel Guest Experience [Corporate]. Kobby. https://hotels.kobby.ai/

Kuusi, O., & Heinonen, S. (2022). Scenarios from artificial narrow intelligence to artificial general intelligence—Reviewing the results of the international work/technology 2050 study. *World Futures Review*, *14*(1), 65–79. DOI: 10.1177/19467567221101637

Law, R., Sun, S., & Chan, I. C. C. (2020). Hotel technology: A perspective article. *Tourism Review*, *75*(1), 286–289. DOI: 10.1108/TR-05-2019-0150

Leocádio, D., Guedes, L., Oliveira, J., Reis, J., & Melão, N. (2024). Customer service with AI-powered Human-Robot Collaboration (HRC): A literature review. *Procedia Computer Science*, *232*, 1222–1232. DOI: 10.1016/j.procs.2024.01.120

Lin, I. W., Sharma, A., Rytting, C. M., Miner, A. S., Suh, J., & Althoff, T. (2024). IMBUE: Improving Interpersonal Effectiveness through Simulation and Just-in-time Feedback with Human-Language Model Interaction. *Annual Meeting of the Association for Computational Linguistics*. DOI: 10.48550/ARXIV.2402.12556

Liu, P. (2024). Reflections on automation complacency. *International Journal of Human-Computer Interaction*, *40*(22), 7347–7363. DOI: 10.1080/10447318.2023.2265240

Macnamara, B. N., Berber, I., Çavuşoğlu, M. C., Krupinski, E. A., Nallapareddy, N., Nelson, N. E., Smith, P. J., Wilson-Delfosse, A. L., & Ray, S. (2024). Does using artificial intelligence assistance accelerate skill decay and hinder skill development without performers' awareness? *Cognitive Research: Principles and Implications*, *9*(1), 46. DOI: 10.1186/s41235-024-00572-8

Marriott. (2013). Marriott launches "Travel Brilliantly" campaign with new brand logo to engage next generation guests. Hospitality Net. https://www.hospitalitynet.org/news/4061971.html

Marriott. (2025a). How Marriott's AI initiatives will empower event planners [Corporate]. Marriott. https://marriottbonvoyevents.com/news-and-highlights/article/674/how-marriott-s-ai-initiatives-will-empower-event-planners

Marriott. (2025b). Meet RENAI [Corportate]. Marriott. https://www.marriott.com/en-us/marriott-brands/portfolio/meet-renai.mi

McCartney, G., & Kwok, S. S. H. (2023). Closing the gap between hospitality industry and academia research agendas: An exploratory analysis case study. *Journal of Quality Assurance in Hospitality & Tourism*, *24*(2), 192–210. DOI: 10.1080/1528008X.2021.2024782

Milgram, P., Takemura, H., Utsumi, A., & Kishino, F. (1995). In Das, H. (Ed.), *Augmented reality: A class of displays on the reality-virtuality continuum* (pp. 282–292)., DOI: 10.1117/12.197321

Mills, M. (2025, August 28). Replaced by bots? No, AI needs academics more than we need it. Times Higher Education (THE). https://www.timeshighereducation.com/depth/replaced-bots-no-ai-needs-academics-more-we-need-it

Monteith, S., Glenn, T., Geddes, J. R., Whybrow, P. C., Achtyes, E., & Bauer, M. (2024). Artificial intelligence and increasing misinformation. *The British Journal of Psychiatry*, *224*(2), 33–35. DOI: 10.1192/bjp.2023.136

Morch, A. (2024, January 7). From chatbots to smart rooms: How AI is personalizing and transforming your next hotel stay [News]. Hospitality Net. https://www.hospitalitynet.org/opinion/4122644.html

Myers, P., Starr, A., & Mullins, K. (2018). Flight simulator fidelity, training transfer, and the role of instructors in optimizing learning. *International Journal of Aviation, Aeronautics, and Aerospace*. Advance online publication. DOI: 10.15394/ijaaa.2018.1203

Nam, K., Baker, J., & Dutt, C. S. (2023). Does familiarity with the attraction matter? Antecedents of satisfaction with virtual reality for heritage tourism. *Information Technology & Tourism*. Advance online publication. DOI: 10.1007/s40558-023-00273-w

Nam, K., Dutt, C. S., & Baker, J. (2022). Authenticity in objects and activities: Determinants of satisfaction with virtual reality experiences of heritage and non-heritage tourism sites. *Information Systems Frontiers*. Advance online publication. DOI: 10.1007/s10796-022-10286-1

Nam, K., Dutt, C. S., Chathoth, P., Daghfous, A., & Khan, M. S. (2021). The adoption of artificial intelligence and robotics in the hotel industry: Prospects and challenges. *Electronic Markets*, *31*(3), 553–574. DOI: 10.1007/s12525-020-00442-3

Nazareth, L. (2024, January 12). A new era of customer relationship management. Hospitality News Magazine. https://www.hospitalitynewsmag.com/a-new-era-of-customer-relationship-management/

Pashaie, S., Mohammadi, S., & Golmohammadi, H. (2024). Unlocking athlete potential: The evolution of coaching strategies through artificial intelligence. Proceedings of the Institution of Mechanical Engineers, Part P: Journal of Sports Engineering and Technology, 17543371241300889. DOI: 10.1177/17543371241300889

Peng, S., Zhu, S., Yang, M., Huang, H., Liu, D., Wen, Z., Li, X., & Fan, B. (2022). AdaCoach: A virtual coach for training customer service agents (Version 1). arXiv. DOI: 10.48550/ARXIV.2204.12935

Peters, J.-H. (2023, March 17). Transforming vocational education with AI and VR [News]. Hospitality Net. Hospitality Net. https://www.hospitalitynet.org/opinion/4119175.html

Roberts, K. (2024, May 3). Hotel Management education and the future of simulated learning spaces [Corporate]. Torrens University Australia. https://www.torrens.edu.au/stories/blog/bmihms/hotel-management-education-and-the-future-of-simulated-learning-spaces

Seekda. (n.d.). Seekda Stay [Corporate]. Seekda. Retrieved October 15, 2025, from https://www.seekda.com/en/seekda-stay-ai-voice-assistant-hotels/

Shiohira, K. (2021). Understanding the impact of artificial intelligence on skills development. Education 2030. (No. ED612439). UNESCO-UNEVOC International Centre for Technical and Vocational Education and Training. https://eric.ed.gov/?id=ED612439

Shumeiko, N. V., & Osadcha, K. P. (2024). Application of artificial intelligence in higher education institutions for developing soft skills of future specialists in the sphere of information technology. *Journal of Physics: Conference Series*, *2871*(1), 012027. DOI: 10.1088/1742-6596/2871/1/012027

Sigala, E. G., Gerwin, P., Chroni, C., Abeliotis, K., Strotmann, C., & Lasaridi, K. (2025). Reducing food waste in the HORECA sector using AI-based waste-tracking devices. *Waste Management (New York, N.Y.)*, *198*, 77–86. DOI: 10.1016/j.wasman.2025.02.044

Skarbez, R., Smith, M., & Whitton, M. C. (2021). Revisiting Milgram and Kishino's reality-virtuality continuum. *Frontiers in Virtual Reality*, *2*, 647997. DOI: 10.3389/frvir.2021.647997

Stamer, T., Steinhäuser, J., & Flägel, K. (2023). Artificial intelligence supporting the training of communication skills in the education of health care professions: Scoping review. *Journal of Medical Internet Research*, *25*, e43311. DOI: 10.2196/43311

Sufi, T., Sigala, M., Rojas-Rivas, E., & Tirkey, A. (2025). Investigating industry-academia collaborations for enhancing tourism & hospitality graduates' employability: A technological perspective from industry professionals. *Journal of Hospitality & Tourism Education*, *37*(2), 154–164. DOI: 10.1080/10963758.2025.2456634

Supervity. (2025). Supervity [Corporate]. Supervity. https://www.supervity.ai/ai-agents-for-hospitality

Talukder, M. B., Kabir, F., & Jibon, F. A. (2024). AI-driven personalized room management in the modern hotel industry. In Chiwaridzo, O. T., & Masengu, R. (Eds.), *Advances in Hospitality, Tourism, and the Services Industry* (pp. 59–82). IGI Global. DOI: 10.4018/979-8-3693-5678-4.ch003

Trav, A. I. (2025). TravAI [Corporate]. TravAI. https://travai.co/use-cases/hotel/

Vadisetty, R., & Polamarasetti, A. (2024). AI-augmented skill development roadmaps: Tailoring 12-month learning paths for future-ready careers in education 4.0 and industry 4.0. 2024 13th International Conference on System Modeling & Advancement in Research Trends (SMART), 655–661. DOI: 10.1109/SMART63812.2024.10882483

Virgin Hotels. (2025). Meet luxury, Our free app [Corporate]. Virgin Hotels. https://virginhotels.com/about-the-app/

Wang, X., & Huang, R. "Tammy," Sommer, M., Pei, B., Shidfar, P., Rehman, M. S., Ritzhaupt, A. D., & Martin, F. (2024). The efficacy of artificial intelligence-enabled adaptive learning systems from 2010 to 2022 on learner outcomes: A meta-analysis. *Journal of Educational Computing Research*, *62*(6), 1348–1383. DOI: 10.1177/07356331241240459

Winnow. (2025). Winnow [Corporate]. Winnow. https://www.winnowsolutions.com

Woltering, R.-O. (2025). AI Learning Assistant: Revolutionizing Personalized, 24/7 Learning Support [Corporate]. EHL. https://pedagogy.ehl.edu/pedagogical-excellence/ai-learning-assistant

Xie, B., Liu, H., Alghofaili, R., Zhang, Y., Jiang, Y., Lobo, F. D., Li, C., Li, W., Huang, H., Akdere, M., Mousas, C., & Yu, L.-F. (2021). A review on virtual reality skill training applications. *Frontiers in Virtual Reality*, *2*, 645153. DOI: 10.3389/frvir.2021.645153

Zhai, X., Chu, X., Chai, C. S., Jong, M. S. Y., Istenic, A., Spector, M., Liu, J.-B., Yuan, J., & Li, Y. (2021). A review of artificial intelligence (AI) in education from 2010 to 2020. *Complexity*, *2021*(1), 8812542. DOI: 10.1155/2021/8812542

Section 3
Case Studies and Scenarios

Chapter 12
From Paper Fairs to Predictive Paths:
Ethical AI Across Generations in Career Development

Mahala Geronasso
http://orcid.org/0009-0006-2197-7832
Abu Dhabi Hospitality Academy-Les Roches Global Hospitality Education, Abu Dhabi, UAE

Stefania Escobar
Abu Dhabi Hospitality Academy-Les Roches Global Hospitality Education, Abu Dhabi, UAE

Joan Aviso
http://orcid.org/0009-0009-2612-9404
Abu Dhabi Hospitality Academy-Les Roches Global Hospitality Education, Abu Dhabi, UAE

Christopher Dutt
http://orcid.org/0000-0003-0219-0277
Abu Dhabi Hospitality Academy-Les Roches Global Hospitality Education, Abu Dhabi, UAE

ABSTRACT

Artificial Intelligence (AI) has become a pervasive tool in higher education, assisting students as a 24/7 tutor, proof editing, and writing assistant. Increasingly, students are using AI to guide career planning and professional growth. These technologies provide personalized insights, real-time feedback, and scalable support that can enhance self-awareness and employability. However, their growing presence intro-

DOI: 10.4018/979-8-3373-5112-4.ch012

duces significant ethical and pedagogical concerns. Questions persist regarding the accuracy and reliability of AI-generated career recommendations, the quality of guidance for skill development, and the reinforcement of pre-existing social or algorithmic biases. This chapter explores the opportunities and challenges associated with AI-enabled career development, highlighting the need for transparent, fair, and ethically governed systems balancing technological efficiency with human judgment. Central to this approach is the human-in-the-loop principle, in which AI serves as a complementary tool rather than a substitute for professional counsellors.

INTRODUCTION

AI at the Crossroads of Efficiency and Ethics in Career Counselling

Artificial Intelligence (AI) has emerged as one of the most transformative technologies of the 21st century, reshaping the way individuals learn, work, and navigate their professional lives. Within higher education, the integration of AI has extended far beyond administrative efficiencies, encompassing teaching, learning, and, critically, career counselling and development (Jawhar et al., 2025; Pandya & Wang, 2024; Wasnik et al., 2025). In an era defined by rapid technological innovation and digital transformation, AI systems are increasingly employed to support students in preparing for careers, building employability skills, and connecting with global opportunities (Pandya & Wang, 2024). While these advancements offer unprecedented efficiency and scalability, they also bring into sharp focus complex ethical questions concerning transparency, accountability, and fairness. Specific adoption data of AI in career services is not currently available however, as more companies begin exploring the use of AI in different aspects of the business, it is likely that evidence will become much more apparent (McKinsey & Company, 2025). This is likely to be particularly evident in the GCC (Gulf Cooperation Council countries) and Asia Pacific, where adoption rates are currently among the global highest (BCG, 2025; Nair, 2025).

The hospitality industry provides a particularly relevant context for examining the intersection of AI and career development. As a sector deeply rooted in human interaction and service quality, hospitality education and employment pathways depend not only on technical competencies but also on interpersonal skills, emotional intelligence, and cultural awareness (Baum et al., 2016; Dogru et al., 2023). This dual reliance on both human and technological capacities creates a unique tension: how can AI-driven career tools support the employability of future hospitality professionals without eroding the essential "human touch" that defines the industry?

Addressing this question is vital, as the hospitality sector has historically been a major employer of younger generations entering the workforce, who are now engaging with AI-powered career platforms at an accelerating pace (Seyfi et al., 2024).

These tensions are documented in hospitality research. Generative AI has been described as a "double-edged sword" that can open new opportunities for efficiency and value creation, while at the same time risking the erosion of trust and fairness when implemented without ethical foresight (Dogru et al., 2023). This perspective highlights how technology, if left unchecked, can compromise the very sustainability it promises to enhance. On the human side of this equation, studies show that employees' awareness of AI adoption often translates into heightened job insecurity, stronger intentions to leave, and declines in psychological well-being (Bakir et al., 2025). For students on the threshold of entering the workforce, these dynamics underscore an important reality: preparing for an AI-mediated career path involves not only mastering digital tools but also navigating the ethical, emotional, and professional dilemmas that accompany them.

The rise of generative AI tools, including ChatGPT, AI-driven résumé builders, and predictive career guidance platforms, has significantly altered how students approach their professional development. These systems can provide instant feedback on résumés, simulate job interviews, and even recommend tailored learning pathways based on algorithmic assessments of skills gaps (Omar et al., 2024). However, while such applications streamline processes and enhance personalization, they also raise critical ethical challenges. For instance, questions arise about the accuracy of AI-generated content, the risks of misinformation, the potential amplification of bias, and the erosion of student agency in decision-making (Jobin et al., 2019; Monteith et al., 2024).

The purpose of this chapter is therefore to critically examine the ethical implications of AI in career counselling and career development within higher education globally, with a particular emphasis on hospitality contexts. By examining generational shifts, mapping current AI applications, identifying key ethical challenges, and providing recommendations for best practices, this chapter seeks to strike a balance between technological innovation and the integrity of career support systems. Ultimately, it argues that while AI presents promising opportunities for enhancing employability and access to career resources, its ethical deployment requires careful consideration of issues such as authenticity, fairness, and human oversight.

The chapter proceeds as follows: Section 2 traces historical and generational shifts; Section 3 maps current AI applications in career counselling; Section 4 interrogates core ethical challenges; Section 5 advances implications and recommendations for universities, employers, and policymakers; Section 6 synthesizes the discussion for hospitality's people-centric context; and Section 7 concludes with a call for responsible, human-centered adoption.

HISTORICAL CONTEXT AND GENERATIONAL SHIFTS

From Career Fairs to ChatGPT: Generational Transformations in Career Development.

Broader societal and technological shifts have always influenced career counselling and professional development. Beyond describing behavioral differences, generational theory provides explanatory depth for how technological adoption and ethical perceptions evolve over time. Mannheim's (1952) concept of "fresh contact" and Twenge's (2010) cultural shift framework explains how successive cohorts reinterpret technology as an extension of their socialization environment. Building on this, Benítez-Márquez et al. (2022) demonstrate that digital trust varies systematically across generations, influencing not only how individuals use AI tools but also how they judge their ethical legitimacy. Such theoretical integration clarifies that attitudes toward AI are shaped not only by exposure but also by value systems and lived experience.

For Generation X and early Millennials, career services in higher education were characterized by manual processes, such as face-to-face appointments with career advisors, physical career fairs, and paper-based résumé submissions. Verification of credentials and employment histories often requires time-intensive checks, with employers relying on direct references or institutional records. These processes, while slower and less scalable, emphasized authenticity and interpersonal engagement, reinforcing the importance of trust and relationship-building in professional advancement (Brown & Lent, 2013).

By contrast, Generation Z and Generation Alpha have entered the workforce in a digital-first environment, where AI-driven tools are increasingly central to career preparation. These students are digital natives who expect instant feedback, personalized recommendations, and globally networked opportunities (Benítez-Márquez et al., 2022). Tools such as ChatGPT can generate cover letters in seconds, résumé builders can optimize documents to match applicant tracking systems, and AI-powered job boards can recommend positions aligned with skill profiles (Deshmukh & Raut, 2024; Gray, 2025; Pandya & Wang, 2024). These innovations have transformed the traditional dynamics of career development, reducing barriers to entry and democratizing access to resources that human advisors previously mediated.

In hospitality, this generational transition carries particular significance. Attracting and retaining Generation Z talent already requires rethinking traditional workforce strategies, as their expectations around technology, flexibility, and career progression differ sharply from previous cohorts (Goh & Okumus, 2020). When combined with the rapid adoption of AI tools in education and employment, these evolving expectations add complexity to how career counseling and development should be designed.

Yet, these generational shifts are not without trade-offs. While AI enhances efficiency, scalability, and accessibility, it also raises concerns about the loss of authenticity. For Gen Z and Alpha, professional narratives may increasingly be shaped by algorithmic outputs rather than personal reflection, potentially diluting the individuality and credibility of applications (Berkelaar & Buzzanell, 2014). Employers, too, face new challenges in distinguishing genuine human capabilities and AI-enhanced representations of skills and experience. For instance, AI-generated résumés may embellish achievements or present unverifiable claims, complicating recruitment decisions.

The ethical implications of these generational shifts are profound. For earlier generations, the slower, human-centered processes allowed for natural checks on accuracy and personal accountability. In contrast, today's students face a paradox: the very tools designed to enhance employability may also increase anxiety about career stability and fairness (Bakir et al., 2025; Hosseini & Lichtinger, 2025). Employees in the hospitality industry often perceive AI adoption as a threat to their roles, which can lead to diminished well-being and heightened turnover intentions (Bakir et al., 2025). Empirical evidence supports this tension. Xie and Ma (2025) found that while AI adoption in hotels improved efficiency and decision-making, it also required redefined workforce roles and significant training investments to maintain employee trust and adaptability. For students preparing to enter such environments, these patterns signal a growing psychological burden as they navigate AI-dominated workplaces. Moreover, generative AI's adoption in hospitality can simultaneously create and destroy value, depending on whether stakeholder concerns are recognized and addressed (Dogru et al., 2023).

Consequently, hospitality education sits at the heart of this transformation. As institutions prepare students for careers where trust, interpersonal skill, and service authenticity remain vital, the challenge is to integrate AI thoughtfully, leveraging its advantages without undermining the human qualities that define the field. This calls for both critical awareness of AI's limitations and the implementation of ethical safeguards that preserve fairness and credibility across generations.

In short, the progression from manual, human-centric career counseling to AI-mediated, digital-first approaches mirrors wider societal changes in technology use and generational values. What has been gained in efficiency, scalability, and access must now be weighed against what has been lost in authenticity, human connection, and ethical oversight. This tension sets the stage for the ethical dilemmas explored in the following sections.

AI APPLICATIONS IN CAREER COUNSELLING

Résumés in the Age of Algorithms

AI is reshaping career counseling, especially in résumé creation and enhancement. Leveraging natural language processing (NLP) and machine learning, contemporary tools analyze job descriptions, extract salient keywords, and offer personalized feedback to applicants (Huntr, 2025; KickResume, 2025; ResumeAI, 2025; Zety, 2025). Beyond streamlining applications, these platforms approximate aspects of human advising, helping users align materials with evolving employer expectations, an imperative in service-intensive fields where adaptability and digital fluency are increasingly valued.

For instance, AI-driven résumé screening systems, such as those utilizing Sentence-BERT (S-BERT), demonstrate how semantic similarity models can significantly improve the accuracy and efficiency of candidate evaluation. These systems optimize résumé formatting, enhance content relevance, and ensure compatibility with applicant tracking systems (ATS), offering scalable solutions for institutions focused on employability outcomes (Deshmukh & Raut, 2024).

In addition, platforms such as ResumeAI, Huntr, Zety, and KickResume use semantic search and contextual analysis to parse resumes and suggest targeted improvements (Huntr, 2025; KickResume, 2025; ResumeAI, 2025; Zety, 2025). These tools simulate aspects of career advising by identifying skill gaps, recommending enhancements, and tailoring resumes to specific roles. General-purpose AI tools, such as Grammarly and Microsoft Copilot, also contribute meaningfully: Grammarly refines clarity, tone, and professionalism (Grammarly, 2025), while Copilot assists users in drafting and polishing resumes within productivity platforms, offering contextual suggestions based on job descriptions and user input (Microsoft, 2025)

Identifying Skills and Bridging Gaps Through AI

The literature indicates that AI is effective in supporting the development of personalized career plans and in identifying individual skill-development needs (Córdova-Esparza, 2025; Pandya & Wang, 2024). There are two potential areas of AI in skill development, in particular, that deserve further consideration. First, building AI literacy itself can bolster long-term career sustainability (Ahmad & Bilal, 2025). Emerging platforms, even those that validate AI skills or match talent to AI-enabled roles, signal where the labor market is heading (Zeff, 2025). Second, AI can accelerate early-career capability building. In firms adopting AI, junior employees proficient with these tools were less likely to quit and more likely to be promoted than peers in non-adopting firms, suggesting recognition and mobility for AI-skilled entrants (Hosseini & Lichtinger, 2025).

For those entering the workforce, there is likely to be increasing pressure to begin their careers with a broader range of knowledge and competencies, yet with a shorter period allowed for adjustment. As AI may soon be expected to start work with the equivalent expertise of two to three years' experience, ready to assume responsibilities once reserved for more senior colleagues. Organizations and individuals should therefore integrate AI into training to ensure early-career professionals are genuinely job-ready. Encouraging students to use AI thoughtfully during their studies not only strengthens employability but also develops applied, market-relevant skills.

For more senior staff, AI can function as a form of reverse mentoring, offering a private, always-available channel to stay current on tools, behaviors, and trends (Goh & Richardson, 2024). Although formal reverse-mentoring programs create valuable intergenerational learning, senior employees may hesitate to participate if they perceive juniors as lacking sufficient context or experience. AI can complement (not replace) these programs by serving as an impartial, low-friction advisor that supports continuous professional development and fosters a culture of lifelong learning across generations.

AI as Interview Coach and Career Mentor

Recent scholarship underscores the expanding role of AI-powered platforms in academic career counselling, offering scalable, personalized, and data-driven guidance for both students and job seekers. These intelligent systems utilize machine learning and natural language processing to evaluate user profiles, analyze skill sets, and recommend career trajectories that align with individual strengths, motivations, and aspirations (Wasnik et al., 2025). In addition to personalized guidance, such platforms generate real-time analytics on labor-market trends and emerging competencies, enabling students to make more informed decisions regarding future roles and the evolving demands of the global workforce.

Within higher education, AI-based applications such as VMock are increasingly employed to provide instant feedback on résumés, LinkedIn profiles, and interview performance. These tools employ sophisticated algorithms to assess content, structure, and presentation, enabling students to refine their application materials and prepare more effectively for recruitment processes (Wasnik et al., 2025). AI-powered mock interview platforms further enhance this preparation by simulating realistic interview scenarios, generating adaptive questions, and offering immediate, actionable feedback on communication style, body language, and overall delivery. Such systems help students build confidence and readiness for professional encounters in competitive job markets (Córdova-Esparza, 2025; Xiao & Zheng, 2025).

Similar patterns are evident in the hospitality sector, where luxury hotels increasingly deploy AI tools to streamline recruitment and candidate evaluation processes. For instance, Marinakou et al. (2025) document how Greek luxury hotels use AI-driven screening to accelerate hiring while emphasizing the continued need for human judgment to ensure fairness and service quality.

In parallel, AI chatbots and virtual mentors deliver 24/7 support, answering career questions, recommending targeted upskilling, and flagging relevant opportunities, broadening access to individualized guidance at scale (Córdova-Esparza, 2025).

AI adoption in hospitality recruitment and career development is gaining traction across global brands. Hilton Worldwide, for instance, uses AI-powered chatbots to screen early-stage candidates, answering common questions and assessing language fluency, while maintaining human oversight for cultural fit and emotional intelligence. Marriott International has implemented predictive analytics tools to identify high-potential management trainees, improving placement speed while confronting ethical questions about algorithmic bias in candidate scoring. In higher education, Les Roches Global Hospitality Education has piloted AI-driven résumé and interview platforms (VMock) to help students refine applications, with faculty acting as human verifiers. These examples illustrate both the opportunities for scalability and the ethical tensions surrounding fairness, transparency, and authenticity in people-centric service industries.

Predictive Pathways and Career Scenario Modelling

Beyond guiding individuals and students in developing their skills to support a specific career choice, AI is being used to offer suggestions on potential career paths. OpenAI's new job platform could showcase a variety of career paths and, based on users' data (such as experience and education), offer recommendations of relevant careers (Zeff, 2025). By further integrating AI in the career development process, students could use AI to run various career scenarios and what-ifs to help them choose an ideal future career or lifestyle, then plan the process needed to achieve this result (Gray, 2025).

AI can thus function as a virtual career consultant, capable of offering tailored advice on progression opportunities, skill enhancement, or transitions into new sectors. Numerous tools exist within this space, from the generic of GPTs such as ChatGPT or Gemini, to the more specific, such as LinkedIn's AI search tool (Komljenovic, 2019), Coach, Careerflow, Musely, or Job Hunt Mode[1]. Together, these applications make career planning more dynamic, data-rich, and interactive, empowering students to visualize and design their professional futures with greater clarity.

Branding, Networks, and the AI-Enhanced Professional Identity

The increasingly challenging and volatile job market emphasizes the need for student career counselling and development in hospitality education to be intertwined with personal branding and social media optimization (Gorbatov et al., 2024; Harrison & Peters, 2025; Johnson, 2021; Leo et al., 2024; Lexis et al., 2023). Indeed, evidence suggests that many employers actively seek prospective employees who demonstrate a strong individual brand image, as this is perceived as an indicator of potential future value creation (Happonen et al., 2022). Consequently, cultivating personal branding strategies becomes particularly valuable for students entering the workforce.

AI-enabled platforms, such as LinkedIn, Canva AI, BrandYourself, and Crystal Knows, help students refine brand voice, produce professional assets, and strengthen networks through immediate, personalized feedback (Brewer & McCarthy, 2024; Harrison & Peters, 2025). LinkedIn's AI features can suggest content, surface relevant groups and alumni, and streamline strategic connections (Komljenovic, 2019). BrandYourself and Canva AI support the creation of digital portfolios, personal websites, and branding materials (Johnson, 2021). Empirical studies highlight the value of these tools. For instance, LinkedIn significantly contributes to building a connected identity and social network literacy in students, helping them overcome a lack of confidence in professional networking (Lexis et al., 2023).

Consequently, these tools serve as pedagogical instruments: they enhance employability skills, support reflective identity work, and increase students' confidence as they transition to the workforce (Jackson & Wilton, 2017; Johnson, 2021; Tomlinson & Jackson, 2021; Zhou et al., 2024).

Critical Synthesis: Opportunities and Ethical Risks in AI-Driven Career Development

The expanding integration of AI into career counselling presents a dual narrative of opportunity and caution. On one hand, AI democratizes access to personalized guidance, enhances employability analytics, and empowers students to visualize diverse professional trajectories through data-driven insights. On the other hand, these same systems raise enduring concerns about bias, authenticity, and over-reliance. Efficiency and personalization may come at the cost of transparency when users are unable to evaluate how recommendations are generated or to what extent algorithms reflect historical inequities. In hospitality education, where interpersonal sensitivity and service authenticity are central, this tension becomes even more pronounced: tools that enhance professional readiness can also depersonalize reflection and flatten individuality. Consequently, while AI extends the reach of career development support, ethical vigilance and human mediation remain essential to ensure that technology amplifies rather than diminishes human potential.

ETHICAL CHALLENGES

Accuracy and Authenticity: When AI Polishes Too Much

In hospitality recruitment, AI résumé parsers have occasionally flagged applicants incorrectly when translation software altered job-title wording, leading to mismatched placements and credibility issues for international candidates.

Concerns around the accuracy and authenticity of user-provided data have gained prominence as AI becomes more integrated into career counselling and recruitment processes. AI resume screening systems rely heavily on the information submitted by candidates, yet these systems often lack mechanisms to verify the truthfulness of credentials, experiences, or achievements. This opens the door to embellishment or fabrication, which can undermine the integrity of both career guidance and hiring decisions. In addition, while natural language processing and semantic search have improved the parsing and contextual understanding of resumes, they remain vulnerable to inconsistencies and unverifiable claims embedded in unstructured data. The challenge lies in distinguishing between genuine qualifications and strategically exaggerated content, especially when AI systems are trained to optimize matches based on keyword relevance rather than factual validation (Dadaboyev et al., 2025).

Furthermore, the automation of career services introduces ethical risks, particularly when AI tools are used to assess candidate suitability without human oversight (Wilson et al., 2022). The lack of verification mechanisms can lead to unfair advantages for individuals who manipulate their profiles, while disadvantaging honest applicants. Moreover, the reliance on algorithmic matching may inadvertently reinforce superficial metrics or biased over substantive evaluation (Chen, 2023). Addressing these concerns requires the integration of cross-referencing systems, human review protocols, and ethical design principles that prioritize transparency and accountability. As AI continues to evolve, ensuring the authenticity of career data will be essential to maintaining trust and fairness in career development practices.

Bias and Fairness in Algorithmic Recruitment

When a global hotel chain piloted AI screening for management trainees, accent-based transcription errors in video interviews disproportionately lowered scores for non-native English speakers, an example of algorithmic bias that required human-in-the-loop correction.

The increasing use of AI-driven recruitment tools has raised critical concerns about discriminatory outcomes based on gender, ethnicity, or language style (Chen, 2023; Drage & Mackereth, 2022). While these tools are often promoted as mechanisms to enhance efficiency and fairness in hiring, evidence suggests that they can inadvertently reproduce or even amplify existing social biases (El Mimouni & Bouhdadi, 2025; Hall & Ellis, 2023). For instance, algorithms trained on historical hiring data may replicate patterns of gender and ethnic exclusion, particularly in male-dominated industries (Martin, 2022).

In addition, studies have shown that natural language processing systems used in résumé screening can penalize applicants whose language style deviates from dominant cultural norms, disadvantaging non-native speakers or individuals from minority backgrounds (Raghavan et al., 2020). Furthermore, research indicates that bias may occur both in candidate selection and in performance prediction models, where proxies for race, gender, or socioeconomic background are embedded within supposedly neutral data (Barocas & Selbst, 2016).

Such findings highlight the need for critical analysis, transparency, and bias mitigation strategies in the deployment of AI tools in recruitment strategies. Without such measures, tools designed to democratize hiring processes risk reinforcing the labor market inequalities they aim to address.

Transparency and Explainability: Opening the Black Box

A resort group's AI matching system was suspended after applicants complained that its selection logic was opaque; publishing "explainability statements" restored trust among users and recruiters alike.

Information-wise, one major concern that should be considered by everyone, regardless of the setting, is the inaccuracy of AI's responses. Despite sounding intelligent and human, AI models do not understand the words they generate and can make errors in semantics and facts (Monteith et al., 2024). Erroneous facts may lead to poor career advice, which, if not checked, can have detrimental outcomes.

Concerns also arise regarding the source of information or the way an AI model summarizes its suggestions. If prompted correctly, a model can clearly explain the reason behind a suggestion and provide appropriate sources. However, this is dependent on correct prompts, due diligence in cross-checking the information, and assumes those using AI still retain sufficient skill to assess the suggestions (Macnamara et al., 2024). Without understanding how AI generates its suggestions, it is possible that poor career choices will be made or that the wrong skills will be focused on due to erroneous AI outputs. With AI models being trained on available data, incorrect or biased information may be incorporated into the AI models' responses (El Mimouni & Bouhdadi, 2025; Jobin et al., 2019; Martin, 2022; Monteith et al., 2024). With a sufficient quantity of misinformation, the degree of inappropriateness may increase.

Privacy and Data Security in AI-Mediated Careers

Universities partnering with hotel brands to share student data for internship matching had to implement encrypted data-exchange portals to meet new GCC data-protection rules.

The ethical management of personal data is becoming increasingly central to the design and deployment of AI-powered career counselling systems. These platforms rely on sensitive user information, such as academic records, employment history, and career preferences, to generate personalized guidance, making robust data governance essential (Pandya & Wang, 2024; Wasnik et al., 2025). While this data-driven approach enhances the relevance and accuracy of career recommendations, it also introduces risks related to privacy, consent, and potential misuse. Encrypted cloud-native databases and secure data pipelines are particularly important to ensure confidentiality and prevent unauthorized access during data processing.

Equally critical is transparency: users may trust AI-generated career recommendations without understanding how their data are being used, leading to issues of informed consent and potential overreliance on opaque systems (Gedrimiene et al., 2023; Macnamara et al., 2024). Ethical AI deployment also requires mechanisms for data minimization, user control, and bias mitigation, alongside continuous monitoring and inclusive design practices (Sharma, 2025). Together, these measures enable AI systems to deliver transformative, personalized guidance while upholding fairness, privacy, and user autonomy (Gedrimiene et al., 2023; Sharma, 2025; Wasnik et al., 2025).

Over-Reliance and the Risk of Dehumanization

Some career centers noted students submitting AI-generated résumés that no longer reflected their personality or communication style, prompting reflective workshops on balancing automation with authenticity.

While AI-driven tools in student career development can offer personalized feedback, they may inadvertently diminish interpersonal, tailored support that human advisors traditionally provide (Mishra, 2024). Algorithmic systems struggle to replicate certain elements that make human guidance essential, such as interpreting nuanced student needs, offering emotional support, and boosting critical reflection (Klimova & Pikhart, 2025). For instance, AI-powered career platforms, such as automated résumé evaluators or interview simulators, can provide rapid feedback on technical skills but may fail to address context-specific concerns, such as cultural nuances, motivational barriers, or emotional preparedness (Holmes et al., 2019).

Excessive reliance on automation risks displacing mentorship, collaborative learning, and the trust-based relationships that are crucial to developing professional confidence (Luckin et al., 2016). Moreover, standardized datasets limit the extent to which AI can tailor advice to individual experiences (Selwyn, 2019). Consequently, AI should not replace human counselors but complement them, improving its efficiency and reach while preserving the empathy and context sensitivity that characterize authentic human guidance. Integrating AI within a human-supervised framework remains the most sustainable path to ensuring that technological progress strengthens, rather than diminishes, the human core of career development.

Ethical Challenges Synthesized

The ethical risks discussed, such as bias, transparency gaps, and over-reliance, carry particular significance for hospitality, a field defined by interpersonal competence and emotional intelligence. In hospitality recruitment and training, where empathy, adaptability, and cross-cultural understanding are essential, algorithmic systems often struggle to recognize or measure these human dimensions. For example, AI résumé screening may undervalue non-verbal communication, teamwork, or service recovery experience, which are qualities central to guest satisfaction but difficult to quantify. Bias in training data can also distort assessments of soft skills, penalizing candidates from diverse linguistic or cultural backgrounds. Consequently, ethical AI implementation in hospitality must not only mitigate data-driven inequities but also preserve the social and emotional competencies that technology cannot replicate. Embedding these people-centered values within AI design and evaluation criteria ensures that innovation supports, rather than supplants, the relational essence of the industry.

Table 1. Ethical challenges and mitigation strategies in AI-mediated career development for hospitality education

Ethical Challenge	Manifestation in Hospitality Career Context	Potential Impact	Mitigation Strategies
Accuracy & Authenticity	AI résumé tools fabricate or over-polish content	Misrepresentation; trust erosion	Verification checks; AI-use disclosure forms
Bias & Fairness	Algorithms replicate cultural or language bias	Exclusion of diverse candidates	Diverse training data; human review panels
Transparency & Explainability	Users can't see how recommendations are generated	Low trust; perceived opacity	Explainability statements; audit trails
Privacy & Data Security	Sensitive student/employer data mishandled	Data breaches; regulatory risk	Encryption; consent policies; minimal data storage
Over-Reliance & Dehumanization	Loss of mentoring and emotional engagement	Reduced interpersonal skill development	Human-in-the-loop counselling; reflective exercises

This summary table (Table 1) underscores that ethical risks and their mitigations are not abstract but operational decisions that directly shape student experiences and organizational credibility in hospitality education.

IMPLICATIONS AND RECOMMENDATIONS

Universities as Gatekeepers of Ethical AI Literacy

Universities hold a pivotal responsibility in preparing students to navigate an AI-mediated career landscape, particularly in fields like hospitality, where employability depends on both technical proficiency and interpersonal capability. Institutions should take a leading role in establishing ethical guidelines for AI use in career counseling, emphasizing transparency, disclosure, and accountability. For instance, students could be required to disclose when and how AI was used in producing résumés, cover letters, or digital portfolios, thereby promoting honesty while enabling them to benefit from technological assistance.

Structured workshops and curricular modules focused on AI literacy can demystify algorithmic processes, teach students to critically evaluate AI-generated outputs, and highlight key risks related to bias, privacy, and authenticity. Research shows that higher levels of AI literacy reduce job-seeking anxiety and improve employment confidence, underscoring the need for formalized, evidence-based training (Li et al., 2025). Beyond technical competence, universities should embed reflective exercises and case studies that prompt students to consider how AI shapes their professional identity, decision-making, and ethical responsibility. This dual emphasis, on capability and conscience, ensures that graduates approach AI as a tool for empowerment rather than dependence.

Career counselors and academic advisors can operationalize ethical AI literacy by incorporating short simulations or workshops where students critically evaluate AI-generated résumés and interview transcripts, identifying ethical red flags such as bias or misrepresentation. Embedding these reflective exercises into employability modules helps students practice human oversight in real contexts rather than learning AI ethics abstractly.

Employers as Verifiers of Authenticity

Employers, meanwhile, must complement academic preparation by reinforcing robust verification processes. In hospitality, recruiters face unique challenges: AI-enhanced résumés may appear polished but may not accurately represent service orientation, teamwork capacity, or cultural adaptability, qualities central to the industry. To address this, employers should implement layered assessments that go beyond algorithmic résumé screening, including behavioral interviews, situational judgment tests, and live service simulations that reveal interpersonal competencies.

Verification mechanisms should extend beyond résumé parsing to include digital credentialing systems that authenticate academic qualifications and professional certifications, reducing risks of misrepresentation. Crucially, human oversight must remain present in all high-stakes hiring decisions: AI can assist in filtering large applicant pools, but the ultimate judgment should rest with experienced professionals capable of interpreting nuance. Without these safeguards, hiring outcomes risk being driven by embellished, unverifiable, or biased AI-generated representations, undermining both fairness and trust (Bakir et al., 2025).

For hospitality recruiters, actionable steps include creating shared databases of verified digital credentials across partner institutions, developing bias-checklists for algorithmic screening tools, and training HR staff to interpret AI outputs critically. Pilot programs in hotel management training could pair automated evaluation with peer review or mentor feedback to ensure ethical alignment and consistency across hiring decisions.

Taken together, universities and employers form the dual foundation of ethical AI adoption in career development, one preparing ethically aware graduates, the other validating authenticity and human judgment in professional selection. Yet these efforts require broader systemic alignment to ensure consistency and accountability across education and industry.

Policymakers as Guardians of Transparency and Accountability

Policymakers play a defining role in shaping the ethical landscape for AI in education and employment. Regulatory frameworks can mandate transparency by requiring AI systems to disclose how recommendations or hiring decisions are generated, ensuring that both students and employers understand the underlying processes. The European Union's AI Act, for example, demonstrates a tiered regulatory approach that classifies AI systems by risk level and imposes stricter compliance requirements for high-stakes uses, such as recruitment and career counseling (Dogru et al., 2023). This model balances innovation with consumer protection and offers a blueprint for policymakers globally to adapt in sector-specific contexts.

In hospitality, transparency carries both legal and cultural significance: trust and authenticity are integral to service relationships. Students must have confidence that AI-mediated career guidelines reflect fair, unbiased assessments, and employers must be assured that recruitment tools do not compromise equity or misrepresent candidates' potential. Policymakers can reinforce this trust by setting clear standards for auditability, accountability, and disclosure. Mandating that AI-driven recruitment platforms provide audit trails and publish annual fairness reports, similar to requirements under the EU's AI Act, would improve clarity, reduce bias, and sustain confidence among all stakeholders (Jobin et al., 2019).

Furthermore, independent auditing and certification of AI tools should become standard practice in high-stakes applications. As with financial reporting or food safety, periodic third-party assessments can validate the integrity, fairness, and reliability of AI systems. These audits reassure employers and applicants alike that ethical standards are being met, and that algorithmic decisions remain subject to external scrutiny.

Frameworks for Responsible AI: Human-in-the-Loop and Beyond

At the practical level, ethical frameworks such as the human-in-the-loop principle should guide AI adoption across education, recruitment, and policy.

Definition Box: Human-in-the-Loop (HITL)

A design and governance principle in which humans retain meaningful oversight of AI- assisted processes and final responsibility for consequential decisions. In practice, HITL requires clear checkpoints for review, challenge, and override of model outputs; traceable rationales (audit trails); and escalation to human judgment when stakes are high or uncertainty is elevated, safeguarding fairness, context sensitivity, and accountability in career counselling and recruitment.

This principle requires that humans remain actively involved in decision-making processes, using AI as an aid rather than a replacement. For instance, while AI can suggest career pathways or flag skills gaps, counsellors should interpret and contextualize those insights, embedding ethical reflection and cultural awareness. In the workplace, recruiters might employ AI to streamline candidate searches but still rely on managers and HR professionals to make the final decisions. Scholars emphasize that successful AI integration depends not only on technical safeguards but also on leadership and stakeholder engagement, which can mitigate risks of job insecurity, value co-destruction, and loss of trust while enabling long-term sustainability (Bakir et al., 2025; Pandya & Wang, 2024).

Beyond HITL, scholars have proposed frameworks that stress stakeholder engagement, continuous monitoring, and adaptive governance. Hospitality institutions, for instance, could establish "responsible AI boards" composed of faculty, employers, and student representatives to oversee the integration of AI in career services. These boards could evaluate not only the technical accuracy of AI systems but also their impact on student well-being, diversity outcomes, and alignment with the people-centric values of hospitality education. Embedding such frameworks creates an environment where AI adoption is not a one-time decision but an ongoing process of ethical reflection and adjustment. This approach ensures that while efficiency and innovation are harnessed, the foundational qualities of authenticity, trust, and fairness remain at the heart of hospitality career development (Seyfi et al., 2024).

When guided by these principles, AI can enhance efficiency, inclusion, and opportunity without compromising authenticity or trust. Ethical frameworks thus serve as both compass and guardrail, directing innovation while preserving the interpersonal essence that remains the hallmark of hospitality education and practice.

DISCUSSION

Balancing Efficiency with Integrity in Career Counselling

The central dilemma for AI in career counselling is balancing efficiency with integrity. On one hand, AI platforms provide scalable solutions that expand access to personalized guidance and real-time labor market insights. By automating résumé reviews, job-matching processes, and even mock interviews, these tools can help institutions serve larger student populations at lower costs, making career support more accessible than ever before. For students in hospitality, where competition for placements and early career opportunities is often intense, this kind of rapid, data-driven support is particularly attractive (Pandya & Wang, 2024).

The other side of this equation involves authenticity and fairness. Over-reliance on AI risks compromising the integrity of the career counselling process by prioritizing keyword optimization or algorithmic matching over holistic assessments of human potential. In hospitality, this trade-off is especially acute: while AI can efficiently screen candidates, it cannot replicate the nuanced human judgment required to assess cultural fit, emotional intelligence, or service orientation, traits that are central to success in people-driven environments (Bakir et al., 2025). Moreover, opaque algorithms may unintentionally reproduce existing labor market inequalities, amplifying systemic biases.

The solution is not to reject automation but to embed AI within hybrid, human-centered frameworks. AI can process data on a scale, offering analytics and labor-market insights, while human counselors interpret those outputs with nuance, contextual awareness, and ethical consideration. In this configuration, efficiency amplifies human expertise rather than replacing it. Ultimately, AI should act as a co-pilot, an analytical assistant that augments, not automates, professional judgment.

Hospitality's People-Centric Imperative in an AI Era

Few industries embody the human touch as deeply as hospitality. The sector thrives on empathy, attentiveness, and interpersonal connection, qualities that resist codification and defy algorithmic replication. As AI becomes more integrated into hospitality education and career services, maintaining this people-centric ethos becomes both a challenge and an ethical imperative.

AI tools can undoubtedly enhance employability training. They can identify skills gaps, simulate interviews, and suggest personalized development plans. However, they cannot fully evaluate the nuances of guest interaction, emotional resilience, or service recovery, the dimensions of hospitality that distinguish excellence from adequacy. When students depend excessively on AI-generated résumés or interview scripts, they risk weakening the very competencies employers prize most: genuine engagement, teamwork, and emotional intelligence (Bakir et al., 2025).

Moreover, as generative AI influences both educational and professional practices, its deployment can either create or destroy value. Applied thoughtfully, AI can expand opportunity and inclusion, helping international or first-generation students access high-quality career support on a scale. Used carelessly, it can reinforce inequities, depersonalize preparation, and replace mentoring with mechanized feedback loops (Dogru et al., 2023). The task for hospitality educators and leaders is therefore not simply to integrate AI but to humanize its implementation, framing technology as a complement to, not a substitute for, the social intelligence that defines the industry.

To bridge academic theory and industry practice, hospitality organizations can play a proactive role in shaping ethical AI adoption. For instance, hotel chains and tourism companies can pilot hybrid recruitment systems where AI tools handle data-driven screening, but final candidate assessments include live service simulations or peer evaluations to preserve the human element. Internship programs can integrate AI-assisted learning portfolios, allowing students to document both digital competencies and soft-skill development. These applied collaborations not only strengthen employability pipelines but also position the hospitality sector as a testbed for ethical, human-centered innovation.

Looking Ahead: Hybrid Models of Career Guidance

The future of career counselling will most likely see a hybrid approach where human counsellors make use of AI analytical capabilities as tools to deliver more comprehensive, personalized, data-driven guidance to students (Al-Abri & Sidhu, 2023; Jawhar et al., 2025; Zhou et al., 2024). On the one hand AI tools, such as machine learning and natural language processing, will provide facilitating and supporting roles in providing real-time data related to labor market trends, emerging industries, in-demand skills, and potential career opportunities. Human counselors, in turn, interpret this information, translating data into personalized strategies that address each student's strengths, aspirations, and ethical considerations.

Such collaboration ensures that technological efficiency is harnessed without sacrificing relational depth. Students benefit from timely, evidence-based insights while retaining opportunities for mentorship, reflection, and interpersonal growth. Over time, hybrid systems can also foster lifelong learning: AI-powered platforms help graduates identify skill gaps and pursue tailored upskilling opportunities, keeping them agile amid evolving market demands.

By 2035, this human-AI partnership may redefine career development across higher education, shifting it from a static advising model to a continuous, adaptive process that supports professionals at every career stage. For hospitality, this approach carries even deeper promise. When combined with experiential learning, service simulations, and cross-cultural mentorship, hybrid career models can produce graduates who are not only digitally literate but also empathetically grounded, equipped to lead in an industry where technology and humanity must coexist in balance.

These recommendations can be summarized in the following table 2, which reflects the considerations different stakeholders should take into account. These considerations have been categorized in terms of the Purpose of using AI, the Process of using AI, the role of People, and steps to ensure user Protection,

Table 2. Practical framework for ethical AI adoption across key stakeholders in hospitality education and employment

Stakeholder	Purpose (Why AI is used & intended goals)	Process (How AI tools are selected, used, and reviewed)	People (Human oversight, skills, fairness, inclusion)	Protection (Privacy, security, authenticity, compliance)
Educators	• Clarify when AI is intended to support learning vs. automate tasks. • Ensure AI use aligns with hospitality's people-centric values. • Disclose to students the appropriate and inappropriate uses of AI in career preparation.	• Vet AI tools used in classrooms for accuracy, bias, and transparency. • Integrate AI literacy modules that teach prompt evaluation, fact-checking, and ethical reasoning. • Require students to indicate when and how AI has been used in résumés, cover letters, or portfolios.	• Provide human feedback on AI-generated work to avoid over-reliance or skill loss. • Support students who are non-native speakers or unfamiliar with AI tools to avoid inequities. • Establish responsible-AI committees/boards to monitor educational use.	• Ensure compliant data practices for student analytics platforms. • Teach students about digital footprint, consent, and the risks of sharing data with third-party AI tools. • Promote authenticity by discouraging over-polished, misleading AI-produced career materials.
Career Counsellors	• Use AI to enhance, not replace, guidance and decision-making. • Define boundaries: AI for insights, humans for interpretation and relational support. • Ensure AI contributes to holistic development rather than purely efficiency.	• Employ HITL checkpoints for any AI-derived recommendation. • Evaluate model outputs for accuracy and relevance before presenting to students. • Audit AI platforms regularly for biases in career pathway suggestions. Require clear evidence to justify claims	• Provide empathetic, contextualized advice that AI cannot replicate. • Train students to critically evaluate AI feedback and avoid over-dependence. • Ensure equitable access and avoid disadvantaging students with less digital fluency.	• Explain clearly to students how their data will be used in AI-powered tools. • Use only institution-approved, secure AI systems for storing career information. • Avoid uploading identifiable student data into public generative AI platforms.

continued on following page

Table 2. Continued

Stakeholder	Purpose (Why AI is used & intended goals)	Process (How AI tools are selected, used, and reviewed)	People (Human oversight, skills, fairness, inclusion)	Protection (Privacy, security, authenticity, compliance)
Recruiters / Employers	• Define AI's function (e.g., initial screening, skills matching) and disclose this to applicants. • Ensure AI adoption aligns with organizational ethics policies, service excellence, and fairness goals.	• Use AI only for preliminary filtering; retain human judgment for all (HITL) consequential decisions. • Validate AI outputs with layered assessments (interviews, simulations, behavior tasks). • Conduct regular third-party audits of recruitment algorithms and vendor tools.	• Train hiring teams on algorithmic bias and fairness in evaluation. • Review flagged candidates manually to prevent rejection from false negatives or biased scoring. • Ensure AI does not prioritize keyword optimization over service orientation or emotional intelligence.	• Implement digital credential verification to confirm authenticity of AI-polished résumés. • Store applicant data securely and minimize unnecessary data collection. • Clearly communicate AI usage, data retention, and candidate rights (e.g., appeal or human review).

CONCLUSION

Artificial intelligence is fundamentally reshaping how career counseling and professional development are conceived and delivered within higher education. Its influence is particularly profound in hospitality, a field where employability depends not only on technical and managerial proficiency but also on empathy, emotional intelligence, and service authenticity. As this chapter has shown, the integration of AI into career services marks a decisive shift from human-centered, manual processes to dynamic, data-driven ecosystems that promise speed, personalization, and scalability. Yet, these same systems introduce new ethical dilemmas surrounding accuracy, bias, privacy, authenticity, and overreliance on automation (Jobin et al., 2019; Wilson et al., 2022).

The challenge, then, is not whether AI will shape career development, it already has, but how it can be governed to enhance, rather than erode, human potential. Efficiency without integrity risks undermining trust; innovation without ethics risks inequity. The key lies in adopting a balanced, hybrid approach that treats technology as an amplifier of human insight rather than a substitute for it. AI can analyze data, detect trends, and personalize pathways, but only humans can interpret those insights with empathy, context, and moral judgment.

The review of applications, such as résumé enhancement, skills diagnostics, mock interviews, and predictive pathway exploration, demonstrates meaningful benefits when AI is used to augment reflection and strategy rather than to replace them (Pandya & Wang, 2024). Yet those same systems can mislead when outputs are accepted uncritically, when keyword optimization substitutes for genuine capability, or when opaque models reproduce historical inequities in hiring and progression (Barocas & Selbst, 2016; Raghavan et al., 2020). In hospitality, the stakes are heightened because qualities such as cultural fluency, empathy, and service recovery are not easily inferred from text embeddings or synthetic polish, making human judgement an ethical necessity rather than a discretionary add-on (Baum et al., 2016).

The ethical issues identified, including accuracy and authenticity, bias and fairness, transparency and explainability, privacy and security, over-reliance and dehumanization, are not abstract; they manifest in students' confidence, employers' trust, and staff well-being (Bakir et al., 2025; Monteith et al., 2024). Evidence that AI awareness can heighten job insecurity and turnover intentions in hospitality reminds us that adoption choices reverberate psychologically and organizationally, not just technically (Bakir et al., 2025). Equally, studies linking AI literacy with reduced job-seeking anxiety suggest a practical lever universities can pull to realize benefits while mitigating harm (Li et al., 2025).

Accordingly, the chapter proposed a shared responsibility model. Universities should set clear norms for disclosure, integrate AI literacy with verification and critical reflection, and assess not only outputs but also students' reasoning about when and how AI was used (Li et al., 2025). Employers should pair automated screening with job-relevant simulations, structured interviews, and verifiable credentials, ensuring a human in the loop at high-stakes decision points to protect fairness and authenticity (Wilson et al., 2022). Policymakers should require auditability, impact assessments, and avenues for redress, so that high-impact recruitment and counselling systems meet transparency and accountability standards commensurate with their risks (Jobin et al., 2019). Across settings, the guiding design pattern is consistent: augment, verify, disclose (Pandya & Wang, 2024).

For hospitality education specifically, the way forward is to treat AI as a service amplifier that frees time for coaching, experiential learning, and interpersonal feedback, while embedding safeguards that keep character, context, and culture at the center of employability decisions (Seyfi et al., 2024). Generative AI can create value or destroy it depending on governance and stakeholder alignment; programs that pair technical enablement with ethical foresight will be best positioned to sustain trust and long-term performance (Dogru et al., 2023).

Ultimately, responsible adoption of AI is not a final destination but an ongoing practice, a cycle of monitoring, explanation, human oversight, and adaptation. Integrity must remain the constraint within which efficiency is optimized, not the other way around. In this way, the hospitality sector can lead by example, showing that the future of technology in education is not about replacing human intelligence, but about refining and elevating it.

For practitioners, the message is clear: technology should serve hospitality's values, not redefine them. Industry leaders who embed ethical safeguards such as bias audits, human-in-the-loop protocols, and transparent data practices into recruitment and talent development can achieve both efficiency and authenticity. By modeling responsible AI integration, hospitality organizations demonstrate that innovation and empathy are not opposing forces but mutually reinforcing drivers of service excellence.

A people-centered, ethics-first approach is not merely a philosophical preference, it is the very condition that makes lasting innovation possible.

REFERENCES

Ahmad, B., & Bilal, S. (2025). Knowledge of AI as a future work skill for career sustainability. *Journal of Career Development*, *52*(2), 134–152. DOI: 10.1177/08948453241307384

Al-Abri, K., & Sidhu, M. (2023). Conceptual model of hybrid neural expert system for career counselling. *International Journal of Application on Sciences, Technology and Engineering*, *1*(1), 28–35. DOI: 10.24912/ijaste.v1.i1.28-35

Bakir, S., Dogru, T., Bilgihan, A., & Ayoun, B. (2025). AI awareness and employee-related outcomes: A systematic review of the hospitality literature and a framework for future research. *International Journal of Hospitality Management*, *124*, 103973. DOI: 10.1016/j.ijhm.2024.103973

Barocas, S., & Selbst, A. D. (2016). Big data's disparate impact. *California Law Review*, *104*(3), 671–733. DOI: 10.15779/Z38BG31

Baum, T., Kralj, A., Robinson, R. N. S., & Solnet, D. J. (2016). Tourism workforce research: A review, taxonomy and agenda. *Annals of Tourism Research*, *60*, 1–22. DOI: 10.1016/j.annals.2016.04.003

BCG. (2025, October 30). *Asia Pacific leads the world in AI adoption while grappling with job fears, BCG survey finds* [Corporate]. BCG. BCG Global. https://www.bcg.com/press/30october2025-asia-pacific-leads-ai-adoption

Benítez-Márquez, M. D., Sánchez-Teba, E. M., Bermúdez-González, G., & Núñez-Rydman, E. S. (2022). Generation Z within the workforce and in the workplace: A bibliometric analysis. *Frontiers in Psychology*, *12*, 736820. DOI: 10.3389/fpsyg.2021.736820

Berkelaar, B. L., & Buzzanell, P. M. (2014). Cybervetting, person–environment fit, and personnel selection: Employers' surveillance and sensemaking of job applicants' online information. *Journal of Applied Communication Research*, *42*(4), 456–476. DOI: 10.1080/00909882.2014.954595

Brewer, S. W., & McCarthy, K. (2024). Teaching networking skills in an introductory course: Impact of a LinkedIn assignment on student perceptions and behaviors. *Marketing Education Review*, *34*(1), 23–30. DOI: 10.1080/10528008.2023.2187669

Brown, S. D., & Lent, R. W. (Eds.). (2013). *Career development and counseling: Putting theory and research to work* (2nd ed.). John Wiley & Sons.

Chen, Z. (2023). Ethics and discrimination in artificial intelligence-enabled recruitment practices. *Humanities & Social Sciences Communications*, *10*(1), 567. DOI: 10.1057/s41599-023-02079-x

Córdova-Esparza, D.-M. (2025). AI-powered educational agents: Opportunities, innovations, and ethical challenges. *Information (Basel)*, *16*(6), 469. DOI: 10.3390/info16060469

Dadaboyev, S. M. U., Abdullayeva, J., Abbosova, N., Suleymenova, A., & Mamadjanova, K. (2025). Role of artificial intelligence in employee recruitment: Systematic review and future research directions. *Discover Global Society*, *3*(1), 1–16. DOI: 10.1007/s44282-025-00246-w

Deshmukh, A., & Raut, A. (2024). Enhanced resume screening for smart hiring using sentence-bidirectional encoder representations from transformers (S-BERT). *International Journal of Advanced Computer Science and Applications*, *15*(8). Advance online publication. DOI: 10.14569/IJACSA.2024.0150825

Dogru, T., Line, N., Mody, M., Hanks, L., Abbott, J., Acikgoz, F., Assaf, A., Bakir, S., Berbekova, A., Bilgihan, A., Dalton, A., Erkmen, E., Geronasso, M., Gomez, D., Graves, S., Iskender, A., Ivanov, S., Kizildag, M., Lee, M., & Zhang, T. (2023). Generative Artificial Intelligence in the hospitality and tourism industry: Developing a framework for future research. *Journal of Hospitality & Tourism Research (Washington, D.C.)*, *49*(2), 235–253. DOI: 10.1177/10963480231188663

Drage, E., & Mackereth, K. (2022). Does AI debias recruitment? Race, gender, and AI's "eradication of difference.". *Philosophy & Technology*, *35*(4), 89. DOI: 10.1007/s13347-022-00543-1

El Mimouni, S., & Bouhdadi, M. (2025). Fairness and bias in AI: A sociotechnical perspective. *Journal of Information. Communication and Ethics in Society*, *24*(1), 77–94. DOI: 10.1108/JICES-12-2024-0182

Gedrimiene, E., Celik, I., Mäkitalo, K., & Muukkonen, H. (2023). Transparency and trustworthiness in user intentions to follow career recommendations from a learning analytics tool. *Journal of Learning Analytics*, *10*(1), 54–70. DOI: 10.18608/jla.2023.7791

Goh, E., & Okumus, F. (2020). Avoiding the hospitality workforce bubble: Strategies to attract and retain generation Z talent in the hospitality workforce. *Tourism Management Perspectives*, *33*, 100603. DOI: 10.1016/j.tmp.2019.100603

Goh, E., & Richardson, S. (2024). Developing effective mentoring programs in hospitality higher education: A practical perspective using the mentoring framework. *Journal of Teaching in Travel & Tourism, 24*(2), 179–188. DOI: 10.1080/15313220.2024.2304748

Gorbatov, S., Oostrom, J. K., & Khapova, S. N. (2024). Work does not speak for itself: Examining the incremental validity of personal branding in predicting knowledge workers' employability. *European Journal of Work and Organizational Psychology, 33*(1), 40–53. DOI: 10.1080/1359432X.2023.2276533

Gray, K. (2025, July 4). *Helping students design their future with AI-powered career and life design*. National Association of Colleges and Employers. https://www.naceweb.org/career-development/best-practices/helping-students-design-their-future-with-ai-powered-career-and-life-design?

Hall, P., & Ellis, D. (2023). A systematic review of socio-technical gender bias in AI algorithms. *Online Information Review, 47*(7), 1264–1279. DOI: 10.1108/OIR-08-2021-0452

Happonen, A., Manninen, L., Hirvimäki, M., & Nolte, A. (2022). Expectations for young job applicants' digital identity related to company's social media brand development strategies. *Small Enterprise Research, 29*(2), 87–108. DOI: 10.1080/13215906.2021.2000482

Harrison, M., & Peters, C. B. (2025). *Leveraging AI to audit, build, and grow a student's personal brand*. Center for Curriculum Redesign. DOI: 10.1080/10528008.2025.2547003

Holmes, W., Bialik, M., & Fadel, C. (2019). *Artificial intelligence in education: Promises and implications for teaching and learning*. The Center for Curriculum Redesign.

Hosseini, S. M., & Lichtinger, G. (2025). *Generative AI as seniority-biased technological change: Evidence from U.S. résumé and job posting data* (SSRN Scholarly Paper No. 5425555). Social Science Research Network. DOI: 10.2139/ssrn.5425555

Jackson, D., & Wilton, N. (2017). Perceived employability among undergraduates and the importance of career self-management, work experience and individual characteristics. *Higher Education Research & Development, 36*(4), 747–762. DOI: 10.1080/07294360.2016.1229270

Jawhar, M., Almotairi, M., Miller, J. R., & Jawhar, S. (2025). AI-Powered career matching system for university students: Bridging education and employment. *2025 IEEE/ACIS 23rd International Conference on Software Engineering Research, Management and Applications (SERA)*, 113–117. DOI: 10.1109/SERA65747.2025.11154544

Jobin, A., Ienca, M., & Vayena, E. (2019). The global landscape of AI ethics guidelines. *Nature Machine Intelligence, 1*(9), 389–399. DOI: 10.1038/s42256-019-0088-2

Johnson, K. M. (2021). Using LinkedIn to teach students how to build their professional network and enhance their personal brand. *Global Research in Higher Education, 4*(2), 83. DOI: 10.22158/grhe.v4n2p83

Klimova, B., & Pikhart, M. (2025). Exploring the effects of artificial intelligence on student and academic well-being in higher education: A mini-review. *Frontiers in Psychology, 16*, 1498132. DOI: 10.3389/fpsyg.2025.1498132

Komljenovic, J. (2019). Linkedin, platforming labour, and the new employability mandate for universities. *Globalisation, Societies and Education, 17*(1), 28–43. DOI: 10.1080/14767724.2018.1500275

Kuusi, O., & Heinonen, S. (2022). Scenarios from artificial narrow intelligence to artificial general intelligence—Reviewing the results of the international work/technology 2050 study. *World Futures Review, 14*(1), 65–79. DOI: 10.1177/19467567221101637

Leo, C., Halloran, T., Valdez, C., Martinou, I., Connell, L., & Morin, J. (2024). The LinkedIn effect: Building personal brands, enhancing self-esteem and job search behaviors for the next generation. *Marketing Education Review, 34*(2), 107–120. DOI: 10.1080/10528008.2024.2336453

Lexis, L., Weaver, D., & Julien, B. (2023). STEM students see the value of LinkedIn as a career development tool and continue to use it in the long-term post-assignment. *Journal of Teaching and Learning for Graduate Employability, 14*(1), 53–70. DOI: 10.21153/jtlge2023vol14no1art1510

Li, R., Ouyang, S., & Lin, J. (2025). Mediating effect of AI attitudes and AI literacy on the relationship between career self-efficacy and job-seeking anxiety. *BMC Psychology, 13*(1), 454. DOI: 10.1186/s40359-025-02757-2

Luckin, R., Holmes, W., Griffiths, M., & Corcier, L. B. (2016). *Intelligence unleashed: An argument for AI in education*. Pearson.

Macnamara, B. N., Berber, I., Çavuşoğlu, M. C., Krupinski, E. A., Nallapareddy, N., Nelson, N. E., Smith, P. J., Wilson-Delfosse, A. L., & Ray, S. (2024). Does using artificial intelligence assistance accelerate skill decay and hinder skill development without performers' awareness? *Cognitive Research: Principles and Implications*, *9*(1), 46. DOI: 10.1186/s41235-024-00572-8

Mannheim, K. (1952). The problem of generations. In Kecskemeti, P. (Ed.), *Essays on the Sociology of Knowledge* (pp. 276–320). Routledge and Kegan Paul.

Marinakou, E., Giousmpasoglou, C., & Papavasileiou, E. F. (2025). The use of Artificial Intelligence (AI) in talent acquisition: The case of Greek luxury hotels. *Strategic Change*, *34*(4), 533–543. DOI: 10.1002/jsc.2632

Martin, K. (2022). *Ethics of data and analytics: Concepts and cases* (1st ed.). Auerbach Publications. DOI: 10.1201/9781003278290

McKinsey & Company. (2025). *The state of AI: Global survey 2025* [Corporate]. McKinsey & Company. https://www.mckinsey.com/capabilities/quantumblack/our-insights/the-state-of-ai

Mishra, P. (2024). Revolutionizing education with AI and ML. In C. Reddy, M. Ouaissa, H. Lamaazi, M. El Hamlaoui, & K. K (Ed.), *Advances in Educational Technologies and Instructional Design*, (pp. 53–94). IGI Global. DOI: 10.4018/979-8-3693-8151-9.ch003

Monteith, S., Glenn, T., Geddes, J. R., Whybrow, P. C., Achtyes, E., & Bauer, M. (2024). Artificial intelligence and increasing misinformation. *The British Journal of Psychiatry*, *224*(2), 33–35. DOI: 10.1192/bjp.2023.136

Nair, M. (2025, August 27). *UAE professionals "second highest" in world using AI tools: LinkedIn poll* [News]. Gulf News. https://gulfnews.com/business/markets/uae-professionals-second-highest-in-world-using-ai-tools-linkedin-poll-1.500246696

Omar, Z. F., Mior Harun, M. H., Mohd Ishar, N. I., Mustapha, N. A., & Ismail, Z. (2024). Enhancing professional development and training through AI for personalized learning: A framework to engaging learners. *International Journal of E-Learning and Higher Education*, *19*(3), 115–138.

Pandya, S. S., & Wang, J. (2024). Artificial intelligence in career development: A scoping review. *Human Resource Development International*, *27*(3), 324–344. DOI: 10.1080/13678868.2024.2336881

Raghavan, M., Barocas, S., Kleinberg, J., & Levy, K. (2020). Mitigating bias in algorithmic hiring: Evaluating claims and practices. *Proceedings of the 2020 Conference on Fairness, Accountability, and Transparency*, 469–481. DOI: 10.1145/3351095.3372828

Selwyn, N. (2019). *Should robots replace teachers? AI and the future of education* (1st ed.). Polity Press.

Seyfi, S., Vo-Thanh, T., & Zaman, M. (2024). Hospitality in the age of Gen Z: A critical reflection on evolving customer and workforce expectations. *International Journal of Contemporary Hospitality Management*, *36*(13), 118–134. DOI: 10.1108/IJCHM-01-2024-0035

Sharma, A. (2025). Leveraging big data and AI for personalized career pathways: A systematic literature review. *22nd AIMS International Conference on Management*, 855–861.

Tomlinson, M., & Jackson, D. (2021). Professional identity formation in contemporary higher education students. *Studies in Higher Education*, *46*(4), 885–900. DOI: 10.1080/03075079.2019.1659763

Twenge, J. M., Gentile, B., DeWall, C. N., Ma, D., Lacefield, K., & Schurtz, D. R. (2010). Birth cohort increases in psychopathology among young Americans, 1938–2007: A cross-temporal meta-analysis of the MMPI. *Clinical Psychology Review*, *30*(2), 145–154. DOI: 10.1016/j.cpr.2009.10.005

Wasnik, C., Lakeshri, A., Chaturvedi, M., Jajoo, L., & Soni, R. (2025). AI-powered career coaching system: A data-driven approach to career guidance. *Journal of Emerging Technologies and Innovative Research*, *12*(3), 238–244.

Wilson, M., Robertson, P., Cruickshank, P., & Gkatzia, D. (2022). Opportunities and risks in the use of AI in career development practice. *Journal of the National Institute for Career Education and Counselling*, *48*(1), 48–57. DOI: 10.20856/jnicec.4807

Xiao, Y., & Zheng, L. (2025). Can ChatGPT boost students' employment confidence? A pioneering booster for career readiness. *Behavioral Sciences (Basel, Switzerland)*, *15*(3), 362. DOI: 10.3390/bs15030362

Xie, P., & Ma, L. (2025). How hotel AI adoption shapes employee performance? A study based on the transactional theory of stress and coping. *Journal of Hospitality and Tourism Technology*. Advance online publication. DOI: 10.1108/JHTT-09-2024-0606

Zeff, M. (2025, April 9). *OpenAI announces AI-powered hiring platform to take on LinkedIn.* TechCrunch. https://techcrunch.com/2025/09/04/openai-announces-ai-powered-hiring-platform-to-take-on-linkedin/

Zhou, K., Petsangsri, S., & Sriwisathiyakun, K. (2024). The use of AI counselling to enhance self-esteem in the job seeking process for Chinese undergraduate students. *Eurasian Journal of Educational Research*, (114). https://ejer.com.tr/article-view/?id=2006

KEY TERMS AND DEFINITIONS

Career Counseling: In this chapter, career counseling refers to the activities related to advising students on potential careers, career paths, career skill requirements, and résumés building.

Generative AI: AI which can create original content. This is a type of Artificial Narrow Intelligence (ANI) which can execute specific tasks (Kuusi & Heinonen, 2022). This is distinct from Artificial General Intelligence (AGI) which can learn and execute a range of tasks (Dogru et al., 2023).

Human-in-the-Loop (HITL): A design and governance principle in which humans retain meaningful oversight of AI-assisted processes and final responsibility for consequential decisions.

Natural Language Processing: A field of AI facilitating computer's understanding and generation of human-sounding language.

ENDNOTES

1 LinkedIn: https://training.talent.linkedin.com/page/ai-powered-features#language_english

2 Coach: https://www.aicareercoach.org/

3 Careerflow: https://www.careerflow.ai/organizations/career-coaches

4 Musely: https://musely.ai/tools/career-planner

5 Job Hunt Mode: https://jobhuntmode.com/ai/career-planning/pathways/

Chapter 13
The Impact of Consumer Trust in AI on Hotel Brand Perception

Julien Morange
http://orcid.org/0009-0000-4056-7181
Les Roches Global Hospitality Education, Crans-Montana, Switzerland

ABSTRACT

This chapter explores how consumer trust in artificial intelligence (AI) shapes hotel brand perception. Integrating the AIDUA model with foundational trustworthiness dimensions, the author proposes a framework where AI interactions function as critical brand touchpoints. Trust evolves sequentially: primary appraisals (social influence, anthropomorphism) establish judgments of integrity and benevolence, while secondary appraisals (performance, effort) determine perceived ability. Findings indicate that perceived ethics and emotion are stronger determinants of acceptance than utility; crucially, established brand trust is a prerequisite for guest engagement with AI. Consequently, hospitality education requires curriculum reconception. Future professionals must develop competencies in AI ethics, transparency management, and strategic brand-AI alignment. By preparing students to balance data personalization with privacy, educators ensure graduates can leverage AI to enhance trust while maintaining the authentic human connection central to successful hotel brands.

INTRODUCTION

This chapter examines the critical relationship between consumer trust in AI technologies and hotel brand perception. As hotels integrate AI-powered solutions,

DOI: 10.4018/979-8-3373-5112-4.ch013

from chatbots and dynamic pricing to personalized recommendations and automated check-ins, understanding how trust influences brand perception becomes essential for hospitality educators, students, and industry practitioners.

The chapter addresses how emerging AI technologies like generative AI, advanced robotics, and predictive analytics impact trust considerations and brand perception. As Sébastien Bazin, Chairman & CEO of Accor, notes: "Before you come into the hotel, after you leave the hotel, you will be 90% AI-driven" (Pymnts, 2025). Voice-activated assistants, AI-powered concierge services, and predictive maintenance systems create new trust touchpoints that directly influence how guests perceive and evaluate hotel brands.

Unlike other industries where AI interactions may be brief, hotel stays involve extended engagement where guests form deeper relationships with service providers. This creates multiple touchpoints where AI systems can either build or erode trust, directly impacting brand perception. Understanding these dynamics is crucial for hospitality students navigating an increasingly AI-driven industry where brand equity depends heavily on successful AI-trust management.

Theoretical Grounding: The AIDUA Framework and Brand Equity

Traditional hospitality has been built on personal relationships and human-to-human trust. The introduction of AI systems creates new paradigms where guests must develop trust in non-human entities while maintaining confidence in the overall brand experience. As Naveen Manga, Global CIO of Marriott International, emphasizes: "We want this tech to be powered by trust" (Wilkinson, 2025).

This chapter employs the Artificial Intelligence Device Use and Acceptance (AIDUA) model alongside brand equity theory to understand how AI interactions shape hotel brand perception and introduces the concept of "AI brand authenticity" as a key determinant of guest evaluations.

Educational Implications

The rapid integration of AI in hospitality has profound implications for hospitality education. Academic programs must evolve to prepare students for an industry where managing the trust-brand perception nexus in AI contexts is as fundamental as traditional hospitality skills.

Hospitality students must acquire competencies extending beyond operational knowledge to encompass strategic thinking about AI's impact on brand perception, ethical decision-making regarding data usage and algorithmic transparency, and maintaining brand integrity while leveraging technological innovation.

Chapter Objectives

By the end of this chapter, readers will be able to:

- Understand how consumer trust in AI influences hotel brand perception through the AIDUA framework
- Identify key factors influencing guest trust and brand evaluations of AI-enabled hotel services
- Implement evidence-based strategies to build consumer trust in AI applications while strengthening brand equity
- Evaluate ethical and data governance considerations essential to protecting brand reputation
- Recognize educational implications of AI adoption and competencies hospitality students must develop

The Double-Edged Sword of AI

During the Paris 2024 Olympics, Google aired an advertisement featuring Gemini AI helping a father draft his daughter's letter to an Olympic athlete (Duffy, 2024). The advertisement generated substantial public backlash, with viewers expressing discomfort about AI's intrusion into such a personal interaction. This incident exemplifies how AI applications can undermine consumer trust and damage brand perception when they conflict with consumer values.

In August 2025, a La Quinta Inn & Suites in Miami faced criticism after a viral video revealed guests were checked in via a virtual kiosk connected to a remote employee in India (Herzlich, 2025). The incident sparked widespread criticism about the loss of personal touch in hospitality. Wyndham Hotels & Resorts clarified that the independently owned hotel's virtual check-in system was not brand-approved, emphasizing that brand standards require physical staff presence. This example illustrates how poorly managed outsourcing can severely damage trust and brand perception.

These incidents underscore why training hospitality educators and students to navigate AI implementation responsibly while protecting brand equity is critical for the industry's future.

LITERATURE REVIEW

Theoretical Foundation: AI Adoption, Trust, and Brand Perception

Evolving Beyond Traditional Technology Acceptance Models. The Technology Acceptance Model (TAM) (Davis, 1989) and the Unified Theory of Acceptance and Use of Technology (UTAUT) (Venkatesh et al., 2003) have been widely adopted in hospitality research and education. TAM proposes that perceived usefulness and ease of use facilitate technology adoption, while UTAUT extends this by incorporating social influence and facilitating conditions. Several studies have employed these models to assess hospitality students' behavioral intentions toward technology use and educators' intent to adopt technology in their courses (Hasanein, 2025).

However, academics increasingly debate the theoretical validity of these models for understanding AI adoption (Alam et al., 2024). TAM was designed for non-intelligent technology like self-service systems, and its core construct of ease of use becomes irrelevant in AI contexts where users do not need to learn how to use the technology (Lu et al., 2019). Mogaji et al. (2024) question whether traditional acceptance models remain relevant in the generative AI era. These models are criticized for their limited scope and inability to capture the unique characteristics of advanced AI technologies within hospitality contexts (Mogaji et al., 2024).

While alternative frameworks like Task-Technology Fit (TTF) theory emphasize evaluating actual adoption performance in specific tasks (Wan et al., 2025), frameworks that explicitly address the emotional and trust dynamics unique to AI interactions offer more comprehensive insights for hospitality contexts.

Trust and Acceptance: The AIDUA Framework in AI-Powered Hospitality. The Artificial Intelligence Device Use and Acceptance (AIDUA) model provides such a framework, specifically explaining customers' willingness to accept AI device use in service encounters (Gursoy et al., 2019). Unlike traditional models, AIDUA integrates cognitive factors (what the AI does) and emotional factors (how the AI makes users feel), recognizing that users' emotions toward AI ultimately drive their adoption or rejection decisions. Chi et al. (2022) validate the AIDUA model in hedonic (hotels) and utilitarian (airports) service settings, finding that social influence plays a particularly prominent role in the hotel industry. Recognizing the centrality of trust in AI adoption, Chi et al. (2022) and Della Corte et al. (2023) have extended the AIDUA model by incorporating trust constructs, with Chi et al.'s (2022) findings suggesting that trust in interaction with AI is a significant higher-order construct influencing intention of use.

Traditional hospitality has been built on personal relationships and human-to-human trust. The introduction of AI systems creates new paradigms where guests must develop trust in non-human entities while maintaining confidence in the overall service experience. As Naveen Manga, Global CIO of Marriott International, emphasizes: "We want this tech to be powered by trust. We want to deploy technology that is responsible, ethical and lawful" (Herzlich, 2025).

Figure 1. AIDUA model (Gursoy et al., 2019)

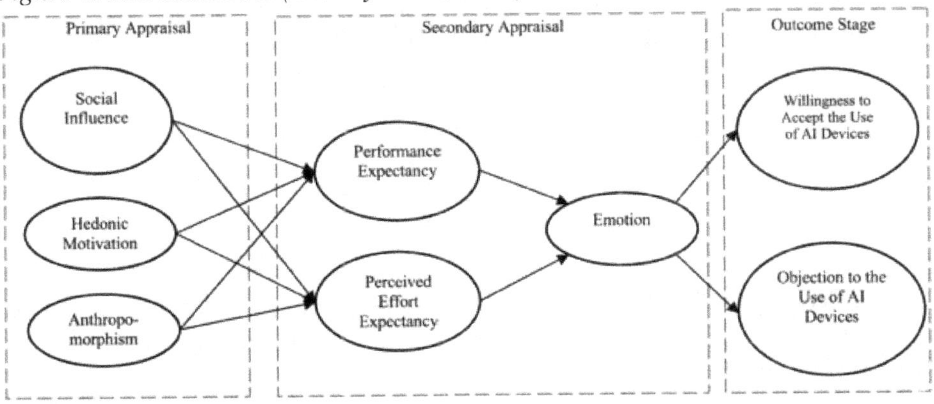

Within the AIDUA framework, trust formation occurs primarily during the primary appraisal stage, where users evaluate AI systems' reliability, competence, and alignment with their expectations. Trust emerges as a critical prerequisite for consumer engagement. However, substantial evidence indicates that AI systems are trusted less than human counterparts (Sands et al., 2022), and AI-related trust concerns negatively impact brand engagement behaviors (McLean et al., 2021). Consumers exhibit reduced trust when disclosing information to AI systems, driven by perceptions that AI shares information with broader audiences, heightening feelings of exploitation (Lefkeli et al., 2024).

Given that information disclosure concerns are central to consumer trust issues with AI, this chapter adopts Lee's (2005) definition of trust as willfully placing confidence in a party while providing personal information. To complement the AIDUA framework, this research employs the Integrative Model of Organizational Trust proposed by Mayer et al., (1995). Their three dimensions of trustworthiness (ability, benevolence, and integrity) map distinctly onto the cognitive appraisal stages of AIDUA. Ability aligns with utilitarian evaluations of performance and effort expectancy, while benevolence and integrity capture the social and moral dimensions of trust triggered by anthropomorphism, providing a comprehensive lens for understanding the emotional and cognitive drivers of AI acceptance.

Figure 2. Mayer et al. (1995) model of trust

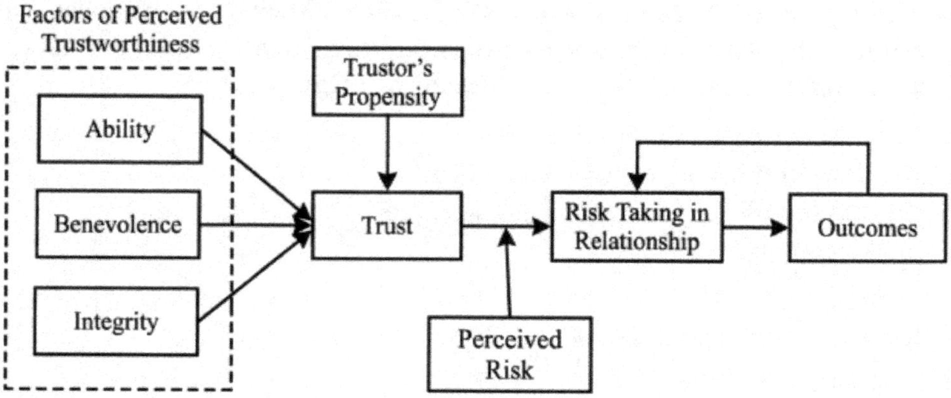

AI as Brand Touchpoint: Linking Trust to Brand Equity. The trust dynamics identified through the AIDUA framework have direct implications for hotel brand equity. Improper AI deployment can harm brand reputation and guest satisfaction, particularly if hotels fail to align AI with customers' unique needs across different segments and locations (Deloitte UK Report, 2024). When guests experience trust deficits during AI interactions, these negative evaluations cascade into broader brand perceptions, ultimately eroding brand equity.

Building on brand equity theory (Aaker, 1991; Aaker, 2012), this chapter explores how AI interactions serve as critical touchpoints shaping hotel brand perception. AI integration creates new dimensions of brand experience where guests evaluate brands based on AI sophistication, the seamlessness of human-AI collaboration, and whether AI systems enhance hospitality experiences while maintaining brand authenticity. The emotional responses and trust evaluations that emerge from AI encounters, as conceptualized in AIDUA, directly influence whether guests perceive the brand as trustworthy, innovative, and aligned with their values. Liu et al. (2024) found a matching effect between hospitality brand image and AI service agents on brand attitude, demonstrating that adoption of AI by cool brands can foster positive feelings and enhance consumers' positive brand attitudes.

Strong brand equity means customers recognize, trust, and prefer the brand, leading to higher sales, pricing power, and competitive advantage. The chapter examines "AI brand authenticity" as a key construct linking the trust formation processes identified in AIDUA's primary appraisal to long-term brand equity outcomes, demonstrating how guests evaluate whether AI implementations align with a hotel's brand values and positioning.

Designing Effective Human-AI Service Integration. Employee awareness of potential AI replacement increases job insecurity and deviant behavior (Zhang et al., 2025; Zhou & Yi, 2025), with older luxury hotel employees struggling more with adoption (Jung et al., 2025). Organizations should develop AI adoption strategies encouraging employee training (Xie & Ma, 2026), while perceived organizational support reduces turnover intention (Hou & Fan, 2024; Li & Khan, 2025).

The most trusted AI implementations feature seamless human backup systems (Wong et al., 2023). Successful implementations blend AI efficiency with human warmth, deploying AI for routine tasks while freeing staff for meaningful interactions (Gajić et al., 2025; Wang & Zhang, 2025). AI with high automated social presence mitigates consumer alienation, while high-autonomy AI exacerbates it (Mou et al., 2025), underscoring the importance of anthropomorphic design that builds consumer trust (Li et al., 2023) and drives acceptance (Pelau et al., 2021; Upadhyay & Kamble, 2024).

AI Performance Dimensions and Hotel Brand Trust. AI usability demonstrates substantial positive effects on consumer trust and brand perceptions. Convenience and ease of use enhance trust and satisfaction (Mari et al., 2024; Uzir et al., 2021), influencing brand experiences and repurchase intention (Ho & Chow, 2024; McLean et al., 2021). AI responsiveness deepens brand intimacy (Lin & Wu, 2023) and increases brand love (Upadhyay & Kamble, 2024), while effectiveness positively influences brand outcomes through information quality and problem-solving ability (Ho & Chow, 2024; Yuan et al., 2023).

Beyond functional performance, AI relational qualities significantly impact trust. AI social presence positively influences brand engagement (McLean, et al., 2021), while parasocial interactions and media richness determine perceived trust and authenticity (Hsieh & Lee, 2021; Vo et al., 2024). AI attractiveness fosters attachment (Yim, et al., 2024), with baby-schema increasing benevolence trustworthiness and warm colors strengthening emotional trust (Chan et al., 2023). AI entertainment strengthens customer-brand relationships (Cheng & Jiang, 2022), while empathy increases trust and task delegation intentions (Mari et al., 2024).

The Risks of Over-Automation and Uniform AI Implementation. Over-automation risks undermining consumer trust, as AI generally exhibits lower trust than humans. Consumers experience reduced trust in AI advice (Riedel et al., 2022; Sands et al., 2022) and decreased brand trust when disclosing information to AI agents (Lefkeli et al., 2024).

Consumer responses to AI vary significantly across segments. High technology readiness demonstrates greater brand trustworthiness (Ghazali et al., 2024), while cultural background shapes acceptance (Fang et al., 2024). Three distinct consumer profiles emerge (Morosan, 2025): "Safeguards" exhibit low disclosure willingness, "Balancers" demonstrate selective disclosure, and "Disclosers" selectively share when perceiving service value. Hotels must tailor AI implementation according to customer profiles and cultural backgrounds.

Brand Trust as Foundation for AI Trust. Brand trust serves as the foundation for AI trust. Users' positive attitude toward the parent brand positively associates with perceived AI authenticity and usage intention (Vo et al., 2024). Hotel trust strongly influences consumer engagement with AI-based systems (Morosan & Dursun-Cengizci, 2024). For cool hospitality brands, AI adoption reinforces their modern image and fosters positive brand attitudes (Liu et al., 2024), while AI can serve as a strategic positioning theme for luxury-independent AI-themed hotels (Yi et al., 2025). Strategic alignment of AI capabilities with loyalty objectives sustains competitive advantage (Bilgihan et al., 2025).

Transparency, Falsity, and AI Trust Management. Maintaining brand trust requires careful transparency management. Initial disclosure of AI-generated content leads to unfavorable attitudes (Baek et al., 2024), though this diminishes when AI appears more human-like. Conversely, transparency in AI digital endorsers positively influences purchase intention (Wang & Qiu, 2024), while lack of transparency reduces acceptance of AI hotel recommendations (Huang et al., 2025).

The absence of clear AI legislation has led to cautious interest among hotel managers (Wang, 2025). Hotels must proactively embrace transparent AI disclosure and build trust strategies exceeding minimum compliance requirements, as discovering undisclosed AI usage creates perceptions of falsity. Falsity negatively impacts brand engagement (Aljarah et al., 2024), while perceived risk decreases brand loyalty and chatbot trust (Hasan et al., 2021; Li et al., 2023).

Implications of AI-Driven Trust for Hospitality Education

Understanding how to effectively teach consumer trust in AI and its impact on hotel brand perception requires examining pedagogical approaches within hospitality education. Kara (2025) found that every education dimension of AI is positively related to sustainability in hospitality education, concentrating on three major learning aspects: knowledge, practical implementation, and value-based orientation. Results demonstrate that hospitality students with moderate technical abilities and high sustainability values outperformed those possessing high digital abilities without integrity value-based alignment. These findings reveal that formal AI education serves as a stabilizing force in hospitality programs, encouraging more consistent and sustainability-focused attitudes, underscoring the significance of educational models combining technical skills with ethical and environmental consciousness.

Xie (2025) identified three major issues when generating assignments with ChatGPT in hospitality education: accuracy and reliability, ethical implications, and the shifting role of the educator. Despite these challenges, ChatGPT presents opportunities for revolutionizing hospitality education by enabling personalized learning, enhanced accessibility, and industry-specific knowledge. Zhu and Yu (2025) highlight how large language models facilitate hands-on knowledge development, innovative thinking, and technology-driven scenarios in hospitality education.

Fathy et al., (2025) emphasized ChatGPT's positive impacts in hospitality learning environments, including its ability to address individual learning needs, its versatility in enhancing digital marketing skills, and its practical utility for role-play and cultural competency development. However, challenges include concerns about academic dishonesty, technological limitations, and ethical considerations, highlighting the current lack of ethical guidelines and personalized learning frameworks.

Addressing these educational gaps requires comprehensive competency frameworks for hospitality programs. Papageorgiou et al., (2024) propose models encompassing six core competency categories: communication, operational knowledge, cultural diversity, human resource management, leadership, and information technology. Wan et al., (2025) further suggest that hospitality education should retain courses enhancing students' soft competencies while strengthening those cultivating advanced communication skills, and should add subjects related to data analytics, strategic decision-making, and AI applications.

Ethical and Responsible AI as Foundations of Consumer Trust and Brand Perception

Teaching the relationship between consumer trust in AI and hotel brand perception fundamentally requires addressing ethical AI frameworks and responsible implementation practices. Ali and Ali (2025) identify agentic AI systems, characterized by autonomy, contextual reasoning, and adaptive decision-making, as poised to transform the hospitality and tourism industry. They propose a typology of five functional agentic AI roles: service agents, planning agents, monitoring agents, engagement agents, and meta-agents. While these systems offer opportunities for enhanced personalization and efficiency, their adoption introduces critical risks including data privacy concerns, algorithmic bias, cultural misinterpretation, and workforce displacement, necessitating governance strategies emphasizing ethical design, human-AI collaboration, and regulatory adaptation.

Law et al., (2025) illustrate the translation of general ethical AI principles into hospitality and tourism business management by providing a framework with five key ethical principles for the hospitality and tourism industry, designed to mitigate potential issues across various stages of the AI evolution trajectory.

Figure 3. Ethical AI principles for hospitality and tourism (Law et al., 2025)

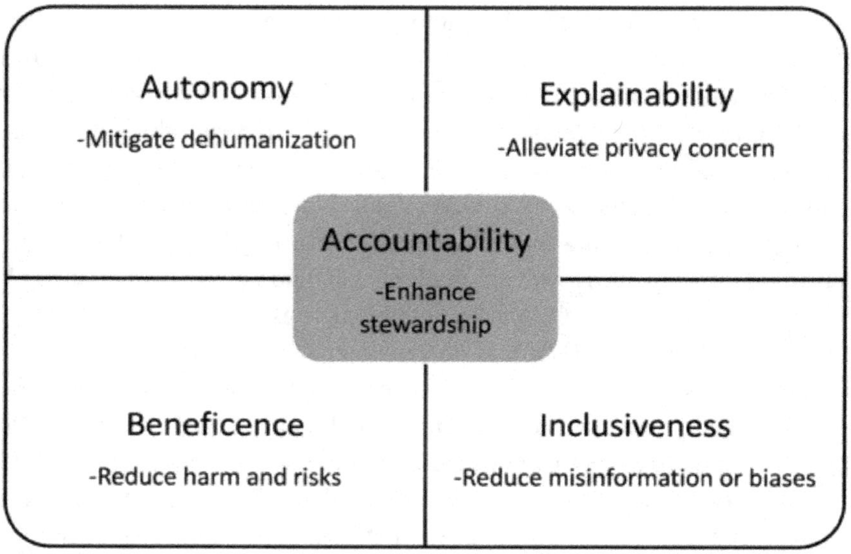

Morosan and Dursun-Cengizci (2024) found that the most important determinant of hotel guests' acceptance of technology agency was perceived ethics, followed by benefits. Risks of using AI-based systems had a negative impact on acceptance, with perceived loss of competence and unpredictability having relatively strong impacts.

Xu et al. (2025) propose a full-cycle AI ethics education system integrating three core components: an updated four-dimensional ethics framework focused on Gen-AI challenges in hospitality education (research review, data privacy, algorithmic fairness, intellectual property); a "cognition-behavior" dual-loop training mechanism combining theoretical learning with hands-on simulated practice; and a full life-cycle education platform featuring tools like virtual laboratories to support experiential learning. Yan et al., (2025) conducted a systematic review of AI ethics in education that identifies stakeholder-specific ethical tensions and highlights gaps in empirical validation, geographical diversity, and policy implementation. Their findings cluster into four solution domains: AI education ethical frameworks, ethical assessment frameworks, AI education literacy frameworks, and literacy assessment frameworks.

Conceptual Framework: Consumer Trust in AI and Hotel Brand Perception

This chapter proposes a process-oriented conceptual framework examining how consumer trust in artificial intelligence (AI) shapes hotel brand perception. The framework integrates the Artificial Intelligence Device Use and Acceptance (AIDUA) model (Gursoy et al., 2019) with Mayer et al., (1995) dimensions of trustworthiness to establish a direct pathway from AI trust formation to brand equity outcomes. Unlike utilitarian-focused models such as TAM or UTAUT, AIDUA's grounding in cognitive appraisal theory captures the social and emotional dimensions critical to hospitality contexts, where AI interactions serve as brand touchpoints that shape overall guest perceptions.

The framework unfolds across three sequential stages. In the primary appraisal stage, consumers initially evaluate AI's inherent characteristics through social influence, hedonic motivation, and anthropomorphism (Gursoy et al., 2019). Trust formation at this stage derives from benevolence and integrity assessments (Mayer et al., 1995). High anthropomorphism functions as a heuristic signaling moral trustworthiness, leading consumers to attribute positive intentions to both the AI and, critically, the hotel brand deploying it. This initial appraisal establishes the foundation for brand-AI alignment perceptions.

Building on these initial impressions, the secondary appraisal stage involves consumers assessing performance expectancy and effort expectancy (Gursoy et al., 2019), which directly map onto ability judgments (Mayer et al., 1995). Uniquely, AIDUA integrates emotional responses at this stage: systems demonstrating high ability while evoking positive emotions reinforce experiential trust that transfers to the hotel brand, whereas functional failures damage both AI credibility and brand perception simultaneously.

These appraisals culminate in the outcome stage, where acceptance or rejection signals whether consumers perceive sufficient ability, benevolence, and integrity (Mayer et al., 1995). Sustained acceptance solidifies trust that extends beyond the device to enhance hotel brand equity. Conversely, rejection signals trust breach that erodes brand perception and loyalty.

This framework advances hospitality research by explicating how AI trust dynamically shapes brand equity rather than treating technology adoption as isolated from brand outcomes. It establishes trust as the mechanism through which AI interactions translate into lasting brand perceptions, providing actionable insight for hotels balancing technological innovation with brand integrity. Given AIDUA's relatively recent introduction to hospitality research, this framework demonstrates its utility for understanding the complex interplay between AI acceptance and brand outcomes in service contexts.

Figure 4. Conceptual framework integrating the AIDUA framework (Gursoy et al., 2019) and Mayer et al. (1995) three factors of perceived trustworthiness

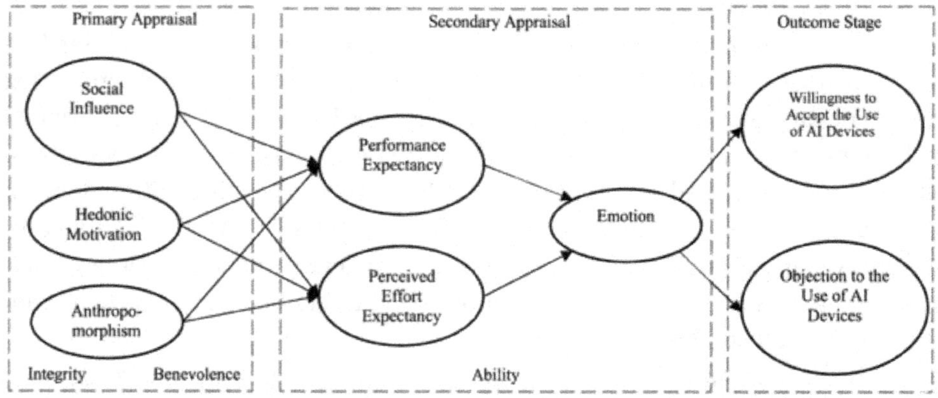

DISCUSSION: CONSUMER TRUST IN AI AND HOTEL BRAND PERCEPTION

Primary Appraisal of AI and Trust Signals in Hotel Brands

Social Influence. Integrity. AI acceptance by hotel workforce is critical for implementation success. Since AI increases job insecurity and deviant behavior (Zhang et al., 2025; Zhou & Yi, 2025), employee training must ensure company integrity remains perceptible to consumers. Older employees in luxury hotels require priority training (Jung et al., 2025), while organizational support reduces AI-induced stress (Hou & Fan, 2024; Li & Khan, 2025).

Consumer responses to AI vary significantly across segments. Higher religiosity shows greater trust in AI-using companies (Minton et al., 2022), while cultural background shapes acceptance: Chinese consumers accept facial scanning whereas Europeans prioritize data privacy (Fang et al., 2024). Three distinct consumer profiles emerge (Morosan, 2025): "Safeguards" exhibit low disclosure willingness, "Balancers" demonstrate selective disclosure, and "Disclosers" share when perceiving service value.

Managers must ensure company integrity through employee interactions during AI implementation. Priority training should target vulnerable groups while organizational support mechanisms reduce stress. Hotels must tailor AI implementation according to customer technology readiness, disclosure profiles, and cultural backgrounds.

Hospitality curricula must address AI-workforce integration as a core competency. Programs should develop cultural intelligence modules addressing cross-cultural AI acceptance variations and consumer segmentation frameworks identifying guest technology readiness. Case studies examining cultural misinterpretation teach students to recognize warning signs and implement corrective measures.

Benevolence. AI trust starts with hotel brand trust, and AI can be part of brand positioning though it must align appropriately. Hotels should invest in staff training ensuring employees collaborate effectively with AI systems. Training must emphasize continued knowledge sharing (Zhang et al., 2025) while maintaining employee passion (Xu et al., 2025). AI services should feature high automated social presence to mitigate consumer alienation while maintaining lower autonomy (Mou et al., 2025).

Hotels should invest in comprehensive staff training for AI collaboration. Managers must calibrate AI with high automated social presence while maintaining lower autonomy. Hotels must develop protocols ensuring AI is quickly backed up by human intervention (Wong et al., 2023).

Consumer alienation, manifesting as social isolation and powerlessness (Mou et al., 2025), requires educational intervention. Programs must integrate emotional intelligence training within AI service contexts. Curricula should include service recovery modules addressing AI-related failures. Students should analyze cases like Marriott's Aloft Hotels' Alexa-enabled rooms and Hilton's Connie to understand how brands balance automation with human touchpoints (AWS, 2018) Practical training should develop ability to calibrate AI service parameters, managing tension between automated social presence and system autonomy.

Hedonic Motivation. Integrity. Personalization through data acquisition positively impacts brand experience and equity (Armutcu et al., 2024; Ho & Chow, 2024), though privacy concerns persist (Wang, 2025). Successful personalization depends on selecting less privacy-sensitive data types while delivering tangible value, as demonstrated by Sensei Lanai's thermographic sensors.

Managers must balance personalization benefits with privacy protection using less privacy-sensitive data types while delivering tangible value.

Hospitality programs must address the personalization-privacy paradox as a core curriculum element. Students need training in data ethics and privacy regulations. Case studies like Sensei Lanai demonstrate how hotels achieve personalization without compromising privacy. Students must learn to recognize when data requests cross privacy thresholds that could damage brand trust.

Anthropomorphism. Integrity. Over-automation risks undermining consumer trust, as AI exhibits lower trustworthiness than humans. Consumers experience reduced trust in AI advice (Riedel et al., 2022; Sands et al., 2022) and decreased brand trust when disclosing information to AI agents (Lefkeli et al., 2024). However, AI demonstrates advantages in specific contexts: service robots reduce consumer discomfort when ordering wine (Lu et al., 2024), and AI influencers appear more authentic than human counterparts (Allal-Chérif et al., 2024).

Hotels must resist over-automation driven purely by cost reduction. Managers should strategically deploy AI where it demonstrates advantages while maintaining human service as the default. Ethical AI autonomy principles should mitigate dehumanization (Law et al., 2025).

Students must learn decision frameworks identifying contexts where AI advantages outweigh trust concerns. Programs should analyze cases teaching students to recognize situational factors determining optimal service delivery methods. Students need analytical skills evaluating when AI deployment enhances rather than diminishes service quality.

Benevolence. Anthropomorphic design builds consumer trust (Li et al., 2023), enhances warmth perceptions (Kim & Hur, 2024), and drives acceptance and brand love (Pelau et al., 2021; Upadhyay & Kamble, 2024), as exemplified by Aloft Hotels' Botlr. AI social presence positively influences brand engagement (McLean et al., 2021) and increases trust in recommendations (Mari et al., 2024). AI attractiveness influences engagement and fosters attachment (Yim et al., 2024), with baby-schema increasing benevolence trustworthiness and warm colors strengthening emotional trust (Chan et al., 2023).

Hotels should prioritize anthropomorphic design elements when implementing AI interfaces. Managers must understand that AI relational qualities significantly impact brand outcomes.

Hospitality programs must integrate AI design principles into curricula, teaching students how anthropomorphic features influence consumer trust. Students should learn to evaluate AI interfaces based on design elements like social presence, attractiveness, empathy, and baby-schema features. Meaningful human interaction becomes increasingly relevant as AI relieves employees of routine tasks (Wang & Zhang, 2025). Practical training should include analyzing successful implementations like Aloft Hotels' Botlr, examining how anthropomorphic design choices influenced guest reception.

Secondary Appraisal with AI Systems and Trust Formation

Performance Expectancy. AI systems face ability concerns regarding complex interactions, local culture incorporation, service contingency responses, and meeting generational preferences (Wang, 2025). Data privacy protection represents another significant concern. Ethical AI explainability and inclusiveness principles should alleviate privacy concerns and reduce misinformation (Law et al., 2025).

Managerial Implications. Hotels must demonstrate AI capabilities while acknowledging limitations. Managers should ensure staff remain trained to handle situations where AI falls short. Data privacy protection protocols must be robust.

Educational Implications. Hospitality programs must prepare students to manage AI limitations in complex service contexts. Curricula should develop competencies in handling situations where AI capabilities prove insufficient. Programs should integrate the five functional agentic AI roles: service agents, planning agents, monitoring agents, engagement agents, and meta-agents (Ali & Ali, 2025). Students must learn to manage risks linked to data privacy concerns, algorithmic bias, and cultural misinterpretation while leveraging opportunities for enhanced personalization and efficiency.

Perceived Effort Expectancy. AI usability demonstrates substantial positive effects on consumer trust. Perceived convenience and ease of use enhance trust and satisfaction (Mari et al., 2024; Uzir et al., 2021), influencing brand outcomes (Ho & Chow, 2024; McLean et al., 2021). AI responsiveness deepens brand intimacy (Lin & Wu, 2023) and increases brand love (Upadhyay & Kamble, 2024). AI entertainment strengthens customer-brand relationships (Cheng & Jiang, 2022) and enhances booking intentions (Alam, 2025), as demonstrated by Paramount Hotel Dubai's immersive digital art installations (StandardVision, n.d.). Making AI more entertaining reduces perceived effort expectancy.

Managerial Implications. Hotels should prioritize AI usability, convenience, and responsiveness. Managers must understand that entertainment elements reduce perceived effort. Staff should be trained to classify consumers into technology readiness categories and tailor AI implementation accordingly.

Educational Implications. Hospitality programs must teach students that AI usability directly impacts brand perception. Curricula should cover how convenience, responsiveness, and effectiveness influence brand intimacy and loyalty. Students need frameworks classifying consumers into categories like "Safeguards," "Balancers," and "Disclosers" (Morosan, 2025), enabling adaptive AI deployment. Programs should analyze cases like Paramount Hotel Dubai's digital art installations, examining how entertainment elements strengthen customer-brand relationships.

Emotion. Brand trust serves as the foundation for AI trust. Users' positive attitude toward the parent brand positively associates with perceived AI authenticity and usage intention (Vo et al., 2024). Hotel trust strongly influences consumer engagement with AI-based systems (Morosan & Dursun-Cengizci, 2024).

For cool hospitality brands, AI adoption reinforces their modern image and fosters positive brand attitudes, though this matching effect disappears under service failure conditions (Liu et al., 2024). AI can serve as a strategic positioning theme, with technology-related qualities proving attractive for luxury-independent AI-themed hotels (Yi et al., 2025). To avoid guest anxiety that reduces acceptance (Huang et al., 2025), hotels must demonstrate ability to manage transparency carefully, even if initial disclosure can lead to unfavorable attitudes (Baek et al., 2024).

Managerial Implications. Managers must recognize that brand trust precedes AI trust. AI deployment must align with brand positioning, as mismatched implementations damage brand equity. Hotels should demonstrate transparency management capabilities while selecting more human-like AI applications to reduce negative disclosure impacts.

Educational Implications. Hospitality curricula must integrate AI considerations into branding courses, teaching students the interconnection between brand positioning and AI applications. Students need competencies evaluating brand-AI fit. Programs should analyze cases like cool brands successfully deploying AI and traditional brands where AI implementation felt inauthentic. Training should cover transparency management strategies, teaching students how to disclose AI usage ethically while minimizing guest anxiety.

Since vested interests shape AI policy in education (Mochizuki et al., 2025), hotel schools should proactively establish ethical guidelines for AI usage in hospitality. Students should develop competencies creating organizational AI ethics frameworks tailored to hotel operations.

Outcome Usage Stage of AI and Its Impact on Brand Perception

Strategic alignment of AI capabilities with loyalty objectives sustains competitive advantage (Bilgihan et al., 2025). Judicious data usage for personalization can reassure guests while increasing repetitive use of hotel AI devices, translating into brand loyalty.

The EU's AI Act (2024) explicitly requires informing users when they interact with AI-generated content that could be mistaken for human-generated material, establishing a transparency precedent reflected in platform policies globally. Discovering undisclosed AI usage creates perceptions of falsity. Falsity negatively impacts brand engagement (Aljarah et al., 2024), while perceived risk decreases brand loyalty (Hasan et al., 2021). Morosan and Dursun-Cengizci (2022) found that perceived ethics was the most important determinant of hotel guests' acceptance of technology agency, followed by benefits.

Managerial Implications. Hotels must balance data-driven personalization with transparent disclosure practices. Managers should implement ethical AI practices aligned with emerging regulations while offering opt-out options with human alternatives. Hotels must prioritize perceived ethics in AI implementations.

Educational Implications. Hospitality curricula must emphasize the balance between personalization through data acquisition and maintaining high data safety standards. Students need comprehensive training in evolving AI regulations, including the EU AI Act requirements and platform-specific disclosure policies. Programs should integrate regulatory compliance training covering international variations. Training must emphasize avoiding falsity situations, teaching students that undisclosed AI usage severely damages brand trust. Programs should develop competencies in ethical AI decision-making, prioritizing perceived ethics over operational efficiency when these conflict.

Hospitality Education Specific

Preparing students to build consumer trust in AI-enhanced hotel environments requires comprehensive educational frameworks addressing three core dimensions: knowledge acquisition, practical implementation, and value-based orientation (Kara, 2025).

Curriculum Design for Trust-Building Competencies. Hotel school curricula must combine technical skills with ethical consciousness while accommodating students' differential technical abilities (Kara, 2025). Programs should retain courses enhancing soft competencies essential for maintaining human warmth alongside automation, while strengthening advanced communication skills enabling transparent dialogue about AI capabilities. Adding subjects related to data analytics, strategic decision-making, and AI applications equips students to make informed choices protecting brand reputation (Wan et al., 2025).

Ethics Education for Brand Protection. Understanding how ethical AI practices influence consumer trust requires a comprehensive ethics education system integrating three components (Xu et al., 2025): an updated four-dimensional ethics framework addressing Gen-AI challenges (research integrity, data privacy, algorithmic fairness, intellectual property); a "cognition-behavior" dual-loop training mechanism combining theoretical learning with hands-on simulated practice; and a full life-cycle education platform featuring virtual laboratories where students experience how ethical breaches erode brand perception.

Pedagogical Applications Supporting Trust Development. Educators should leverage AI as a pedagogical tool to enable personalized learning and provide industry-specific knowledge (Xie, 2025). AI can facilitate innovative thinking (Zhu & Yu, 2025) and positively impact education by addressing individual learning needs, enhancing digital marketing skills, and improving cultural competency development (Fathy et al., 2025).

Training Priorities for Trust Management. Student training must prioritize competencies directly relevant to fostering consumer trust. Programs should develop digital marketing skills that communicate AI benefits transparently and build cultural competency for managing diverse guest comfort levels with automated systems (Fathy et al., 2025). Advanced communication skills enable students to address guest concerns and know when human intervention strengthens brand perception (Wan et al., 2025).

Addressing Risks to Consumer Trust. Hospitality educators must address challenges including accuracy and reliability issues in AI systems, ethical implications of AI adoption, and the shift in the educator's role (Xie, 2025). Additional concerns include academic dishonesty risks, technological limitations, and broader ethical considerations (Fathy et al., 2025).

By addressing knowledge, practical implementation, and value-based orientation comprehensively, hospitality education can prepare students to strengthen consumer trust in AI while maintaining the authentic human connection that differentiates successful hotel brands and sustains positive brand perception in an increasingly automated industry.

CONCLUSION

This chapter examined how consumer trust in artificial intelligence shapes hotel brand perception, proposing that AI interactions function as critical brand touchpoints where trust assessments directly influence brand equity. By integrating the AIDUA model with Mayer et al., (1995) trustworthiness dimensions, the framework establishes that AI trust formation and brand perception are inseparable. Each AI encounter represents a moment where guests evaluate not merely technological functionality but the hotel brand's competence, care, and integrity.

The framework demonstrates how trust evolves sequentially. During primary appraisal, consumers evaluate AI through social influence and anthropomorphism, forming initial judgments about organizational benevolence. Secondary appraisal maps performance and effort expectancy onto ability judgments, where emotional responses uniquely amplify functional evaluations. Systems demonstrating capability while evoking positive emotions reinforce experiential trust transferring to the hotel brand, whereas functional failures disproportionately damage both AI credibility and brand perception. Critically, brand trust precedes AI trust; hotels require established credibility before guests willingly engage with automated systems. Strategic alignment between brand positioning and AI deployment is essential, as mismatched implementations damage brand equity regardless of technical sophistication.

This framework advances hospitality research by identifying perceived ethics as the strongest determinant of AI acceptance, outweighing functional benefits. Unlike utilitarian models such as TAM, AIDUA's grounding in cognitive appraisal theory captures the social and emotional dimensions critical to hospitality. Operational efficiency proves meaningless if guests feel deceived, a vital insight as AI deployment accelerates while consumer trust remains fragile.

For hospitality education, these findings necessitate curriculum reconception. Programs must develop competencies spanning technical knowledge, practical brand-AI fit, and ethical decision-making. Curricula should integrate comprehensive AI ethics—addressing privacy and fairness—with hands-on simulated practice. Students require cultural intelligence modules and transparency management skills to balance regulatory compliance with emotional reassurance. By leveraging AI as both curriculum content and a pedagogical tool, educators can prepare professionals to manage the paradox of data-driven personalization versus privacy. This approach ensures graduates can strengthen consumer trust in AI while maintaining the authentic human connection that differentiates successful hotel brands.

As this research synthesizes existing literature, quantitative validation is required across diverse hotel segments and cultural contexts. Future research should examine how trust-brand perception relationships vary across property types and generational cohorts, and use longitudinal studies to illuminate how initial AI encounters shape cumulative trust. As the regulatory landscape evolves, understanding how disclosure practices influence trust formation remains essential for both industry practice and the educational preparation of future professionals.

REFERENCES

A. W. S. (2018, June 20). *Amazon helps hotels offer new, engaging guest experiences with Alexa for hospitality*. Hospitality Net. https://www.hospitalitynet.org/news/4089005.html

Aaker, D. A. (1991). *Capitalizing on the value of a brand name*. New York, 28(1), 35-37.

Aaker, D. A. (2012). *Building strong brands*. Simon and Schuster.

Alam, S. S. (2025). Impact of customer willingness to co-create and co-creation value of AI- oriented live streaming on hotel booking intention. *International Journal of Hospitality Management, 130*, 104246. DOI: 10.1016/j.ijhm.2025.104246

Alam, S. S., Masukujjaman, M., Mohamed Makhbul, Z. K., Helmi Ali, M., Ahmad, I., & Al Mamun, A. (2024). Experience, trust, eWOM engagement and usage intention of ai enabled services in hospitality and tourism industry: Moderating mediating analysis. *Journal of Quality Assurance in Hospitality & Tourism, 25*(6), 1635–1663. DOI: 10.1080/1528008X.2023.2167762

Ali, F., & Ali, L. (2025). Agentic AI in Hospitality and Tourism: Opportunities, Risks, and Research Pathways. *Journal of Travel Research*, •••, 00472875251392915.

Aljarah, A., Ibrahim, B., & López, M. (2024). In AI, we do not trust! The nexus between awareness of falsity in AI-generated CSR ads and online brand engagement. *Internet Research, 35*(3), 1406-1426. https://doi.org/10.1108/INTR-12-2023-1156.

Allal-Chérif, O., Puertas, R., & Carracedo, P. (2024). Intelligent influencer marketing: How AI- powered virtual influencers outperform human influencers. *Technological Forecasting and Social Change, 200*, 123113. DOI: 10.1016/j.techfore.2023.123113

Armutcu, B., Tan, A., Ho, S. P. S., Chow, M. Y. C., & Gleason, K. C. (2024). The effect of bank artificial intelligence on consumer purchase intentions. *Kybernetes, 54*(10), 5529-5553. https://doi.org/10.1108/K-01-2024-0145

Baek, T. H., Kim, J., & Kim, J. H. (2024). Effect of disclosing AI-generated content on prosocial advertising evaluation. *International Journal of Advertising*, •••, 1–22.

Bilgihan, A., Ostinelli, M., Zhang, Y., & Lorenz, M. (2025). Artificial intelligence (AI) agents and the future of customer loyalty. *International Journal of Contemporary Hospitality Management, 37*(9), 3240–3262. DOI: 10.1108/IJCHM-03-2025-0373

Chan, K. W., Septianto, F., Kwon, J., & Kamal, R. S. (2023). Color effects on AI influencers' product recommendations. *European Journal of Marketing*, *57*(9), 2290–2315. DOI: 10.1108/EJM-03-2022-0185

Cheng, Y., & Jiang, H. (2022). Customer–brand relationship in the era of artificial intelligence: Understanding the role of chatbot marketing efforts. *Journal of Product and Brand Management*, *31*(2), 252–264. DOI: 10.1108/JPBM-05-2020-2907

Chi, O. H., Gursoy, D., & Chi, C. G. (2022). Tourists' attitudes toward the use of artificially intelligent (AI) devices in tourism service delivery: Moderating role of service value seeking. *Journal of Travel Research*, *61*(1), 170–185. DOI: 10.1177/0047287520971054

Davis, F. D. (1989). Perceived usefulness, perceived ease of use, and user acceptance of information technology. *Management Information Systems Quarterly*, *13*(3), 319–340. DOI: 10.2307/249008

Della Corte, V., Sepe, F., Gursoy, D., & Prisco, A. (2023). Role of trust in customer attitude and behaviour formation towards social service robots. *International Journal of Hospitality Management*, *114*, 103587. DOI: 10.1016/j.ijhm.2023.103587

Duffy, C. (2024, July 29). *Google's Olympics ad went viral for all the wrong reasons | CNN business*. CNN. https://www.cnn.com/2024/07/29/tech/googles-ai-olympics-ad-backlash/index.html

Fang, C. H., Lin, J. Y., & Lin, T. M. (2024). Exploring the impact of AI-translated hotel reviews: The roles of reviewer nationality, cosmopolitanism, and review dispersion. *Asia Pacific Journal of Tourism Research*, *30*(10), 1266-1281. https://doi.org/10.1080/10941665.2024.2405136

Fathy, E. A., Zidan, H. A. K. Y., El Sayed, A. H., & Fouad, A. M. (2025). Integrating ChatGPT in tourism and hospitality education: A systematic and bibliometric analysis of research trends, applications, and implications. *Tourism and Hospitality Research*, *0*(0) 1–28. DOI: 10.1177/14673584251357510

Gajić, T., Ivanišević, A., & Knežević, S. (2025). *Employee perceptions of BI and AI tools for service transformation: Evidence from the Serbian airline and hotel industries*. International Journal of Industrial Engineering and Management, in-press.

Ghazali, E., Mutum, D. S., & Lun, N. K. (2024). Expectations and beyond: The nexus of AI instrumentality and brand credibility in voice assistant retention using extended expectation-confirmation model. *Journal of Consumer Behaviour*, *23*(2), 655–675. DOI: 10.1002/cb.2228

Gursoy, D., Chi, O. H., Lu, L., & Nunkoo, R. (2019). Consumers acceptance of artificially intelligent (AI) device use in service delivery. *International Journal of Information Management*, *49*, 157–169. DOI: 10.1016/j.ijinfomgt.2019.03.008

Hasan, R., Shams, R., & Rahman, M. (2021). Consumer trust and perceived risk for voice- controlled artificial intelligence: The case of Siri. *Journal of Business Research*, *131*, 591–597. DOI: 10.1016/j.jbusres.2020.12.012

Hasanein, A. M. (2025). Responses to the AI Revolution in Hospitality and Tourism Higher Education: The Perception of Students Towards Accepting and Using Microsoft Copilot. *European Journal of Investigation in Health, Psychology and Education*, *15*(3), 35. DOI: 10.3390/ejihpe15030035 PMID: 40136774

Herzlich, T. (2025, August 5). *Major hotel chain faces backlash for allegedly outsourcing check-ins - to India*. New York Post. https://nypost.com/2025/08/05/business/major-hotel-chain-faces-backlash-for-allegedly-outsourcing-check-ins-to-india/

Ho, S. P. S., & Chow, M. Y. C. (2024). The role of artificial intelligence in consumers' brand preference for retail banks in Hong Kong. *Journal of Financial Services Marketing*, *29*(2), 292–305. DOI: 10.1057/s41264-022-00207-3

Hou, Y., & Fan, L. (2024). Working with AI: The effect of job stress on hotel employees' work engagement. *Behavioral Sciences (Basel, Switzerland)*, *14*(11), 1076. DOI: 10.3390/bs14111076 PMID: 39594376

Hsieh, S. H., & Lee, C. T. (2021). Hey Alexa: Examining the effect of perceived socialness in usage intentions of AI assistant-enabled smart speaker. *Journal of Research in Interactive Marketing*, *15*(2), 267–294. DOI: 10.1108/JRIM-11-2019-0179

Huang, G. I., Wong, I. A., Zhang, C. J., & Liang, Q. (2025). Generative AI inspiration and hotel recommendation acceptance: Does anxiety over lack of transparency matter? *International Journal of Hospitality Management*, *126*, 104112. DOI: 10.1016/j.ijhm.2025.104112

Jung, H. S., Yoon, H. H., & Cho, M. (2025). Addressing the needs of an aging workforce in luxury hotels with a focus on perceived job insecurity and AI attitudes. *Journal of Hospitality and Tourism Technology*, *16*(5), 1085–1102. DOI: 10.1108/JHTT-09-2024-0614

Kara, T. (2025). How Does AI Education Shape Sustainability Attitudes Among Generation Z? Evidence from Istanbul's Move Toward Hospitality 5.0. *Sustainability (Basel)*, *17*(22), 10246. DOI: 10.3390/su172210246

Kim, W. B., & Hur, H. J. (2024). What makes people feel empathy for AI chatbots? Assessing the role of competence and warmth. *International Journal of Human-Computer Interaction*, *40*(17), 4674–4687. DOI: 10.1080/10447318.2023.2219961

Law, R., Ye, H., & Lei, S. S. I. (2025). Ethical artificial intelligence (AI): Principles and practices. *International Journal of Contemporary Hospitality Management*, *37*(1), 279–295. DOI: 10.1108/IJCHM-04-2024-0482

Lee, T. (2005). The impact of perceptions of interactivity on customer trust and transaction intentions in mobile commerce. *Journal of Electronic Commerce Research*, *6*(3), 165.

Lefkeli, D., Karataş, M., & Gürhan-Canli, Z. (2024). Sharing information with AI (versus a human) impairs brand trust: The role of audience size inferences and sense of exploitation. *International Journal of Research in Marketing*, *41*(1), 138–155. DOI: 10.1016/j.ijresmar.2023.08.011

Li, B., Yao, R., & Nan, Y. (2023). How do friendship artificial intelligence chatbots (FAIC) benefit the continuance using intention and customer engagement? *Journal of Consumer Behaviour*, *22*(6), 1376–1398. DOI: 10.1002/cb.2218

Li, Y., & Khan, M. S. (2025). Extension of the POS-TI relationship–in the context of contemporary hotels with AI applications. *Journal of Hospitality and Tourism Technology*, *17*(1), 29–54. DOI: 10.1108/JHTT-06-2024-0354

Lin, J. S. E., & Wu, L. (2023). Examining the psychological process of developing consumer-brand relationships through strategic use of social media brand chatbots. *Computers in Human Behavior*, *140*, 107488. DOI: 10.1016/j.chb.2022.107488

Liu, Y., Wang, X., & Qin, H. (2024). When cool hospitality brand meets AI: Exploring the matching effect of service agents and brand images on brand attitude. *International Journal of Contemporary Hospitality Management*, *36*(7), 2367–2384. DOI: 10.1108/IJCHM-04-2023-0516

Lu, L., Hua, M., Sun, X., Zou, R., & Lin, B. (2024). AI robots over sommeliers? Exploring the service provider effect on diners' wine ordering decisions at restaurants. *International Journal of Hospitality Management*, *122*, 103879. DOI: 10.1016/j.ijhm.2024.103879

Mari, A., Mandelli, A., & Algesheimer, R. (2024). Empathic voice assistants: Enhancing consumer responses in voice commerce. *Journal of Business Research*, *175*, 114566. DOI: 10.1016/j.jbusres.2024.114566

Mayer, R. C., Davis, J. H., & Schoorman, F. D. (1995). An integrative model of organizational trust. *Academy of Management Review*, *20*(3), 709–734. DOI: 10.2307/258792

McLean, G., Osei-Frimpong, K., & Barhorst, J. (2021). Alexa, do voice assistants influence consumer brand engagement?–Examining the role of AI powered voice assistants in influencing consumer brand engagement. *Journal of Business Research*, *124*, 312–328. DOI: 10.1016/j.jbusres.2020.11.045

Minton, E. A., Kaplan, B., & Cabano, F. G. (2022). The influence of religiosity on consumers' evaluations of brands using artificial intelligence. *Psychology and Marketing*, *39*(11), 2055–2071. DOI: 10.1002/mar.21727

Mochizuki, Y., Bruillard, E., & Bryan, A. (2025). The ethics of AI or techno-solutionism? UNESCO's policy guidance on AI in education. *British Journal of Sociology of Education*, •••, 1–22. DOI: 10.1080/01425692.2025.2502808

Mogaji, E., Viglia, G., Srivastava, P., & Dwivedi, Y. K. (2024). Is it the end of the technology acceptance model in the era of generative artificial intelligence? *International Journal of Contemporary Hospitality Management*, *36*(10), 3324–3339. DOI: 10.1108/IJCHM-08-2023-1271

Morosan, C. (2026). Who discloses personal information to generative AI in hotels? Insights from a latent profile analysis. *Journal of Hospitality and Tourism Insights, 9*(1), 419-437. https://doi.org/10.1108/JHTI-01-2025-0208

Morosan, C., & Dursun-Cengizci, A. (2024). Tips and trips: A structural model of guests' intentions to stay and tip for AI-based services in hotels. *Journal of Hospitality and Tourism Technology*, *15*(1), 170–194. DOI: 10.1108/JHTT-10-2022-0293

Mou, Y., Wang, J., Ding, Z., Huang, J., & Wang, Z. (2025). When automation backfires: Exploring the impact of consumer resistance to AI application in hybrid service agents. *Journal of Hospitality Marketing & Management*, *34*(7), 1043–1074. DOI: 10.1080/19368623.2025.2532488

Papageorgiou, G., Marneros, S., & Efstathiades, A. (2024). Predicting career success in the hospitality industry of Cyprus: A competency-based approach. *Journal of Teaching in Travel & Tourism*, *24*(3), 236–268. DOI: 10.1080/15313220.2024.2341616

Pelau, C., Dabija, D. C., & Ene, I. (2021). What makes an AI device human-like? The role of interaction quality, empathy and perceived psychological anthropomorphic characteristics in the acceptance of artificial intelligence in the service industry. *Computers in Human Behavior*, *122*, 106855. DOI: 10.1016/j.chb.2021.106855

Pymnts. (2025, June 13). *Expedia and Accor CEOS: Ai to reinvent the future of Travel.* PYMNTS.com. https://www.pymnts.com/news/artificial-intelligence/2025/expedia-accor-ceos-ai-reinvent-future-travel/

Riedel, A., Mulcahy, R., & Northey, G. (2022). Feeling the love? How consumer's political ideology shapes responses to AI financial service delivery. *International Journal of Bank Marketing, 40*(6), 1102–1132. DOI: 10.1108/IJBM-09-2021-0438

Sands, S., Campbell, C. L., Plangger, K., & Ferraro, C. (2022). Unreal influence: Leveraging AI in influencer marketing. *European Journal of Marketing, 56*(6), 1721–1747. DOI: 10.1108/EJM-12-2019-0949

StandardVision. (n.d.). *Immersive 16K digital art installation at DAMAC Paramount Hotel in Dubai.* https://standardvision.com/damac-paramount-hotel

Upadhyay, N., & Kamble, A. (2024). Why can't we help but love mobile banking chatbots? Perspective of stimulus-organism-response. *Journal of Financial Services Marketing, 29*(3), 855–872. DOI: 10.1057/s41264-023-00237-5

Uzir, M. U. H., Al Halbusi, H., Lim, R., Jerin, I., Hamid, A. B. A., Ramayah, T., & Haque, A. (2021). Applied Artificial Intelligence and user satisfaction: Smartwatch usage for healthcare in Bangladesh during COVID-19. *Technology in Society, 67*, 101780. DOI: 10.1016/j.techsoc.2021.101780 PMID: 34697510

Venkatesh, V., Morris, M. G., Davis, G. B., & Davis, F. D. (2003). User acceptance of information technology: Toward a unified view. *Management Information Systems Quarterly, 27*(3), 425–478. DOI: 10.2307/30036540

Vo, D. T., Nguyen, L. T. V., Dang-Pham, D., & Hoang, A. P. (2024). When young customers co-create value of AI-powered branded app: The mediating role of perceived authenticity. *Young Consumers, 25*(5), 557–578. DOI: 10.1108/YC-06-2023-1759

Wan, F., Li, Z., Chen, Y. F., & Lei, C. F. (2025). Charting the Course in the Digital Transformation: Navigating the Intersection of the Hospitality Industry and Education. *Journal of Hospitality & Tourism Education, 37*(2), 214–227. DOI: 10.1080/10963758.2024.2433067

Wang, P., & Hou, Y. (2025). The effects of hotel employees' attitude toward the use of AI on customer orientation: The role of usage attitudes and proactive personality. *Behavioral Sciences (Basel, Switzerland), 15*(2), 127. DOI: 10.3390/bs15020127 PMID: 40001758

Wang, S., & Zhang, H. (2025). Generative AI in international hotel marketing: Impacts on employee creativity and performance. *International Journal of Contemporary Hospitality Management, 37*(8), 2601–2626. DOI: 10.1108/IJCHM-10-2024-1595

Wang, T., Cheng-Xi Aw, E., Wei-Han Tan, G., Sthapit, E., & Li, X. (2025). Can AI improve hotel service performance? A systematic review using ADO-TCM. *Tourism and Hospitality Research*, •••, 14673584251356817. DOI: 10.1177/14673584251356817

Wang, X., & Qiu, X. (2024). The positive effect of artificial intelligence technology transparency on digital endorsers: Based on the theory of mind perception. *Journal of Retailing and Consumer Services*, *78*, 103777. DOI: 10.1016/j.jretconser.2024.103777

Wilkinson, L. (2025, September 4). Marriott checks out AI agents amid technology transformation. *CIO Dive*. https://www.ciodive.com/news/marriott-international-AI-strategy-agentic-cloud-cybersecurity

Wong, I. A., Zhang, T., Lin, Z. C., & Peng, Q. (2023). Hotel AI service: Are employees still needed? *Journal of Hospitality and Tourism Management*, *55*, 416–424. DOI: 10.1016/j.jhtm.2023.05.005

Xie, P., & Ma, L. (2026). How hotel AI adoption shapes employee performance? A study based on the transactional theory of stress and coping. *Journal of Hospitality and Tourism Technology*, *17*(1), 176–191. DOI: 10.1108/JHTT-09-2024-0606

Xie, P. F. (2025). Incorporating ChatGPT into Hospitality and Tourism Education: A Comparative Student and AI Study. *Journal of Hospitality & Tourism Education*, •••, 1–10. DOI: 10.1080/10963758.2025.2512430

Xu, X., Meng, F., & Gou, Y. (2025). From Theoretical Navigation to Intelligent Prevention: Constructing a Full-Cycle AI Ethics Education System in Higher Education. *Education Sciences*, *15*(9), 1199. DOI: 10.3390/educsci15091199

Yan, Y., Liu, H., & Chau, T. (2025). A systematic review of AI ethics in education: Challenges, policy gaps, and future directions. [JGIM]. *Journal of Global Information Management*, *33*(1), 1–50. DOI: 10.4018/JGIM.386381

Yi, B., Shi, D., & Li, G. (2025). What makes an AI-themed hotel successful? New evidence from a sequential research design. *International Journal of Contemporary Hospitality Management*, *37*(3), 783–804. DOI: 10.1108/IJCHM-05-2024-0743

Yim, A., Cui, A. P., & Walsh, M. (2024). The role of cuteness on consumer attachment to artificial intelligence agents. *Journal of Research in Interactive Marketing*, *18*(1), 127–141. DOI: 10.1108/JRIM-02-2023-0046

Yuan, C., Wang, S., & Liu, Y. (2023). AI service impacts on brand image and customer equity: Empirical evidence from China. *Journal of Brand Management*, *30*(1), 61–76. DOI: 10.1057/s41262-022-00292-8

Zhang, Y., Wang, J., & Zhang, J. (2025). Impacts of AI awareness on proactive service behavior and tacit knowledge sharing among hotel employees. *International Journal of Contemporary Hospitality Management*, *37*(12), 3935–3951. DOI: 10.1108/IJCHM-03-2025-0420

Zhou, S., & Yi, N. (2025). How and when does AI awareness affect hotel frontline employee's Unethical Pro-organizational Behavior? Insights from two longitudinal studies. *International Journal of Hospitality Management*, *130*, 104267. DOI: 10.1016/j.ijhm.2025.104267

Zhu, J., & Yu, S. (2025). Generative AI for tourism and hospitality education. *Current Issues in Tourism*, ●●●, 1–9. DOI: 10.1080/13683500.2025.2500730

ADDITIONAL READING

Chhatwal, P. (2024, February 13). *Embracing the future: AI's transformative role in hospitality*. Deloitte. https://www.deloitte.com/uk/en/Industries/consumer/blogs/embracing-the-future-ais-transformative-role-in-hospitality.html

Dixit, S. K., Lee, K. H., & Loo, P. T. (2019). Consumer behavior in hospitality and tourism. *Journal of Global Scholars of Marketing Science*, *29*(2), 151–161. DOI: 10.1080/21639159.2019.1577159

McKinsey & Company, & Skift Research. (2025, September 16). *Remapping travel with agentic AI*. McKinsey & Company. https://www.mckinsey.com/industries/travel/our-insights/remapping-travel-with-agentic-ai

Rust, R. T., & Huang, M. H. (2021). The feeling economy. In *The Feeling Economy: How Artificial Intelligence Is Creating the Era of Empathy* (pp. 41–61). Springer International Publishing. DOI: 10.1007/978-3-030-52977-2_4

KEY TERMS AND DEFINITIONS

AIDUA Framework: A model explaining how customers decide to accept or reject AI devices in service settings, based on both what the AI does (cognitive factors) and how it makes them feel (emotional factors).

Anthropomorphism: Attributing human characteristics, emotions, or behaviors to non-human entities like AI systems or robots.

Brand Equity: The value a brand adds to a product or service based on consumer perceptions, recognition, and loyalty—essentially what makes customers choose one brand over another.

Brand Positioning: How a brand distinguishes itself in the market and in consumers' minds relative to competitors, defining what the brand stands for and who it serves.

Consumer Engagement: The level of involvement, interaction, and emotional connection a customer has with a brand or service over time.

Consumer Trust: The willingness of customers to place confidence in a brand or service and share personal information with it, based on perceptions of reliability, competence, benevolence, and integrity.

Falsity: When consumers discover that content or interactions they believed were human-created are actually AI-generated, without the brand having disclosed this upfront.

Perceived Contingency: The user's sense that the AI system is responding specifically to their individual inputs rather than providing generic, pre-programmed responses.

Responsiveness: The speed and appropriateness with which a system or service reacts to user requests or needs.

Social Presence: The degree to which a technology feels like interacting with a real person, creating a sense of human connection despite being mediated by technology.

Technology Readiness: An individual's propensity to embrace and use new technologies, including their optimism about technology and comfort with adopting innovations.

Usability: How easy and intuitive a system is to use, including how quickly users can learn it and accomplish their goals without frustration.

About the Contributors

Marius Vlad holds a Doctorate in Education from the American International University, alongside a Master's in Business Administration from the Hotel and Management Institute in Soerenerg. His hotel industry experience includes training and operations in various 5-star independent properties, chain hotels, and institutions in countries like Greece, the United States, Switzerland, the United Arab Emirates, P.R. China, and his home country, Romania. At the Les Roches Global Hospitality Education Marbella campus, his main responsibilities are academic research, guiding the students on the honours path in completing their dissertations, coordinating master applied projects, and teaching a variety of Rooms Division operations and management courses for undergraduate and postgraduate students.

Edmund Goh is a distinguished academic and award-winning leader in hospitality and tourism management. Currently serving as Assistant Dean, Research and Innovation, he plays a pivotal role in strengthening industry engagement and bridging the gap between academia and practice. With a wealth of experience in higher education, Professor Goh has held several senior leadership positions, including Associate Dean, Head of Academic Studies, Deputy Head of School, and Deputy Research Director at Torrens University, Edith Cowan University, and Bond University Australia. He earned his PhD in Tourism and Hospitality from the University of Queensland, Australia, and has made significant contributions to the field with over 100 publications in top-tier journals and conferences. He is ranked within the top 2% of researchers globally in 2020-2024. Passionate about advancing hospitality education and research, Professor Goh continues to shape the future of the industry through his leadership and scholarship.

Rachel Germanier is a Professor at Les Roches, and has a solid record of accomplished teaching and supervising of student research work, some of which has been published at conferences and in academic journals. Her overarching aim is to bring the best out of all my students, aiming high, always. She is passionate about advancing the scholarship of teaching and learning, and is proud to lead faculty development through all our campuses. Her academic rigour is also recognised in the wider academic field through her work as an external examiner.

***

Albian Albrahimi is Assistant Dean of Graduate Programs at Les Roches and a faculty member teaching corporate finance and hospitality financial analysis. His work focuses on hospitality finance education, revenue strategy, and the integration of analytics and artificial intelligence into curriculum and assessment. He is a certified STR trainer (CHIA and CAHTA) and holds the CMA Certification. His current research interests include hospitality financial forecasting and modelling.

Joan Aviso is currently the Manager of the Learning Resources Center, overseeing academic support services and resource development to improve student learning. With over 20 years of experience in academic resources and learning services, she has depth expertise in digital transformation and scholarly communication. She also teaches academic writing and communication skills, guiding students to articulate their ideas with precision, coherence, and academic rigor. Joan holds a Master of International Studies degree from the University of Wollongong and Bachelor's degree in Education and Information Sciences.

Ahmed Bakri is an international finance and real estate trainer with over 15 years of global teaching and consulting experience. He specializes in capital budgeting, corporate finance, real estate investment, hospitality finance, valuation, and data-driven decision-making. He holds a PhD in Finance and an MSc in International Finance from the University of Dundee, where his doctoral research focused on capital budgeting and investment decision-making, a core pillar of real estate finance. He also holds a Certificate in Real Estate Investment from the University of Oxford, further strengthening his expertise in real estate markets and investment analysis. Dr. Bakri is an active researcher with several published academic articles in international journals. He trains executives across Europe and the Middle East and teaches at leading institutions including Les Roches Marbella, Glion London, EAE Business School Madrid, and Universidad Europea. His programs are known for their practical, analytics-driven approach, using applied cases and advanced Excel-based financial models.

Sarah Belanger is a Senior Practical Arts Lecturer at Abu Dhabi Hospitality Academy – Les Roches (United Arab Emirates). She teaches across hospitality and service-related modules, with a focus on experiential learning and industry-aligned skills development. Her research interests include hospitality education, curriculum innovation, and the use of artificial intelligence to support teaching, assessment, and student engagement, particularly in the context of wine and fine dining education.

Leonardo Roman serves as Practical Arts & Events Manager at Abu Dhabi Hospitality Academy – Les Roches. A Certified Culinary Educator (CCE) by the Worldchefs Organization and Senior Member of the Emirates Culinary Guild, Chef Leonardo has a perfect blend of academic knowledge with practical experience. He holds a master's degree in management and education in Food and Nutrition and is dedicated to designing high-impactful, real-world training that equips students to thrive in the global hospitality industry.

Raul Santiago Castro-Lopez, FHEA is a seasoned academic and hospitality management professional with over 15 years of teaching experience across vocational, undergraduate, and postgraduate levels, including at the Master's level. He began his academic career in the United Kingdom at the renowned University College Birmingham (UCB), where degrees were conferred by the University of Birmingham. Since relocating to Spain in 2019, Raul has held academic positions at Endicott International University and Schiller International University. He currently serves as both Assistant Dean and Clinical Professor at Les Roches Global Hospitality Education. As a Fellow of the Higher Education Academy (FHEA), Raul has demonstrated a commitment to maintaining high standards in teaching and learning within higher education. Raul is in the final stages of completing his PhD in Tourism, Economics, and Management, complementing his extensive academic credentials, which include a Postgraduate Certificate in Education and a Master's degree in Tourism Business Administration and Management. Beyond academia, Raul brings over two decades of experience in establishing and managing international partnerships with distinguished organizations across B2B, B2C, and B2G sectors. He has also served as Director of the Erasmus Program.

Christopher S. Dutt is an Associate Professor at Abu Dhabi Hospitality Academy – Les Roches in Abu Dhabi, UAE. He holds a PhD in Management Studies from the University of Exeter in the UK. His research interests include tourism impacts, technology in hospitality and tourism, expatriation, and sustainability in hospitality and tourism. His research has appeared in Information Systems Frontiers, Information Technology and Tourism, the Journal of Hospitality and Tourism Management, and the Journal of Travel and Tourism Marketing, among others. In 2020, he won the Emerald/EFMD Outstanding Doctoral Research Award - Tourism and Hospitality Management Award.

Stefania Denise Escobar is an Academic Lecturer at Abu Dhabi Hospitality Academy Les Roches. She holds a PhD in Management and Economics from the Free University of Bozen-Bolzano where she also completed her postdoc. She is a visiting researcher at AUS and has been a visiting research scholar at Bangor University (UK), University of Aveiro (Portugal), New York University (USA) and Free University of Brussels (Belgium). Her research lies at the intersection of management, smart hospitality, tourism and sustainability. Her research has been presented at TTRA, EURAM and AOM. Her work has appeared in the Current Issues in Tourism, Cities, International Journal of Public Sector Management and Journal of Knowledge Management.

Mahala Geronasso is an Academic Lecturer at Abu Dhabi Hospitality Academy, Les Roches, and holds a Ph.D. in Hospitality Management from the University of Central Florida. Her research focuses on the intersection of finance, technology, and innovation in the hospitality industry, with particular attention to digital transformation, artificial intelligence, and firm performance. She has published in leading hospitality and tourism journals and is passionate about integrating ethical and data-driven perspectives into teaching and practice. Dr. Geronasso combines academic expertise with industry experience, having held leadership roles across hospitality operations and international business ventures.

Nansy Kouroupi is a researcher and lecturer with over a decade of teaching in Switzerland, Greece, and Cyprus. She brings more than twenty years of management and entrepreneurial experience across the broader services sector, including co-founding an award-winning hospitality venture. Her academic credentials currently include a BSc in Tourism and Hospitality Management; an MBA in Business and Law focused on marketing and CSR; and an MSc in Entrepreneurship and Innovation. A certified educator (PGDE, PGCE), she designs practice-based learning and mentors students and professionals. Her research interests include metaverse-enabled tourism, digital service design, digital transformation and new business models, consumer behaviour, and brand engagement.

Jon Loiti is the Academic Dean at the Marbella campus. He joined Les Roches in 2007 and has taught different subjects related to his expertise in HR, Management skills, Strategic Human Resources and Professional Development. He has a passion for teaching and has helped shape the graduate program portfolio.

Jonathan Meehan is a Senior Lecturer at Les Roches Global Hospitality Education with over 25 years of teaching experience at Bachelor's and Master's levels, alongside professional training experience as a coach and facilitator for several multinational companies. His teaching spans Marketing, Business Communication,

Ethics, and Artificial Intelligence applied to Business Innovation. His research interests focus on leveraging artificial intelligence to enhance critical thinking skills among university students.

Julien Morange is a marketing executive and researcher with over 15 years of international experience spanning APAC and North America. He holds a Doctorate in Business Administration from KEDGE Business School and Hong Kong Polytechnic University, specializing in AI-driven marketing and brand management. His research explores the transformative impact of artificial intelligence on consumer engagement and brand strategy. Julien combines academic rigor with practical leadership, bringing a unique perspective to the intersection of technology and marketing. Education: PhD in Management Sciences, Aix-Marseille-Toulon University (CERGAM), France Doctorate in Business Administration (DBA), KEDGE Business School & Hong Kong Polytechnic University Master in Management Research, KEDGE Business School & Hong Kong Polytechnic University MBA, KEDGE Business School & Shanghai Jiao Tong University

Abdul Rehimane is a Practical Arts Instructor at Abu Dhabi Hospitality Academy – Les Roches. With more than 20 years of experience in the hospitality industry, Abdul Rehimane brings both passion and expertise to his role at Abu Dhabi Hospitality Academy – Les Roches. He specializes in practical arts training, guiding students through hands-on learning experiences that merge classroom knowledge with real-world application. Abdul's background includes wide-ranging experience in culinary operations, event management, cost control, and supply chain management. Known for his dedication to excellence and student development, he helps future hospitality professionals build the confidence and skills needed to succeed in the industry.

Roberto Rodriguez-Garcia holds a PhD in Economics from the Universitat Jaume I of Castellón (Spain). He is Master Degree in Sustainability and Corporate Social Responsibility from Universitat Jaume I of Castellón (Spain). He is a senior lecturer in sustainability in the graduate programs at Les Roches Global Hospitality Education in Marbella (Spain). He is also responsible for the Career Services and Internship Department at Les Roches Marbella. His research focuses on sustainability in the hospitality industry.

Zaid Rouby is a Rooms Division and Events Instructor. He contributes to hospitality education by integrating extensive industry experience with academic practice. His work focuses on preparing students for real-world hospitality environments through experiential learning, industry-aligned curricula, and competency-based training. Zaid's professional and research interests include luxury service standards, soft skills development, emotional intelligence, leadership communication, and the responsible integration of emerging technologies, including AI-driven simulations, in hospitality education. He is particularly interested in exploring the balance between human-centered service and technology-enhanced learning. By combining operational expertise, sales insight, pre-opening experience, and pedagogical innovation, Zaid remains dedicated to advancing hospitality education and supporting the development of future hospitality professionals.

Krisztina Soreg is a professor, economist and business analyst, holding a Ph.D. degree in Economics and Management Sciences from the University of Sopron, Hungary, as well as a graduate degree from the Budapest University of Technology and Economics with 10+ years of teaching experience. Since March 2022, she has been an integral part of Les Roches, where she delivers lectures as an Associate Professor on various subjects in Data Analytics and Economics to undergraduate and postgraduate students, while also overseeing dissertation projects across a spectrum of topics.

Alexandru Stoinea is a Senior Career Counselor and Visiting Lecturer in Economics at Les Roches Crans-Montana. His work sits at the intersection of higher education and industry, with a focus on graduate employability, recruitment processes, and the growing use of generative artificial intelligence in CV screening and candidate assessment. His experience combines academic teaching with hands-on career advising.

José Luis Ximénez de Sandoval holds a PhD in Tourism and Bachelor's Degree in Economics and Business Administration, he is a university professor with more than 15 years of experience as a lecturer and researcher. He is currently a full-time professor at Les Roches Marbella and a part-time professor at the University of Málaga. As a lecturer, he has taught undergraduate, postgraduate, and master's programmes. In recent years, he has delivered, among others, the following courses: Data Insights and Analytics, Market Research Analytics, Financial Management for Business, and Methods of Research Inquiry. As a researcher, he has participated in numerous international conferences and has published several book chapters as well as multiple articles in academic journals. His two main research areas focus on online hotel rankings (TripAdvisor, Booking) and new technologies applied to university education in tourism and hospitality. As a professional in accounting and finance, he has worked as an international financial controller in Poland, Germany, Turkey, and Morocco.

Index

A

B

C

T

U

V

X

www.ingramcontent.com/pod-product-compliance
Lightning Source LLC
LaVergne TN
LVHW062214200926
848484LV00006B/1392